D0707703

Life, the Universe, and Everything

Life, the Universe, and Everything

An Aristotelian Philosophy for a Scientific Age

RIC MACHUGA

CASCADE *Books* · Eugene, Oregon

LIFE, THE UNIVERSE, AND EVERYTHING
An Aristotelian Philosophy for a Scientific Age

Cascade Books
An Imprint of Wipf and Stock Publishers
199 W. 8th Ave., Suite 3
Eugene, OR 97401

www. wipfandstock.com

ISBN 13: 978-1-60899-812-8

Cataloging-in-Publication data:

Machuga, Ric.

    Life, the universe, and everything : an Aristotelian philosophy for a scientific age / Ric Machuga.

    xvi + 308 p. ; cm. 23 — Includes bibliographical references and index.

    ISBN 13: 978-1-60899-812-8

    1. Aristotle. 2. Thomas, Aquinas, Saint, 1225?–1274. 3. Thomists. 4. Philosophy. 5. Science—Philosophy. 6. Ethics. 7. Metaphysics. 8. Knowledge, Theory of. I. Title.

B485 M2416 2011

Manufactured in the U.S.A.

To Kathy

Contents

Preface

ALL MY FORMAL PHILOSOPHICAL training was done within the tradition of analytic philosophy. But when I began teaching in a Great Books honors program thirty years ago, I was forced to read Plato, Aristotle, Augustine, and Aquinas in a way that I had never done before. The rationale for the program was that we could still learn much about freedom, justice, and a well-lived life from these ancient authors. But these sorts of "big questions" were not the sorts of questions I was taught to ask (much less try to answer) in graduate school.

The program also required that we read and teach *whole* books, not analyzing small fractions or individual arguments. That too was a new experience. When I was a student, it was standard fare to read the three pages of Aquinas' *Summa Theologica* that contained his "five ways" of proving the existence of God and then to evaluate soundness of these arguments. The fact that we had only read a tiny fraction of the *Summa* in which these arguments were found seemed beside the point. "After all," as good analytic philosophers we said, "arguments must stand on their own two feet—either their individual premises entail their conclusion or they don't."

The dynamics of twenty years of reading these philosophers with lower division students changed all that. Though students were initially enamored with the idea of reading the "Great Books," they soon began to baulk at the discipline this required. And when they read a sentence in Aquinas like, "The cause of the causality of the efficient cause is the final cause," the spirit of rebellion became palpable. And it was toward *me* that the rebellion was directed because now it was me who was *making* them read these "dead white males" who knew nothing of space travel, much less the internet! I learned much about "refuting" ancient philosophers in graduate school; making them intelligible and/or believable was something I had to learn on my own.

More than any other book, it was Plato's *Republic* that taught me how to teach in Butte College's honors program. Though I must confess, at first I shared some of my students' skepticism. Plato's world was not our world. What could I possibly learn from a book that asked and answered *all* the "big questions" in ethics, political theory, epistemology, metaphysics, and the philosophy of mind in a mere 300 pages? All my previous training taught me to ask *little* questions. And it seemed like the smaller the question I addressed, the better my grade. If Plato had submitted his *Republic* as a dissertation, I mused, it never would have been accepted.

So though I began "by faith" believing that Plato had something important to teach us today, and in time I began to see that what he had to say about "curriculum selection" for future rulers (my students called it "censorship") had connections with what he had to say about the dialectical justification of epistemological assumptions. Soon other connections began to emerge. For example, in Plato's mind, it was impossible to think clearly about the virtues and vices of liberal democracies until questions in the metaphysics of "truth" had been asked and answered. Oh how my "analytic" self rebelled! It seemed that in Plato all philosophical questions were connected. However, in time, my conversion was complete. Even though colleagues might scoff, I now openly proclaimed that "big questions" could both be asked and answered, provide that they were approached *synthetically.*

Though parts of Plato's ideal republic still seem misguided, he fully convinced me that ideas always exist in an ecosystem. No philosophical idea, no matter how small, can live by itself. Ideas always gain their force, power, and life from their surrounding ideas. Nothing living in an ecosystem lives by itself.

The ecosystem of ideas in this book comes largely from Aristotle and his medieval interpreter, Aquinas. Aristotle, of course, was a pagan. He knew nothing about the God of Abraham, Isaac, and Jacob. Aquinas, on the other hand, was a devout Christian who never looked to philosophy for the ultimate truth. But this never caused him to disparage the penultimate truths that he discovered in Aristotle.

Yet, how can students growing up with the wonders of modern science *not* disparage both Aristotle and Aquinas? After all, both were firmly convinced that the earth was the center of the universe and that biological species were eternally fixed and immutable. Since they were so obviously wrong about these matters, why should we try to figure out what they had to say about other matters? Philosophy, as one of the characters in Plato's *Republic* says, is appropriate for youngsters, but when one grows up we should address adult questions in an adult fashion. Today, this pretty much means that as adults in college we should ask (1) "scientific" questions about how the universe works or (2) "economic" questions about how to make a lot of money. Like it or not, that's where my students are "at" so I always begin there, as does this book.

After a very quick summary of two fundamental principles of logic in the first chapter, the next two chapters discuss "the scientific method" as Newton and Darwin employed it. We conclude that *the* scientific method does not exist—the reasoning of Newton and Darwin was no different from the reasoning of ancient philosophers, modern lawyers, and skilled auto mechanics. Yes, college students should study the universe in a "scientific" way, but they should not assume the very narrow understanding of science perpetuated by the positivism of the previous century.

On the other hand, we must avoid a simple relativism that assumes that all ideas—both of philosophers and of scientists—are nothing more than a "social construct." My strategic response has been to flesh out the implications of three simple propositions: 1) plants and animals exist; 2) square circles and other contradictions do not exist; and 3) nothing comes from nothing. These common sense propositions have become my "sound bite" summary of Aristotelian philosophy. No matter how predisposed to relativism today's students are, the vast majority still accept these common sense propositions. While they may be bored, they see no reason to question their truthfulness, even after I inform them that modern philosophy began with René Descartes' rejection of all three propositions.

At this point, patience is required. The next three chapters sketch the philosophical implications of these fundamental propositions. Though their point may not be immediately evident, they lay the groundwork for a philosophical alternative to both positivism and relativism. It is called *Aristotelian realism*. And while examining metaphysical and epistemological assumptions can be tedious, it must be done—otherwise philosophy is reduced to "come let us rap together."

With chapter 7—What does it mean to be human?—we return to an intrinsically interesting question. I've been polling students now for many years, and the vast majority initially answer this question as would Plato or Descartes: to be a human being is to have an immaterial soul that controls the body during this life and escapes to a better life when the body dies. Scientific materialism may reign among the scientific and philosophical elite, but it does not with the students.

Dualism and materialism, however, are not the only options. Aristotle argued that soul is the form of the body. While the body is a necessary condition for being human, it is not a sufficient condition. Without an essentially immaterial intellect we would not be human. So the most serious challenge to the Aristotelian understanding of the soul still comes from modern science—why talk about immaterial souls when functional MRIs can literally picture, in real time, what's happening in the brain when a person prays, philosophizes, or fantasies about philandering? Such a question deserves an answer.

Chapter 8 most directly addresses my student's second assumption about the kind of questions adults ought to study: how to make money? Of course, the vast majority of students want to be moral and they care a great deal about "values." So making money is not their *only* goal. It is just that "values" are understood to be intrinsically *personal*—I have my values, and they have their values. So who am I (or Aristotle) to tell them what they should or should not value? And, in one sense, my students are right. I fly radio-controlled airplanes in my free time, but that's no reason for *them* to fly radio-controlled airplanes in their free time.

But no Aristotelian would suggest that they should. Rather, Aristotelians are like physicians who tell their patients to take vitamin D supplements to maintain their health. The assumption here is that everyone prefers a healthy to an unhealthy life. So too, Aristotelians tell their students to cultivate the virtues of courage, temperance, justice, and practical wisdom if they want to flourish as human beings and be all they were meant to be. In short, if you want to be happy, practice the classical virtue. But there is no *single* way to flourish as a human being. While some pursuits (like power and fame) are always inimical to long term happiness, Aristotelians are the first to encourage students to follow their individual interests and talents—whether it is motorcycles or music. It is just that these must be pursued in the right way, at the right times, and in the right manner.

Just as the vast majority of my students are Cartesian dualists with regard to the soul, they are also philosophical libertarians with regard to free will. They assume that true freedom means that no person or thing (including brain states) is *causing* them to act one way or the other. No matter what functional MRIs show, they believe humans' free will *proves* that somewhere deep down in the brain there are gaps in the causal chain. And it is in these gaps that our freedom is found.

Aristotelians tell a quite different story. Yes, humans have a free will, but, No, it does not reside in gaps in the causal sequence of events. The relation between our soul (free will) and our body/brain is the same relation that exists between the meaning of a word and the ink with which it is written. By itself, this makes little sense. But having sloughed their way through the earlier chapters, the basic idea is fairly clear: in-*form*-ation in our minds is real and powerful, but it is not a physical thing nor is it subject to the laws of physical causation. Though we must immediately add that in-*form*-ation does not *violate* the laws of physical causation. In-*form*-ation is ascientific, without being unscientific. (My hyphenating "information" is simply a way of reminding the reader of the fundamental Aristotelian distinction between form and shape—technically called hylomorphism—that is developed in chapters 4 through 6.)

With chapter 10, we leave Aristotle behind and pick up Aquinas. Though Aristotle is convinced that an Unmoved Mover (god) is philosophically required, the god of Aristotle bears only a faint resemblance to the God of Aquinas. For Aristotle, god is the ultimate final cause which moves everything else without itself moving; it is like a bowl of food which "moves" a hungry dog to come and eat without itself moving. For Aquinas, God is not only a final cause, but also the efficient cause (Creator) of all that exists.

In one sense, chapter ten is a defense of the third and fifth of Aquinas' "five ways" for proving the existence of God that I (somewhat contemptuously) mentioned earlier. However, in another sense, the argument here will bear little resemblance to the analytic approach I pursued in graduate school. The power and life of Aquinas' argument comes not from their logical entailments, but from their interconnection with everything in the preceding chapters. While the premises are not obviously true *considered by themselves*, they are nonetheless extremely plausible in light of the *whole* of the philosophy in which they are embedded. Here, more than any place else, the "ecology of ideas" becomes apparent.

And here, too, is the "robustness" of Aristotelian realism most evident. While I emphasize the interconnection of philosophical ideas,

Aristotle was definitely *not* interested in creating a deductive system where each proposition logically followed from its premises. Such a "system" is like a chain: it is only as strong as its weakest link. "Systems" like this lack redundancy, and hence, they lack robustness. Aristotle's philosophy is more like a black widow's web—messy in some respect, yet so interwoven that it can withstand wounds to many of its strands.

The last two chapters are all about Aquinas and his Christian predecessor, Augustine. Chapter 11 asks a question Aristotle never asked— If a good and all-powerful God exists, why is there so much pain and suffering? For contemporary Christians, the most common response to the problem of evil is grounded in a libertarian conception of freedom. Among analytic Christian philosophers this is even truer. However, it is not the path taken by Augustine and Aquinas since neither of them was a libertarian with respect to free will. Augustine, for essentially theological reasons, argued that God's providential control of the *whole* of creation precludes the idea that humans are autonomous agents, or at least, they were not autonomous when they were doing good. "The good that I do," Augustine famously prayed, "is done by You in me." Aquinas would whole hearted agree.

And Aquinas had a second reason for rejecting a libertarian conception of freedom—it's the third of the three fundamental principles of Aristotelian realism, namely, nothing comes from nothing. Or, in more contemporary terms, mass/energy is always conserved; it can be neither created nor destroyed.

For both these reasons chapter 11 develops a privation theory of evil. Evil is a real "hole" in the created ordered; it hurts and causes much suffering. But evil is not something God either does or could create. So why are there are "holes" in creation? Simply put, there are "holes" because not even an infinite God can create a second "God." By definition, there can only be *one* Creator of all that is. So an infinite creation, without any "holes," would be perfect and complete unto itself—a second "God." But this is not possible. Though we must be clear, such a philosophical response to the problem of evil is *not* intended to provide "existential" comfort. For that, Augustine and Aquinas look to faith in Christ and the power of his resurrection.

The final chapter is all about faith and making sense of Augustine's prayer. As we said, it begins, "The good that I do is done by You in me." But it concludes, "The evil is my fault." How can that be? Is this not a "heads I win, tails you lose" proposition? The salvation for which Christians pray has always been understood to be a gift of grace—it is not something one earns or works for; rather it is an "unmerited favor" bestowed by God alone. While salvation comes by faith, faith itself is a gift from God. But, again, how can the "good" that we do come from God, while the "bad" is our fault? Before this can be believed, it must be understood. A person can *verbally* say "Procrastination lays lazily understand the seven." But nonsense sentences like this cannot be believed. The final chapter seeks to make *believable* Augustine's and Aquinas' understanding of grace.

Throughout this book I write as a kind of layman. I have taught for thirty years at a two-year public college in California, which means that I have been paid to *teach* philosophy to lower division students. While my job provides much leisure to read and write, unlike professional philosophers working at universities, there is no expectation to publish in professional journals. Instead, I write for my students. So to call myself an "academic philosopher" doing "original research" is a little misleading. I prefer to think of myself as a good journalist trying to interest a thoughtful audience in a story that has not yet been widely reported.

And like all good journalism, sources should be named. So my footnotes are fairly extensive, and perhaps even excessive. But these footnotes can easily be ignored without detracting from the story. I have also included summaries at the beginning of each chapter. In some ways these are redundant and can also be ignored. However, some readers may want to read through all the chapter summaries before reading the text itself. This book, after all, is all about the "big picture" and the interconnection of ideas. It is not a mystery novel, so having a sneak peep at how the story ends may make it easier to connect the intervening dots.

Being a book about the "big picture," one of my goals is to ensure that students do not lose slight of the forest because they are looking so intently at the trees. As Aquinas said in the prologue to his *Summa Theologica* (a book he said was addressed to "beginners") students have frequently "been hampered by what they have found written by other authors, partly on account of the multiplication of useless questions, articles, and arguments." Of course, I would be rich if I had the proverbial dime for each of my students who said *that* about Aquinas' *Summa*! So finding the proper balance between precision and lucidity is always tricky. This is especially the case with the terms "Aristotelian realism," "positivism," "relativism," and "idealism" that are used throughout the book. Though each of these generic terms are distinguishable into countless different species, for pedagogical purposes I have tried to resist the temptation to multiply distinctions.

Finally, I want to acknowledge the Butte College Board of Trustees who approved the funding for a team-taught Honors Programs. So much of this book grows out of many years of teaching with Silvia Milosevich and Roger Ekins. Many of the chapters in this book were first presented at the Chico Triad, a discussion group on science and religion initially funded by the Templeton Foundation and Bidwell Presbyterian Church. Rev. Greg Cootsona, Dan Barnett, and Bill Martin deserve special mention for commenting on several chapters and, even more, for their ongoing friendship. And, then, there is my wife, Kathy, who spent untold hours typesetting earlier versions for use by my students and creating all but two of the figures in the book. The exceptions are my colleague Mike Findley's drawing of homologous forelimbs in chapter 3 and my daughter Christy Caldwell's photograph of cells in the same chapter.

What Is a Good Argument?

Good arguments are public, honest, and have as their goal the best (not perfect) answer to the problem being discussed. When they succeed, good arguments improve our understanding of reality. However, philosophical relativists do not believe good arguments are possible. Following Nietzsche, they say that "truth" is nothing more than "a mobile army of marching metaphors." "Reality," according to relativists, is a social construct that people and cultures create; it is not something philosophers discover.

Though relativists may disagree about the possibility of having a good argument, the logic of deductive proof is not in dispute. First, proofs must have a valid form; second they must have true premises. And it is important to note that "valid" does not *mean "true." Rather it means that if the premises are true, then it is* absolutely impossible *for the conclusion to be false. Such certainty is only possible because the conclusions of valid arguments never assert more than is already given in the premises.*

So while deductive proofs produce logical certainty, they can never expand our knowledge. New knowledge only comes from inductive arguments. Yet, inductive arguments only establish their conclusion to a greater or lesser degree of probability. Even with the best inductive argument it is always possible for all the premises to be true, yet, by a kind of bad luck, the conclusion turns out to be false.

This creates a dilemma: Deduction produces certainty but presupposes we already know the premises to be true. Induction can show that premises in a deductive argument are probable, *but can never provide* proof. *So how is knowledge possible?*

Philosophical idealists, realists, and positivists give different answers. Idealists ground knowledge in "clear and distinct ideas." Positivists ground it in the experimental method of the sciences. And realists ground it in common sense propositions like (1) plants and animals exist, (2) square circles do not exist, and (3) nothing comes from nothing. A preliminary discussion of the pluses and minuses of these three answers follows.

Relativists, on the other hand, argue that real knowledge (at least when it comes to ethical, philosophical, and religious issues) is impossible. The best we can hope for is to present our "arguments" in rhetorically powerful ways so that other people are persuaded. It is futile, they say, to ask if our most persuasive opinions correspond to "reality."

CLOUDS ARE A NECESSARY condition for rain, but they are not sufficient. It will never rain without clouds, but being cloudy does not guarantee rain. The same relation exists between logic and philosophy. Philosophy requires logic, but logic by itself does not make a philosopher.

In this regard, logic is related to philosophy as mathematics is related to science. Mathematics allows scientists to reason rigorously about all things that can be *quantified*. However quantifiable measurements presuppose *good* data and "goodness" is not observable with a camcorder; it requires good judgment which only comes from much experience under the tutelage of good teachers. Without this, science is impossible. Likewise, logic allows philosophers to reason rigorously about the *qualities* of things. Qualities tell us what something *is*; they specify a thing's essential nature. So, just as sophisticated mathematics by itself produces no interesting scientific results; logic by itself produces no interesting philosophical results. Nevertheless, we must begin with logic, because without it, good philosophy is impossible.

1.1 "GOOD ARGUMENTS" AND RELATIVIST CRITICS

Logic is the study of arguments. Frequently we use the term "argument" to refer to verbal fights where voices are raised, insults are hurled, feelings are hurt, and relations are ruptured. But that is *not* how it is being used here. Throughout this book "argument" refers to a public dialogue in which the participants are honestly seeking the best solution to a problem or answer to a question. In this sense, an argument is a good thing; it should produce a lot of light with very little heat.

So understood, there are three elements of a good argument: (1) it must be *public*, (2) the participants must be *honest*, and (3) their goal must be the *best* (as opposed to a perfect) solution or answer. We will be saying much more about these three requirements as we proceed. For now, suffice it to say that the first requirement excludes appeals to "private knowledge or experience." Suppose, for example, someone says that God told him that the world was going to end next year on April 15th. Perhaps he will be proven right and perhaps he really did know this by divine revelation. But it would be impossible to have a philosophical discussion about the truth or falsity of such a proposition since it is based on a *special* revelation that, by definition, was not available to everyone (i.e., it was private).

That is not to say that philosophy is anti-religious. It is only to say that religious discussions are different from philosophical discussions. All great religions have established criteria, many of them public in nature, for discerning between true and false prophets. The most common criteria are moral virtue coupled with "signs and wonders." But the evaluation of a prophet's virtue and miracles is an essentially historical, not philosophical, matter.

Though philosophers frequently discuss God and other theological issues, their discussions are deliberately limited to reasons, data, and evidence which are public and equally available to everyone.[1] In chapter 10 we will sympathetically discuss two philosophical arguments for the existence of God. Of course, most people who believe in God do so by faith, not as the result of philosophical arguments. Though we will say much more about the nature of faith in chapter 12, for now we will not quibble with this distinction between religious faith and philosophical argumentation.

The second requirement for a good argument is that all participants are honestly looking for the best solution or answer; they are *not* trying to win a debate. In a good argument, everyone wins because everyone gains a better understanding of reality. But when victory is the goal, everyone loses. Verbal "muggings" shut down reasoned discussion. And when reason shuts down, everyone's understanding is diminished.

Only when all the participants are honestly and in good faith searching for the truth will problems get solved and questions answered. If

---

1. An apparent exception is philosophical discussions of the soundness of "religious experience." Many philosophers have defended the reasonableness of God choosing to reveal himself to individual people. But while the person's experience of "God speaking to them" is essentially private, the philosophical arguments defending the legitimacy of such experiences are essentially public.

some of the participants are only trying to convince others to adopt *their* solution or answer, we will have moved from logic to rhetoric. We are not suggesting that all rhetoric is bad. Once the best solution or answer has been discovered, then it is quite appropriate to use the most effective means possible to communicate to others what's been discovered. But good rhetoric always *follows* good reason; it should never *replace* good reason.

Not surprisingly, many will disagree about this characterization of good arguments. Relativists say there are no answers to big philosophical questions concerning God, immortality, and free will, so rhetoric is all that is left. Some will go so far as to claim that *all* appeals to "truth" are nothing more than the social constructs of those in power. These philosophers adopt Friedrich Nietzsche's (1844–1900) definition of "truth" as nothing more than "a mobile army of marching metaphors." So defined, "truth" is not something to be *discovered* by philosophers; it is something *created* by the rich and powerful to control, oppress, and marginalize the masses. We will have much to say about this in subsequent chapters, but for now we are simply acknowledging an objection to our definition of a "good argument" as one where the participants are seeking truth, not victory.

The third characteristic of a "good argument" is that it seeks the *best* solution or answer, not a perfect or absolutely certain answer. Perfection is frequently the enemy of the good. Humans are finite and fallible. If our goal is absolute and infallible knowledge, we are sure to end up frustrated, if not cynical. And frustration frequently results in aggression, while cynicism leads to sarcasm—neither of which is conducive to a good argument.

Once again, there will be objections. Beginning with René Descartes (1596–1650), many philosophers have argued that knowledge requires certainty. And clearly these philosophers have had a powerful influence in public discourse. Every time the retort, "you *might* be wrong," is used to rebut an argument, Descartes' ghost is near by. The only alternative, they say, to turning knowledge into mere opinion is to ground knowledge in an absolutely firm foundation. Without arguments that establish their conclusions with absolutely certainty, the door is left wide open for relativists who say that "truth" is anything a person or culture sincerely *believes*. This is unacceptable to classical foundationalists.

We will have much to say about the classical foundationalism of Descartes in chapter 6, but here we will simply note that Aristotelian realists disagree. They argue that foundationalists have created a false dichotomy. Complete relativism and absolute foundations are not the only alternatives. The third alternative, say philosophical realists, is reasonable (though not infallible) conclusions based on good arguments.

Of course, realists face problems too. They say with a straight face: "10 percent of what I'm telling you is probably false, but I do not know which 10 percent." To foundationalists, this is nothing more than disguised relativism. If you admit that *some* of what you claim to know is probably wrong and if you cannot specify in advance which portion that is, then you cannot really be said to *know* anything. Realists respond: "But the 90 percent which turns out to be true I really will have known; the 10 percent which turns out to be false only proves that all humans are fallible." A recurrent theme of realism is that knowing is a human activity which requires truth, not certainty. Claims to "know" are *not* ipso facto claims to "*know* that we know."

To recap, according to realists, "good arguments" are public, honest, and seek the best (not an absolutely certain) answer to our philosophical questions. However, before we proceed, one corollary and a qualification must be added.

The corollary to honesty is patient diligence. Both are moral virtues and both are required for a good argument. There is always a strong temptation when one begins to ask philosophical questions to race ahead to the exciting and "sexy" issues about God, freedom, and immortality before mastering the more basic points of logic. To resist such temptation takes discipline. Without such discipline, philosophical "arguments" will generate much heat, but little light. Plato would not allow anyone under thirty who has not already master mathematics to study philosophy. "You must have seen how youngsters, when they get their first taste of it [philosophy], treat argument as a form of sport solely for purposes of contradiction."[2] So in addition to being honest, good philosophers

---

2. Plato continues, "When someone has proved them wrong, they copy his methods to confute others, delighting like puppies in tugging and tearing at anyone who comes near them. And so, after a long course of proving others wrong and being proved wrong themselves, they rush to the conclusion that all they once believed is false; and the result is that in the eyes of the world they discredit, not themselves only, but the whole business of philosophy." Plato *Republic* VII.539.

will be self-disciplined and patient in their pursuit of answers to big questions.

And one final qualification is necessary. We said earlier that good arguments are public dialogues. Now we need to refine that statement. With big philosophical questions, it is always wise to begin by considering what previous philosophers have said. Failure to do so is simple arrogance. This is part of what it means to say that philosophical arguments require diligence.

But sometimes we ignore what others have said not out of arrogance, but out of despair over the manifest diversity of positions taken by previous philosophers. If even the "great philosophers" are unable to reach agreement on the big questions, why should we lesser lights even try?

Our answer depends upon the meaning of "even try." If by this one means, "try to convince everyone else," then despair is inevitable. It is utterly utopian to think we will put to rest an important philosophical debate. But, if by "even try" one means, "try to discover *for oneself* the best answers to big questions," then such a goal is achievable, and perhaps even obligatory. As the Greeks frequently said, "the unexamined life is not worth living." Besides, who has not asked themselves big philosophical questions about the meaning of life, the significance of death, and how we "got here" in the first place? These are questions which humans can only pretend to avoid.

There is, however, a second reason one might not "even try" which requires a different kind of answer. This second source of despair is grounded in one of the most fundamental of all philosophical disputes. It is the dispute between realists who believe in good arguments and relativists who only believe in rhetoric.

This fundamental dispute begins with the truism that there is no such thing as a "view from nowhere." All observations assume a particular perspective. We must view elephants either from the front, side, rear, top, or bottom. This alone does not mean that all statements about elephants must begin with "*To me* an elephant looks like ..." If we happen to be viewing an elephant from the front, there is nothing preventing us from taking a second look from another perspective. And when we look at an elephant from all the various perspectives, then we can safely claim to know what an elephant looks like without having to add, "This it how it looks *to me*."

But suppose we are looking for something bigger? Suppose we are looking for Truth, Goodness, Freedom, or even God? How is it possible to approach such big philosophical issues from any perspective other than our own? If we were born in America and raised in a Christian family, we are going to look at God from a Christian perspective. If we were born Thailand and raised in a Buddhist monastery then we are going to look at "God" from a quite different perspective. Is there any reason to suppose that "good arguments" might change one's "perspective" with respect to God? So, when it comes to these big philosophical questions, relativists insist that we preface all our statement with, "*To me* God is . . ." or "*To me* Freedom is . . ."

Well, prefacing all our philosophical statements with "to me" is certainly one philosophical perspective. But this is not the only philosophical perspective. The pagan Greek philosopher, Aristotle (384–322 BCE) and his medieval Christian interpreter, Thomas Aquinas (1225–1275) had a quite different perspective. They endorsed the motto of the TV series, *The X-Files*: "The truth is out there." Though they never claimed to have discovered the whole truth—absolutely free of error—these two founders of philosophical realism did claim that some answers to the big philosophical questions are better than others. It remains to be seen if they succeed. But we have already learned one thing: there are different philosophical perspectives about what constitutes a perspective. The important question is: whose "perspective" accounts for more of the data— the Relativists or the Realists? In all succeeding chapters, this question will be lurking in the background so we will not attempt an answer it here. However, we can be clear about what is at stake.

Relativists argue that all answers to big questions about Truth, Goodness, Freedom, and God are relative to the person (or culture) making the claim. What's "true" for one person with respect to a big philosophical question need not be "true" for someone else. If a person sincerely believes that humans are free and that God exists, then for *that* person (or culture) this is the "truth," but it need not be the "truth" for a different person (or culture). Relativists support this position by arguing that "reality" is not something that exists independent of people and their unique perspectives. Instead, "reality" is something that people create for themselves.

Reality, say relativists, is like cookie dough. When a baker cuts out Christmas cookies in the shape of trees, bells, and candy canes, these do not pre-exist *in* the dough. The dough is any combination of trees, bells, and candy canes that the baker *chooses* it to be. So too, "reality" does not come with a pre-existing set of categories just waiting to be discovered. No, "reality" is something that each person and/or culture creates for themselves.

Aristotle and Aquinas disagree. First, while it is obviously true that many of our categories, perhaps even most, are created by individuals and cultures who have "imposed" their categories upon reality, this is not *always* the case. Realists argue, for example, that the distinction between things which are alive and things which are not, or the distinction between animals that are capable of feeling pain and plants that are incapable of feeling pain, are *not* humanly constructed categories. And if such distinctions are grounded in reality-as-it-is-in-itself, then it is at least possible that there are distinctions that go deeper than mere human conceptions between good and evil, freedom and determinism, God and random chance. So the only way to know if these distinctions are real is to have a "good argument."

This leads to a second point. While sincerity is a virtue, it is possible to be sincerely wrong. The most sincere people are the first to admit that they are sometimes mistaken. The fact that the vast majority of people and philosophers who lived prior to the sixteenth century *sincerely believed* that the earth was in the center of the universe did not make their belief true. While they are certainly not to blame for their error, it was an error nonetheless.

We must, however, remember that philosophical realists are *not* "absolutists." They are the ones who insist that humans are finite and fallible, and that none of our knowledge is absolutely certain. We can never know *all* there is to know about morality, freedom, and God until history comes to an end. Somewhat paradoxically this means that it is the relativists, not the realists, who bestow a kind of infallibility on humans. According to realists, humans sometimes bump into an independent existing reality that can refute their previous beliefs. But according to relativists, no such "reality" exists; only "sincere beliefs" about reality exist. The most that a relativist can bump into are other people who have a different set of beliefs. However, the fact that others believe X would hardly be a reason for him to give up his sincere belief in Y.

The disagreement between relativists and realists is fundamental and it will not go away any time soon. Much of what is popularly referred to as the "culture wars" grows out of this ancient dispute. So time spent studying these opposing philosophies is not wasted. In fact, it might even be a civic duty for those living in a pluralistic democracy.

But now we are faced with a dilemma—how can one fairly articulate and describe such a fundamental dispute without already "taking sides"? The answer is that one cannot. There is no such thing as a "neutral" description of any philosophical dispute. "A view from nowhere" is impossible; everyone must think and write from *within* a philosophical tradition. What is important is that we do so self-consciously. Only then will we realize that what seems so obvious to us may not be obvious to other philosophical traditions. With this sort of self-awareness, good arguments are possible. So in the interest of full disclosure, we will declare up front that this book is written from within the tradition of Aristotle and Aquinas.

But writing from within a philosophical tradition is not the same as writing with a "bias" and/or "prejudice." In fact, openly acknowledging one's "perspective" is the first step in avoiding such shortcomings. A healthy self-consciousness of one's own tradition is more conducive to an honest consideration of contrary positions than a pseudo-objectivity that pretends to be "above the fray."

Once again, we see the centrality of "honesty" in good arguments. And once again it is worth noting that the most important philosophical arguments are not those that try to convince others. Openly acknowledging that one is *part* of an ongoing dispute means that one has (or at least should!) renounced the role of judge and jury. Realism may be true, but the final verdict will only be returned at the end of history. The most anyone can do is to allow their best judgments to become the guiding light for all they believe and do. When it comes to ultimate verdicts, both realists and relativists "live by faith." The only difference is that realists believe there will be an ultimate verdict on their philosophy, relativists do not.

1.2 DEDUCTIVE PROOFS

The two indispensable distinctions in logic are between (1) valid and true and (2) deductive and inductive reasoning. First, validity only concerns the *form* of an argument; it has nothing to do with the truth or falsity of either its premises or conclusion. Second, the criteria for evaluating deductive and inductive arguments are radically different. Sound deductive arguments produce proof; the best inductive arguments only produce probability. To expect proof from induction is like expecting orange juice from a bushel of apples. The remainder of this section explains the distinction between valid and true. Section 1.3 explains the distinction between deduction and induction.

The logician's distinction between "true" and "valid" and the biologist's distinction between "fish" and "mammal" are both *stipulative*. In ordinary discourse, "true" and "valid" are frequently used interchangeably, just as "fish" is used interchangeably with "lives and swims in water." But all logicians know that arguments with a true conclusion can be invalid just as all biologists know that not all animals that live and swim in water are fish. Similar "exteriors" can hide radically different "interiors": On the outside, tunas and dolphins look a lot alike, but when you cut them open, they are quite different—tunas have gills, while dolphins have lungs. So too, cut open two arguments with true premises and a true conclusion and it may very well be the case that only one of them is valid.

"True" and "valid" are related like "heavy" and "purple." A ball can be purple without being heavy or it can be heavy without being purple or it can be *both* heavy and purple. So too, a deductive argument can have true conclusions and premises without having a valid form (like example #1 below) or it can have a valid form without having true conclusion and premises (like example #2 below) or it can have *both* a true conclusion and premises and a valid form. Only in the last case does the argument *prove* its conclusion.

While this may seem needlessly complex, a simple example from math will illustrate its importance. When fifth grade teachers correct their students' math homework they check for two things: first, did the student get the correct answer, and second, did the student *do* the calculations correctly? Suppose a student's long division homework looks like this:

$$25\overline{)1250} \quad \begin{array}{r} 50 \\ \hline 23 \\ \underline{26} \\ 0 \end{array}$$

Figure 1.1

The student's answer is correct, but his "method" or "process" of getting to the answer is not. This student has made a couple of mistakes. (First, 5 x 25 is not 123, and second, 26 divided by 25 does not equal 0.) It just happens that these two mistakes cancel out so that the answer, *by sheer luck*, turns out to be correct. In this example, getting the correct answer is not the same as doing long division correctly. So too, having a true conclusion is not the same as *proving* the conclusion to be true. A deductive argument can have a true conclusion and true premises *and yet still be invalid.* For example,

> *Example #1*
> 1. All dogs are animals, and
> 2. All Golden Retrievers are animals.
> 3. Therefore, all Golden Retrievers are dogs.

Conversely, arguments whose form or structure is valid can have a false conclusion and premises. For example,

> *Example #2*
> 1. All reptiles are black, and
> 2. All dogs are reptiles
> 3. Therefore, all dogs are black.

The arguments in examples #1 and #2 are both bad arguments, but they are bad for very different reasons. The first argument is bad because its form is invalid, even though its conclusion and premises are all true. The second argument is bad because its conclusion and premises are false, even though its form is perfectly valid.

So how can an argument in which everything is false nonetheless be perfectly valid? Answer: A valid deductive argument is one which is structured in such a way that *if the premises were true*, it would be absolutely impossible for the conclusion to be false.

Grammatically, this definition is a subjunctive conditional. "If it were to rain, Bill would get wet" does not assert that Bill will *in fact* get wet since the truth of a subjunctive conditional is quite consistent with its antecedent being false, i.e. it is not raining. So too, to assert that an argument is valid is quite consistent with its premises and conclusion being false. In Bill's cases, what is asserted is the existence of a causal relation between rain and getting wet. In the case of a deductive argument, what is asserted is the existence of a logical relation between premises

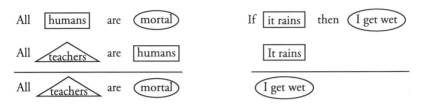

Figure 1.2

and the conclusion. Here are two examples of valid (i.e., logical) relations between premises and conclusions.

> *Example #3*
> 1. All humans are mortal, and
> 2. All teachers are humans.
> 3. Therefore, all teachers are mortal.

> *Example #4*
> 1. If it rains, then I will get wet.
> 2. It is raining.
> 3. Therefore, I will get wet.

The form of these two arguments becomes more apparent if we use circles, squares, and triangles to represent the logical relationship between crucial terms (see figure 1.2). In representing the form of an argument, the premises are placed above the line and the conclusion below the line.

When logicians evaluate deductive proofs, they are not concerned with the *content* of the argument ("humans," "mortals," "it rain," "I get wet," etc.). The logicians only concern is with the arrangement of the circles, squares, and triangles. They think of these shapes as empty containers into which all different kinds of content can be placed. Their arrangement represents the argument's structure or form. This arrangement is the logicians' *only* concern. When the containers are arranged in a logically proper structure the argument is valid. When they are not properly arranged the argument is invalid. In short, validity concerns the *form* (i.e. structure) of an argument, while truth concerns the *content* of an argument (i.e. what is placed inside the containers).

How, then, can we know if an argument is validly structured? Logicians have two methods—one is fairly simple, but not absolutely conclusive; the other is absolutely conclusive, but not as simple.

The conclusive method requires the use of Venn Diagrams and/or other specialized tools of logicians. Though we will not take the time to explain these, what they show is that in all valid arguments the conclusion is already "contained" or "given" in the premises. In other words, all valid arguments are ultimately reducible to an argument like this:

> *Example #5*
> 1. Roses are red.
> 2. Violets are blue.
> 3. Therefore, roses are red.

Clearly, it is absolutely impossible for an argument like this to have true premises and a false conclusion because the conclusion simply repeats what is already stated in the premises. The conclusion of *all* deductively valid arguments—no matter how complex and sophisticated— never assert anything that has not already been asserted in the premises. That is why logicians can say with total confidence that in a valid deductive argument it is *absolutely impossible* for the premises to be true and the conclusion to be false.

However, we do not need Venn Diagrams or any other special tools to demonstrate that an argument is invalid. A simple example can illustrate this. Remember, invalid arguments prove nothing, even if their conclusion happens to be true (See #1 above). Consider, for example, the following argument with a true conclusion and true premises.

> *Example #6*
> 1. If the earth is round, then we would see the tops of ships' sails first as they approach from a distance.
> 2. We do see the tops of ships' sails first when they approach from a distance.
> 3. Therefore, the earth is round.

In both #1 and #6 the premises and conclusion are all true. (If you have doubts about the first premise in #6, consider the figure 1.3 below. A "rounded" earth has a "hump" that cuts off our vision of the bottom of the ship without cutting off our vision of the top of the ship.)

However, simple counterexamples prove both arguments to be invalid. There are two steps to producing a counterexample. First, we abstract their structure/form. (#1 is on the left and #6 on the right in figure 1.4.)

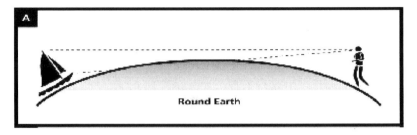

Figure 1.3

Second, we construct a counterexample, i.e. an argument of the same form, but with new content such that the premises are obviously true and the conclusion obviously false. For example:

> *Example 1A*
> 1. All mothers are parents, and
> 2. All fathers are parents.
> 3. Therefore, all fathers are mothers.

and

> *Example 6A*
> 1. If John F. Kennedy was beheaded, then he would be dead.
> 2. John F. Kennedy is dead.
> 3. Therefore, John F. Kennedy was beheaded.

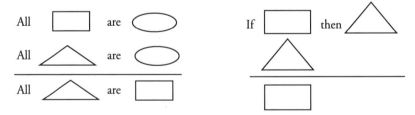

Figure 1.4

Arguments #1A and #6A are obviously not good arguments since both conclusions are false. But there are only two things that can go wrong with a deductive argument: (1) a false premise or, (2) an invalid structure/form. Since the premises in #1A and #6A are all true, by a process of elimination, the problem must in the structure/form. And since arguments #1 and #6 are of the exact same structure/form as the arguments

#1A and #6A, we must conclude that arguments #1 and #6 must themselves be invalid *even though their premises and conclusions are all true.* Put affirmatively, a valid structure/form is one for which no counterexample can be constructed. In a valid argument, no matter what "content" is placed in the circles, squares, and triangles, if the premises are true, it is absolutely, cross your heart, hope to die, impossible for the conclusion to be false.

But the reverse is not true. The fact that a particular argument has not yet been proved invalid with a counterexample does not, strictly speaking, prove that it is valid. It may only mean that we have not looked hard enough. But once a counterexample is discovered, we have absolute proof that the form is invalid.

Though determining the validity or invalidity of an argument is fairly simple, determining whether the premises are true is anything but simple. For that we need more than deductive logic; we need to reason inductively.

1.3 INDUCTIVE ARGUMENTS

Imagine a carpenter who is also a fairly good cabinetmaker. One day he dies without any heirs. His house, and everything in it, is sold at auction. One of the last items to sell is a piece of furniture: an Early American style buffet that he made for his mother. The buffet is purchased by Mr. Philistine who takes it to his stable, straps a heavy anvil to a corner and then starts pounding out horseshoes. By the third horseshoe, the corner of the buffet collapses. After uttering a few expletives, the Philistine exclaims, "Whoever made this certainly is a poor craftsman!" Clearly, by taking the criteria for evaluating a work bench and (mis)applying them to a piece of furniture, the Philistine is acting like his namesake. What makes a buffet good is *not* what makes a workbench good. So too, what makes a deductive argument good is *not* what makes an inductive argument good.

We will say much more about inductive arguments in succeeding chapters (especially chapters 2, 3, and 6). Here, we will only explain why one must never hold inductive arguments to the same standard as we do deductive arguments.

By definition, inductive arguments only establish their conclusion with a greater or lesser degree of *probability*. Probability is always a more-or-less affair, while validity is always an all-or-nothing affair. (It makes no more sense to say of a deductive argument that it is almost valid than it does to say of a woman that she is a little bit pregnant.) Inductive arguments are never valid proofs, no matter how strong the argument. The best inductive argument never establishes its conclusion with certainty. Unlike valid deductive arguments—where it is absolutely impossible for the premises to be true and the conclusion false—it is quite possible in the *best* inductive argument for all the premises to be true, and yet—by a kind of "bad luck"—for the conclusion turns out to be false.

To illustrate, suppose that a person is offered an even odds bet that a single honest die, when rolled, will come up less than six. A person will win such a bet five out of six times or 83 percent of the time. Clearly, those are pretty good odds. And if one is a gambler, then it would be quite rational to make such a bet. Now suppose the bet is made, the die is thrown and it comes up six. Does that mean that the person who made the bet was reasoning poorly? No, it just means that he was reasoning inductively and that bad luck got in the way. Inductive reasoning is always subject to such "bad luck," *but that does not mean that one was reasoning poorly.*

Second, unlike deductive arguments, the *content* of an inductive argument must always be considered. While the *validity* of a deductive proof has nothing to do with the content of the premises, the *strength* of an inductive argument has everything to do with the content of its premises.

Suppose Fred is in the market for a fuel-efficient car, but he cannot afford to spend much money. His neighbor owns an old V.W. Rabbit with a five-speed transmission, radial tires, and diesel engine which consistently gets over fifty miles per gallon. So Fred checks E-Bay and finds a V.W. Rabbit with a five-speed transmission, radial tires, and a diesel engine. Formally considered, we have an argument that looks like this:

Example #7
1. Neighbor's car = VW + Rabbit + five-speed + radials + diesel → fifty m.p.g.
2. E-Bay's car = VW + Rabbit + five-speed + radials + diesel → ? ? ?

From these premises Fred reasons inductively and draws the conclusion that his newly purchased E-bay car will also get around fifty miles per gallon just like his neighbor's. Is Fred reasoning well? Here there is no philosophically neutral answer. As we will see in later chapters, there are very important and significant philosophers—like René Descartes (who we already mentioned) and David Hume (to be considered later)—

who would be critical of Fred's reasoning. Though interestingly, their criticisms of Fred's reasoning are totally different. On the other hand, Aristotelian realists would say, without hesitation, that Fred has reasoned well. (This dispute between Descartes' classical foundationalism, Hume's positivism, and Aristotelian realism will be considered in chapter 6.)

But there is another sort of case where we can all agree. Suppose Fred wins a multimillion dollar lottery, yet he retains his environmentalist conscience and wants a car that will get good mileage. Once again he reasons inductively about his neighbor's car. Only this time, his premises concern the fact that his neighbor's car is red, has bucket seats, a moon roof, racing strips, a CD player, and gets fifty miles per gallon. Fred then concludes that if he purchases a red Ferrari with bucket seats, a moon roof, racing strips, and a CD player that he too will get around fifty miles per gallon. Formally, his second argument goes like this:

Example #8
1. Neighbor's car = red + bucket seat + moon roof + racing strips + CD → fifty m.p.g.
2. Ferrari = red + bucket seat + moon roof + racing strips + CD → probably fifty m.p.g.

Again, we ask: Is Fred reasoning well? This time everyone agrees that he is not. Why? The problem with Fred's second argument has nothing to do with its form. Were we to draw circles, squares, triangles, etc. for both arguments, we would see that their *form* is identical (compare example #7 and #8). What makes Fred's second argument (example #8) extremely weak is the *content* of the circles, squares, triangles, etc. In the first argument, the content of the premises is causally *relevant* to its conclusion; in the second argument it is not. Therefore, in two structurally/formally identical inductive arguments, one may be good, while the other is bad. That's why inductive arguments can never be evaluated by their "logic" alone. (And we will argue later that it is deductively impossible to determine what is or is not causally relevant.)

Here again we see why the words "valid" or "logically proves" should never be used in connection with inductive arguments. Though there are rough and ready rules of thumb called "informal fallacies" that are frequently used in the evaluation of inductive arguments, these can never be more than a starting point. By themselves, informal fallacies are never conclusive.

For example, generally speaking it is an *ad hominem* fallacy to criticize public policy proposals by criticizing their author. Bad people can have good policy proposals and good people can have bad policy proposals. Does this mean that the House of Representatives was reasoning fallaciously when they impeached President Clinton for his illicit sexual behavior? Maybe it does and maybe it does not. It depends on whether one's "moral character" is more-or-less important than one's policy proposals when it comes to questions about one's fitness to lead. This is not a question of logic, but a difficult question about the relation between personal virtue and public leadership. (Actually, we will have much to say about such questions in chapter 8.) And this point can be generalized: it is never possible to determine the strength of an inductive argument *solely* with a check list of informal fallacies. The very name *in*-formal fallacy (i.e., not formal) makes this clear. Form alone never determines the strength of inductive reasoning; we must always consider its contents, i.e., what the argument is about. What may constitute legitimately disqualifying behavior by a religious leader may or may not constitute legitimately disqualifying behavior for a college professor.

Perceptive readers will notice a dilemma: Deductive arguments logically prove their conclusions only *if* we know their premises are true. But to establish the truth of premises in a deductive argument, we must reason inductively. However inductive arguments, no matter how strong, never logically *prove* their conclusion. So how can we ever *know* anything?

Relativists simply accept the skeptical dilemma and conclude that there is no independently existing "truth" the way that realists understand the term. All that exists are various opinions. This is one of the reasons relativists say that "truth" is always relative to a person's beliefs. If a person sincerely believes that "X" is true, then X is true for him. While if another person sincerely believes that "not-X" is true, then not-X is true for them.

There are three ways to avoid this skeptical dilemma and the relativist's conclusion—*idealism, realism,* and *positivism*.

A chief proponent of idealism is René Descartes, the same philosopher we mentioned earlier as a critic of all "*merely* inductive" arguments. His criticism of induction was grounded in his claim that we ought never to accept merely probable arguments. In his uncompleted *Rules for the Direction of the Mind*, his second rule was to "trust only what is completely known and incapable of being doubted." The effect of Descartes' rule is that all knowledge must ultimately be grounded in deductive proof. His way out of the skeptical dilemma was to look for premises which were "clear and distinct" so that they could not possibly be false.

His first "clear and distinct" idea was his absolute certainty that he existed as a thinking being. Why? Imagine, he said, that an evil genius with superhuman powers existed whose sole goal in life was to deceive mere mortals. Such a Being could easily deceive us about many, if not most, of the things we believe to be true. For example, right now I'm absolutely convinced that I am sitting in front of a computer with my fingers typing on a keyboard. However, it would not be difficult for a superhuman evil genius to deceive me about such a belief—perhaps I am drugged or perhaps I am sound asleep in my bed and only dreaming that I am working on my book. Contemporary philosopher's have updated Descartes' argument and asked: Can we know for certain that we are not brains in a vat connected by electrodes to a gigantic computer so that all our conscious thoughts are the product of the evil genius' machinations? (Movie fans will correctly see in this the inspiration for The Matrix.) Nonetheless, there is one belief, Descartes argued, of which we can be absolutely certain—namely, I exist as a conscious being (whether or not I have a body is a different question altogether). Why? Because if I did not exist as a conscious being, there would be nothing for the evil genus to deceive!

Second, Descartes said that we all have a clear and distinct idea of a Supreme Being (i.e. a being than which none greater can be conceived). Descartes then argued that as soon as we have such an idea of a Supreme Being (i.e. God) we know that this being *must* exist. Why? Because if we say that the Supreme Being only exists in our consciousness, not in reality, then we have contradicted ourselves. A being that exists *only* in our consciousness is not as great as one who exists *both* in our consciousness and in reality. Since there is a direct contradiction in thinking that a merely fictional being is the greatest possible being, it is logically certain that God exists.

Having established the existence of a perfect God, Descartes takes his argument further: No perfect and Supreme Being would allow his creatures to be continually deceived by an evil genius. Therefore, the majority of our conscious perceptions must in fact correspond to reality.

The point here is not to defend Descartes' solution to the skeptical dilemma posed above, nor even to make his particular argument sound plausible. We summarize Descartes' arguments only to illustrate how philosophical idealists *begin* with ideas in the mind (not an independently existing reality outside the mind). They begin here because they believe only consciousness can provide an absolutely firm foundation upon which to build one's philosophy. According to idealists, ideas and their deductive consequences are *the* ultimate reality. Inductive arguments, based on observations, of every day things like plants and animals, they say, are both unnecessary (since we can ground a philosophy solely in "clear and distinct idea" and their deductive consequences) and untrustworthy (because our observations are always fallible).

Realists like Aristotle and Aquinas reject the idealist's solution to the relativist's dilemma. Instead of starting with our *ideas* about things, realists insist that we begin with the things themselves. There is no good reason, according to realists, not to begin with the common sense assumption that things like plants and animals exist independent of and prior to our ideas about them. To the old riddle—If a tree falls in the forest and no one hears it, does it make a sound?—realists answer without hesitation, "Of course, it does!" Reality and our consciousness of reality are utterly distinct and different. No Aristotelian realist feels compelled, like Descartes, to *prove* that plants and animals really exist. The fact that we see them is sufficient. The only thing realists attempt to "prove" is that the doubts and arguments of Descartes are unfounded. We'll say more about this later (chapter 6).

Philosophical positivists propose a different solution to the relativist's dilemma. Instead of grounding a philosophy exclusively in ideas and deductive proofs (like idealists), or relying on common sense observations (like realists), they turn to science and its specialized methods of measurement, hypothesis formation and experimental testing. Only science, they say, can produces results that are positively verified.[3] The

---

3. Positivism is not a modern view. Aristotle also had to contend with the view that ethics and other disciplines which employ final causes are not really sciences, i.e. genuine forms of knowledge. Aristippus, says Aristotle, argued that since mathematics is the most noble of sciences and the only genuine method of obtaining knowledge, and since it has no recourse to final causes, that therefore, a discipline like ethics, which does have recourse to final causes, must be considered inferior. Aristotle, *Metaphysics*, 3.2.

"Freud had captured the spirit of a positivist outlook when he had written that his science was no illusion, but 'an illusion it would be to suppose that what science cannot give us we can get elsewhere.'" Brooke, *Science and Religion,* 326.

ultimate goal of positivists is to formulate rules for inductive argument which will *guarantee* their conclusions in the same way that valid deductive argument *guarantee* deductive conclusions. They take inspiration from scientists and their method which seems to produce positive results upon which all can agree.

(Realists argue that "the positive" results of the "scientific method" are largely an illusion. In the next chapter we will argue that cutting edge science always involves more than guaranteed conclusions based on measurable observations. It involves good judgment and rational insight into the nature of things. Neither of these can be reduced to a logical or a mathematical formula.)

1.4 RHETORICAL PERSUASION

As much as Aristotelian realists, idealists, and positivists disagree about the means, they all agree on the end—a *true* understanding of reality. Realists and positivists both believe that physical reality exists prior to and independent of our ideas about reality. The difference, however, is that positivists argue that science is the *only* source of knowledge whereas Aristotelian realists argue that there are other legitimate sources of knowledge. Idealists have yet a third method. They believe that our ideas *are* the ultimate reality. Physical things like plants and animals, they say, are either products of consciousness or inferences from consciousness. Therefore, it is only by relying on our ideas alone that we discover the truth about reality. But all three philosophical traditions assume that discovering the truth is philosophy's goal.

Philosophical relativists, on the other hand, reject the very concept of a human-independent "reality" and of discoverable "truth." They follow Protagoras (c. 490–420 BCE) who said long ago, "Man is the measure of all things: of things which are, that they are, and of things which are not, that they are not." Nothing is simply true—it is always "true *for me*" or "true *in our culture.*" Of course, it is hard to believe that all "truths" are determined by what a person or culture believes. Believing that one can fly like a bird is not going to save someone who jumps off the Golden Gate Bridge. So, today, most relativists limit their skepticism to moral and philosophical issues. It is only when we are talking about questions like—Are humans truly free? Is the soul immortal? Does God exist?— that a proposition becomes "true" if a person or group sincerely believes it is true.

Rather than wasting time studying what past philosophers have written about such questions, relativists counsel us to focus on questions that can be answered in a wholly pragmatic fashion: "How can I get what I want?" "How can we convince people to be more tolerant?" These are the sorts of questions we ought to be considering. In these cases, what is required is rhetorical skill, not philosophical arguments. What is important is not discovering capital "T" Truth; that's impossible. Instead, we need to learn to *convince* other people to adopt our own point of view. And the way to do this is to study the art of rhetorical persuasion, not the arguments of philosophers.

Though relativism is virtually the default position of most Americans, it faces two significant difficulties. The first is its apparent incoherence. It seems that relativists are *arguing* that there are no good arguments.[4] How can relativists *know* that all knowledge is impossible? If they *know* that all "knowledge" is mere opinion, then there is at least one proposition that is more than a mere opinion. On the other hand, if they are only of the *opinion* that all knowledge is impossible, then that is hardly a reason for others to become relativists. Their position, it seems, is in danger of refuting itself.[5]

The second difficulty is the relativist's attempt to sharply distinguish between facts and values. It is hard to take seriously someone who says that sincerely believing that one can fly like a bird will make it true. Therefore, most relativists temper their position and claim that it is only "value judgments" in philosophy and ethics where sincere belief makes something "true for me." But how do we know what's a "fact" and what's only a "value"? Suppose Ralph continually interrupts others when they are speaking. Suppose too that Ralph is frequently and deliberately impolite to strangers. Finally, suppose Ralph has the habit of being vulgar, even to the point of being obscene, even in the most formal of settings. Is it a "fact" or "value" to describe Ralph as rude? Our hesitancy in answering such a question demonstrates, at least in many philosophers' minds, that a rigid distinction between "facts" and "values" is anything but obvious. Besides, how many of us are willing, without equivocation,

4. "For he who 'destroys reason,' must uphold its significance, because he can only express what he denies by speaking and by signifying something." Aquinas, *Commentary*, sec. 611, vol. 1, 248.

5. Of course, this will not silence sophisticated philosophical relativists. But it turns some into ironists. "Sure, go ahead with your logic-chopping if it makes you feel better and I'll go with head-in-hand to defeat!"

to say that disapproving of gang rape and genocide is merely a "value" that some of us happen to embrace? Are claims such as "gang rape is wrong" not moral *facts*?

Whether or not these are insurmountable objections to relativism is something we will be discussing throughout this book, beginning with the next chapter. There we will be considering the "scientific method" because surely, if there is any place we can learn to distinguish facts from values, it will be from scientists.

1.5 SUMMARY

We have not attempted to answer any difficult philosophical questions in this chapter. We have only defined various philosophical positions. But when the question concerns deductive logic, there is universal agreement. The distinctions (1) between valid form and the truth of propositions, and (2) between deductive proofs and inductive arguments are no more controversial than the claim that two plus two equals four. And the reason they are not controversial is that *by itself* neither logic nor mathematics can answer significant philosophical questions. It is only when we provide content for premises in deductive arguments that real knowledge is produced. Unfortunately, it is precisely this "content" that causes philosophical disagreements.

Finally, let me suggest, as a kind of mnemonic device with no disrespect intended, that we think of realists, positivists, and relativists respectively as "double knowers," "single knowers," and "know nothings."

Philosophical realists are "double knowers" who argue that there are at least two sources of content—observation and rational insight. We will say much more about the nature of "rational insight" as we proceed. For now we will only define it as that uniquely human ability to understand *what* an observed object is. Understanding the "whatness" of things is highly controversial among philosophers. The "whatness," or essential nature, of an object is *qualitatively* different from what is observed by a camcorder or any other sophisticated scientific instrument. That is why talk of whatness/essential natures is often considered highly suspect in a scientific age.

Nonetheless, realism was the dominant position in the ancient and medieval world and it is currently gaining support among professional philosophers. And, as long as the topic is not morality, philosophy, or religion, realism is still the default position of most people. After all, what could be more obvious than the proposition that rocks are essentially different from trees and that trees are essentially different from animals?

Positivists and philosophical idealists are "single knowers." They argue that there is only a single source of knowledge. According to positivists, that single source is the kind of observations made by scientists and their sophisticated instruments. According to philosophical idealists, that single source is the ideas in the human mind.

In the nineteenth century, idealism had many proponents. But in the West today, idealism has few advocates—though classical Hinduism bears close resemblance to philosophical idealism and it obviously has many proponents in the East. Positivism, on the other hand, has strong support in the academic world, especially in the sciences. And though its influence among professional philosophers has considerably softened since its hay day in the first half of the twentieth century, it still has significant support today. However, given the limited influence of idealism in the West today, throughout the rest of this book I shall use the phrase "single knowers" to refer to Positivists.

Relativists are "know nothings." They say that all "knowledge" of an independently existing world is impossible. Answers to the big philosophical question are always "socially constructed"; they are not the product of either scientific or philosophical investigations. Put slightly differently, relativists argue that the *content* we insert into our logical rules and mathematical formulas is something humans create or invent; it is not something they discover. While philosophers attempt to provide elaborate and sophisticated "arguments" for their own positions, in the end relativists claim that all that is left is rhetorical persuasion because all "arguments" ultimately rest on premises which are nothing more than personal beliefs and preferences.

Relativism certainly has a strong voice in the academic world. So it is not surprising that the general public thinks of "philosophy" as merely "giving opinions" about controversial issues. Starting with chapter 4 much of our attention will be focused on the dispute between realists and relativists. However, we cannot ignore the fact that we live in a "scientific age" which makes positivism a powerful force. So our next two chapters will consider the central questions that ushered in modern science: Does the earth *really* revolve around the Sun? And is evolution true?

2

Has Science Made Philosophy Obsolete?

All positivists and many relativists draw a distinction between "facts" and "values" or between "science" and "philosophy." "Facts" are propositions which are provable by science, whereas "values" are merely the opinions of philosophers. This chapter challenges the fact/value distinction by considering the rotation of the earth around the sun. When and how did this become a "fact"?

We know that motion of the earth was not a "fact" according to ancient Greeks for the simple reason that they did not believe it to be true. Instead, they believed that the earth was "fixed" at the center of the universe. Their argument was based on three interconnected and symbiotically related ideas: 1) the stars and planets are composed of a super-subtle ethereal substance that naturally revolves in circles; 2) everything on the earth is composed of earthly, watery, airy, and fiery substances that naturally move toward and away from the center of the universe; 3) the idea of "empty space" (a place where "nothingness" exists) is a contradiction. These three ideas are the foundation for the "Two Sphere" theory of the universe.

While Two Sphere theory made a lot of sense and accounted at the time for the observational data just as well as the modern theory, it contains at least three anomalies that were known even to the ancients. First, its explanation for the motion of projectiles is somewhat forced. Second, its mechanism for explaining the motion of the planets seemed to be needlessly complex. Third, it could not explain the origin of new stars. All these lead philosophers/scientists to look for a better theory.

It is frequently thought that our modern, sun-centered theory was somehow "proven" by either experiments or new observations. This is mistaken; there are no "crucial experiments" in the history of science. Any attempt to verify a new theory necessarily commits the logical fallacy of affirming the consequent. And conversely, any attempt to falsify an existing theory ignores the fact that all theories presuppose a set of "background assumptions" or auxiliary hypotheses. This means that any theory can be saved from falsification simply by modifying one of the auxiliary hypotheses instead of the theory itself.

Defending an existing theory with this sort of ad hoc hypothesis, say positivists, is illegitimate. Positivism, however, assumes that there are logical criteria for "ad hocness." Yet, they have never produced such criteria. Furthermore, the history of science is replete with examples of hypotheses which were considered ad hoc to one generation of scientists but not ad hoc to the next generation.

Instead, both philosophical and scientific theories must be judged as organic wholes by the three C's of consistency, comprehensiveness, and coherence. But no theory is (or ever will be) perfectly consistent, comprehensive, and coherent. Therefore, old theories are never replaced by new theories until a more consistent, comprehensive, and coherent theory is purposed.

The modern theory of Copernicus—proposing a sun-centered universe—was immediately recognized as more coherent than the older Two Sphere theory, largely as a result of its mathematical elegance. However, Copernicus' theory also implied the existence of a stellar parallax which its seventeenth- and eighteenth-century advocates could never observe, even with their telescopes. It was only after Newton combined the astronomy of Copernicus, the observations of Kepler, and the physics of Galileo into a single theory that the sun-centered theory of the universe gained scientific acceptance. But even then, there were serious problems with Newton's theory.

MOST RELATIVISTS DISTINGUISH QUESTIONS about morality and philosophy from simple, factual propositions that can, in principle at least, be proved scientifically. It is only when we are making moral judgments or when we are making philosophical pronouncements, they say, that "truth" is relative. However, realists argue that a rigid distinction between "facts" and "values," or between science and philosophy, is itself dubious, and hence, so is this sort of relativism.

Our test case will be the motion of the earth. Is the motion of the earth around the sun a simple, factual proposition proved by science? Most people today would say that it is, though this was not always so. In fact, the vast majority of relativists in Protagoras' own era would have disagreed. *To them* the motion of the earth around the sun was nothing more than the wild philosophical speculation of people like Aristarchus (310–230 BCE).

Theories concerning the motion of the earth have a long, detailed, and fascinating history. We can only review this history in a most cursory fashion. Not too much attention will be paid to exactly who said what when, though more details can be found in the footnotes. Instead, our focus will be the interplay of ideas and arguments concerning the questions: *When* did it become a simple, factual proposition that the earth moves around the sun? And *how* was this "proved"?

There was certainly no "proof" when Aristarchus first proposed the idea. Even though his conclusion was correct, his arguments were weak, inconclusive, and hardly even persuasive. We will have to wait almost two thousand years before the majority of people believed the motion of the earth was a *fact*. And contrary to popular opinion, it was *not* Galileo who proved that the earth moves. To understand what Galileo did and did not contribute to our modern understanding of the universe, we must begin much earlier. In fact, we must begin with the ancient Greek Two-Sphere conception of the universe.

2.1 THE TWO SPHERE UNIVERSE

Five planets are observable by the naked eye. From the time of the ancient Greeks, philosophers/scientists have wanted to understand their motion. These five planets typically move gradually from west to east through the constellations of the fixed stars. However, at various times during the year, each of them—individually and at different times—mysteriously reverse course for a short period and move from east to west. Mercury engages in this retrograde motion once every 116 days. Venus retrogresses every 584 days. Mars, Jupiter, and Saturn exhibit retrograde motion every 780, 399, and 378 days, respectively. It is because of these irregular motions that the Greeks called Mercury, Venus, Mars, Jupiter, and Saturn "wandering stars." We translate the Greek term as "planet."

The ancient Greeks were also puzzled by the behavior of liquids in containers. To efficiently drain beer from a barrel requires *two* holes. With only a single hole the beer will eventually drain, but it comes out in irregular spurts which spill all over. The solution to this problem has been known for ages—simply put another hole near the top to allow air to freely flow into the barrel. But while the solution to the pragmatic problem was known to the Greeks, a persuasive explanation as to *why* two holes solve the problem was not. Why should a hole *above* the beer cause the beer to flow freely? While it is obvious that it has something

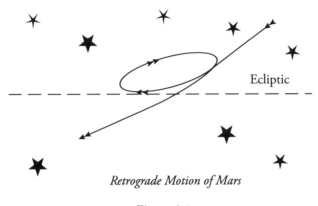

Retrograde Motion of Mars

Figure 2.1

to do with vacuums, how can a vacuum—which is literally nothing—hinder the beer from flowing freely? How can "nothingness" prevent beer from flowing?

Obviously most Greeks did not worry about the heavens out of a love for mere abstract theory. It is important for purely pragmatic reasons to understand the motion of the moon, sun, and stars. Without understanding the basic facts of astronomy, it is impossible to construct a calendar. Without a calendar, agriculture is impossible. And without agriculture, people are reduced to hunting and gathering which simply cannot sustain large groups of people in cities, i.e., civilization.

However, the retrograde motion of the five wandering stars has no bearing on the construction of an accurate calendar. So why worry about it? The same goes with respect to draining beer from barrels. Once we know how to solve the pragmatic problem, what else do we need to know? But the more philosophically inclined Greeks were interested in both *how* things work and *why* things work. As Aristotle said at the very beginning of *Metaphysics*, humans by nature desire knowledge.

So how did the philosophically minded Greeks answer questions about the motion of the planets and the behavior of beer in barrels? Their answer began with a Two-Sphere theory of the universe. The outer sphere was the sphere of the stars; the inner sphere was the earth. The earth was thought to be stationary, while the outer sphere revolved around the earth once every day. In between these two spheres were the moon, sun, and planets. The area between the moon and the outer sphere

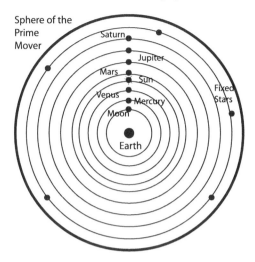

Figure 2.2

was called the celestial realm, while the area between the moon and the center of the earth was called the terrestrial realm.

Here is some more of the observed data which lead to this theory:

1. Any clear sighted Greek willing to stay up most of the night observed that the vast majority of the stars (i.e., all except the "wandering stars" or planets) appear to revolve as a group around the North Star. Today we do not need to stay up all night—a time exposure picture of the night sky nicely reveals the circular motion of the stars.

2. For as far back as we have records, people have reported that the stars were moving from west to east. But things on earth have never been observed to move for more than a short period of time. Plants, animals, and humans can move themselves for a while, but eventually (if only at death), their movement stops. Arrows shot from bows or rocks thrown from slings move for a while, but they too eventually fall back to earth and remain motionless. In short, the heavens move eternally; things on earth do not.

3. While the motion of the stars is eternal, the stars themselves are stable and changeless. The seven stars of the Big Dipper have always been in the same relative position with respect to each other. And the number of stars in the Big Dipper and elsewhere in the heavens has remained

constant. But in the terrestrial realm, things are always changing. People are born and then they die. New civilizations are born which outlive any of their citizens, but these also come and go. Rocks formed in volcanoes may outlast civilizations, but eventually, even they will be ground into sand.

4. The next observation has two parts. First, when tall sailing ships come into port, clear sighted people see the top of the ship before they can observe the bottom of the ship. Second, when the earth is observed to eclipse the moon, the shadow cast by the earth is always semi-circular.

Like any theory, the Two-Sphere theory did more than simply gather up all the data in a long list. Any good theory must also *explain* the data in a way that makes good sense. The Greeks made sense of the data in terms of two spheres.

The inner sphere was the earth. They argued that the earth could not be flat because (1) when sailing ships come in from sea we can see the top of their mask before we can see their bow, and (2) the earth casts a semi-circular shadow. The best explanation of these observations is that the earth is really a *sphere*. Since light travels in a straight line, a person's line of sight to the top of the ship will be clear, while their line of sight to the bottom of the ship will be blocked by the curvature of the earth (see *figure 1.3*). And obviously, only a spherical surface can cast the round shadow we see during an eclipse.

The second sphere was that of the stars. Since the stars are always moving together, it is reasonable to infer that they are part of a single system. Though the precise nature of the system is unclear, the best explanation seemed to be that the stars are located on a large and rotating crystalline sphere. To observers on the stationary earth, this would give the stars the appearance of motion around the axis of the north and south poles. It would also explain why the stars are grouped in constellations.

The unchangeable number of the stars can best be explained, said the Greeks, by assuming that the celestial and terrestrial realms are composed of different kinds of substances. It also suggests that they are composed of a single substance. When things are composed of several different substances (like plants and houses), they are easily "broken," i.e., their pieces come apart. However, diamonds which seem to be composed of only a single substance are much less easily broken. So, when we observe over countless generations that the stars never "come apart" it makes sense to suppose that they are composed of only a single substance. The Greeks called the single substance in the celestial realm *aether*.

While not much could be known about aether, it was obvious that aether was utterly unlike the earth, water, air, and fire which make up the things on earth. When earthy and watery substances are left unsupported, they are *typically* observed to move toward the center of the earth, while airy and fiery substances are *typically* observed to move away from the center of the earth. Things composed of aether, however, are always observed revolving around the center of the earth.[1] And like us, what typically happens the Greeks thought of as natural.

Though it would be anachronistic to say that the Greeks thought of these typical motions as "natural laws," they did share with today's scientists the assumption that what happens "naturally" does not itself need explanation. Galileo, for example, said that all objects continue to move in a straight line unless acted upon by some external force. Science teachers today call this the law of inertial motion. But if challenged to explain *why* all things move in a straight line unless acted upon by some external force, they would have nothing more to say than that is just what things *do*; the "law of inertial motion" is a rock-bottom, fundamental principle of physics. So too, the Greeks believed that the center of the earth was unique. It was that point toward and away from which all terrestrial elements naturally moved. This was *their* rock-bottom fundamental principle of physics because, again, that is just what elements on earth *do*. The center of the earth was also unique because it was the point around which all things composed of aether revolve. This was the

---

1. "The common name, too, which has been handed down from our distant ancestors even to our own day, seems to show that they conceived of it in the fashion we have been expressing … And so, implying that the primary [heavenly] body is something else beyond earth, fire, air, and water, they gave the highest place a name of its own, *aether*, derived from the fact that it 'runs always' for an eternal time." Aristotle *On the Heavens* bk. 1, ch. 3, 361–62.

The Greeks were not the only ones who posited aether. James Maxwell, the formulator of the modern laws of unifying electricity and magnetism, wrote: "Whatever difficulties we may have in forming a consistent idea of the constitution of the aether, there can be no doubt that the interplanetary and interstellar spaces are not empty but are occupied by a material substance or body, which is certainly the largest and probably the most uniform body of which we have any knowledge." Maxwell, "Ether," 443. See also notes 37 and 38.

rock-bottom, fundamental principle of astronomy. It is just what the elemental aether *does*.

There is one more thing to be said about aether. Since things composed of aether never stop revolving around the earth, they must be extremely light and subtle. If they were not, what keeps them in motion? After all, things made of terrestrial substances only move when pushed, and the heavier they are, the harder they are to push. And in all cases, they eventually come to rest. Since aether never rests and always moves, it must be virtually weightless and hence able to move effortlessly in circles around the earth.[2]

Moderns often criticize this conception of the universe because it gives humans a "privileged" place at the center of the universe. This criticism is exactly backwards. In truth, if there was a "privileged" place for the Greeks, it was the outermost sphere of the stars because they were "nearest" to the Unmoved Mover, what some would call "God." Some even went so far as to suggest that the alacrity of the stars' journey around the earth every twenty-four hours is the result of their *nearness* to "God." The Greek theory of the universe, far from arrogantly giving us a special place, in fact consigns us to the place which is *least* important because it is most remote from the gods.[3]

Though there is nothing arrogant in the Greek notion that the earth resides in the center of the universe, it is a pivotal idea with crucial implications. As we have seen, all motion—both of the stars and on the earth—is explained with reference to the center of the universe. Aether always circles around the center of the universe, while earthy, watery, airy, and fiery stuff always moves toward or away the center of the universe. Furthermore, if the universe has a center, then it must be *finite* in size; it is meaningless to talk about the center of something that is infinitely big. A stick one foot long has a center, as does a stick one hundred miles long. But a stick which is infinitely long has no center. So too, for the universe to have a center it must be finite.

And the implications do not stop here. We tend to think of "space" as an empty container of infinite extent because we have unconsciously imbibed much of Newton's and Kant's philosophy. But the idea that

---

2. Again, "aether" literally means "runs away" (see note above). And if the notion of "weightless matter" seems silly, strange, or primitive, then it is worth remembering that that is exactly how contemporary scientists describe the photon.

3. Lovejoy, *Great Chain of Being*, 102ff., 122.

"space" is an infinitely large empty container would make no sense to a Greek. After all, they would have said, how can nothing (empty space) itself be "something"?

So instead of thinking of "nothingness" as itself something, the Greeks thought of space as the realm of things that move. "Space" was a wholly relative term describing the relation between two things. In this regard, "space" is like the word "father." Empty "space," according to the Greeks, can no more exist than a father can exist without a son or daughter. The idea of a place where there was nothing seemed absurd. All "space," they argued, is filled with aether, a super-subtle, elastic, and luminous substance which pervades the whole universe. Where there is no aether, there is literally nothing, not even "space."[4]

This may sound paradoxical to us, but it should not. Though we *moderns* have no problem talking about a place where there is nothing, this is a fact about *us*. It is not something we have observed. Try to think, with fresh ears, about the phrase "place where there is nothing." It is easy to understand the phrase "place where there is a lot of dirt" or "place where there is a lot of smog." Both "dirt" and "smog" are physical things. While dirt is tangible in a way that smog is not, both are things that can move. Contrast this with concepts like the number seven (not a physical representation of the numeral seven, but the concept itself). These sort of "things" are neither in a particular place nor capable of moving from one place to another.

So the question becomes: Is "nothing" more like "dirt" and "smog" or like the concept "seven"? If you are thinking that "nothing" is like a super-subtle, intangible, wholly transparent "smog," then you are think-ing like a Greek. That's exactly how they described aether. But if you say that "nothing" is more like the concept of "seven," then your ideas would strike a Greek as senseless. "Concepts" are not physical things, so they cannot surround or bound or be located in any place or space. According to the Greeks, "space" is literally *no thing*; it can no more be a "place" than procrastination can be blue or the square root of ten can be heavy.

4. "Matter and space are inseparable, two sides of the same coin. There can be no space without matter. In Aristotle's more cumbersome words, 'there is no such thing as a dimensional entity, other than that of material substance' . . . Without a concept that indissolubly united matter and space, the Aristotelian would be forced to admit the infinity of the universe." Kuhn, *Copernican Revolution*, 88–89. See also Aristotle *Physics* bk 4, chapters 6–9, pp. 292–97.

We need not decide whether *our* Newtonian conception of space as an empty container or the Greek's conception of space as the realm of things that move is the most sensible. But it is important to understand how these two contrasting conceptions of "space" illustrate the inter-related and symbiotically connected nature of philosophical/scientific ideas. One idea both supports and in turn is supported by other ideas. And like the ecology of a stream or forest, in the "ecology of ideas" a seemingly small and insignificant change in one place can have a ripple effect throughout the whole theory.

The Greeks' understanding of "space as the realm of things that move" forced them to reject the possibility of empty space, or what they called the *void*. If voids really existed, then beyond the sphere of the star the "void" would extend infinitely. But if space is infinite, then it can have no center. And if space has no center, then it would make no sense to say that terrestrial objects always move toward and away from the center of the universe and celestial objects eternally revolve around the center. In other words, if "voids" really exist, then the Greek's fundamental theory of motion would have been undermined with nothing to put in their place. And conversely, conceiving of "space" as an infinite but empty container requires all the interconnected ideas of Newtonian physics, which we will consider later in this chapter.

We are finally in a position to answer our original question—why do the planets wander and why are two holes required to efficiently drain beer from a barrel?

The outermost sphere is the fixed stars. It revolves eternally around the center of the universe because (1) that is its nature, and (2) it has the privileged location closest to the Unmoved Mover, i.e., "God." The planets, sun, and moon also revolve eternally on their own spheres because (1) they, too, are composed of aether (whose natural motion is circular), and (2) the motion of the fixed stars is communicated to them via the intervening aether. Remember, there can be no empty space between the stars and the planet. So once the outermost sphere of the stars is revolving, its motion is passed on to the interior spheres of the planets, sun, and moon through the aether. In this respect, the celestial realm is like a round swimming pool. The stars are like children who march around the outside creating a whirlpool. And the planets are like floating toys which are moved by the whirlpool.

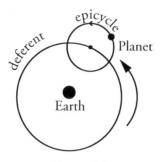

Figure 2.3

The individual planets ride, so to speak, on a band of aether.[5] But inside this band of aether, the planet itself revolves upon another circle, what is called an epicycle. By varying the size of this epicycle, the Greeks were able to predict both the timing and the duration of each planet's retrograde motion (see *figure 2.3* below and several fine computer simulations available on the internet). And when we say "predicted" we do not mean "surprisingly well for their time." We mean that they predicted the retrograde motion so well that Copernicus' contemporaries made no substantial improvements.[6] In fact, they had even built a machine calculator now called the "Antikythera Mechanism" to predict the retrograde motion of the planets and the times of eclipses (Again, a Google search provides several good simulations).

With respect to the beer in barrels, the Greek account should be obvious: by attempting to drain beer from a barrel with only one hole a person is *ipso facto* attempting to create a void, i.e., a place where there is nothing. But no human can flout the most fundamental principle of

---

5. Actually, the Ptolemaic and Aristotelian explanations of the retrograde motion are different. Aristotle assumed the existence of concentric spheres with their axis at different angles to each other. The advantage was that it could explain the retrograde motion of the planets without one sphere having to "pass through" the other. A disadvantage is that it is very difficult to picture. Cf. Hetherington, *Planteary Motions*, 26 for a nice diagram.

While the Ptolemaic explanation for the retrograde motion in terms of epicycles is much easier to picture, it is much less plausible as a physical explanation (as opposed to merely a calculating device) of the planets motions—How are the crystalline spheres suppose to "pass through" each other? See also note 21.

6. Both the Ptolemy's and Copernicus systems had errors of about one percent. Mason, *History of Science*, 131, 159. See also note 22.

the universe by creating a void. Therefore, nature only permits the beer to drain in fits and starts.

In sum, the retrograde motion of the planets and the fact that two holes are required to efficiently drain liquids from barrels can be explained in terms of *three interrelated and symbiotically connected ideas*, what we might call the ancient's "three laws of motion":

1. In the celestial realm, uniform circular motion is natural (a "given").

2. In the terrestrial realm, motion toward or away from the center of the universe is natural (a "given").

3. Nature abhors a vacuum, i.e., "empty space" cannot exist.

2.2 PROBLEMS WITH THE TWO-SPHERE THEORY

The Two Sphere theory of the universe makes a lot of sense, but some of the observational data only fits awkwardly. One awkward fit is the motion of thrown projectiles. According to ancient physics, terrestrial objects only move when pushed or when some force is acting on them. But when rocks and arrows are released from slings and strings they continue in motion for a sizable distance. Why? After all, nothing is pushing them once they leave the sling or the string.

One answer appeals to nature's abhorrence of vacuums. A moving rock or arrow displaces the air in front of it. Conversely, behind it there will be a gap in the air. Since a vacuum would be a violation of the most fundamental principle of nature, the displaced air in front of the projectile rushes in to fill the gap behind the projectile and in doing so pushes the rock or arrow forward. This process will then be repeated until the resistance of the air eventually brings the motion to a stop.[7]

At first blush this explanation seems to make sense, but by the fourteenth century its awkwardness was becoming evident. Jean Buridan, for example, pointed out that this account cannot explain the motion of a spinning top. Even though the top is moving, it is not displacing

---

7. "Aristotle had insisted on continuous contact between the mover and the body forced to move in a direction other than that of its natural motion . . . [This] made it difficult to explain how an arrow shot from a bow continued in motion without continuing contact between the mover and the moved. Somehow, air pushed forward by the arrow had to get around to the rear of the arrow and then push the arrow from behind . . . Philoponus found this convoluted explanation bordering on the fantastic." Hetherington, *Planetary Motions*, 84. See also note #24.

any air. So what is it that keeps the top spinning after the initial force is removed? Secondly, if the ancient explanation is correct, then a javelin with a flat tail should travel farther and faster than one with both ends pointed. Why? Because the one with a flat tail would receive more of the "push" from the air rushing to fill the vacuum than the javelin with a pointed tail. But if thrown by the same person, both javelins will in fact travel about the same distance.

If such "reasoning" appears too philosophical, a simple experiment proves the same point. Throw a javelin with a paper streamer attached to the tail. If the old explanation is correct, we would predict that the air rushing in to fill the vacuum would push both the javelin *and* the streamer forward. But in fact, we observe the streamer trailing behind.

Buridan and his colleagues in the universities developed an alternative to the ancient explanation. It was the theory of impetus. "Impetus" was defined as a property acquired by all bodies merely by their being in motion. It was often compared with heat. Both are a quality that objects can acquire from something else. For example, in the case of heat, a metal poker becomes hot when it is placed in a fire. In the case of a rock, the rock acquires an impetus when it is placed in motion.

In both instances, the heat and the impetus gradually fade away. Though the theory of impetus provides a better explanation of the motion of tops and javelins, it has no place in the larger scheme of things. There is no large set of *interrelated and symbiotically connected* ideas. "Impetus" arrives like a *deus ex machina* to save the day, but its role is singular—it plays no other role in the narrative. So, for at least two more centuries, the problem of projectile motion and the possibility of "impetus" remained an item of debate.

A second awkwardness in the Two-Sphere universe was evident from the start. At first, it did not seem too troublesome. But, like an itch, over the centuries it became more and more unbearable. The problem was the complexity of the epicycles that were necessary to accurately predict the motion of the planets. By the time Ptolemy finished calculating the motion of the planets, more than eighty epicycles were necessary. The ancient astronomy was beginning to look more like a Rube Goldberg Invention than the work of a divine craftsman with even a modicum of intelligence.[8]

8. Strictly speaking, it was not the epicycles, but eccentrics and equants that Copernicus objected to. An eccentric is a geometric device whereby the center of the

But on the other hand, what does an artistic taste for simplicity have to do with astronomy? As Mersenne, a contemporary critic of Galileo, said, "If I could be convinced that God always did things in the shortest and easiest way, then I should certainly have to recognize the fact that the world does move."[9]

---

circle is offset from the center of the earth. An equant is a geometric device whereby the angular motion of a planet remains uniform, even though the velocity of the planet in not uniform. This is accomplished by offsetting the point from which the angular motion is calculated from the center of the earth. The need for all these stemmed from the fact that all astronomers, from Aristotle and Ptolemy to Copernicus and Galileo, assumed that uniform circular motion was the foundation for all celestial motion. It was not until Kepler and Newton that astronomers realized that the planets revolved around the sun in elliptical orbits and that their velocity was not constant.

Copernicus put his objection like this: "But even if those who have thought up eccentric circles seem to have been able for the most part to compute the apparent movement numerically by those means, they have in the meanwhile admitted a great deal which seems to contradict the first principles of regularity of movement. Moreover, . . . they are in exactly the same fix as someone taking from different places hands, feet, head, and the other limbs—shaped very beautifully but not with reference to one body and without correspondence to one another—so that such parts made up a monster rather than a man" (*Revolutions*, 507). As this quote makes clear, Copernicus' precise objection was not the epicycles which his own theory required. "Koestler correctly points out that only Galileo created the myth that the Copernican theory was simple (Koestler, 1959, 476); in fact, 'the motion of the earth [had not] done much to simplify the old theories, for though the objectionable equants had disappeared, the system was still bristling with auxiliary circles.'" Lakatos, "Falsification," 117.

9. Quoted in Butterfield, *Origins*, 96. Cardinal Bellarmine expressed a similar point in his letter to Foscarini, dated April 12, 1615: "Third, I say that if there were a true demonstration that the sun was in the center of the universe and . . . the earth circled around the sun, then it would be necessary to proceed with great caution in explaining the passages of Scripture which seemed contrary, and we would rather have to say that we did not understand them than to say that something was false which has been demonstrated. But I do not believe that there is any such demonstration; none has been shown to me." Quoted in Langford, *Galileo*, 61. And as we will see in the rest of the chapter, in 1615 there were no good "scientific" reasons for believing that the earth moved.

This willingness of theologians to defer to scientists on "scientific" matters goes back to at least Augustine. He wrote: "One does not read in the Gospel that the Lord said: I will send to you the Paraclete who will teach you about the course of the sun and moon. For He willed to make them Christians, not mathematicians." Quoted in Langford, *Galileo*, 65.

Paul Feyerbend says that the decision of the Catholic Church at the trial of Galileo "concerned two points: what would today be called the *scientific content* of the doctrine and its *ethical (social) implications*. On the first point the experts declared the doctrine to be 'foolish and absurd in philosophy' or, to use modern terms, they declared it to be unscientific. This judgment was made without reference to the faith, or to church doctrine, but was based exclusively on the scientific situation of the time . . . *and it was*

Finally, there was new data. In 1572 a new star was observed. And in 1609, a Dutch lens grinder stumbled on a new way to combine two lenses to magnify distant objects. Shortly thereafter word reached Galileo. When he made one of these new telescopes and pointed it toward the sky, spots were visible on the sun and mountains casting shadows were observable on the moon. The celestial realm, it seemed, was no longer utterly unique and perfect when compared to the terrestrial realm. It too seemed to be subject to the same sorts of forces and changes observable here on earth.[10]

Prior to Galileo, few people would have thought that lens grinding would have any connection with astronomy. Such surprising connections anticipate a point we will develop in chapter 6. There we will argue that since we can never know what the future will bring, it is utterly silly to claim finality for any scientific or philosophical theory. No theory is complete until history ends and all the data is in. On the other hand, it makes no sense to immediately abandon existing theoretical explanations, in either science or philosophy, with the discovery of each new

---

correct when based on the facts, the theories and the standards of the time." Feyerbend, *Against Method,* 132.

10. But there are at least three problems with Galileo's telescopic "observations." The first is factual. "The first telescopic observations of the sky are indistinct, indeterminate, contradictory, and in conflict with what everyone can see with his unaided eyes. And the only theory that could have helped to separate telescopic illusions from veridical phenomena was refuted by simple tests . . . It needs only a brief look at Galileo's drawings, and a photograph of similar phases [of the moon], to convince the reader that 'none of the features recorded . . . can be safely identified with any known markings of the lunar landscape.'" Feyerbend, *Against Method,* 89, 97. See also Hetherington, *Planetary Motions,* 116.

The second is theoretical. With respect to Galileo's claim to have observed mountains on the moon, thereby contradicting the tradition's claim that the heavens are "faultless" crystalline spheres, Lakatos points out, "But his 'observations' were not 'observational' in the sense of being observed by the—unaided—senses: their reliability depended on the reliability of his telescope—and of the optical theory of the telescope—which was violently questioned by his contemporaries. It was not Galileo's—pure, untheoretical—observations that confronted Aristotelian theory but rather Galileo's 'observations' in the light of his optical theory that confronted the Aristotelian 'observations' in light of their theory of the heavens." Lakatos, "Falsification," 98.

The third concerns Galileo's special pleading. His telescope is assumed to be accurate when it confirms his ideas, but inaccurate when it conflicts with his ideas. Galileo was firmly committed to the circular motion of all heavenly bodies. But the orbit of comets was obviously not circular. So Galileo argued that comets were not heavenly bodies! Instead, he argued that "they were merely optical phenomena produced by the refraction of the sun rays in the upper atmosphere." Langford, *Galileo,* 107.

piece of contrary evidence. Until a better theory is proposed, contrary evidence is a mere anomaly.[11]

2.3 NO CRUCIAL EXPERIMENTS

And if the connection between lens grinding and astronomy was unexpected, the connection between mining silver and astronomy was even more unexpected. Nonetheless, the connection is real.

Long before the seventeenth century people had noticed that suction pumps do not work perfectly even for short distances, and that for vertical distances of around thirty-four feet they do not work at all. Everyone assumed that the problem lay in the design and construction of the pumps. No one spent much time trying to explain why suction pumps stop sucking at around thirty-four feet. It appeared to be one of those interesting, but trivial, questions like—why is the sky blue or why do the stars twinkle? But at the start of the seventeenth century, newer and deeper silver mines were dug, and it became a pressing economic problem to find efficient ways to pump the water out of deep mines. All attempts to create better suction pumps with new technology failed. What once appeared to be an isolated anomaly had now become a pressing problem for both entrepreneurs and philosophers.

An Italian named Torricelli (1608–1647) thought he had the answer. Under the old theory, liquids get sucked up by a pump because the liquid rush in to the fill the vacuum created by the pump. His new theory postulated what he called a "sea of air." According to Torricelli, water is not sucked up by a pump; rather it is pushed up. This explanation appealed to a "teeter-totter" effect (see *figure 2.4*). He said that water rises in a tube when a vacuum is created because the teeter-totter has become unbalanced. Outside the tube, the sea of air surrounding it is pressing down the water. The amount of pressure that the air exerts outside the tube is determined by its weight. (The greater the depth in the "sea of air" the higher it will push the liquid under suction.) However, inside the tube where the air is being sucked out, there is less air, or even no air

---

11. Lakatos is explicit: "Contrary to naïve falsificationism, *no experiment, experimental report, observation statement or well-corroborated low-level falsifying hypothesis alone can lead to falsification. There is no falsification before the emergence of a better theory* . . . This shows that '*crucial counter-evidence*'—or '*crucial experiments*'—can be recognized as such among the scores of anomalies only *with hindsight*, in the light of some superseding theory." Lakatos, "Falsification," 119, 120.

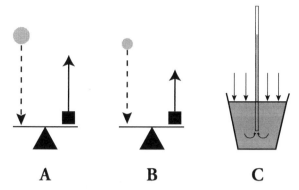

Figure 2.4: The ball in A is bigger than the ball in B, so the corresponding block in A is pushed up higher than the block in B.

(if the vacuum is perfect) exerting a downward pressure on the water. This unbalances the "teeter-totter." Since the weight pressing down on the water inside the straw is less than the weight pressing down outside the straw, the water inside the straw rises.

But why should this new theory of Torricelli be preferred to the old theory of nature abhorring a vacuum? One common answer that will not do is this: the old theory is unscientific because it uses purposeful language (see chapter 5.3, "Causes are also Real"). According to this criticism, nature has no desires and it certainly does not "abhor" a vacuum. Only people (and maybe other animals) can *abhor* anything. So talk of nature "abhorring" is nothing more than a crude, unscientific metaphor. Yet the Greeks could make the same response to our own scientific language. Is not it silly, they might say, to talk of the *law* of gravity. Only people make *laws*. Talk of nature meeting in a legislative session to create "laws" is nothing more than a crude, unscientific metaphor!

Nonetheless, Torricelli did make one significant advance over the older theory. His theory provided a plausible explanation of the fact that nature only seemed to "abhor" a vacuum up to thirty-four feet. On the old theory, this was simply a brute fact of nature that had no explanation. Torricelli's theory was able to make this previously puzzling fact intelligible by making it part of our understanding of weights and balances. The reason water can only be "sucked up" about thirty-four feet is that there is only a finite amount of weight (air) pushing it up. When the weight of the air doing the pushing and the weight of the water being pushed are equal, the water will rise no further.

This new theory made good intuitive sense. But, then, the older theory had a lot going for it too. Was there anything Torricelli could do to logically *prove* his new theory? He thought so. If water rises in a tube only to a height such that the weight of the air equals the weight of the water, then a liquid like mercury (which is fourteen times heavier than water) should only rise one-fourteenth as high as water (which is about thirty inches). This relation between the weight of water and the weight of mercury suggests an experiment—create a vacuum above a column of mercury and see how high it will rise. If it will only rise about thirty inches, then we know that Torricelli theory is true. When Torricelli performed such an experiment, he got the precise results predicted by his theory.

If this were not enough to prove his theory, consider the additional experiment suggested by another philosopher/scientist, Pascal (1623–1662). He saw a further implication of Torricelli's explanation. Pascal began with a simple fact—as one climbs up a mountain, there is less air above. With this as a premise, he reasoned that according to Torricelli's theory, if he carried a column of mercury topped with a vacuum (the original barometer) up a mountain, then the mercury should start to fall as he climbed higher because the amount of air pushing down would decrease. And again, when this experiment was tried, the results were exactly as Torricelli's theory predicted.

Many science textbooks present Torricelli's work (or similar experiments by other scientists) as a model of "the scientific method." This usually involves five steps.

1. Making observations (water can only be lifted thirty-four feet with a suction pump).

2. Formulating a question (why does not nature abhor a vacuum above thirty-four feet?).

3. Framing a hypothesis ("Sea of air" theory).

4. Making a prediction on the basis of the hypothesis (mercury will only rise thirty inches at sea level and even less on top of a mountain).

5. Testing the prediction (the experiments confirming the theory).

It seems obvious that if the experiment gets the results predicted by the hypothesis, then the theory must be true. And if the results are not what were predicted, then the theory is false. However, this "obvious" answer is logically wrong. Both of Torricelli's arguments are deductively *invalid*.

> *Argument #1*
> 1. If there is a "sea of air," then mercury will only rise about thirty inches.
> 2. Experiments show that mercury will only rise about thirty inches.
> 3. Therefore, there is a "sea of air."

> *Argument #2*
> 1. If there is a "sea of air," then mercury will not even rise thirty inches on top of a mountain.
> 2. Experiments show that mercury does not rise even thirty inches on top of a mountain.
> 3. Therefore, there is a "sea of air."

As we saw in chapter 1 (*figure 1.4*), both of these arguments are invalid because both of these arguments "affirm the consequent." They are of the form:

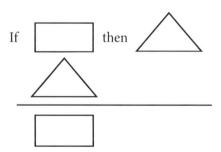

Figure 2.5

A simple counterexample proves that all arguments that affirm the consequence, including Torricelli's, are logically fallacious.

1. If anyone gets hit by a bazooka shell, they will die.
2. Fred died.
3. Therefore, Fred got hit by a bazooka shell.

Of course, this does not mean that Torricelli's conclusion is false. But it does mean that even though his "sea of air" theory makes good sense, there is nothing about Torricelli's experiments which *proves* it to be true.

However, more sophisticated and positivistically inclined defenders of the "scientific method" argue that the difference between philosophy and science is that scientific theories are falsifiable, whereas philosophical theories are not. Their argument begins with the common sense principle—"nothing ventured, nothing gained." For example, let us suppose someone seriously theorized that on April 15, 1950 the entire universe doubled in size. As part of their theory, they "predicted" that no one would notice this doubling because at that very moment the universe doubled in size, they too became twice as tall, their clothes became twice as big, their yard sticks became twice as long, etc. According to positivists, the problem with such a theory is not that it is false, but that it is *meaningless*. There is absolutely no way it could be proven false. Since a theory about the universe doubling in size does not rule out any conceivable set of observations, such a theory is devoid of empirical content.

One philosopher famously illustrated the problem such a theory poses for religion like this. Suppose someone says that a loving heavenly Father rules over the universe. Before we can ask whether this is true or false, we must first ask what such a statement *means*. When a child contracts cancer, we see his earthly father rushing into action doing everything possible to save his child's life. Yet no one sees his heavenly Father doing anything. So the believer adds some qualifications: "God's love is not like human love," or "God's love transcends what we can understand," or "God's love is inscrutable." While such qualifications save the believer's statement from falsification, they do so by turning what at first appeared to be a claim about the real world—that it is ruled by a loving God—into what is now little more than an emotionally comforting platitude.[12] Since the religious believer will not allow contrary evidence

---

12. This is a paraphrase of Antony Flew's famous essay, "Theology and Falsification."

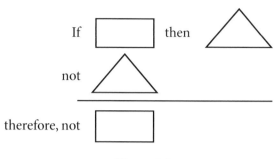

Figure 2.6

to refute his theory, it falls prey to the dictum—nothing ventured, nothing gained. Or, as one philosopher said, it dies the death of a thousand qualifications.

Scientific theories, on the other hand, really do increase understanding because they really do venture claims which can be proved wrong. While *direct* attempts to prove a theory true always commits the fallacy of affirming the consequent, the falsification of theories based on *modus tollens* (see *figure 2.6*) is a perfectly valid deductive form.

So, according to sophisticated positivists, both philosophers and scientists produce theories which cannot be deductively proved. But they differ in this: philosophers' and theologians' theories are immune to falsification because (1) they are so laden with qualifications and/or (2) their proponents are simply unwilling to give them up when contrary evidence is produced. Scientists, on the other hand, are obligated to (1) produce theories with sufficient specificity that they *could* be falsified, and (2) reject theories when they are proven wrong by observable data. So, once a scientist's theory is published, other scientists immediately begin to look for flaws and experimental evidence that would falsify the theory. If, after years of efforts and countless experiments by other scientists, one's own theory has not been falsified, then we can say that it is scientifically demonstrated, even if it is not "proven" in a strictly deductive sense.[13]

13. Karl Popper's name is most frequently associated with a "falsificationist" account of science. But in the end, even Popper repudiated such an account. "I no longer think, as I once did, that there is a difference between science and metaphysics regarding this most important point [i.e., testability]. I look upon a metaphysical theory as similar to a scientific one. It is vaguer, no doubt . . . But, *as long as a metaphysical theory can be ratio-*

Formally speaking, positivists acknowledge that we cannot deductively *prove* that the earth is round. The best we can offer is a logically fallacious argument (affirming the consequent) like this:

1. If the earth is round, then we would see the tops of sailing ships (that are approaching from a distance) first.
2. In fact, we do see the tops of sailing ships (that are approaching from a distance) first.
3. Therefore, the earth is round.

But we can prove with *modus tollens* (a universally agreed valid form) and simple observations that the earth is not flat. For example,

1. If the earth is flat, then we would see the tops and bottoms of sailing ships (that are approaching from a distance) at the same time.
2. In fact, we do not see the tops and bottoms of sailing ships (that are approaching from a distance) at the same time.
3. Therefore, the earth is not flat.

However, there is a huge problem with the positivist's use of *modus tollens*. While the argument is perfectly valid and the second premise is observed to be true, the first premise is incomplete. What positivists ignore is that the reasonableness of the first premise comes from certain auxiliary or "background" assumptions, e.g., that light travels in a straight line. If light had weight and was pulled down by strong gravitational fields, then light would bend, and the same results would occur (i.e. we would see the tops of ships before we saw the bottoms of ships) (see *figure 2.7*).

In other words, the hypothesis of a round earth with light that travels in straight lines (top of figure) and the hypothesis of a flat earth with "sagging" light (bottom of figure) *both* account for the fact that we observe the tops of ship before we see their bottoms. Therefore, there is no purely observational or experimental method to determine which hypothesis is best. More generally, attempts to empirically falsify large, theoretical explanations will always be in the form:

1. If (theory *and* auxiliary assumptions), then empirical effect.
2. No observable or experimental effect.
3. Therefore, either theory is wrong *or* auxiliary assumptions are wrong.

---

nally criticized, I should be inclined to take seriously its implicit claim to be considered, tentatively, as true." Popper, *Quantum Theory*, 199.

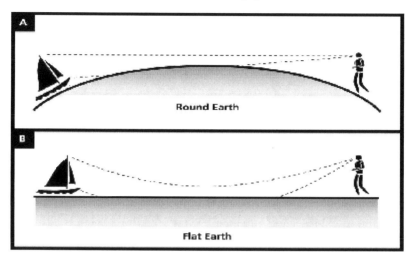

Figure 2.7

From a wholly formal (i.e., deductive) point of view, *any* theory can be saved from falsification by simply abandoning or modifying one of the auxiliary assumptions. True, believers in a loving God sometimes save their beliefs from falsification by adding auxiliary hypotheses to the effect that God's love is not the same as human love. But there is no rule of logic that prevents equally sophisticated scientists from saving their theories with auxiliary assumption (e.g., light is bent in the presence of a strong gravitational field).[14] This means that from a purely deductive (i.e., formal) point of view, there can never be a "crucial experiment" for deciding between competing theories, be they "scientific" or philosophical.[15]

However, while all auxiliary hypotheses are logically equal, from a broader perspective of what "makes good sense," some auxiliary hypoth-

14. Lakatos writes, "For even if experiments *could* prove experimental reports, their disproving power would still be miserably restricted: *exactly the most admired scientific theories simple fail to forbid any observable state of affairs.*" Lakatos, "Falsification," 100.

15. "It is also worth pointing out that Popper repeatedly claims that the famous eclipse experiment [supporting General Relativity] was an *experimentum cruces* ... In fact, the experiment produced four sets of results; depending on which of the (poor quality) photographs one trusted, one got Einsteinian deviation, Newtonian deviation, and even double Einsteinian deviation! ... That general relativity was accepted before there were decisive experiments in its favor of course contradicts completely the whole Popperian account, which can be characterized as mythological." Putnam, *Fact/Value Dichotomy*, 180.

eses are better than others. Sometimes an auxiliary hypothesis seems to "come out of nowhere" or to resemble the "miraculous" appearance of the hero in a cheap B-movie. Such hypotheses play no other part in an interrelated and symbiotically connected set of ideas. Instead, they appear to have been introduced solely for the purpose of saving one's preferred theory from falsification. When this happens, the hypothesis is said to be *ad hoc*. Good theories always avoid *ad hoc* assumptions.

The important point here is that there is no purely logical or purely experimental and/or observational way to distinguish good assumptions from *ad hoc* assumptions.[16] What's needed is "good judgment." Only then will we be able to distinguish between good assumptions and *ad hoc* assumptions. Since "good judgment" is not something that can be put in a bottle and examined under a microscope, realists argue that positivists have not succeeded in drawing a clear line distinguishing scientific and philosophical theories. As we continue our story, we will see more examples where good judgment about what does and does not "make sense" is a necessary part of "scientific proof." But before returning to the narrative, we should say a little more about ideas "making sense."

2.4 THE THREE C'S OF CONSISTENCY, COHERENCE, AND COMPREHENSIVENESS

Grant for the moment that all proofs of the earth's motion must ultimately assume good judgment about what does and does not "make sense." What does this mean in light of the fact that there are many examples of ideas which were once thought to "make sense" but are now widely believed to be totally false—astrology, slavery, the natural inferiority of women, etc.? And, of course, there are countless contemporary examples of cultures which have radically different ideas about what "makes sense" or "seems true." So the question arises: Is the philosophical realist's notion of "good judgment" any different from the relativist's notion that all "arguments" are ultimately ground in mere opinion?

---

16. "The flaw in . . . falsificationism has been pointed out by Willard van Orman Quine, using the arguments anticipated in the writings of Pierre Duhem, to formulate what has become known as the Quine-Duhem thesis." Wallace, *Modeling of Nature*, 248. *The Routledge Encyclopedia of Philosophy* explains it like this: "About a century ago, Henri Poincare and others stressed the significance of the fact that, through any finite number of points, indefinitely many curves could be drawn. This made it clear that indefinitely many alternative hypotheses were compatible with (indeed, deductively entailed by) any given body of data" ("Underdetermination").

The realist's argument begins with the three Cs of consistency, coherence, and comprehensiveness. For a person to merely assert that "*to me* this makes sense" is insufficient. Unless one's judgment is grounded in the *universal* principles of consistency, coherence, and comprehensiveness, then the relativist is right—one's judgment is nothing more than personal preference.

Consistency is purely a matter of logic. No good argument can contain contradictory premises. If one premise asserts that light always travels in a straight line and another premise asserts that light does not always travel in a straight line, we know by pure logic that *one* of these premises must be false, even though logic alone can never tell us *which* one is false. Therefore, any theory which has contradictory premises must have at least one false premise, and no argument with a false premise *proves* its conclusion.

The assumption that nature is coherent goes beyond mere consistency, and hence, it goes beyond mere logic. (This is part of the reason we said at the very beginning of the first chapter that logic is a necessary, but not a sufficient, condition for doing philosophy well.) Coherence is nonetheless an ancient criteria for "making sense." Though much changed with the scientific revolution started by Copernicus, Kepler, and Galileo, both ancient and modern scientists assume that a true account of nature would exhibit simplicity, unity, and reasonableness.[17] Here are the maxims that permeated the writings of these revolutionary scientists:

- Nature loves simplicity.

- Nature loves unity.

- Nature has integrity.

- There never appears in nature anything purposeless or unnecessary. Nature always achieves what it can through the easier route, never through difficult meanderings.[18]

17. Einstein said, "I do not by any means find the chief significance of the general theory of relativity in the fact that it has predicted a few minute observable facts, but rather in the simplicity of its foundation and in its logical consistency." Hetherington, *Planetary Motions*, 64–65.

18. Burtt, *Metaphysical Foundations,* 46. Newton put it like this: "We are to admit no more causes of natural things than such as are both true and sufficient to explain their appearances. To this purpose, the philosophers say, that nature does nothing in vain, and more is in vain when less will serve; for nature is pleased with simplicity, and affects not the pomp of superfluous causes." Newton, *Principles,* 270.

These principles were not discovered by modern science. They were all a well-accepted part in the natural philosophy of the classical and medieval period. Though they are clearly related, let us first consider them individually.

Nature's love of simplicity means that given two equally good explanations, the simplest explanation is most likely to be true. For example, suppose that Sally Smith arrives home two hours late from her senior prom. Her mother asks for an explanation. The following dialogue results:

> *Mother*: Why were you so late?
>
> *Sally*: We had a flat tire.
>
> *Mother*: It does not take two hours to change a tire.
>
> *Sally*: It took so long because the jack in the car was stolen.
>
> *Mother*: You mean someone broke into the truck to steal a ten-dollar jack? And why do I not see any pry marks on the car?
>
> *Sally*: Because the thieves first stole the keys from my purse.
>
> *Mother*: I understand stealing your purse for money, but why steal a purse just so you can then steal a ten dollar jack?
>
> *Sally:* The thieves must have thought there were drugs in the jack.
>
> *Mother:* I think you were just out "partying" and lost track of time.

Sally and her mother have different explanations for a two-hour late arrival. Though both are logically consistent, her mother's explanation is more likely to be true because it is considerably simpler.

Nature's love of unity is also illustrated in the dialogue between Sally and her mother. One of the reasons her mother's explanation is more likely is that Sally's explanation lacks unity. Sally's argument does not "hold together" (i.e., it lacks integrity), especially the part about stealing a purse to steal a jack to then obtain drugs. Though possible, this seems highly *ad hoc*. But again, there is nothing logically inconsistent with Sally's story.

Of course, the mother's argument to the best explanation is not infallible. Inductive arguments like this always assume a *ceteris paribus* or "other things being equal" clause. If we learn that police had recently been pursuing a drug cartel which used automobile jacks to smuggle drugs, then the integrity of her argument would be improved and we would be forced to reconsider Sally's explanation.

Finally, and this is really just another way of praising the virtues of simplicity and unity, a good explanation should not "meander without purpose." This really an expression of the firm conviction that nature is not a Rube Goldberg contraption. Instead, nature is intelligently ordered. The principle of coherence follows from the assumption that we live in a cosmos, not a chaos.[19]

Though we will occasionally refer to these maxims individually, they are so closely related that it is best to think of them as a single principle of coherence. A good theory (other things being equal) will have a simple elegance that provides a unified account of the phenomena in question without meandering off track.[20]

The third principle is comprehensiveness. This principle states that of two equally consistent and coherent theories, the theory that explains more phenomena is better. We saw an example of this already in the "Sea of Air" theory. It could explain why suction pumps could only draw water about thirty-four feet, while the abandoned theory about nature abhorring a vacuum could not explain this fact. (On the other hand, Torricelli's

---

19 We will say more about the intelligent ordering of nature in chapter 10. It is also worth noting Whitehead's claim that it was Christianity's firm faith that the universe was the product of a rational God that made Western science possible. "[T]he faith in the possibility of science, generated antecedently to the development of modern scientific theory, is an unconscious derivative from medieval theology." Whitehead, *Science and the Modern World*, 14.

20. The current resident of Newton's chair of Mathematical Physics, Stephen Hawking, explains scientists' reluctance to abandon a theory in light of the experimental data like this: "In practice, people are very reluctant to give up a theory in which they have invested a lot of time and effort. They usually start by questioning the accuracy of the observations. If that fails, they try to modify the theory in an *ad hoc* manner. Eventually the theory becomes a creaking and ugly edifice." On the other hand, Einstein was driven to the idea of four-dimensional space-time "not so much by the experimental results as by the desire to make two parts of the theory fit together in a consistent whole . . . I do not think Einstein, or anyone else in 1905, realized how simple and elegant the new theory of relativity was." Hawkings, "My Position," 42–43.

Paul Dirac (1933 Nobel Prize for Physics) famously put it like this: "It is more important to have beauty in one's questions than to have them fit experiments . . . It seems that if one is working from the point of view of getting beauty in one's equations, and if it has a really good insight, one is on a sure line of progress." Dirac, "Physicist's Picture," 47.

More recently, Steven Weinberg (1979 Nobel Prize for Physics) put it like this: "The kind of beauty that we find in physical theories is of a very limited sort. It is, as far as I have been able to capture it in words, the beauty of simplicity and inevitability—the beauty of perfect structure, the beauty of everything fitting together, of nothing being changeable, of logical rigidity. It is a beauty that is spare and classic, we find it in the Greek tragedies." Weinberg, *Dream*, 149.

"sea of Air" theory was less comprehensive since it abandoned the third principle of ancient science—"Nature abhors a vacuum"—which was required to explain the motion of the planets.) Finally, sometimes two theories will explain the same number of phenomena, yet one will open up new lines of plausible and fruitful investigation or experimentation. Preferring the more fruitful theory is also included in the principle of comprehensiveness.

2.5 NEWTONIAN PHYSICS

With the three Cs of consistency, coherence, and comprehensiveness in mind, let us now return to our narrative. Modern science begins with the sixteenth century dispute between Copernicus and the supporters of the Two-Sphere or Ptolemaic system. In 1543, Copernicus published his great work, *On the Revolutions of the Heavenly Bodies*. It was a highly technical book designed to be read by other professional mathematicians.[21] In it he argued that contrary to previous scientific thought, and

21. "The Aristotelian classification of the sciences, which was endorsed up to the time of Copernicus, regarded mathematical astronomy as separate from physical cosmology. The former discipline was dedicated to developing mathematical models to predict the positions of celestial bodies; the latter was the branch of natural philosophy devoted to ascertaining the nature and causes of celestial motion. In consequence of this demarcation, the task of mathematical astronomers was not primarily to provide accounts of celestial phenomena that were literally true. Copernicus's theory, like Ptolemy's, was put forward as a contribution to mathematical astronomy." McAllister, *Beauty*, 165.

Arthur Koestler explains why Ptolemy thought of his theory as merely mathematical: "Ptolemy also makes it clear why astronomy must renounce all attempts to explain the *physical* reality behind it: because the heavenly bodies, being of a divine nature, obey laws different from those to be found on earth. No common link exists between the two; therefore we can know nothing about the physics of the skies." Koestler, *Sleepwalker*, 74.

Averroes, a twelfth-century Islamic philosopher, said, "The astronomer must, therefore, construct an astronomical system such that the celestial motions are yielded by it and that nothing that is from the standpoint of physics impossible is implied ... Ptolemy was unable to set astronomy on its true foundations ... The epicycle and the eccentric are impossible. We must, therefore, apply ourselves to a new investigation concerning that genuine astronomy whose foundations are principles of physics ... actually, in our time astronomy is nonexistent; what we have is something that fits calculation but does not agree with what is." Quoted in Duhem, *To Save the Phenomena*, 31.

Averroes' critique, says Duhem, seems to have inspired Aquinas when he wrote: "the assumptions of the astronomers are not necessarily true. Although these hypotheses appear to save the phenomena, one ought not affirm that they are true, for one might conceivably be able to explain the apparent motions of the stars in some other way of which men have not as yet thought." Duhem, *To Save the Phenomena*, 41.

contrary to all common experience, the earth is moving through space at thousands of miles an hour in its orbit around the sun.

On what did Copernicus base this revolutionary theory? Had he discovered some new "fact" that earlier astronomers had overlooked? Had he detected some mistake in their calculations? Had he made more careful observations from which he then made more accurate predictions of the motions of the stars and planets? The answer to all these questions is unequivocal—No.[22] Instead, he argued that his theory contained "mathematical harmonies" which were more simple, beautiful, and elegant than his competitors. In short, it was more coherent and comprehensive.

Why was it more coherent? First, Copernicus's theory was simpler because he needed fewer epicycles to make his calculations than did Ptolemy.[23] And it was more comprehensive because it unified more phenomena with a single theory. For example, Copernicus's theory could explain the phases of Venus more readily than Ptolemy's.[24]

Nonetheless, these two facts did not settle the issue. One of the reasons is that Copernicus's theory was inconsistent with at least one piece of observed data, namely, the lack of observable stellar parallax. A stellar

---

22. "In modern science, the usual suspect for the role of crucial anomaly resisting conformity with theory is a new observation. In Copernicus's time, however, no startling new astronomical observations refuted Ptolemaic astronomy. Nor did Copernicus's heliocentric system provide a better match between theory and observation than had Ptolemy's geocentric system. Copernicus, himself, acknowledged that Ptolemy's planetary theory was consistent with numerical data." Hetherington, *Planetary Motions,* 93. And again, "The two theories [i.e., Ptolemy's and Copernicus's] were thus equally correct with respect to prediction of future planet positions within the then current error of observation of at least 1/6 degree of arc." Holton and Brush, *Physics,* 22.

23. We have, again, considerably simplified the story at this point. It was actually the equants Ptolemy's theory used that Copernicus found most objectionable. Furthermore, it was only the major epicycles that Copernicus eliminated. The minor epicycles necessary to compute the planets' elliptical obits using only circles were not eliminated in Copernicus's system. Thomas Kuhn was blunt: "Copernicus did not solve the problem of the planets." Kuhn, *Copernican Revolution,* 169.

24. Here again, we are grossly oversimplifying. Tycho Brahe proposed a system that was geometrically equivalent to Copernicus's system, yet it did not require a "moving earth." In Brahe's system, the sun revolved around the earth, but the two minor planets, Mercury and Venus, revolved around the sun. As Kuhn says, "the Tychonic system, at least, provides as good an explanation as the Copernican for the observed phases of and distance to Venus. Therefore, the telescope did not prove the validity of Copernicus' conceptual scheme. But it did provide an immensely effective weapon for the battle. It was not proof, but it was propaganda." Kuhn, *Copernican Revolution,* 202, 224.

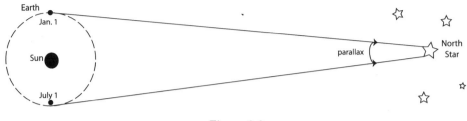

Figure 2.8

parallax is a change in the observed angular position of a star due to the rotation of the earth around the sun. For example, if the earth is revolving around the sun, then the angle at which we observe the North Star on January 1st ought to be slightly different from the angle we observe it six months later because the earth will have traveled half-way around the Sun (see *figure 2.8*).[25]

If, as positivists argue, scientists are obligated to reject a theory as soon as they discovered falsifying data, then Copernicus' theory would never have seen the light of day. Even with the newly discovered telescope, no parallax was observed.[26] Formally stated, Ptolemy's followers argued like this:

1. If the earth moves around the sun, then we ought to observe a stellar parallax.
2. There is no observable stellar parallax.
3. Therefore, the earth does not move around the sun.

The argument is valid (i.e., *modus tollens*), the first premise seems quite reasonable and the second premise was in fact true—no one before, during, or for almost three centuries after Copernicus had ever observed any stellar parallax. Yet, Copernicus had anticipated this objection and thought he had a good response. He said that we cannot observe a stellar

25. This objection dates back to Aristotle. In, *On the Heavens* bk. 2, ch. 14. He wrote: "But if this were so [i.e., if the earth was moving], there would have to be passings and turnings of the fixed stars. Yet no such thing is observed. The same stars always rise and set in the same parts of the earth." That is, the earth does not move because there is no observable stellar parallax. See also bk. 2, ch. 10.

26. The traditional date for the first time a parallax was detected was by Bessel in 1838, long after the dispute was settled in Copernicus's favor. A Catholic priest, Calandrelli actually did it earlier in a work published in 1806 dedicated to Pope Pius VII. Wallace, "Science and Religion."

parallax because the stars were so incredibly far away that our instruments were simply not sensitive enough.[27]

Copernicus's response undoubtedly strikes a responsive note for contemporary westerns who are fully accustomed to thinking in terms of thousands, and even millions, of light-years.[28] (A light-year equals the distance traveled by light in one year—approximately 5.8 trillion miles.) But what does that prove? To Copernicus's contemporaries, who were accustomed to thinking of a finite universe with the sphere of the stars only one sphere removed from the orbit of Saturn, such a response must surely have seemed as *ad hoc* as our imaginary flat-earthers' assumption that light is bent by strong gravitational fields (see *figure 2.7* above).

There was another problem with a sun-centered theory of the universe. What kept such massive bodies like the earth and the planets revolving eternally around the sun? Copernicus had no answer. When it came to explaining the physics (as opposed to the mathematics) of a moving earth, Copernicus's theory was *less* comprehensive. On the older earth-centered theory, the earth did not have to move and the other planets were composed of a totally different kind of material, aether, whose natural state was to revolve in perfect circles.

Historian Stephen Mason summed the situation well. "The Copernican system had not been widely accepted during the sixteenth century as it gave predictions of planetary positions which were no more accurate than those given by the Ptolemaic scheme, and it embodied

27. Here are Copernicus' actual words explaining the lack of an observable stellar parallax: The stars are "at an immense height away, which makes the circle of annual movement or its image disappear from before our eyes since every visible thing has a certain distance beyond which it is no longer seen, as is shown in optics." Quoted in Hetherington, *Planetary Motions,* 105.

28. "The Copernican universe must be vastly larger than that of traditional cosmology. Its volume is at least 400,000 times as great. There is an immense amount of space between the sphere of Saturn and the sphere of the stars. The neat functional coherence of the nesting spheres of the traditional universe has been violated, though Copernicus seems to remain sublimely unaware of the break." Kuhn, *Copernican Revolution,* 160.

Yet, in another sense, there was nothing *ad hoc* about Copernicus's estimation of the size of the universe—it came straight from his neo-platonic philosophy. The God of Aristotle and Aquinas displayed his perfection in his ordering of the cosmos. But the God of the Neoplatonists displayed his perfection by his fecundity. Again, Kuhn puts it like this: "To many Neoplatonists the finitude of Aristotle's universe was therefore incompatible with God's perfection." Kuhn, *Copernican Revolution,* 132. So much for the positivist's claim that science and philosophy/theology operate according to radically distinct methods!

suppositions that appeared to be unsound from the point of view of the traditional mechanics. Moreover, it was only a specialist departure from the integrated Aristotelian philosophy of nature; it was not yet part of a coherent view of the world as a whole."[29]

By 1650 Galileo had developed a theory of inertial motion, i.e. the property of bodies to remain either at rest or in motion in a straight line unless acted upon by an outside force. So, with regard to the *physics* of the earth's motion, Galileo's contribution to our modern theory was significant.[30] However, mathematically he took a step backwards because he himself stubbornly held to old idea that the motion of the planets was a perfect circle.[31] Furthermore, his crowning "proof" that the earth really revolved around the sun was the tides. Galileo argued that the earth's two distinct motions (its annual motion around the sun and its daily motion on its axis) were the best explanation of the tides. Hence, the earth had to move! Of course, Galileo's account of the tides was not only wrong, but it contradicted his own theory of inertial motion.[32] In short, while Galileo's explanation of the physics of terrestrial motion was pretty good, his astronomical account of celestial motion was fundamentally flawed.[33]

29. Mason, *History*, 159.

30. However, even here, it is a mistake to think of Galileo as a great *experimental* scientist. "Galileo never computed the acceleration of a freely falling body by taking the limit of motion on an inclined plane. He *said* that he had timed a freely falling body dropped from a tower. An iron ball weighing one hundred pounds, he said, 'in repeated experiments falls from a height of one hundred yards in five seconds.' These data contain an error of about 100 percent. We may well understand that when one of Galileo's contemporaries, Father Mersenne, tried to repeat these experiments, he found that he could never get the same result that Galileo had reported." Cohen, *New Physics*, 105–6. Is it any surprise that some in the Catholic Church had doubts about the soundness of Galileo's demonstration of the earth's motion?

31. "The mind shudders," wrote Copernicus in his masterwork *De Revolutionibus* (1543), at any theory postulating non-circular, non-uniform motion, "since it is quite unfitting to suppose that such a state of affairs exists among things which are established in the best system." Galileo wrote, "I therefore conclude that only circular motion can naturally suit bodies which are integral parts of the universe constituted in the best arrangement." Galileo, *Two Chief World Systems*, 32.

32. Butterfield, *Origins*, 82.

33. Galileo's physics requires the qualifier "*pretty* good," because he held on to Copernicus's and Aristotle's idea that circular motion is in some sense natural, and hence, need not be explained. Galileo asks us to imagine a boat given a push in a frictionless sea. Certainly it will not move is a straight line in *absolute* space. If it did that, it would fly into outer space just as a line touching a circle on the tangent. Instead, the boat will continue forever in a *circle* around the earth of the earth. See Galileo, *Two Chief World Systems*, 134–35, and Butterfield, *Origins*, 97.

On the other hand, by the mid-seventeenth century, Johannes Kepler (1571–1630) had already produced convincing evidence that the planets revolved around the sun in ellipses, not circles. With this discovery, Kepler could not only decrease the number of epicycles used by Copernicus and Galileo to mathematically describe the motion of the planets, he could eliminate them. However, while his astronomy was correct, his physical explanation for the planets' motion involved the mystical power of sun rays, clearly a step backwards.[34] Terrestrial and celestial physics had yet to be unified into a single theory.

It took Isaac Newton's (1642–1727) theory of universal gravity to combine the theories of Copernicus, Kepler, and Galileo into a single coherent and comprehensive explanation of both terrestrial and celestial motion. The famous story of an apple falling on his head may well be apocryphal, but it nonetheless makes a crucial point—the same force which pulls an unsupported apple toward the center of the earth also pulls the planets around the sun. Newton's theory of gravity could explain both the orbits of the planets and the motion of unsupported apples here on earth with a single theory. Older theories of gravity were not unified into a single theory. In the Two-Sphere theory, celestial and terrestrial motion did not cohere. Rather, they required one theory for explaining the motion of the sun, stars, and planets, and another theory for explaining the motion of things here on earth. Newton's theory was more comprehensive.

Newton's theory of gravity was also prodigiously fruitful in suggesting new avenues for research, another important element in comprehen-

---

34. "Copernicus and Galileo achieved uniformity by applying the traditional conception of natural circular celestial motions to the earth. Kepler achieved the same effect more fruitfully by applying the ancient conception of violent force-governed terrestrial motions to the heavens. Guided by his ever-present Neoplatonic perception of the sun, Kepler introduced forces emanating from the sun and planets to provide a causal foundation for planetary motion." Kuhn, *Copernican Revolution*, 245.

Furthermore, "Despite the Copernican transformation, Kepler could still argue for a unique earth. It was the planet with the central *orbit* in a system that had as its focus a symbol of the living God: the most resplendent sun in the universe. Bruno's vista of an infinite plurality of star systems, scattered through an infinite universe, was unacceptable because of it relativistic implications. Accordingly, when Kepler first heard of Galileo's telescopic observations, he was alarmed lest the satellites reported should be planets orbiting another sun. How great his relief when he learned they were moons of Jupiter!" Brooke, *Science and Religion*, 28.

siveness.[35] The most famous example was the discrepancy in the orbit of the planet Uranus. Uranus' motion occasionally departed from Newton's predicted path. Adams and Le Verrier reasoned that the problem was not with Newton's theory, but rather, that some unknown planet's gravitational field must be disturbing Uranus's orbit. Using Newton's theory, Adams and Le Verrier calculated exactly where this previously unobserved planet would be. On the basis of these calculations, Galle and Encke discovered planet Neptune in 1846.[36]

The discovery of Neptune, however, did not eliminate all the problems in Newton's theory. One of these involved its philosophical coherence. Though Newton's theory of gravity was tremendously successful in providing a unified explanation of terrestrial and celestial motions, many philosophers, scientists, and even Newton himself, were troubled by his definition of gravity.

In Newton's theory, gravity was defined as an essential property of matter that had an instantaneous effect on objects millions of miles away *without any direct contact*. This was, to say the least, mysterious. Some of Newton's detractors went so far as to say that Newton's theory of "action at a distance" was no better than the occult properties of medieval philosophers and theologians.[37] Newton himself wrote, "It is inconceivable, that inanimate brute matter should, without the mediation of something

---

35. One of the first avenues of researched Newton's theory opened up concerned the "expansion" of Jupiter's orbit. Newton knew that this was caused by the gravitational pull of Saturn. However, he thought that it was only divine intervention that would keep Jupiter and Saturn from eventually colliding. Pierre Laplace (1749–1827) famously quipped, "I have no need for that hypothesis." Why? Because he had laboriously calculated the gravitational interactions of the Sun, Jupiter, and Saturn. "Using Newton's laws and the step-by-step iterative technique, Laplace calculated that the effect of all this was to reverse the overall changes seen in the orbits of the two planets every 929 years— after 929 years with the orbit of Jupiter expanding and the orbit of Saturn shrinking, there is an interval of 929 years with the orbit of Jupiter shrinking while the orbit of Saturn expands, and so on. Laplace thought that he had restored order to the Solar System." Gribbin, *Deep Simplicity*, 13–16.

36. See Stanley Jaki's, *The Relevance of Physics* for more examples of the fruitfulness of Newton's theory.

37. According to Einstein, no theory "involving actions-at-a-distance . . . merits serious consideration . . . [Thus] we will not be able to do without the ether in theoretical physics, i.e., a continuum which is equipped with physical properties; for the general theory of relativity, whose basic points of view physicists surely will always maintain, excludes direct distant action. But every contiguous action theory presumes continuous fields, and therefore also the existence of an 'ether.'" Einstein, "On the Ether," 15–20.

else, which is not material, operate upon, and affect other matter without mutual contact." And again, "that one body may act upon another, at a distance through a vacuum, without the mediation of anything else, by and through which their action and force may be conveyed from one to another, is to me so great an absurdity, that I believe no man who has in philosophical matters a competent faculty of thinking, can ever fall into it. Gravity must be caused by an agent acting constantly according to certain laws; but whether this agent be material or immaterial, I have left to the consideration of my readers."[38]

Newton also considered his own theory to be incomplete in that it failed to explain the origin of the planets orbits. "And though gravity might give the planets a motion of descent towards the Sun, either directly or with some little obliquity, yet the transverse motion, by which they revolve in their several orbits, required the divine Arm to impress them according to the tangents of their orbits."[39]

Another problem concerned the nature of space and the gravitational paradox. Newtonians thought of space as an infinite "container" that existed quite apart from any matter. We have already seen how paradoxical such a conception of space is. But putting such objections aside, even according to Newton's own principles there is a seemingly fatal inconsistency in his theory. According to Newton, the universe is composed of an infinite number of gravitational centers all instantaneously exerting a gravitational force on all other bodies. This is part of what philosophers and scientists were calling Newton's assumption of "action at a distance." But if this assumption is true, then why does not the universe collapse into a single mass? Here's Newton's solution: "And lest the systems of fixed stars should, by their gravity, fall on each other, he [God] hath placed those systems at immense distances from one another."[40] Many of Newton's contemporaries argued such an "auxiliary hypothesis" was totally *ad hoc*. Once again, Newton's theory looks more theological than scientific, at least as positivists understand those terms.

A final problem with Newton's theory was its inability to explain the perihelion of Mercury, another slight irregularity in planetary mo-

---

38. Newton, "Third letter to Bentley," 302–3. Hence, something like the ubiquitous aether of the Two-Sphere universe is required for even Newtonian mechanics. See also, Decaen, "Aristotle's Aether," 375–429.

39. Newton, "Fourth letter to Bentley," 310–11.

40. Newton, *Principles*, 370.

tion. Many scientists tried to solve this problem in the same way they had previously solved the irregularities in Uranus's orbit, namely, by positing another planet. By this time, scientists were so confident that Newton's theories had produced the last word in physics and astronomy that they already had a name for this yet to be observed planet—they called it Vulcan.[41]

But Vulcan does not exist. And how can scientists be so sure? Though the story cannot be told here, it begins with Max Planck, a nineteenth-century student who wanted to study physics. Planck's teachers knew that he was an excellent student so they counseled him to find some other field of study because they were afraid that Planck would be bored with physics since "nothing fundamentally new can still be discovered"![42] Fortunately, Planck did not follow the counsel of his professor and began doing graduate work in physics. There he discovered discrepancies in the radiation of black bodies. These puzzling observations led to Einstein's theories of relativity and a yet more coherent and comprehensive theory of gravity than Newton's. Among other things, Einstein's theories explained the irregularities in Mercury's orbit without positing another planet.[43]

So what sorts of conclusions do realists draw from this historical narrative? First, there is no hard-and-fast distinction between the methods of scientists and philosophers when they are addressing the cutting-edge problems of their respective fields. Both philosophers and scientists attempt to find the most consistent, coherent, and comprehensive explanation available for the data at hand. The difference, therefore, is not in their method, but in the sorts of questions that they address. Scientists are primarily concerned with that which can be quantifiably measured and/or observed. Often times this involves the use of highly sophisticated instruments or travel to far and distant lands.

Philosophers, as we will see, also deal with observable data. But it is the sort of data that is readily available to everyone. Examples of such

41. See Richard Baum and William Sheehan, *In Search of Planet Vulcan*, for an extremely readable account of the whole story.

42. Jaki, *Relevance of Physics*, 88.

43. Though ironically, Einstein's ideas were in some ways a throw-back to Aristotle. "Perhaps by mere coincidence, the spatial concepts embodies in Einstein's general theory of relativity are, in important respects, closer to Aristotle's than to Newton's. And Einstein's universe may, like Aristotle's and unlike Newton's, be finite." Kuhn, *Copernican Revolution*, 99.

data are: (1) plants and animals exist, (2) square circles do not exist, and (3) nothing comes from nothing. Such truths are not the product of sophisticated instruments or travel to exotic places. Nonetheless, trying to "make sense" of all that is implied by such seemingly simple propositions is not easy. And, when we do begin to make sense of them, we discover that they have some rather surprising implications about freedom, morality, and God.

Second, "good judgment," "making sense," "preferring simple and elegant explanations to Rube Goldberg accounts," and "rejecting *ad hoc* hypotheses" are necessary elements to *all* good reasoning, both in science and philosophy.[44] Furthermore, none of these can be reduced to a deductive formula. But just because we are not reasoning in a deductive, truth-guaranteeing fashion does *not* mean, as relativists claim, that we are reasoning in a wholly subjective fashion. Good reasoning always involves the three Cs of consistency, coherence and comprehensiveness. So there is no need to preface all our philosophical conclusions with "*To me . . .*" The three Cs are universal—they are not proprietary products of any particular era or culture.

---

44. "Galileo says [in *Discourses and Demonstrations Concerning Two New Sciences*] furthermore that 'in the investigation of naturally accelerated motion we were led, by the hand as it were, in following the habit and custom of nature herself, in all her various other processes, to employ only those means which are most common, simple and easy.' Galileo was invoking a famous principle here, one that actually goes back to Aristotle, that nature always works in the simplest way possible, or in the most economical fashion." Cohen, *New Physics*, 97.

A contemporary philosopher of science puts it like this: "In short, judgments of coherence, simplicity, and so on are presupposed by physical science. Yet coherence, simplicity, and the like are values. Indeed, each and every one of the familiar arguments for relativism in ethics could be repeated in connection with these epistemic values." Putnam, *Fact/Value Dichotomy*, 142.

3

What Is a "Scientific" Proof?

This chapter continues our discussion of the nature of scientific "proof" by considering the history of biology. Up until Darwin in the mid-nineteenth century, biological species were universally believed to be fixed and immutable. And, contrary to popular opinion, the fixity of species was not defended primarily on religious grounds. Once again, the fixity of species was a theory which had widespread scientific acceptance because it was an integral part of an interconnected and symbiotically justified set of propositions.

Today we call this older theory the "Great Chain of Being." Its fundamental propositions were: 1) nothing exists without a cause; 2) the observed goodness of creation implies and is implied by the existence of a good and powerful Divine Craftsman; 3) biological species are hierarchically ordered in such a way that there are no "gaps" in the chain of being because the Divine Craftsman was not jealous that his creation would overshadow his own glory. All this means that biological species must be fixed and immutable because the coming to be of new species would imply that there were either mistakes or gaps in the original creation. And note: this was a philosophical/scientific theory that long preceded the religious dominance of Christianity in the West.

However, the nineteenth century produced puzzling new data. First, no one had ever observed living dinosaurs, mammoths, or saber tooth tigers. Second, rudimentary eyes in moles were observed, but they were covered with fur and thus utterly useless. Third, the forelimbs of bats, whales, chimps, and humans were observed to have similar bone structure. Finally, marsupials were observed (almost) exclusively in Australia. All of these were anomalies on the Great Chain of Being account.

Darwin significantly reduced the anomalous nature of this new data by purposing that all our observations are nothing more than a snapshot taken at a single point in time. After all, the entire re-

corded human observations have taken place within the last seven or eight thousand years and this is a mere drop in the bucket of geological time.

While evolutionary biologists have proved that species are not fixed and immutable, this is not a conclusion they deduced from observed "facts." Instead, they have proven their point in the same way lawyers build a case to prove their point beyond a reasonable doubt. Lawyers do this by convincing a jury of unbiased peers. But where does one find such a jury for a big biological theory? Big "scientific" questions inevitably have implications for big "philosophical" questions. And big "philosophical" questions are always self-involving in a way that is impossible to ignore.

While our full discussion of self-involving propositions will have to wait, the problem of "bias" can be significantly reduced by focusing on the smaller components of evolution, for example: are species eternally fixed? If not, was the change relatively gradual? If so, how important is natural selection as an explanation for this change?

Neither Newton nor Darwin proved their theories with deductive certainty. Yet Newton's theory concerned repeatable events that were mathematically predictable. Darwin's theory concerned unrepeatable, once in the history of the earth, events which were in no way predictable. Therefore the convergence of smaller, independent theories into a single consistent, comprehensive, and coherent theory was even more significant than it was in Newton's case.

THERE IS CERTAINLY NO agreement about whether or not God exists. But, today, there is nearly universal agreement that even if God does exist, his existence cannot be "scientifically proved." It was not always so. In the ancient and medieval world, "scientific" proof of God' existence was taken for granted. So who is right—us or them? This is a big philosophical question we will consider in chapter10. But in this chapter we will continue our discussion of the crucial preliminary question: What is a "scientific" proof?[1]

As we saw in the last chapter, positivists have a fairly clear definition of the "scientific method," and hence, are pretty sure they know what constitutes a "scientific proof." Relativists, on the other hand, deny that

1. "Every evolutionist who has had a discussion with lay people has been asked: 'Has evolution been proven?' or 'How do you prove that man descended from apes?' he is then obliged first to discuss the nature of scientific proof." Mayr, *Growth of Biological Thought*, 27.

there is such a thing as "scientific proof." All "proofs," they say, are an illusion. To say that a proposition has been "proved" only means that a group of people strongly *believes* the proposition to be true, which is not the same saying that it is universally true. And, of course, what one group strongly believes some other group will strongly disbelieve.

Realists chart a middle course. Contrary to relativists, realists argue that scientists really have demonstrated, for example, that the earth moves. But contrary to positivists (as we saw in chapter 2), scientists did *not* follow the five step "scientific method" that most of us were taught in elementary school. With big questions like, "Does the earth revolve around the Sun?" their only "method" was to construct the best explanation using the three Cs of comprehensiveness, consistency, and coherence. When all of these converge and point to the same solution to our puzzle, as they did with Newton, we can be quite confident about our answer.

3.1 THE GREAT CHAIN OF BEING

This chapter will continue to make the case for an Aristotelian realist understanding of science by considering the nature of biological arguments. Plato and Aristotle are largely responsible for the older theory of biology and Charles Darwin is largely responsible for the newer theory which corrected, expanded, and even revolutionized the older understanding. Like the previous chapter, our treatment will be greatly simplified, loosely historical, and directed primarily at understanding the logic (not the details) of biological explanations.

The key to understanding what we will call the old explanation (i.e., the dominant explanation prior to the nineteenth century) is the "Great Chain of Being." The idea dates back to Plato (427–347 BCE) who was Aristotle's teacher. In the *Timaeus,* Plato wrote, "Now everything that becomes or is created must of necessity be created by some cause, for without a cause nothing can be created."[2] This is the first premise. The second premise is that simple observation demonstrates that our universe is in a state of "becoming"—we are born and then we die; we build temples of stone, only to have them destroyed by an earthquake. From these two premises it follows that our universe must have a creator. And since it would be blasphemous to think of the Creator as less than

---

2. Plato *Timaeus,* 28A.

supreme goodness itself, says Plato, the creation must also be good. "He [the divine Craftsman] was good, and the good can never have any jealousy of anything. And being free from jealousy, he desired that all things should be as like himself as they could be. This is in the truest sense the origin of creation and of the world, as we shall do well in believing on the testimony of wise men: god desired that all things should be good and nothing bad, so far as this was attainable."[3]

Before we can understand what Plato meant by saying that "all things should be good" we must distinguish between describing and naming. When parents *name* a child "Johnny" they are doing something fundamental different than when they *describe* Johnny as good. "Johnny" as a name is use to pick out or refer to a single, particular person whereas "good" as a descriptor refers to many, perhaps even an infinite number, of particular people or things. Words like "good" refer to a *universal* essence while names like "Johnny" refer to a *particular* person or thing.

Plato's own example to illustrate the difference between a universal and a particular was the Triangle. We deliberately capitalize "Triangle" since Plato is not referring to any particular triangle a person might see drawn in the sand or cut out of a piece of cardboard. Rather, Plato wants us to think about the *idea* of Triangle which serves as the plan, blue print, or archetype for all *physical* triangles. The Triangle has interior angles which equal *exactly* 180 degrees whereas any particular physical triangle will only have interior angles which *approximate* 180 degrees. The Triangle is eternal and unchanging whereas any particular physical triangle exists in a continual state of flux. And what's true of the Triangle will be true of all words which describe things in our physical world. This is Plato's famous theory of Ideas or Forms

One of the most famous disputes between a teacher and student is the dispute between Plato and Aristotle about the "location" of the universal essences. It has been famously illustrated by Raphael's "School of Athens." In this painting Plato is the old man in the center pointing toward the heavens and Aristotle is the middle aged man next to him with his hand signaling to slow down and pay more attention to things of earth. Plato's hand is pointing upwards because he believed the universal essences (Ideas) resided in an eternal realm completely separate from the physical realm. Aristotle's hand is pointed somewhat downward because

---

3. Ibid., 29E–30A. We will discuss the difference between a divine Craftsman and a Creator God in chapter 10.

he believed that the universal essences resided *in* the physical world, but not as a physical part of the world. (Aristotle thought that essences are *in* things the way meaning is *in* words, not the way dirt is *in* rugs. We will say *much* more about this in the succeeding chapters.) But for now, it is their agreement that is important. Both Plato and Aristotle believed that humans gain a true understanding of reality when we are able to "divide nature at its joints" so that the universal essences of things are clearly revealed.

Now the first point Plato made about the divine Craftsman (Plato's actual term was "Demiurge" or "worker for the people") is that he *really* was good, i.e. "goodness" was part of his essential nature; it was not a mere name (or as we would say a "value judgment"). The second point Plato made is that the divine Craftsman is "without jealousy." In other words, he has no need of denigrating others in order to glorify himself. According to Plato, the divine Craftsman is both good and without peer. Thus, he will make as many different kinds of things as possible. The divine Craftsman has no fear of competitors. So, instead of making a rather paltry world with only humans, a single kind of animal, a single kind of plant, and a single kind of mineral, the divine Craftsman creates a "Great Chain of Being" which includes the richest possible diversity of humans, animals, plants, and minerals.

This leads to a third point. If a young child dumps a box of Scrabble letters on the floor, there will be a lot of diversity—some will be face up, others will be face down; a few might be in a straight line, but most will land at random angles with respect to the others; and, of course, there will be much diversity in the letters we see. The point is this: without some ordering principle, mere variety or diversity constitutes a chaos, not a cosmos. But the divine Craftsman is not like a child who dumps a box of letters on the floor. No, our universe is composed of an immeasurable number of distinct species arranged to form a Great Chain of Being. The highest link in the chain is the form of Goodness itself (an uncreated spirit); the lowest link is mere matter. In between reside all the various grades of life beginning with created pure spirits (angels[4]),

---

4. The belief in angels is not only part of the western religious tradition, but it is also part of our philosophical tradition. God is an uncreated pure spirit. Humans are created beings with bodies and spirits. Given the assumption of the Great Chain of Being, that means that there is a "gap" between God and humans, namely, created pure spirits. Since only a "jealous" Creator would fail to create all possible creatures, we can feel confident that he must have created angels or pure spirits.

then there are created beings with both a body and a spirit (humans). Following these are all the various animal species arranged from the lion down to the worm, all the species of plants from magnificent orchids to mere moss, and finally all lifeless minerals arranged from gold to sand.

The "Great Chain of Being" was both a product of Plato's quasi-religious intuitions and a result of a fairly natural inference from common experience.[5] The "goodness" of creation is evident in the simple fact that the vast majority of people prefer life to death, i.e. they view their own existence as a good gift. We can also see the great joy other creatures take in life—consider a dog running to catch a frisbee, a seagull soaring over the waves, or a leaping dolphin entertaining the passengers on a ship. Second, simple observation confirms the great diversity of life. There is no physical or "scientific" reason why life on earth *had to be* so rich and various. There could have been only a hand full of mammals, reptiles, birds, and fish. Instead, we observe such a wonderful diversity of living creatures that it seems like every kind of creature that could be made has been made.

Finally (though it is difficult to find words which will not cause modern ears to cringe) there seems to be a cosmic ordering of species where the lower is intended to serve the higher *and* the higher is intended to benevolently guide the lower. Think here of a boy throwing a stick for his dog or the Native American thanking the deer he just killed for providing food during a harsh winter. In the ancient world the relation between the ruler and the ruled was one where the ruler had not only the *right* to the respect, honor, and service from those ruled, but the ruler also had the *obligation* to protect, guide, and ensure the general welfare of those he ruled. Among humans such relations were consciously set down in the laws and traditions governing societies. In the sub-human world these relations were more metaphorical, though they were nonetheless real. The cow eats the grass for food, thereby destroying it. Yet the cow also provides manure for the field, thereby ensuring that new grass will grow tall. Today we call the study of these mutual relations "ecology" and the ordering from top to bottom the "food chain."

---

5. "Often it is rather difficult even to distinguish external from internal factors [in biological thought]. The Great Chain of Being (*scala naturae*) was a philosophical concept which clearly had an impact on concept-formation in the case of Lamarck and other early evolutionists. Yet, Aristotle had developed this concept on the basis of empirical observations of organisms." Mayr, *Growth of Biological Thought,* 4.

One immediate consequence of the notion of a Great Chain of Being is the fixity of biological species.[6] If new species came into existence, then that would mean that the original ordering of the world was incomplete. On the other hand, if one of the original species became extinct, then that would leave a gap in the "chain of being" which would mean that the present ordering of the world was incomplete. Either alternative would be a denial of the goodness and power of the divine Craftsman. Thus, the job of ancient biologists was to classify and properly order species in terms of their dignity (what we today call "complexity") so as to most clearly exhibit plan or blueprint of the divine Craftsman.

3.2 PUZZLING NEW DATA

However, by 1800, the task of biologists was beginning to change.[7] First, biologists were becoming more ambitious, seeking not only to describe nature but also to explain what they observed. True, there is an explanatory element in the Great Chain of Being. There is great diversity of species *because* God is not jealous. But Plato would be the first to admit that the "mind of God" transcends human understanding and does very little to *explain* what we observe on earth. In this regard, an explanation in terms of God's lack of jealousy is like the famous Sidney Harris cartoon in which a scientist has scribbled a long equation across a blackboard. But in the middle of the equation are the words, "And then a miracle occurs" to which a second scientist points and responds, "I think you ought to be more explicit."

And note: the point of the cartoon is *not* that miracles are impossible. Rather, its point is that miracles do not explain the physical causes behind our observations. Plato may be absolutely correct about the di-

6. "All of Darwin's teachers and friends were, more or less, essentialists . . . Virtually all philosophers up to Darwin's time were essentialists. Whether they were realists or idealists, materialists or nominalists, they all saw species of organism with the eyes of an essentialist. They considered species as 'natural kinds,' defined by constant characteristics and sharply separated from one another by bridgeless gaps. The essentialist philosopher William Whewell stated categorically, 'Species have a real existence in nature, and a transition from one to another does not exist' (184, 3:626). For John Stuart Mill, species of organism are natural kinds, just as inanimate objects are, and 'kinds are classes between which there is an impassable barrier.'" Mayr, *One Long Argument*, 41.

7. Referring to biologists at the beginning of the nineteenth century is slightly anachronistic. Back then they were all referred to as either "naturalists" or "natural historians." It is not until 1833 that English philosopher and historian of science William Whewell coined the term *scientist*.

vine Craftsman not being jealous; but that tells us little about the tools and methods with which he carried out his work.

Second, the biologist's job was changing because new data was accumulating. Here are four examples: (1) no living dinosaurs, mammoths, or saber tooth tigers had ever been observed; (2) moles have rudimentary eyes which they cannot use because they are covered with fur; (3) the forelimbs of humans, chimps, whales, and bats all have similar bone structure; and (4) marsupials were found (almost) exclusively in Australia. Like the anomalies we discussed in 2.2, such data began to cause puzzlement. Though Aristotle himself tried to explain the second,[8] all of these fit rather awkwardly into the idea of a Great Chain of Being.

Today, the answer to the first question seems simple: Living dinosaurs,[9] mammoths, and saber tooth tigers have never been observed by humans because none exist; these species have become extinct. There are two problems with this response—one logical, the other more philosophical.

The logical problem concerns the "proof" of a universal negative. The fact that no one has ever observed a forty foot purple chiliagon (thousand sided figure) does not mean that they do not or cannot exist. Any competent carpenter with a little time and money could build such an object. It would be only slightly more difficult than building a forty foot purple octagon. And there are several non-hypothetical examples in which absence of evidence is *not* evidence of absence. Prior to 1861 there was no physical evidence for the existence of reptiles with feathers. But, then, archaeopteryx was discovered. Prior to 1938 there was no physical evidence for the existence of living coelacanths (a kind of lungfish for which we had much fossil evidence). But, then, off the coast of South Africa, a living coelacanth was caught in the net of a fisherman.

---

8. See Aristotle *History of Animals* bk. 1, ch. 9. "And yet one might assert that, though the mole has not eyes in the full sense, yet it has eyes in a kind of way. For in point of absolute fact it cannot see, and has no eyes visible externally; but when the outer skin is removed, it is found to have the place where eyes are usually situated, and the black parts of the eyes right situated, and all the place that is usually devoted on the outside to eyes: showing that the parts are stunted in development, and the skin allowed to grow over."

9. Strictly speaking, true dinosaur fossils were not discovered until the 1840s, but fossils of mastodons and mammoths (species we now know to be extinct) had been discovered by 1800.

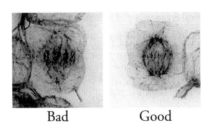

Bad   Good

Figure 3.1

So Thomas Jefferson was hardly being illogical when he expected Lewis and Clark to discover the home of *living* wooly mammoths and the giant sloth.[10] After all, he had observed the bones that had been dug up in the Ohio Valley of these huge mammals. And since they were no longer living there, they must have migrated further west—just where Lewis and Clark were sent to explore.

The more philosophical point is that observations are frequently "theory laden." Today, when paleontologists observe fossils of archaeopteryx they "see" evidence for the existence of an extinct creature that has features of both reptiles and birds. But when Thomas Jefferson observed the giant bones of the mammoth he "saw" evidence for the migration of these creatures further west. The difference is that today's paleontologists work with the assumption that extinction is possible; Thomas Jefferson worked with the older assumption that extinction would create a gap in the chain of being and was therefore impossible.

And it would be wrong to criticize Jefferson for allowing his "assumptions" to prejudice his observations. All significant scientific observations are theory laden. Compare the two photographs of skillfully stained cells taken with a powerful microscope (figure 3.1). Without a theoretical understanding of how staining agents affect cells, mere observation will never reveal that what we "see" in the left picture are disfunctional mircotublues whereas in the right picture they are fully functional.

10. Jefferson wrote to Lacepede on February 24, 1803, that it was "not improbable that this voyage of discovery will procure us further information of the Mammoth, & of the Megatherium also" (Academy of Natural Sciences at http://www.ansp.org/museum/jefferson/megalonyx/history-02.php).

Of course, today many people look back on Jefferson's assumption of a Great Chain of Being as being no more than a piece of outdated "philosophy" which has long since been proven wrong by science. But this begs the question. It assumes that we already understand what "scientific proofs" are, when that is the very question we are currently investigating. Only if we assume (as do the positivists) that all real knowledge is based solely in observation can we know *prior to the examination of the data* that the Great Chain of Being is a piece of dubious philosophy. But look again at the two pictures of cells. Is it the fact that biologists have better *eyes* than philosophers that make them better able to *observe* what is functional and what is not? Hardly. It is only the biologist's *theoretical understanding* of cells and microscopes that enables them to make such distinctions.

However, by rejecting the positivist's assumption we are *not* thereby suggesting that the Great Chain of Being is true or that it is the best theory for understanding the observed data of the living world. As we will argue below, ancient biology has been superseded by more comprehensive, consistent, and coherent theories. We are only suggesting that there are no simple observations which "proved" it to be false, in the same way that there was no observation or set of observations which "proved" the Two-Sphere theory of the universe to be false. Before we can rationally reject the Great Chain of Being, a case must be built against it, in much the same way as a prosecutor builds a legal case against a defendant. There are no shortcuts, as positivist assume, for determining which theories are good "science" and which are not. And remember, mere anomalies will never disprove a scientific theory until a better theory is discovered (chapter 2).

The second piece of data in the case against the Great Chain of Being concerns moles. Why do moles have rudimentary eyes which they never use (because they live underground) nor could they use (because they are covered with skin and fur)? Why would a divine Craftsman make such a creature, unless mole's "eyes" were a sort of joke? But between the time of Aristotle and Darwin few naturalists were willing to think of the divine Craftsman as a jokester. Instead, they considered the "eyes" of moles and several other vestigial organs[11] as nothing more than anomalies waiting for a better explanation.

---

11. The side toes on pigs and horses that do not touch the ground, hip bones in boa-constrictors and whales, and even the "tail bone" in humans are also standard examples of what biologist call vestigial organs.

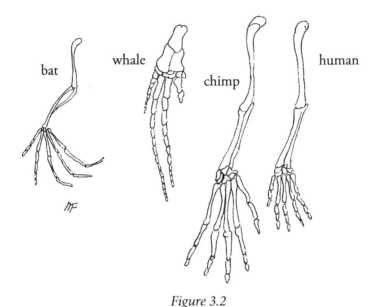

Figure 3.2

The third piece of data concerns the number, shape, and location of the bones in the forelimbs of radically distinct creatures (see figure 3.2).

The arms of humans and chimps, the flippers of whales, and the wings of bats all have the same number of bones. And while these bones are in the same spatial relation to all the rest, their sizes and shapes are quite different. In a word, they are similar, but not the same (or as biologists say, they are homologous).

"Similar," however, is a word unintelligible in both logic and mathematics. The similarity of the bone structure in figure 3.2 is observable, but it cannot be "proved" with either logic or mathematics. Logically speaking, "similar" makes no sense. To say that A is similar to B means that A both *is and is not* the same as B. Mathematically and/or logically this makes no sense. Such a contradiction will cause any computer to crash. Of course, humans can quantify (i.e. assign a numerical rank) observed similarities.[12] But to do so we must first make *qualitative judg-*

12. "The champions of quantification tend to consider the recognition of quality as something unscientific or at best as something purely descriptive and classificatory. They reveal by this bias how little they understand the nature of biological phenomena. Quantification is important in many fields of biology, but not to the exclusion of all qualitative aspects." Mayr, *Growth of Biological Thought,* 55.

ments about what "counts" as a similarity.[13] And this presupposes that we already know which of the infinite number of observed features of the two objects are relevant. And questions of relevancy always require human judgment and understanding. How great is the similarity between a red fire engine and red blood? Is it more or less than the similarity between reddish dirt and brownish dirt?[14]

Instead of trying to quantify "similarities," we would do better to consider the underlining assumption which is largely responsible for the puzzlement. The old assumption was that "bat" and "chimps" name two distinct species of animals because they embody two distinct eternal archetypes (i.e., a Platonic Idea or essential natures). If this is the case, then we are rightfully puzzled as to why a divine Craftsman would, so to speak, "re-shape" the same body parts to form the arms of humans and chimps, flippers of whales, and wings of bats. Why not start from scratch when making parts designed to perform radically different functions— grasping, running, swimming and flying? Failure to do so seems more indicative of incompetence than a practical joke.

But if we move from assuming a *Great* Chain of Being to assuming only a *Little* Chain of Being, the puzzle is largely resolved. The *Great* Chain of Being includes many thousands of different and distinct species of animals (each one with its own eternal archetype). A *Little* Chain of Being includes only a hand full of distinct species.[15] It assumes that plants are distinct from non-living things,[16] and that animals with feelings are distinct from plants which have no feeling, and that humans who can understand things (like chiliagons or tomorrow) which they

13. Darwin, though he sometimes said he followed "the true Baconian method" of observing and counting, in fact knew better. He wrote in a letter to Henry Fawcett: "About 30 years ago there was much talk that geologists ought to observe and not to theorize; and I well remember someone saying that at this rate a man might as well go into a gravel pit and count the pebbles and describe the colors. How odd it is that anyone should not see that all observation must be for or against some view if it is to be of any service!" Mayr, *One Long Argument*, 9.

14. We will say much more about this in 5.2. There we will argue that quantity is itself a quality.

15. See Adler, *Problem of Species*.

16. "Furthermore, all biological processes differ in one respect fundamentally from all processes in the inanimate world; they are subject to *dual causation*. In contrast to purely physical processes, these biological ones are controlled not only by natural laws but also by *genetic programs*. This duality fully provides a clear demarcation between inanimate and living processes." Mayr, *What Makes Biology Unique*, 30.

have never observed are distinct from animals which can only know that which they observe.[17] In short, on this assumption there are only four links in nature—1) non-living things, 2) plants, 3) animals without rational intellects, and 4) animals with rational intellects. With a Little Chain of Being the individual species of animals—dogs, chimps, whales, bats, etc.—are viewed as variations on a single essence. To use a human analogy, the individual species of animals are like the multitudinous makes and models of cars—Mazda Miata, Ford Escort, Toyota Camry, Jeep Grand Sport, etc. Though they differ in size and shape and are all designed to satisfy distinct desires and needs, nonetheless, they are all cars. With such an assumption, it is not especially puzzling that different cars would all have similar looking fuel pumps and radiators.

Furthermore, if we suppose that one of the desires of car owners is to keep the cost down whenever possible, then we should not be surprised or puzzled by the fact that frequently, over a number of years, car manufactures "tinker" with their cars—adding new features here; removing old features there—instead of re-tooling and starting from scratch each year. Finally, if we also suppose that occasionally there are externally imposed constraints—for example, stricter emission standards—then it is hardly puzzling that more and more pumps, hoses, and regulators would be added to the engine in a somewhat haphazard or Rube Goldberg fashion. This would not be a mark of incompetence, but only indicative of the fact that it is very expensive to completely re-designing engines each time the emission standards change.

The comparison of biological homologies to humanly manufactured automobiles suggests that we view the multitude of individual species as a snapshot in a point of time rather than as embodiments of eternal archetypes. In other words, if we start with only a Little Chain of Being, then the observed similarities of the bones in bats, whales, chimps, and humans *point to* historical continuities among animals, not the incompetence of the designer. (Including humans in the genus "animal," of course, says nothing about whether or not humans are es-

17. "Even though we often use the word 'language' in connection with the information transmittal systems of animals, such as the 'language of bees,' actually all of these animal species have merely systems of giving and receiving signals. To be a language, a system of communication must contain syntax and grammar. Psychologists have attempted for half a century to teach language to chimpanzees, but in vain. Chimps seem to lack the neural equipment to adopt syntax. *Therefore, they cannot talk about the future or the past.*" Mayr, *What Evolution Is,* 253 emphasis added.

sentially different from all other animals. That question must wait until chapter 7.)

The final puzzling piece of data for the idea of a Great Chain of Being is that, with only a very few exceptions, marsupials are native only to Australia. Here the divine jokester explanation might work. The fact that the divine Craftsman made polar bears living in the artic regions with white fur and bears living in temperate zones with black and brown fur suggests "good design." Different environments require different color coats. But the environment of Australia is not significantly different from many other places in the world. So why the radically different reproductive design of marsupials and their counterparts elsewhere in the world? Three answers are possible: 1) marsupials are a practical joke, 2) marsupials are an unexplainable, brute fact of nature, and 3) we extend the car analogy and adopt a longer, more historical perspective.[18]

In Europe, 50 percent of the cars manufactured are diesels. In the United States, they are a tiny minority (under 4 percent). It was not always like this. Change began with three political "earthquakes": the Arab oil boycott of 1973, the Iranian Revolution of 1979, and the Iraqi invasion of Iran of 1980. All of these resulted in a sharp increase of oil prices in Europe and the United States. So in the 1980s, the fuel efficiency of diesels were an attractive alternative in both Europe and the United States. But as time went on, the Europeans and Americans gradually went their separate ways with respect to gasoline taxes and emission standards. After three decades gasoline became significantly cheaper in the United States than in Europe. There were also significant differences in the emission standards. These combined to make diesels less and less attractive in the United States, but more attractive in Europe. In time these differences resulted in a large gap in the number of diesels across the ocean.

Might not a similar explanation work for marsupials? Suppose Australia and Asia where once physically connected so that mammals could roam freely in one large super-continent. (This would be analo-

18. "When a biologist tries to answer a question about a unique occurrence such as 'Why are there no hummingbirds in the Old World?' or 'Where did the species *Homo sapiens* originate?' he cannot rely on universal laws. The biologists has to study all the known facts relating to the particular problem, infer all sorts of consequences from the reconstructed constellations of factors, and then attempt to construct a scenario that would explain the observed facts of this particular case. In other words, he constructs a historical narrative." Mayr, *This Is Biology*, 64.

gous to high oil prices in Europe and America at the beginning of the 1980s.) Then suppose Australia and Asia start moving in opposite direction through a process of what today we call plate tectonics. Mammals could no longer roam freely between the two. Over time, as the result of external forces (analogous to the changes in tax laws and emission standards), we might reasonably expect them to slowly develop different means of reproducing, assuming of course that individual species of mammals are *not* physical embodiments of eternal archetypes which cannot change.

3.3 THE LOGIC OF EVOLUTIONARY EXPLANATIONS

Readers of Charles Darwin will have caught on to our ruse several paragraphs ago. The "logic" of our proposed solutions to the four puzzling pieces of data is identical to Darwin's. All we have done is to update the analogies. Since this is a book of philosophy, we will let the biologists flesh out the details and multiply the examples. Our task is to understand the "logic" of this argument.

1) The scare quotes around "logic" are essential. As we have already said and as we will continue to show in succeeding chapters, there is no such thing as the "logic" of inductive arguments. Philosophical positivists have made several attempts to "formalize" inductive reasoning so that inductive conclusions could be established in the same way and with the same certainty as deductive proofs. The last serious attempt was made by Rudolf Carnap in the early 1950s. By all accounts, he failed.[19] We will see why in chapter 6.

But chapter 2 already gives us some understanding of the problem. Deductive attempts to *verify* scientific theories always commit the fallacy of affirming the consequent. On the other hand, deductive attempts to falsify scientific theories presuppose logical (i.e., purely formal, content-neutral) criteria which rule out *ad hoc* hypotheses. Since there are no such criteria, *all* theories, no matter how silly, can logically be saved from falsification by adding an auxiliary hypothesis.

And closely connected is the "theory laden" nature of scientific observations that we already discussed. Sophisticated photographs produced by powerful microscopes (see *figure 3.1*) require much more than a set of good eyes to properly "observe."

19. Putnam, *Fact/Value Dichotomy*, 141, 180.

2) We refer to *this* argument, not *these* arguments. Darwin concluded his *Origin of Species* by describing it as "one long argument." So too, the solution we presented to the four puzzles of the nineteenth century make a cumulative case against eternal archetypes. None of them by themselves refutes the idea that species are eternal and unchanging. Nor do the four of them together, in a strictly logical sense, refute this old theory. But together they build a strong case *against* eternal and unchanging species and conversely build a case *for* a historical understanding of species. And as the individual examples are multiplied for each of four puzzles the overall case is strengthened.

In chapter 2 we discussed the three Cs of consistency, coherence, and comprehensiveness. Here we see more clearly how coherence and comprehensiveness work together when distinct arguments converge to a single solution. At first, the extinction of dinosaurs and mammoths, the rudimentary eyes in moles, the slightly weird structure (from an engineering point of view) of a bird's wings, and the distinct reproductive means of "wolves" in Australia and North America seem to have nothing to do with each other. However, once a historical and developmental perspective is taken, these independent pieces of data begin to converge to a single solution. With respect to method, the case that Darwin built and the case a prosecutor builds in a criminal trial are the same.

3) Darwin's argument does not deductively prove that there are no eternal archetypes for each of the individual species, but that does not mean that his arguments are not extremely powerful. Logicians and mathematicians speak of "proof," as do police detectives and lawyers, but "proof" in these distinct contexts have nothing in common. The sort of proof that logicians and mathematicians demand is impossible to produce in a court of law. Conversely, the sort of proof "beyond a reasonable doubt" that lawyers produce would be of absolutely no interest to a logician or mathematician.

Neither Newton nor Darwin nor Einstein nor quantum physicists have *proved* their theories in a fashion that would satisfy logicians and mathematicians. Yet this hardly means that these scientists have not "proved" their theories in the looser, more general sense of the word.[20] Newton's theory of universal gravity, Darwin's theory of natural selection,

---

20. It was Descartes who first argued that all knowledge must be ground in strict deductive proofs. We will consider his argument in chapter 6.

Einstein's theory of relativity, and Bohr's theory of quantum mechanics, according to philosophical realists, have all been "proved beyond a reasonable doubt."

4) Big theories—in philosophy, physics, astronomy, and biology—are all established (or refuted) by "building a case," in much the same way that police detectives and lawyers "build a case." And to determine whether or not a strong case has been built, we rely on juries of one's peers to determine if the case has been "proved beyond a reasonable doubt."

There are two essential elements to having a "jury of one's peers." First, the jury must be neutral, unbiased, and without a conflict of interest. That's why lawyers spend so much time in jury selection. Such a jury is not always easy to obtain.

Second, the jury must be composed of one's *peers*. Fantasize a moment about a jury composed of absolutely unbiased and extremely intelligent Martians. The only problem is that they are incapable of fear, sorrow, anger, and all the other psychological states that humans experience. Would they make a good jury for a woman charged with the murder of her physically abusive husband? Hardly. Perhaps a jury of Martians could make an accurate assessment of the purely factual question—Did the women kill the husband? But a Martian jury without "feelings" could not make a good judgment about whether or not the woman acted in self-defense. So too, those making judgments about scientific theories must be able to "think and feel" like those who are proposing the theories. That is why, at least today, scientific disputes are largely conducted in peer reviewed journals and books.

So far, so good. A number of readers, however, will object that we have too quickly skated over the first criteria—that jurors be neutral, unbiased, and without a conflict of interest. Critics of evolution will object that it is impossible to find a "neutral jury" because too much is at stake with respect to religion and morality. Thus, each side in the controversy over evolution has a right to their own opinion.

The critic raises an important issue. "Evolution" is clearly a self-involving topic. Individual biases, prejudices, and interest are virtually impossible to avoid. That is why evolution is such a controversial topic. However, much of the controversy is caused by both sides talking past each other. While some of the controversy is caused by individual prejudice, more is caused by the *ill* defined nature of the question. When the questions are *well* defined, fruitful discussions are not impossible.

For example, Darwin's theory of evolution was composed of at least five *explicitly* stated and independent theories: 1) species are not eternally fixed and unchangeable, 2) species have descended from a common ancestor, 3) species only change gradually, 4) species multiply as the result of geographic isolation, and 5) natural selection is the primary mechanism of evolution.[21] And, of course, just below the surface of many debates about evolution is a sixth theory, namely, that evolution "proves" that there is no God.[22]

If we are patient enough to distinguish these six distinct questions, we would see that there is as much agreement among biologists with respect to questions 1, 2, and 4 as there is among physicists with respect to relativity theory and quantum mechanics. With respect to 3 and 5, there is necessarily going to be discussion since the terms "gradually" and "primarily" invite ongoing refinement. And question 6—Does "evolution" disprove the existence of God?—clearly moves beyond mere science. We will discuss this question in chapter 10.

5) No big theory is proved with deductive certainty nor are they irrefutable. The best of juries occasionally convict innocent people. New evidence occasionally turns up and even honest and conscientious jurors can misjudge the evidence. Yet, we continue to punish people convicted of crimes. Waiting for a perfect system of justice is not a viable alternative. Likewise, philosophers and scientists will never know what they

---

21. Ernst Mayr has argued for this five-fold division in several of his books including *One Long Argument*, *This Is Biology*, *What Evolution Is* and *What Makes Biology Unique?* Any reasonably competent biologist could name numerous sub-theories under each of the five theories we have listed.

22. Richard Dawkins' *God Delusion* is only the most recent example of this claim, though with Dawkins the claim is anything but implicit! We must contrast this with Stephen Jay Gould's position: "I have been both amused and infuriated that this issue still haunts us. I understand why American fundamentalist who call themselves 'creation scientists,' with their usual mixture of cynicism and ignorance, use the following argument for rhetorical advantage: (1) evolution treats the ultimate origin of life; (2) evolutionist can't resolve this issue; (3) the question is inherently religious; (4) therefore evolution is religion, and our brand deserves just as much time as theirs in science classrooms. We reply, although creations do not choose to listen or understand, that we agree with points two and three, and therefore do not study the question of ultimate origins or view this issue as part of scientific inquiry at all (point one)." Gould, *Evolutionary Theory*, 101n.

do not know. So they can never know that their "best theories" are the absolute truth because they can never know when new data and new ideas will be discovered.

But, here again, waiting for an irrefutable answer to our big questions is not a viable alternative. We cannot, for example, know with complete certainty that global warming is caused by humanly controllable CO_2 emissions. But, here, the decision is forced. To wait for further evidence is to have already made a decision. And the same is true with big philosophical questions concerning free will, immortality, and God. People must act on their best judgments in these matters without having *all* the evidence because *all* the evidence will only be available when history ends. Our philosophical (and scientific) decisions are forced. To remain "non-committal" on these matters is not an option.

3.4 CONCLUSIONS

We have now considered two of the biggest "scientific ideas"—The Newtonian physics of the Copernican Revolution and the Darwinian explanation for the origin of species. In neither case were scientists convinced by a crucial experiment.[23] Instead, in both instances, competing cases were made by the defenders and critics of Copernicus and Darwin. Then, over decades which stretched into a century in Copernicus's case and just short of a century in Darwin's case,[24] Copernicus's and Darwin's ideas were judged to be the best (not perfect!) explanation for the data at hand.

---

23. "I first learned about August Weismann in high school biology as the man who 'disproved' Lamarckism by cutting off mouse tails for numerous generations and noting the fully retained tails of all offspring (a good example of terrible teaching based upon the myth of crucial experiments as the source of all insight in science). Weismann did perform these experiments (1888, in 1891, 431–61), but they (by his own admission) did little to combat Lamarckism, which is, as supporters parried, a theory about the inheritance of functional adaptations, not of sudden and accidental mutilations." Gould, *Evolutionary Theory*, 201.

24. "The introduction of a new paradigm by no means always results in the immediate replacement of the old one. As a result, the new revolutionary theory may exist side by side with the old one. In fact, as many as three or four paradigms may coexist. For instance, after Darwin had proposed natural selection as the mechanism of evolution, saltationism, orthogenesis, and Lamarckism competed with selectionism for the next eighty years (Bowler, 1983). It was not until the evolutionary synthesis on the 1940s that these competing paradigms lost their credibility." Mayr, *What Makes Biology Unique*, 165.

In both cases, the judgment was *not* made on the basis of uniquely "scientific" criteria.[25] Instead, the competing explanations were judged by the three Cs of consistency, comprehensiveness, and coherence—the same criteria used by auto mechanics to fix cars, elementary school teachers to determine the cause of a playground spat, and philosophers to answer big questions.

And in the case of Darwin, where the central issues concern non-repeatable historical events, there is an especially strong comparison to the methods and procedures of lawyers building a case. Occasionally, trials are decided when the prosecutor produces a "smoking gun." The discovery of archaeopteryx just two years after Darwin wrote the *Origin of Species* was certainly a powerful piece of evidence in his favor. Yet, Lord Kelvin's calculation of the relatively young age of the earth based on the principles of thermodynamics was certainly a powerful piece of evidence against Darwin's theory. But neither were a "smoking gun."[26]

Instead, there was a gradual convergence of independently produced data from explorers (no living mammoths were found), naturalists (moles' "eyes" are covered with fur), anatomists (a whale's flipper is "built" like a human arm) and geographers (marsupials are only found in Australia) that all pointed away from immutability of species and toward their common descent.

But again, the convergence of evidence in favor of Darwin's explanation will never deductively prove his conclusion just as no prosecutor deductively proves a defendant to be guilty. "Proof beyond a reasonable

25. "In other words, the sharp break between science and the nonsciences does not exist." Mayr, *Growth of Biological Thought*, 77.

26. "If my theory be true," writes Darwin, "it is indisputable that before the lowest Silurian stratum [i.e., Cambrian] was deposited, long periods elapsed, as long as, or probably far longer than, the whole interval from the Silurian age to the present day; and that during these vast, yet quite unknown periods of time, the world swarmed with living creatures" (quoted in Gould below). Today, there is no doubt that he was wrong. "Paleontologists have now established a good record of Precambrian life. The world did swarm indeed, but only with single-celled forms and multicellular algae, until the latest Precambrian fauna" writes Stephen Jay Gould. Darwin, on the other hand, wrote: "I cannot doubt that all the Silurian [=Cambrian] trilobites have descended from some one crustacean, which must have lived long before the Silurian [=Cambrian] age." Gould, *The Structure of Evolutionary Theory*, 154. So, what should we say: Darwin's theory was falsified by his own standards? Or Darwin's theory is essentially correct, though mistaken in the particulars? Notice how we might ask the same question about Newton's theory. He was wrong about God having to "fine tune" the orbits of Jupiter and Saturn, but does that falsify the laws of universal gravity?

doubt" is the highest standard that either can satisfy, even when the case concerns matters of life and death.

Chapter 6 will continue our discussion of the appropriate standards of evidence not only for lawyers, but also for scientists and philosophers. Here we will simply remind readers of the argument in chapter 1. A valid *deductive* argument with true premises can never have a false conclusion. However, a perfectly good *inductive* argument with all true premises might very well have a false conclusion. But that does not mean we know nothing. (After all, if we *knew* that we knew nothing then that would mean that we knew something!) It only means that humans—both philosophers and scientists—are fallible.

4

What Is Truth?

Relativists define truth as that which is rhetorically persuasive. Idealists define truth as the largest set of logically consistent propositions. Realists define truth as that which corresponds with reality. This chapter outlines the realist's theory without too much attention to its critics until the very end.

The theory begins by distinguishing between substances and attributes. A substance is anything that can exist by itself. An attribute is something that can only exist in a substance. For example, a red flag can exist on its own; but its "redness" can only exist in the flag (or some other substance). It is important to note that substances are not always "touchable." Rainbows are a substance, even though they cannot be touched.

There are three kinds of attributes. Accidents are attributes which vary in a single kind of substance, e.g., some humans have a lot of hair and others have little. Essential attributes do not vary, e.g., all (normal) humans are rational. (By "rational" we mean no more than able to conceive of things that they have never seen, like a chiliagon or tomorrow.) Properties are attributes which do not in fact vary, but they could, e.g., all humans are featherless bipeds. But if for some strange reason human mothers started giving birth to children with a single feather growing from their tail bone, yet the children were fully rational, we would still have little doubt about their essential humanity.

The distinction between accidents, essences and properties in turn defines two modes of existence. "Contingent" means that a thing's existence, attributes, or actions are dependent upon something besides the thing itself. "Necessary" means that a thing's existence, attributes, or actions are dependent upon nothing except the thing itself.

It is likely that the vast majority of things humans define are not necessary. We can, for example, categorize (define) books, buildings, and baseball bats in many different ways. These are called nominal definitions. However, Aristotelians argue that the distinction between humans, animals, plants, and non-living physical things have real definitions in terms of their essential natures.

Relativists, on the other hand, argue that all definitions are nominal because all definitions are dependent (contingent) upon a culture's conceptual schemes. Nothing has an "essential nature" in-and-of itself according to relativists.

Two thousand years ago, Pontius Pilate asked, "What is truth?" Though his question was in part cynical, it would be uncharitable to suppose that it was not also in part honestly motivated by the philosophical puzzles we will be considering in this chapter.

There are three definitions of truth. Relativists like Protagoras define truth as any consensus that rhetorical persuasion is able to produce. Exactly how wide spread the consensus must be is open to question. Is it sufficient for a single individual to be persuaded that his beliefs are true or must consensus be spread throughout a culture? But whoever needs to be persuaded, once they are persuaded their beliefs are true *for them.*

Philosophical idealists define "truth" as all statements which are included in the largest possible set of consistent ideas. The crucial point here is that idealists *deny* that we can significantly talk about a reality which exists independent of our ideas. Since no one can possibly *see* reality directly, it is meaningless, they say, to think a tree can fall in the forest when nobody sees or hears it fall. As one philosopher famously said, "To be *is* to be perceived." In short, reality and our most coherent ideas about reality are one-in-the-same. Idealists thereby reject as meaningless the question of whether or not those ideas match reality. Though idealism is currently out of favor in the West, it has dominated the East for millennia and was prominent here toward the end of the nineteenth century.

Directly opposed to idealism is philosophical realism. Realists like Aristotle and Aquinas defines "truth" as the correspondence of what we say or think with what *really exists.* Realism is basically a defense of common sense. It is, so to speak, the default position for the vast majority of westerners. After all, what could be more simple, obvious, and true than saying "The cat is on the mat" is true if and only if the cat *really* is on the mat? There are, on the other hand, numerous philosophical critics of realism in the West which we will be considering throughout this book.

But before we consider these criticisms, we must first flesh out the realists' thesis in more detail.

4.1 SUBSTANCES AND ATTRIBUTES

Things exist in a multitude of sizes, shapes, colors, and weights. Some things maintain their individual identity for a fairly long time, like rocks and diamonds. Other things only maintain their identity for a very short period of time, like clouds and subatomic particles. Some things are fairly solid, like books and backdoors. Other things are virtually impossible to touch or feel, like rainbows and light rays. Some things are inanimate and without life, like dirt and sand. Other things are alive and animated, like plants and people.

But perhaps the most fundamental distinction is between substances and attributes.[1] A substance is anything that is able to exist by itself.[2] An attribute is something that is *only* able to exist in a substance. "Substance" literally means that which "stands under," upholds, or supports attributes. "Attribute" refers to everything that "falls to" or "befalls" something else.

Here are some examples of substances and of the many different ways to name them. Individual substances can be given a proper name like "Fido" or "Fred." They can also be referred to with a definite description, like the "fastest man on the team" or the "first President of the United States." Natural groups of substances can be given a common name like "plants" or "animals." Arbitrary groups or clusters of things can also be treated as a substance, for example, "a pile of dirt" or "all the water in all the world's oceans." In all these cases the descriptive words refer to something that exists by and in itself.

Contrast this with the way we refer to their attributes. We might say that Fido "has red fur" or that Fred "weighs 160 pounds." We might also

---

1. Thomas Aquinas, commenting on Aristotle puts it like this: "Blackness itself does not become whiteness, so that, if there is a change from black to white, there must be something besides blackness which becomes white." Aquinas, *Commentary*, sec. 2429; vol. 2, 859.

2. "But the idea of substance itself can still be used to refer to things that can be identified as beings in some sense complete, such as human beings, horses, and houses, to revert back to examples used by Saint Thomas, if not to atomic or subatomic particles. The idea is not derived from physics or chemistry, but is rather presupposed by them, even when they seem to be subverting our naïve representations of it." Blanchette, *The Perfection of the Universe*, 55.

say that the first President of the United States was "born in Virginia" or that a pile of dirt "is brown." In these cases, the descriptive words do not refer to independently existing substances. They only refer attributes *of* a substance. Unlike substances, attributes cannot exist by themselves; they can only exist in a substance. "Weighs 160 pounds" or "is brown" are not "things" which can exist by themselves; they must always exist *in* something else.

Though the italicized words "of" and "in" are short, they are also tricky. We say both that there is dirt *in* a rug and that attributes exist *in* substances. However, the word "in" means something quite different in these two cases. Attributes are not *in* substances the way dirt is *in* a rug. The relation between dirt and a rug is a relation between two physical substances. The relation between substances and attributes is relation that transcends physics. Traditionally it was called a *metaphysical* relation. Today some philosophers sometimes call it a grammatical relation. But whatever we call it, we must not try to form a "mental picture" of the relation of attributes and substances; it cannot be done.

The distinction philosophical realists make between substances and attributes more-or-less parallels the distinction logicians and grammarians make between subjects and predicates. Substances will typically be the subject of a proposition and attributes will typically be the predicate of a proposition. For example, we can say "Fred has red hair" or "The fastest man on the team weighs 160 pounds." But it makes no sense to say of one predicate that it is some other predicate. "Has red hair is weighing 160 pounds" is nonsense.

Though the distinction between substance and attributes may seem trivial, it is the basis of a philosophically crucial (and thus controversial) distinction between three kinds of attributes—accidents, properties, and essences. In the next chapter we will consider the realists claim that these distinct attributes refer to real differences in the nature of things. But for now we will simply consider the way they function in our language.

We will begin by distinguishing accidental and essential attributes. Consider a group of one hundred dinosaurs. Each dinosaur undoubtedly had a slightly different weight, size, and shape, yet they are all referred to as "dinosaurs." The reason is simple: the specific attributes of weight, size, and shape are all *accidental* attributes of dinosaurs. An accident is an attribute which only some members of a group or kind actually possess. In other words, accidental attributes vary among the individual members.

Whether a particular dinosaur weighs 9,534 pounds or 9,535 pounds has no effect on our willingness to refer to it as a "dinosaur." Similar sorts of things could be said about a dinosaur's exact size, shape, color, smell, and so on. These are all accidental attributes which can and will vary among particular members of the species.

However, there are other attributes which all dinosaurs must possess or else they would not be a dinosaur.[3] Every dinosaur was a cold-blooded, egg-laying animal with a backbone. These attributes—being cold-blooded, egg-laying, and having a backbone—are *essential.* There is no variation here among dinosaurs. An essence is an attribute which all members of a species must possess. An animal which was not cold-blooded or did not possess a backbone could not *by definition* be a dinosaur. The essences determine *what* something is, that is, it *defines* a species.

Properties are a third kind of attribute. In one way they are like accidents but in another way they are like essences. Like an essence, a property is an attribute which all members of a species possess. Unlike an essence, a property is not what makes something what it is or defines it as a species. Instead, they only *happen* to have the attribute in question. For example, all past and present human beings have been less than eight feet tall. But "being less than eight feet tall" is not part of human's essential nature. There is nothing incoherent in the suggestion that some day humans might grow to be more than 8 feet tall. This means that properties are like accidents because they *could* vary among individual members of a species without changing the fact that they were all members of the same species. An eight foot tall person would still be a human being.

To recap: An essential attribute is one all members of the species *must* have to be a member of the species; an accidental attribute is one that can and does vary among individuals; a property is an attribute which *could* vary among members of the species, even though in fact it does not.

---

3. "For by the essence of a thing we mean the proper answer which can be given to the question asking what it is. And when we ask what a thing is we cannot give a proper answer by mentioning attributes which belong to it accidentally; for when someone asks what man is, one cannot answer that he is white or sitting or musical. Hence none of those attributes which are predicated of a thing accidentally belong to its essence; for being you is not being musical." Aquinas, *Commentary*, sec. 1309; vol. 2, 506.

4.2 MODES OF EXISTENCE

"Must," "happen," and "could" are common words, but they too are tricky. Logicians call them *modal terms*. Modal words do not refer to the existence or non-existence of a thing or event. They refer instead to the *way* a thing or event either exists or does not exist.

For example, there are two things we can say about all normal humans. First, they are all rational animals. (By "rational" all we mean is "able to understand abstract words like 'tomorrow.'") Second, all humans are featherless bipeds. (*Only* humans and birds are anatomically bipedal.)

The interesting point about attributes like "rational animal" and "featherless biped" is that even though the words mean something different, they both *refer to* exactly the same group of things.[4] It is equally true that all normal humans are rational animals and that all normal humans are featherless bipeds. In other words, every rational animal is a featherless biped *and vice versa*, every featherless biped is a rational animal. This is unusual. Typically when we reverse a subject and predicate in a true sentence, the new sentence will be false. For example, while it is true that "all humans are animals with hearts," it is false that "all animals with hearts are humans."

So, the philosophically crucial (again controversial[5]) point becomes: If the words "rational animal" and "featherless biped" both refer to the same class of things, can they really be significantly different? In short, is there really a difference between an essence and a property? Aristotelians think that there is for the following reasons.[6]

---

4. In the terms of the logician, "rational animal" and "featherless biped" have the same *extension*, though they have different *intensions*.

5. In the jargon of philosophers, the issue concerns the possibility of "intensional" logic. Most "modern logic" is wholly extensional, i.e. it assumes that words which refer to identical groups of things must be logically equivalent. Aristotelian logic does not make this assumption because (among other reasons) it distinguishes between essences and properties. See my *In Defense of the Soul*, 73–75 for short and simple account of this dispute. For a book-length and scholarly treatment, see Veatch, *Intentional Logic*.

6. The classic Aristotelian example of the difference is between humans' rationality (which is an essence) and human's capacity for laughter (which is a property). "Because in every thing, that which pertains to its essence is distinct from its proper accident [i.e. property]; thus in man it is one thing that he is a mortal rational animal, and another that he is an animal capable of laughter." Aquinas, *ST*, I–II 2.6.

A simple thought experiment illustrates the difference. Imagine that at some time in the future mothers, all around the world, started giving birth to children with a single feather growing from the tail bone. This would, to say the least, be highly troublesome. Doctors would be shocked; mothers would be surprised; and biologists would have to do a lot of rethinking about the effects of mutations. But if we suppose that no other changes occur and that these children grow up to live otherwise normal lives, we would have no question about their status as human beings.

But now imagine a different scenario. This time, mothers from all around the world start giving birth to children who are never able to understand the concept "tomorrow" or any other word that refers to things which cannot be perceived or imaged. This would be more than highly troublesome. If humans lost their rational ability to understand abstractions, then even if these "children" which continue to *look* just like human beings could perpetuate their species, it would be a *new* species. There would no longer be a *human* species as we now understand it. The rationality that allows us to understand abstractions is part of our essential nature. If we lose that, we lose our identity as humans. (Of course, this example says nothing about how we should ethically treat this new species in the "transitional period" and it says even less about how we should treat individual humans who lack rational abilities as the result of brain damage or have yet to develop their natural capacities, i.e. infants.)

In sum, while we *happen* to be featherless, we *must* be rational or else we would not be humans. And while we *could* begin to grow feathers and remain human, we *could not* lose our rationality and remain human. Being rational is necessary in order for us to be human beings.

The example above concerns the way (mode) *things exist*. The same point can be made about the way *events occur*. Consider the following example from Hilary Putnam, a Harvard philosopher. He notes that Emerson Hall at Harvard University has been in existence for over one hundred years. Now suppose that during those one hundred years no person has ever walked through the doors of Emerson Hall and been able to speak and understand Inuit, the native language of Eskimos. Thus the statement "everyone who has ever sat in Emerson Hall is unable to speak Inuit" is a true generalization. It is also a true generalization that every pen that has ever been dropped in Emerson Hall falls down, not up. But these two generalizations are not true in the same *way*.

The "mode" of these two events is distinct. It is true that pens *must* fall down (not up); it is not true that people entering Emerson Hall *must* be unable to speak Inuit. If Sam, an Eskimo whose first language is Inuit, wins a scholarship from Harvard and takes a course in Emerson Hall, then he will not suddenly lose his ability to speak and understand Inuit when he sits in Emerson Hall. There is nothing about the nature of Emerson Hall that causes a person to be unable to speak Inuit. And if Sam decides to go to Princeton instead of Harvard and it just happens that no future person who enters Emerson Hall is able to speak and understand Inuit, we would still understand that "being unable to speak and understand Inuit while inside" is a property, not an essence, of Emerson Hall.

These two distinct modes of existence are termed *contingent* and *necessary*. Contingent means that a thing's existence, attributes, or actions are dependent upon something besides the thing itself. Necessary means that a thing's existence, attributes, or actions are dependent upon nothing except the thing itself. It is a *contingent* truth that no person in Emerson Hall has been able to speak Inuit; it has nothing to do with the nature of the building itself. But it is a *necessary* truth that when objects heavier than air are dropped, they move down, not up. (Of course, here we are speaking inductively, i.e., "scientific," and thus there is always an implicit *ceteris paribus* clause. See 2.4 above.)

The important point to remember about modes of existence is that they refer to what is possible, not what actually exists or happens. Just because something always *has* happened does not mean that it always *will* happen. For as long as the earth has existed, the sun has always risen in the east. Yet we know that one day the sun will run out of fuel and will no longer rise in the east. "Rising in the east" is, therefore, a contingent truth about the relative motion of the earth and sun; it is not a necessary truth. In other words, we can say that if something happens necessarily, then we know it will always happen. But we cannot reverse this proposition. We cannot say that if something always happens, then we know that it happens necessarily.

This distinction between contingent and necessary modes of existence allows us to sharpen our definition of accidents, properties, and essences. Both accidents and properties are *contingently* connected to the substances of which they are attributes. Only essences are *necessarily* connected to the substances of which they are attributes. It is a wholly *contingent* truth, for example, that all human beings are featherless bipeds; but it is a *necessary* truth that all human beings are rational animals.

DEFINITION OF HUMAN

	Attribute	Frequency	Mode
Essential Nature	Rationality	Always	Necessary
Property	Featherless	Always	Contingent
Accident	Baldness	Sometimes	Contingent

Figure 4.1

4.3 LIMITS TO WHAT CAN BE DEFINED

According to Aristotelian realists, there are two different kinds of substances: those that exist independent of human action and those that only exist as the direct result of human creativity. Rocks, plants, and animals are all examples of natural substances (sometimes called "natural kinds") whose existence and attributes do not depend upon human action. Guns, snow boards, and grocery stores are examples of artificial substances which, though real, cannot existence independent of human action. Dinosaurs existed before any humans existed, but no gun existed prior to the existence of humans.

The distinction between natural substances and artificial substances introduces a corresponding distinction between real and nominal definitions.

A *real definition* defines a naturally existing substance in terms of its essential attributes. The goal of all real definitions, in Plato's evocative phrase, is to "divide nature at its joints"—that is, to separate and classify the parts of nature as they really exist. The discovery of real definitions is the first step to understanding the natural world and its causal relations. Until we know the essences of things we will never be able to understand how things causally interact. For example, if we do not know *what* a clear, odorless liquid is, then we cannot know whether it will quench our thirst or make us drunk.

A *nominal definition*, on the other hand, merely specifies the words we have *chosen* to attach to a humanly created thing—whether that "thing" is a substance, like a gun, an event, like a baseball game, or a cluster of things, like a baseball team. Nominal definitions never pretend to "divide nature at its joints" because it is not nature that is being *defined*. Instead, it is a human artifact or creation that is being *named*. The fundamental principle here is: you make it; you get to name (or "define") it. Since guns are something humans make, humans get to define the word as broadly or as narrowly as they choose. Of course, after a culture has agreed to the range of things called "guns," if an individual chooses to call a "slingshot" a gun because it, too, can kill people, he is perfectly free to do so. But he is not free to insist that everyone else use the word "gun" to include slingshots.

Heaps and clusters also lack a real definition. Though humans did not create Mount Everest or the Indian Ocean, these too cannot, strictly speaking, be defined; they can only be named. As we will see in the next section, failure to distinguish between real and nominal definitions leads to a serious misunderstanding of realist philosophy.

Individuals and existence itself are also indefinable. Both Fido and Fred can be considered either as members of a natural kind or as individuals. When we say that Fido is a dog or that Fred is a human being we are considering them as members of natural kinds. In doing so, we are also defining the essential natures of Fido and Fred. But when we consider an individual dog or person and *name* them "Fido" or "Fred" we are not defining their essential natures. The parents of Fred in some sense "created" him, and thus they get to name him anything they choose. And if a person chooses to raise a particular dog, then that person, too, earns the right to name the dog. The important point to remember here is that the process of *naming* an individual is fundamentally different from the process of *defining* a natural kind. Names are entirely arbitrary; definitions of natural kinds are not arbitrary.

Specific qualities are also *named*, not defined. For example, humans have agreed to call a specific range on a color wheel red, but in doing so they are not defining the essential nature of red. In fact we cannot define specific qualities like red because there is no non-circular way to specify how *red* is different from other colors. Red and yellow are both colors, but it is not possible to specify the difference between red and yellow except by pointing to examples of things that are red and other things that are yellow. It is an arbitrary and wholly contingent truth about different cultures that they attach different sounds and symbols to various ranges on the color spectrum.

While the use of *names* is arbitrary, real definitions are not arbitrary. Realists happily acknowledge that it is wholly arbitrary whether we use the word "silver" or "*argentums*" to refer to a particular naturally occurring element. But it is *not* an arbitrary human convention that silver (or *argentum*) melts at 5.336 times the temperature at which pure water boils. This ratio between the melting point of silver and the boiling point of water is a truth that we have *discovered* and is not just an arbitrary *convention* about the way we choose to use language.

Normally when we define a word we first locate it in a larger category of things (its genus) and then explain how it differs from other members of the larger category. For example, we define "hammer" as a tool designed to pound nails. Here, "tool" is the larger category (genus) and "designed to pound nails" explains how hammers are different from other kinds of tools. It is impossible to do this with *individuals* (be they people, dogs, or qualities) since as individuals they are a genus unto themselves. When we say (pointing to a particular person) "He is Fred" we are not categorizing something by putting it into a larger genus and then specifying how it differs from other things in that genus. We can know *what* a hammer is through a definition; we can only know *who* Fred is through experience.

A similar problem arises when we reach the most general category.[7] Consider the following sequence (*figure 4.2*):

---

7. "There is a science that investigates being as being and the attributes that belong to this in virtue of its own nature. Now this is not the same as any of the so-called special sciences; for none of these others deal generally with being as being. They cut off a part of being and investigate the attributes of this part—this is what the mathematical sciences for instance do [i.e., they investigate that which can be quantified apart from all matter and the natural sciences investigates that which moves]. Now since we are seeking the first principles and the highest causes, clearly there must be some thing to which these belong in virtue of its own nature . . . *Therefore it is of being as being that we also must grasp the first cause.*" Aristotle *Metaphysics* 4, I, 1003a22–31; emphasis added. It is the emphasized phrased which gives rise to the "cosmological conjecture" in chapter 10.3.

Fred   Human   Animal   Plant   Physical Thing   Existence

Figure 4.2

The four middle terms can each be defined in terms of their genus and specific difference. For example, "human are rational animals"; "animals are living beings capable of self locomotion and consciousness"; "living beings are physical organisms capable of reproduction"; "physical things are beings that exist in time and space." But at the far left hand side, no definition in terms of genus and specific difference is possible.[8] True, we can say that "Fred is a human being." That gives us a genus, but there is no definition until we have a specific difference, i.e., how the term being defined *differs* from other members of the genus into which it is placed by the definition. Again, "Fred" names an individual and individuals can only be *described*; they cannot be defined.

At the far right hand side, an analogous problem arises. Existence can never be defined because there is no larger genus into which it falls. A person who has never seen a chiliagon can still know what it is. A simple definition will work—"It is a thousand-sided geometrical object." With such a definition a person knows all there is to know about chiliagons.

But with existence it is quite different. Existence must be experienced to be "understood." And in this last sentence, the scare quotes are deliberate and necessary. Since existence cannot be defined, we cannot have a *concept* of existence. This means that existence cannot be understood the way other things are understood, namely, in terms of their essential natures. Existence is not, Aristotelians insist, simply another category (genus) of things the way life, consciousness, and rationality are categories of different kinds of things. The reason is simple: the whole point of categorizing things is to distinguish them from other things. But once we reach, so to speak, the largest (i.e., most inclusive) category we can no longer make a distinction between it and something else. Existence is really more like a verb than a noun. Existence is not an attribute of a thing; instead it is what a thing *does*.

---

8. "The only thing that is defined in a proper sense is the species, since every definition is composed of a genus and a difference." Aquinas, *Commentary,* sec. 877; vol. 1, 341.

Furthermore, the "doing" that is existence is a unique activity. Trees do lots of things—they turn light and carbon dioxide into carbohydrates, they grow, their leaves change colors, etc. But as long as we are thinking about a real tree (not an imaginary tree) it is doing something even more fundamental—it is existing. Aristotle called this most fundamental kind of doing *actus*, or actuality. Josef Pieper (1904–1997), puts it like this:

> Anyone who wishes to underline the difference between a real tree and an imaginary one can do no better than to repeat the same phrases: that the real tree exists, that it "actually is," that it is "something real." Existence cannot be defined . . . says Thomas [Aquinas] in his commentary on Aristotle's *Metaphysics*. This means that at this point in our considerations—without the slightest exaggeration of the actual facts—our thinking has encountered the riddle of being, perhaps for the first time. Perhaps, to put it more sharply, our thinking meets the *mysterium* of being."[9]

We will say much more about the "mystery of existence" in succeeding chapters (especially chapter 10), but for now we sum up like this: definitions of things require both a specific difference and a genus. In the case of individual things or specific qualities no real definition is possible because it is impossible to provide a specific difference. In the case of existence itself, no real definition is possible because it has no genus. Real definitions provide knowledge about many things. But individuals and existence itself can only be known through direct experience.

4.4 RELATIVISTS' OBJECTIONS

Until history ends, there will be no end to human creativity. Since makers get to name what they make there are countless objects for which there are no real definitions, only nominal definitions. Relativists claim that what is true in these many cases is really true in *all* cases. According

---

9. Pieper, *Thomas Aquinas*, 136–37. The "mystery of Being" alludes to what Thomists call the "Transcendentals." "What has an essence, and a quiddity ["whatness"] by reason of that essence, and what is undivided in itself, are the same. Hence these three—thing, being, and unity—signify absolutely the same thing but according to different concepts." Aquinas, *Commentary*, sec. 553; vol. 1, 223. In addition to "thing or truth," "being," and "unity" there is a fourth transcendental, namely, "goodness." "Good and being are really the same . . . But good presents the aspect of desirableness, which being does not present." Aquinas, *ST*, I 5.1.

to relativists, classification is *always* based on individual or cultural interests since there are no real essences.

The most common argument for relativism is based on the (alleged) infinite flexibility of conceptual schemes. The notion of a conceptual scheme gets its impetus from Immanuel Kant's (1724–1804) theory that the human mind has certain "built in" categories with which it organizes all experience. Kant argued that the division of things into substances and attributes was not something *discovered* in reality but was something that the categories of the mind *imposed* upon experience.[10] Imagine that everyone was born with blue-colored contact lenses and that no one could see anything without them. In such a situation everyone would *think* everything is blue. We, of course, know better. Reality is not wholly blue. Only imaginary people who view everything through blue lenses think otherwise. But Kant believed that the categories of space, time, substance, and causation were like blue lenses. That is, he thought that these categories were *imposed upon* reality rather than categories the mind *abstracted from* reality.

Few philosophers today believe there is a *single* set of categories that *all* humans impose upon their experience.[11] But many claim that Kant's point—that it is impossible to see reality directly—is borne out because the sets of categories people use vary from culture to culture and these various linguistic categories constitute a culture's own "con-

10. Kant wrote: "Hitherto it has been assumed that all our knowledge must conform to objects. But all attempts to extend our knowledge of objects by establishing something in regard to them a priori, by means of concepts, have, on this assumption, ended in failure. We must therefore make trial whether we may not have more success in the tasks of metaphysics, if we suppose that object must conform to our knowledge." Kant, *Critique of Pure Reason*, 22.

Here are two contemporary philosophers' responses: According to Kant, "there is no knowledge of essences and causes of things-in-themselves; [instead there is] a mere ordering of data in accordance with a conceptual scheme which we ourselves impose and which carries with it no more than a pragmatic justification." Veatch, "Two Logics," 352. And, "For Kant the only things that are independent of the human mind are, in his words, '*Ding an sich*'—things in themselves that are intrinsically unknowable. This is tantamount to saying that the real is unknowable, and the knowable is ideal in the sense that it is invested with the ideas that our minds bring to it to make it what it is." Adler, *Ten Philosophical Mistakes*, 100.

11. The fact that Kant began with "mental categories" makes him a philosophical idealist as we discussed in chapter one. He was not, however, a relativist because he believed all people in all cultures shared the same mental categories. It was only later that relativists loosen the notion of "mental categories" so that they varied among individuals and cultures.

ceptual scheme." Relativists claim the only way we can understand our experiences is through some conceptual scheme *of our own making.*

To see how this might play out, imagine two different cultures. One is very "scientific" and the other is very "religious." The scientific culture distinguishes between animals in terms of their ability to interbreed, and ultimately in terms of their genetic make up. The religious culture, on the other hand, though it knows how animals mate, concerns itself primarily with animals' suitability for use in religious ceremonies. (In this imaginary culture, since it snows too infrequently, only snow-colored pelts can be worn while petitioning the spirits.) Since these cultures have different *interests*, they will also have different "conceptual schemes."

The scientific culture is going to distinguish between rabbits and foxes because of their inability to mate. The religious culture may implicitly realize that rabbits and foxes cannot mate. Yet they may have no word to distinguish between rabbits and foxes because for them what is important is whether their pelts are suitable for petitioning the snow gods. Therefore, they might have a term like "whiterox" and "darrox." A "whiterox" in this culture is the name for all animals with white pelts, i.e. white rabbits and albino foxes. A "darrox" is the name for all dark-pelt animals, i.e., dark rabbits and all non-albino foxes.

According to relativists, there are no "facts," either scientific or philosophical, that require rational people to divide the world up in any particular way.[12] See for example *figure 4.3.*

No matter what characteristics are represented by the letters X and Y, there will always be an alternative set of characteristics by which to divide that world that will be equally rational. Whether we chose to classify things as "X's" and "Y's" or as "Upper case" and "Lower case" is *solely up to us* according to relativists. All conceptual schemes are equally "rational."

Relativists tend to think of the cosmos as a huge piece of cookie dough just waiting to be cut into shapes such as trees or bells. But if trees or bells no longer suffice, the dough can be rolled up and new shapes cut out, even original ones that have no name. The cosmos, too, is in

12. Here is what a contemporary evolutionary biologist has to say about species relativism. "There is no more devastating refutation of the nominalistic [i.e., relativistic] claims than the fact that primitive natives in New Guinea, with a Stone Age culture, recognize as species exactly the same entities of nature as western taxonomists. If species were something purely arbitrary, it would be totally improbable for representatives of two drastically different cultures to arrive at the identical species delimitations." Mayr, *Towards a New Philosophy of Biology*, 317.

World Divided into X's and Y's		World Divided by Upper and Lower cases	
X X X X	Y y y y	X X X X Y	y y y
X X X X	y y y y	X X X X	y y y y
X X X x	y y y y	X X X	x y y y y

Figure 4.3

a perpetual state of flux in which everything is gradually merging and morphing into something else. Nature comes with no real joints so humans are free[13] to categorize "things" in any way they choose. Even the category of "things" is itself a human construct!

Realists, on the other hand, are quite willing to grant the cookie dough analogy for large sections of the cosmos. Objects for which there are only nominal definitions fit the analogy well. And the class of nominal definitions is very large. In fact, there may be only *four* real definitions in the entire cosmos, namely, humans, animals, plants, and the basic physical things out of which everything else is made. These can be defined in terms of genus and specific difference:

- *Physical things*: fundamental stuff with both quantitative and qualitative properties.
- *Plant*: Physical things that are alive.
- *Animal*: Physical things that are alive and capable of consciousness.
- *Human*: Physical things that are alive, capable of consciousness, and capable of using language conceptually.

Why are there so few linguistic categories of really distinct substances? Because there is strong evidence to suggest that Darwin was correct. If so, then the differences between animal species, e.g., between rabbits and foxes, are really only the differences between well marked varieties. Clearly, there is no real difference between Irish Setters and

---

13. Or "*condemned* to be free," in the language of existentialist philosopher Jean-Paul Sartre (1905–1980).

Dachshunds. These two breeds of dogs are "social constructs"; if humans allowed dogs to breed indiscriminately, soon these distinct breeds would disappear and all that would be left would be the mongrel mutt. If Darwin was correct (and only scientific investigation can answer this question), then all species are in some sense arbitrary divisions that humans draw between gradually merging and morphing slices of life here on earth.[14]

But having granted the fundamental correctness of Darwin's theory, realists argue that there are some (i.e., at least five) real joints in nature that are not created by humans. Fundamental potentiality, elements, plants, animals, and humans constitute distinct categories. Realists argue that these distinct categories are created by nature and/or God, and, hence, they are not covered by the principle of "you make it; you get to name it."[15]

4.5 CONCLUSION

So who's right about the nature of *truth*—the realists or the relativists? This is a big philosophical question and it cannot be answered yet. But we can be clear about the precise nature of the question and what is at stake.

The question hinges on the reality of essential natures—realists assert that they exist; relativists, on the other hand, deny the existence of essential nature. They assert that "truth"—*all* categorical propositions— is relative to a "conceptual scheme" and that these schemes are essentially

---

14. Aristotle also understood the problems posed by borderline cases. "Nature proceeds little by little from things lifeless to animal life in such a way that it is impossible to determine the exact line of demarcation, nor on which side thereof an intermediate form should lie ... In regard to sensibility, some animals give no indication whatsoever of it, while others indicate it but indistinctly. Further, the substance of some of these intermediate creatures is flesh-like [such as the sea anemones]; but the sponge is in every respect like a vegetable. And so throughout the entire animal scale there is a graduated differentiation in amount of vitality and in capacity for motion." *History of Animals*, 8.1 588b 4–22.

15. John Searle makes this point even stronger: "Many people find it repugnant that we, with our language, our consciousness, and our creative powers should be subject to and answerable to a dumb, stupid, inert material world. Why should we be answerable to the world? Why shouldn't we think of the 'real world' as something we create, and therefore something that is answerable to us? If all of reality is a 'social construction,' then it is we who are in power, not the world. The deep motivation for the denial of realism is not this or that argument, but a will to power, a desire for control, and a deep and abiding resentment." Searle, *Mind, Language and Society,* 32–33.

arbitrary, or at best, purely pragmatic. If, for example, an American says of his automobile that the engine is under the hood, what he says is true. And if an Englishman says of his automobile that the engine is under the bonnet, what he says is also true. Obviously, the "truth" about the location of cars' engines are relative to the "conceptual scheme" one is assuming.

Now with this sort of example, and countless others, relativists and realists are in complete agreement. There is no right or wrong answer to the question: Are car engines under the hood or the bonnet? Here the answer unequivocally depends on a person's conceptual scheme. Aristotelian realists make precisely the same point when they distinguish between real and nominal definitions. Since "hoods" and/or "bonnets" are human creations, that means that human's are free to name them as they please. In other words, when the question concerns the location of automobile engines we are *not* seeking to "divide nature at its joints." With such questions, there is no underlining reality (essential nature) with which our propositions could or could not correspond.

What is absolutely crucial is that we not create a straw man. This is the fallacy that arises whenever one side of a debate significantly misdescribes their opponents' position, knocks over the straw man, and then claims victory. Unfortunately, such fallacies are common when discussing the nature of truth. Since realism and relativism are in some sense "opposites" it is easy to reason like this:

1. Relativists say that *all* truth is relative to a conceptual scheme.

2. Relativism and realism are "opposite" theories.

3. Therefore, realist must say that *no* truth is relative to a conceptual scheme.

But this argument is fallacious. As we just saw in the preceding paragraph, Aristotelian realists happily acknowledge that the truth of many propositions, if not the vast majority, is "relative" to the nominal definitions (or "conceptual schemes") which are being assumed. It would be difficult, if not impossible, to name a single philosopher who has ever defended the conclusion in the above argument.

The confusion arises because the word "opposite" in the second premise is ambiguous. The language of logicians clearly distinguishes two different meanings of "opposite." Sometimes "opposite" means *con-*

trary. Other times it means *contradictory.* (The contrary of "All S is P" is "No S is P"; the *contradiction* of "All S is P" is "Some S is not P.") Realism and Relativism are *contradictory* theories; they are *not* the contraries. Relativists assert that "*All* truth is relative to one's conceptual scheme"; Realists assert that "*Some* truths are *not* relative to one's conceptual scheme." The only time when "truth" is not relative to a set of nominal definitions and/or conceptual schemes is when the terms being discussed have an essential nature. Then, and only then, do realist think that we both can and must "divide nature at its joints." And as we said at the end of section 4.3, today's realists today no longer assume that biological species are fixed and unchanging.[16] The only *real* divisions in nature that they insist upon are among fundamental potentiality, elements, plants, animals, and humans.

If there are only *five* real definitions of terms, then that means the 99.9 percent of the words we ordinarily use have no real definition, and thus, in 99.9 percent of our arguments about "truth" the relativist is right. Why worry about the remaining 0.1 percent of disagreement?

Because the four cases where they disagree are of supreme significance. For example, when Hitler said that Jews, homosexuals, and gypsies were not truly human, realists insist that he was wrong—what makes someone a human being is not determined by one's "conceptual scheme"; instead, it is determined by nature and/or God. And this is only the most striking example. The existence or non-existence of essential natures has huge implications for how we think about human freedom, the nature of morality and the existence of God. But before considering these *really* big questions, we will address the slightly smaller questions in the next two chapters: 1) Do *any* essential natures exist, and 2) if they do, how can they be known?

16. Many times biologists and other scientists will refer to Aristotle's "essentialism" and then add that it has been thoroughly refuted by modern science. In one sense this is true; in another sense it is false. If essentialism means that each individual species has a fixed and unchangeable "essential nature," then it is true that Aristotle was an "essentialist." (Though it is worth adding that in this sense virtually everyone else prior to the twentieth century, including people like J. S. Mill who is generally considered thoroughly modern, progressive, and "scientific," were also essentialists.) It is also true that essentialism in this sense has been "refuted" by modern science for all the reasons discussed in chapter 3. However, if "essentialism" is the theory that there are *some* (probably as few as five) essential natures and that these essential natures are crucial to thinking well about our world, then it is far from obvious that *this* sense of "essentialism" has been refuted by modern science.

5

What Is Real?

A common sense understanding of the world requires some sort of distinction between form *and* shape. *"Form" refers to a thing's essential qualities; what makes it what it is. "Shape" refers to a thing's quantities; its most complete description in terms of size, shape, mass, electrical conductivity, etc. Without this distinction it would be impossible to say what makes Socrates sitting and Socrates standing the same person.*

Aristotle's own terms were form *and* matter, *but he meant by "matter" a thing's potentiality, which is quite different from what we mean by "matter." Either way, whether we think of "shape" or "matter/potentiality" our language tends to mislead. While the form/shape distinction is absolutely essential, we must remember that we are* distinguishing, *not* separating. *The form/shape distinction is like the distinction between a smile and a face—even though the two are different, a smile cannot exist without a face.*

Positivists object to the form/shape distinction. They argue that a thing's qualities are really nothing more than human's subjective evaluation of things. Ultimate reality, they say, is composed solely of quantities.

Aristotelians argue that positivists have it exactly backwards. In fact, quantity *is itself ultimately a* quality. *There is absolutely nothing that one rock, one corporation, one song, one game, one angel, one dramatic play, one word, and one beautiful day have in common except their* qualitative *integrity, i.e. their unity as a single "thing." Since all numbers are iteration of "one," all quantitative measurement presupposes a* qualitative *understanding of a thing's essential unity.*

Furthermore, there is nothing particularly "objective" or "scientific" about quantitative measurements since the number of objectively measurable "quantities" is infinite. The ratio of a person's height to weight is important for doctors, nutritionists, and insur-

ance actuaries. But does anyone care about the ratio of a person's street address to the number of years he or she has lived at that location? Yet both are equally "objective."

The form/shape distinction also explains the crucial scientific (and common sense) distinction between mere correlation *and real* causation. *There may be, for example, a perfect correlation between people who walk through the doors of Emerson Hall at Harvard University and people who are unable to speak Inuit. Yet there is no causal connection between the two.*

Real causation requires a causal law, or what Aristotelians call a final cause. This last sentence strikes modern readers as highly paradoxical. Ever since Descartes it has been assumed that laws of efficient ("scientific") causation and final causation are incompatible and antithetical. But in fact, efficient causation requires final causation. Unless we know what a turtle is (i.e. a living organism whose goal is reproduction), we will never understand what a turtle is doing when it comes ashore to lay her eggs. To describe a turtle's behavior more "objectively" as coming ashore and laying her eggs is scientifically useless.

THE FIRST GREEK PHILOSOPHERS argued that ultimate reality is just a swirling mass of atoms of varying degrees of complexity—some fairly simple like heaps of sand; other extremely complex like the human body. Contemporary positivists agree and add that modern science provides irrefutable evidence for this sort of materialism. Beginning with Descartes, other philosophers have argued that ultimate reality is composed of at least two kinds of stuff—material things like atoms and immaterial things like minds, souls or spirits. Though philosophical dualists acknowledge the many contributions of modern science, they argue that its implicit materialism destroys human freedom and dignity.

A strong case can be made for both of these answers. Furthermore, it *seems* that logic forces us to choose between materialism and dualism. Materialists argue that reality is ultimately composed of one sort of thing; dualists argue that it is composed of two sorts of things. However, Aristotle argued for a third alternative which seeks to save the best in both answers. This chapter explains Aristotle's realist alternative and fleshes out the notion of "essential natures" that we introduced in the previous chapter.

5.1 FORM AND SHAPE

Aristotle began with the obvious: some things change; some things stay the same; and some things both change and stay the same—that's how common sense understands the world. Yet, beneath the obvious there lurks difficulties. For example, in one sense, a house is like a river. They are both in a continual state of flux. The river in which a person goes fishing today will not be exactly the same river tomorrow. Houses, too, are always changing, though not as fast. Roofs wear out and have to be replaced; paint is stripped from the walls only to be covered with new paint; faucets on the sinks break and new ones are installed.

Yet, in another sense, a house has a kind of permanence. While no house will last forever, Monticello will always be the house that Thomas Jefferson built for as long as it remains intact. Houses, then, both change and stay the same.

Similarly, as long as a dog and a friend remain alive, they will in one sense be changing—sometimes sitting, other times standing; sometimes gaining weight, other times losing weight; sometimes learning new things, other times forgetting old things. But, in another sense, they will be the same Fido or Fred one has grown to know and love until the day they die.

We only mention the obvious because certain philosophers have denied either the reality of change or the reality of permanence. It was the ancient Greek proto-relativist Heraclitus (c. 500 BCE) who first argued that it was impossible to step into the same river twice. His argument against the reality of permanence was simple: Since only experience tells us what is real, permanence cannot be real because experience reveals that the world (and everything in it) is always changing.

On the other hand, Parmenides (roughly Heraclitus' contemporary) was a proto-idealist. He explicitly argued against the reality of change. His argument was equally simple, though it will strike most contemporary readers as less convincing. Parmenides argued that the only real source of knowledge is pure reason. Experience, after all, is frequently deceptive. People who have had too much to drink see pink elephants and those who are asleep have dreams so "real" that they awake in a cold sweat.

But when we put our trust in reason and reason alone, the whole idea of change becomes absurd. Look at it this way, said Parmenides. For something to change is for it to become what it is not. For example, if on

Monday Fido is alive but on Tuesday he is killed by a car, then Fido is no longer a dog but a corpse. Fido has become something he was not. This is the first premise. And the second premise, equally obvious to reason, is that what does not exist is not real. In other words, what *is* exists and what *is not* does not exist, and obviously, if something does not exist, it is not real. The conclusion follows with rational certainty—change is unreal. Here's the argument reduced to a simple deductive syllogism:

1. For something to change means that it becomes what it is not.

2. What "is not" is unreal.

3. Therefore, change is unreal.

Parmenides' conclusion is clearly contrary to common sense,[1] but Heraclitus' claim that only change is real is equally contrary to common sense. If nothing remained the same, then no one could stay married for even a week—not because the divorce rate has skyrocketed, but because every day the husband and wife would become someone else. Aristotle's realism is nothing more than a sustained defense of common sense against these sorts of philosophical attacks. It begins with what we'll call the distinction between form and shape.

We will define "form" as the specific *quality* of a thing that makes it what it is. In other words, forms are the attributes that real definitions name, i.e. they are essential natures. We will use the term shape, on the other hand, to refer to all the *quantifiable* attributes of a thing. With today's computers and scanners it is fairly easy to turn any physical object's shape into a digitized set of coordinates. When this is done the thing's physical shape has been quantified.[2]

But "shape" as we are using it refers to much more than a thing's physical outline. Sophisticated computer programs can scan a hammer and then produce blueprints fully specifying its top, side, and front views. Yet, this would be insufficient for machinists making a hammer.

1. Here is what Aristotle said about Parmenides: "But to investigate this question at all [whether change is real]—to seek a reasoned justification—implies bad judgment of what is better and what is worse, what commends itself to belief and what does not, what is ultimate and what is not." *Physics* 254a30.

2. "Aristotle might have said that instead of ten categories one may speak only of two: quantities and everything else, or, inversely, everything except quantities. He should have also stated emphatically that between those two domains of categories, the difference was such as to render inane any attempt of reducing one to the other." Jaki, *Means to Message*, 33.

Until the material composition of the head, shank, and handle are specified, hammers cannot be made. However, with today's understanding of the chemical composition of various materials, and with our ability to specify all the various elements and their compounds in terms of atomic numbers, the material composition of a hammer can itself be reduced to quantifiable relations. So "shape" will even include more esoteric properties like electrical conductivity and specific gravity since these too can be fully specified in quantifiable terms. In sum, shape refers to a complete description of a thing's material composition and how it physically interacts with other material objects.

In fact, Aristotle's own term for "shape" was matter. But today, "matter" means something quite different from what Aristotle meant by the term. When we think of matter, we are strongly predisposed to think of the most basic, fundamental, independently existing substances out of which things are composed. This is definitely not what Aristotle had in mind. To think like this is to think like a philosophical materialist.

It is better to think of "matter" in the Aristotelian sense as mere potentiality. Pure matter is the potentiality for real existence. [3] According to Aristotle, to turn pure matter into something real it must be in-formed. Only form actualizes matter. Aristotelian matter is a little like rolled out cookie dough which is potentially many differently shaped cookies. But until the dough is stamped with a cookie cutter of a specific shape, there are no actual cookies. Of course, the analogy is misleading because the dough itself has a physical shape and size. Perhaps a better analogy would be an author's great idea that does not become an actual book until words are put on paper. So too, matter does not become a physical object until its potentiality is turned into a specific thing.

Yet here again language betrays us. To speak of form as something that actualizes matter and makes it real suggests that "forms" are themselves "things" which exists in some sort of spiritual realm. And, in fact, that is exactly how idealists like Plato think of them. Forms, or what he frequently called ideas, *were* the ultimate reality. The material world, according to Plato, only existed as a poor imitation of the forms. But that is not Aristotle's theory.

The technical name for Aristotle's theory is hylomorphism. "Hyle" was the Greek word for wood. It became a metaphor for the stuff out

---

3. In this regard, matter is a little like pure energy which contemporary physicists say is convertible with mass.

of which all things were made. "Morph" simply meant form, but again, form did not mean shape. According to Aristotle, absolutely everything we can see, hear, taste, touch, and smell is composed of both matter (i.e., potentiality/quantifiable shape) and form.[4] If one day scientists succeed in identifying a fundamental particle which cannot physically be split, it will still, in Aristotelian terms, be composed of *both* form and shape.

Yet, if it is absolutely impossible to separate a thing's form from its shape, then what sense does it make to say everything is made up of two "things"? Aristotle's answer is that while we can never *separate* a thing's form and shape, we must *distinguish* its form and shape. For example, we distinguish a smile from a face, but it is absolutely impossible to separate a smile from a face. There is no such thing as a smile which is not a smile of a particular face, but that does not mean that the word "smile" and the word "face" refer to one and the same thing.[5]

By now we may be trying some readers' patience. What, some may ask, does all this have to do with ultimate reality and whether or not it includes things like immaterial souls, free will, and God? Good question, but we must remember the magnitude of our quest. Starting down the wrong road would be costly. Sometimes little errors get canceled out. If a student writes ten short essays over the course of the semester, then it does not make a lot of sense for the instructor to agonize over each essay. Small mistakes here will be averaged out in the end. However, if we are flying from San Francisco to Tokyo and our initial heading is just slightly off course, our little mistake in the beginning will be tremendously costly in the end.

We are setting our initial philosophical heading. Here, small mistakes will be costly, so it is worth the effort to be right from the start. Until we can specify what it is that makes Socrates sitting and Socrates standing the same person, it would be rash to tackle truly big philo-

4. "And, in spite of the difficulties to which it gives rise, the distinction of potentiality and act [form], or at least some modern equivalent for it, seems to be unavoidable if we are to discuss the extremely mysterious fact of change without subtly substituting something else for it . . . [Otherwise] we shall be substituting for rich complexity of a universe which, with all its processes of generation and corruption, life and death, persists through time a succession of discrete states without any real continuity." Mascall, *He Who Is*, 43.

5. "This is evident from the fact that all accidents involve the concept of substance, since in the definition of any accident it is necessary to include its proper subject; for example, in the definition of 'snub' it is necessary to include nose." Aquinas, *Commentary*, sec.1768; vol. 2, 654.

sophical questions.[6] In an ordinary setting, we have no difficulty following Socrates through his various postures. But if our quest is for ultimate reality, then our answer to this seemingly simple question is critical. Aristotle's hylomophism is designed to answer this question. Simply put, it goes like this: while the shape of Socrates has changed, his form remains the same. Here's another example. Consider two words—"**TOOL**" written in bold upper case letters and "*tool*" written in italic, lower case letters. Their shapes are different, but they are in-formed with the same meaning, i.e. essential nature.

Of course, there are limits to how much Socrates' shape (matter) can change while he remains the same. When he moves from sitting to standing, one of his accidental attributes changes. However, after he dies, his essential attributes will change—Socrates will cease to be a human being and become a corpse. When this happens, matter loses one form (that of humanity) and gains a different form (that of a corpse). To summarize:

- Only substances exist by themselves.

- All substances are composed of form and shape (i.e. matter/ potentiality).

- Some forms are accidental; others are essential.

- When a thing's essential form changes, it becomes a different substance.

If this sounds less than profound—like nothing more than attaching new words to common sense—so be it. Profundity, according to Aristotle and Aquinas, must be firmly rooted in common sense and common sense must be fully and precisely understood before it will yield its profundity. It is okay if what we have said seems a little boring; what is important is that we have said nothing false. But positivists think we have done precisely that.

5.2 THE POSITIVIST'S OBJECTIONS

Modern science has been extremely successful and its success is largely the result of its focus on quantifiable relations. This has led many philosophers and scientists, starting with Galileo (1564–1642) and John Locke

6. "For if it is not the function of the philosopher, who is it who will inquire whether Socrates and Socartes seated are the same thing?" Aristotle *Metaphysics* IV.2, 523.

(1632–1704), to argue that *only* quantifiable properties are objectively real. They thought that qualities, such as color and smell, only existed in the consciousness of the person making the observation. These were wholly subjective and unsuitable for use in science. They called the quantifiable properties "primary attributes" while qualities like red and green (because they could not be quantified) were called "secondary attributes." This is the origin of our own contemporary penchant for dividing statements into "facts" which are objective and "opinions" which are merely subjective.

Now if Locke, Galileo, and the whole positivistic tradition which followed them are correct, then realism crumbles to the ground because essential natures or forms are qualities, not quantities. And according to the positivist tradition, all qualities are merely subjective "feelings" that only exist in the "eye of the beholder." But if this is true, then real definitions do not exist and all definitions are arbitrary, i.e. nominal.

Realists do not deny that the focus of modern science on quantifiable attributes has paid huge dividends. But they do deny that science itself can function without qualitative attributes and forms. As Stanley Jaki points out, "The mind knows much more than quantities. Indeed, the very knowledge that there is a quantitative knowledge is a nonquantitative knowledge."[7] For example, all numbers are iterations of the number 1. Think about it: 2 is 1 + 1; 3 is 2 + 1; 4 is 3 +1, and so on. But "1" itself can never be defined. In this respect, "1" is just like "existence." We recognize unity when we see it, but we cannot define unity in measurable terms. There is nothing that one rock, one corporation, one song, one game, one angel, one dramatic play, one word, and one beautiful day have in common except their integrity, i.e., their unity as a single "thing."[8]

A second, and closely related, problem with the positivist's attempt to reduce all qualities (including a substance's form) to quantities is their

---

7. Jaki, *Brains, Minds, and Computers*, 5.

8. "If Nominalist theories [the proto-positivism of the thirteenth century] are to be accepted we must believe that the common principles sought for in particular things are fictions. But to abolish the objectivity of universals in *some* sense is to abolish, as St. Thomas would say, the possibility of exploring the nature of anything. He insisted that universals have their foundations in objects and so far are indisputably real. All thinking, he maintained, presupposes certain irreducible modes of unity, and these are not psychical patterns contributed by subjects but essential feature of objects." Carre, *Realists and Nominalists*, 124–25.

failure to note that "objective measurements" exist wherever we choose to look for them. For example, the ratio of the number of square feet in a room to the number of outside doors is an important number. A room which can hold a lot of people but has only one outside door is a fire hazard. On the other hand, the ratio of nail holes in a wall to the number of green tiles on the floor is equally "objective," though it is utterly devoid of scientific significance. Such quantities are just as "subjective" as qualities.

Furthermore, what makes one numerical ratio important and another trivial has nothing to do with "objectivity." No matter where we look or what we consider, the number of objectivity measurable "quantities" is infinite. The ratio of a person's height to weight is important for doctors, nutritionists, and insurance actuaries. For how is the ratio of a person's street address to the number of years he or she has lived in that location of any importance? Yet both are equally "objective."

By itself, being measurable is of no scientific importance since there will always be an infinite number of quantities to measure. Measurement is only important once we know what is *worth* measuring.[9] Without some way of distinguishing essential and accidental attributes, the question is unanswerable. Not withstanding the positivist theory, the fact that scientists (and everyone else) are able to distinguish between attributes which are worth measuring and those that are not *assumes* Aristotle's form/shape distinction; it does not refute it.

What is more, it is the form/shape distinction which explains the crucial scientific distinction between mere correlation and real causation.

5.3 CAUSES ARE ALSO REAL

The shape of things can be captured by an ordinary camcorder. Other tools and instruments can determine a thing's mass, electrical conductivity, temperature, etc. So imagine a super-camcorder that can capture

9. "A fetish for measurement is astir among our contemporaries. We worship at the altar of statistics: the penchant for quantities is a salient characteristic of contemporary Western culture . . . All the same, there are problems here. For quantification is no guarantor of objectivity, simply because numbers, even robustly determined ones, may in fact fail to be effectively meaningful." Rescher, *Objectivity*, 75. See also Darwin's comment about counting pebbles in a gravel pit (chapter 3, note 13).

all the quantifiable attributes of a thing, digitize them, and thereby measure all there is to measure.

On a positivist's understanding of science, such a machine would make scientists obsolete. Since science, they say, deals only with quantifiable and measurable attributes, a super-camcorder would know everything that is objectively true and there would be nothing left for scientists to do. Like Dr. Frankenstein, positivists have unwittingly created a monster which threatens their own existence.

But according to realists, a scientific understanding of reality requires much more than precise and accurate measurements and logical inferences deduced from them.[10] Like Hamlet, they argue that there is more in heaven and earth than is dreamed of by their positivistic peers. Even with a super-camcorder, we would only know things' shapes; their forms would remain an utter mystery. The best a super-camcorder can do is to produce an endless list of numbers, with no distinction made between those numbers which reveal the essential attributes and those which merely measure accidental attributes. Again, without an ability to distinguish between shape and form, we will never know what is worth measuring and what' is not, and hence, a mere measuring machine, no matter how sophisticated, will never be able to distinguish between real causation and mere correlation. Here is why:

Science does more than make lists; it *explains*. The difference between a list of observations and an explanation harkens back to our previous discussion of "modes of existence" (section 4.2). Remember the story about Sam the Eskimo? When he enters Emerson Hall, we know he will not somehow lose his ability to speak Inuit, his first language. But we cannot learn this from a mere list, even a list which establishes a 100 percent correlation between people entering Emerson Hall and being unable to speak Inuit.

The problem, for the super-camcorder, is that it can only record constant conjunctions—A happens and then B happens. But constant conjunction is not the same as causation. There is a difference between "does happen" and "must happen." Without this distinction, it is impos-

---

10. "For to proceed from causes to effects or the reverse is not an activity of the senses but only of the intellect." Aquinas, *Commentary*, sec. 1146; vol. 2, 457. See chapter 7 for further clarification of the crucial Aristotelian distinction between sense and intellect.

sible to correctly answer a simple question like: What would happen if someone whose first language was Inuit entered Emerson Hall?

A little barroom ditty makes a similar point.

> The horse and mule live thirty years
> And know nothing of wines and beers.
> The goat and sheep at twenty die
> And never taste of scotch or rye.
> The cow drinks water by the ton
> And at eighteen is mostly done.
> A dog at fifteen cashes in
> Without the aid of rum or gin.
> The cat in milk and water soaks
> And then in twelve short years it croaks.
> The modes, sober, bone-dry hen
> Lay eggs for noes, then dies at ten.
> All animals are strictly dry;
> They sinlessly live and swiftly die.
> But sinful, ginful, rumsoaked men
> Survive for three-score years and ten;
> And some of them, a very few,
> Stay pickled till they're ninety-two.

If we are simply basing our explanations on our observations—"what does happen"—then we ought to conclude that the consumption of alcoholic beverages increases longevity. But, such observations miss the crucial distinction between essential attributes and purely accidental attributes.

Here's a final, and more serious, example which makes the same point. Imagine two people studying the same turtle, but coming to two distinct conclusions:

- The turtle came ashore *to* lay her eggs.
- The turtle came ashore *and* laid her eggs.

Which is better? Many college freshmen have been taught to say that the second is "scientifically" more accurate. The problem with the first, they have been told, is that by using the word "to" we are implying that turtles are acting out of conscious intent, whereas in fact, they are only reacting to inbred, internal causes that have been produced by millions of years of evolution. Crudely put, turtles who randomly laid their eggs without first coming to shore were not as successful in passing on their genes as those who *merely by chance* laid their eggs on shore. After thousands of generations of improved reproduction, what began as mere chance was "hardwired" into the turtles, i.e., it became the scientifically knowable cause.

There is nothing this account *affirms* which Aristotelians would deny. Yet, ever since Descartes, philosophers and scientists have assumed that it *denies* that the turtle came ashore *to* lay her eggs. "The entire class of causes which people customarily derive from a thing's 'end,'" said Descartes, "I judge to be utterly useless in physics [i.e., science]."[11] And this, they say, is precisely what is wrong with saying, "The turtle came ashore *to* lay her eggs." It misguidedly explains the turtle's behavior in terms of an "end," or a final cause.

Descartes' injunction, however, far from replacing older explanations in terms of final causes, in fact presupposes such causes. As Aquinas pointed out in one of his earliest works, "The cause of the causality of the efficient cause is the final cause."[12] If we did not implicitly presuppose that there was something "special" about pregnant turtles coming to shore, then no series of finite observations would result in the scientist's evolutionary explanation. There is nothing *observational* that distinguishes a turtle which come ashore *and* laid eggs from

11. Descartes, *Meditations*, no. 4.

12. Thomas Aquinas, *Principles of Nature*, chapter 4. A contemporary analytic philosopher puts it like this: "Not only are many teleological concepts irreducible, but a commitment to the reality of objective natures, functions and associated values is presupposed by actual scientific enquiry and speculation. Functional intelligibility—not just invariable succession—is a common presupposition in the life sciences and it brings with it certain orders of value. An animal, organ or vital process admits of objective evaluation by reference to its proper operation or development as a thing of that sort of nature. Far from excluding such ideas real sciences are built around them, and the picture of the world that emerges is one of living things developing in accord with intrinsic teleologies." Haldane, "Rational and Other Animals," 27.

Unlike John Haldane who we just quote, John Searle has no proclaimed allegiance to either Aristotle or Aquinas. Yet, he too writes: "To repeat: there is no nonintentional standpoint from which we can survey the relations between Intentional states and their conditions of satisfaction. Any analysis must take place from within the circle of Intentional concepts." Searle, *Intentionality*, 79. This is another way of saying that it is impossible to eliminate the notion of final causality in our attempt to understand the cosmos.

The French Thomist Gilson summed it up like this: "But teleology does not propose to eliminate determinism; it proposes to explain the existence of the mechanically determined." Gilson, *From Aristotle to Darwin*, 30.

- A turtle came ashore *and* kicked some sand.

- A turtle came ashore *and* stepped on a piece of driftwood.

- A turtle came ashore *and* reflected a photon into the eyes of an owl.

All of these, from a wholly observational perspective, are equally good descriptions of what a turtle did, yet none of them are of any interest to biologists.[13] Why? In Aristotelian terms, the answer is obvious—these latter three descriptions only describe accidental characteristics of a turtle's life, whereas our first description—the turtle came ashore *to* lay her eggs—defines part of the essential nature of all animals, namely, to reproduce their own species.

Though final causes have been much maligned, they should not be.[14] Final causes simply specify "the regular and characteristic actions of the various agents and efficient causes that operate in the natural world."[15] Roughly speaking, an efficient cause specifies *how* something happens; it names the agent which makes something else happen. For example, an artist is the efficient cause of a painting and the heart is the efficient cause of blood circulation. A final cause, again speaking roughly, specifies *why* something happened; it provides the goal, purpose or typical direction of an agent. For example, the goal of an artist may have been to honor his patron, and the purpose of the heart is to circulate the blood and maintain life.

13. "Scientists never ask themselves *why* things happen, but *how* they happen. Now as soon as you substitute the positivist's notion of relation for the metaphysical notion of cause, you at once lose all right to wonder *why* things are, and why they are what they are." Gilson, *God and Philosophy*, 112. But not all scientists have renounced "the metaphysical notion of cause." "Aristotle's *eidos* is a teleonomic principle which performed in Aristotle's thinking precisely what the genetic program of the modern biologist performs." Mayr, *The Growth of Biological Thought*, 88.

14. "If philosophy identifies true knowledge with useful knowledge, as modern scientism [another name for positivism] does, final causality will be by the same stroke eliminated from nature and from science as a useless fiction. Aristotle, who was a Greek, saw things otherwise. In his philosophy final causality occupied a considerable position because its workings were, for him, an inexhaustible source of contemplation and admiration ... Not so much aesthetic beauty ... but first of all and above all the intelligible beauty, which consists in the apperception by the mind of the order which rules the structure of forms and presides over their relations." Gilson, *From Aristotle to Darwin*, 19.

15. Veatch, *Aristotle*, 48. This book contains an excellent discussion of final causes and mocks Descartes' mocking.

Of course, final causes can be mocked. Why do bunnies have white tails—so that hunters have a target to aim at! Why do people have noses—so that eye doctors have something on which to hang their prescriptions! The critic's point here is that only people, and perhaps some of the higher animals, are able to do things "on purpose" or "to reach a goal." To apply such attributes to nature, Descartes would say, is a misguided anthropomorphism. Falling rocks and rushing rivers do not move or act to achieve an end, but only in conformity to the laws of nature.

But the charge of misguided anthropomorphism cuts both ways. When did *nature* convene its (or is it her?) legislative session to propound such laws? And where are these alleged laws written? In truth, the language of "Laws of Nature" is just as "anthropomorphic" as the language of final causes. Of course, no serious scientist believes in a literal legislative session convened in the murky pre-history of our universe; but then, neither do serious Aristotelians believe that rocks and rivers consciously strive to reach some end or goal.

Nonetheless, some criticisms are justified. Sometimes final causes have been invoked to gloss over our ignorance of efficient causes. Others have argued that science's inability to explain extremely complex things like eyes and brains in terms of efficient causes constitutes an argument for a supernatural cause. Still others have argued that unless there are gaps in the series of efficient causes, there will be no room for human freedom or divine action.[16] (We will consider their arguments further in chapters 9 and 10.) But all these arguments are misguided because scientific investigations are prematurely stifled.

However, properly understood, final causes will never stifle science. The reason is simple: efficient causes and final cause never *compete* with each other; they always *complement* each other. Here again, the form/

---

16. "For centuries final causes have been mistaken for scientific explanations by so many generations of philosophers that today many scientists still consider the fear of final causes as the beginning of scientific wisdom. Science is thus making metaphysics suffer for its centuries-long meddling in matters of physics and biology." Gilson, *God and Philosophy,* 129.

Here's why it is a mistake: "Even for the theist, to appeal to divine agency in explanation of why a particular event happened would in most contexts be unhelpful, since . . . God is ultimately responsible for all natural events in any case. It would be rather as though a literary critic said, in explanation of some feature of *Macbeth,* 'That was the way Shakespeare wanted it'—so obviously true as not to be informative, and indeed implicitly, in its implication of arbitrariness, as derogatory to God in the one case as to Shakespeare in the other." Meynell, *Intelligible Universe,* 71.

shape distinction resolves the difficulty. "**TOOL**" in bold, upper case letters and "*tool*" in italic, lower case letters have the same form, even though they have quite different shapes. Yet, these two differently shaped words are carriers of the same in-*form*-ation, namely, they refer to things we call tools. *How* these words were written is irrelevant—one person might have moved his right hand while holding a pen over a piece of paper while another person may have moved fingers on both hands over a keyboard of a computer. *Why* these words were written is all that matters.

True, it is a little wordy to say that a person's goal or intention was the final cause of the word's in-*form*-ation. But once again, we are distinguishing, not separating. Writing is composed of two distinguishable (though not separable) causes. One answers the question—*how* were the lines shaped? The other answers the question—*why* are these lines a word (as opposed to a meaningless scribble)?

Obviously, modern biologists have a much more detailed understanding than Aristotle of the series of efficient causes that results in a word being produced. But no increase in our understanding of efficient causes will ever rid the world of final causes. The meaning of words does not exist in the gaps between the ink molecules; nor do the author's intentions which constitute a word's final cause exist in gaps between brain cells.

In the rush of enthusiasm that followed Newton's and Darwin's grand syntheses, many people assumed that precise observations and experiments had made obsolete the contributions of philosophy in understanding our universe. But with the diminishing (though hardly extinct) influence of positivism, we are coming to realize that observation by itself is insufficient for scientific investigation.[17] Aristotelians have

17. If Hilary Putnam is right, we have understated the case. "To put it very briefly, Carnap wanted to reduce theory choice to an algorithm . . . Today no one holds out any hope for Carnap's project." Again, "In fact, in his response to my 'Degree of Confirmation and Inductive Logic,' . . . Carnap backs away significantly from the hopes for an algorithm that would enable us to reproduce the judgments of an ideal inductive judge he expressed in *Logical Foundations of Probability*, his only book-length treatment of inductive logic." Putnam, *Fact/Value Dichotomy*, 141, 180.

Karl Popper makes a similar point. "Every description uses *universal* names (or symbols, or ideas); every statement has the character of a theory, of a hypothesis. The statement, 'Here is a glass of water' cannot be verified by any observational experience [sense-datum] . . . By the word 'glass,' for example, we denote physical bodies which exhibit a certain *law-like behavior*, and the same holds for the word 'water.' Universals cannot be reduced to classes of experience." Popper, *Logic of Scientific Discovery*, 94–95.

named, articulated, and made explicit what is left out in a positivistic understanding. It is final causation, the corollary of which are the abstracted essences/forms which make some regularities in nature lawful (and hence useful for predictions) while others are mere coincidences.

In the next chapter we answer the question: Since observation by itself never produces knowledge of essences/forms, how is such knowledge to be obtained?

Aquinas classically made the point in one of his first works: "Hence, the end is the cause of the causality of the efficient cause, for it makes the efficient cause be an efficient cause" (*Principles*, chapter 4). One of his contemporary interpreters explains it like this: "The efficient cause is cause of the end with regard to being, because by moving the efficient cause brings it about that the end is. But the end is cause of the efficient cause, not with regard to being, but with regard to the idea of causality. For the efficient cause is cause inasmuch as it acts, but it does not act except by reason of the end. Hence the efficient cause has its causality from the end." Blanchette, *The Perfection of the Universe*, 178.

6

How Do We Know?

We live in an age which assumes that true knowledge requires certainty. This confusion began when Descartes declared that we should no more believe merely probable propositions, no matter how great the probability, than we should believe propositions which are patently false. Only those "clear and distinct ideas" which are known with mathematical certainty, said Descartes, can provide an adequate foundation for a theory of knowledge. His position is called rationalism.

David Hume, an empirically minded and somewhat skeptical philosopher, agreed that knowledge must have an absolutely firm foundation. But rather than grounding knowledge in pure reason, Hume sought to ground knowledge in pure experience. His position is called empiricism.

Aristotle's position is called realism and, once again, it steers a common sense course. First, Aristotelian realists reject Descartes' explicit and Hume's implicit assumption that knowledge (as opposed to mere opinion) requires complete certainty. This "classical foundationalist" assumption, says Aristotelians, is self-refuting. We can only know that we have been wrong in the past if we assume that our present beliefs are adequately justified. Doubt is parasitic on knowledge; without knowledge, we can have no reason to doubt. In short, knowledge requires adequate *justification, not irrefutable proof.*

There are two sources of justification according to Aristotelians—reason and experience. Yet neither is "pure." Rationalists' argue that truths of reason must be devoid of all *experience. Aristotelians see no evidence for this sort of innate knowledge. Instead, they argue that experience is always the* occasion *for coming to know truths of reason (e.g., 2 + 2 = 4), even though it is not its* justification.

Empiricists, on the other hand, seek to purify experience and strip it of all judgment. We never directly see plants and animals, they say; we only see mental images *of plants and animals. (They say this because a person cannot be mistaken about what they* seem *to see.) But this, Aristotelians argue, confuses what we* see *with what we see* by. *A person who is sufficiently near sighted may not be able to see much without their glasses. But when they see plants and animals by means of their glasses it is not their glasses that they are seeing. So too, we see* by means *of mental images; but it is not the mental images that we are seeing.*

Thomas Aquinas summed up the Aristotelian theory of knowledge with a single sentence: "But it should be borne in mind that material substances are not actually intelligible but only potentially; and they become actually intelligible by reason of the likenesses of them which are gotten by way of sensory powers and are made immaterial by the agent intellect." In more contemporary language his three points are: (1) essential natures do not first exist as an eternal archetype in some separate realm as Plato thought; (2) therefore the forms cannot be known apart from experience; but (3) human understanding of essential natures requires more than mere experience; it also requires an agent intellect.

Aristotle himself described the agent intellect as "akin to the divine." Positivists argue that only propositions which are verifiable by the tools of science are knowable. Since the agent intellect is not observable by the tools of science, it follows from the positivist's premise that it cannot be real. Aristotelians respond by arguing that the positivists' own criterion of knowledge cannot be scientifically verified.

Relativists reject both positivism and Aristotelian realism. According to relativists, "truth" is something we create; it is not something we discover. Such a view, they say, will make us more tolerant. But relativism is also in danger of defeating itself. Why should we value tolerance unless tolerance is known to be good?

WE LIVE IN AN age filled with philosophical irony. First, we assume without argument that true knowledge requires God-like omniscience. Unless an argument is proved with deductive certainly, we confidently dismiss it with the quip, "But you cannot know that *for sure!*" Yet we fail to notice that our confident dismissal assumes the same God-like omniscience we deny is possible. It seems we know for sure that nothing can be known for sure. How did we get to such a state?

6.1 RATIONALISM AND EMPIRICISM

Once again, the Enlightenment philosopher, René Descartes (1596–1650), bares much responsibility for our current confusion. His short book, *Meditations*, begins with the firm resolution, "that I should withhold my assent no less carefully from opinions that are not completely certain and indubitable than I would from opinions that are patently false." Unless we can know something with *complete certainty*, Descartes confidently asserts, we should assume that our opinions are utterly groundless, or even "patently false."[1]

Two questions come to mind. First, why would Descartes make such a strange assertion? Are there not *degrees* of certainty? While I am quite certain that Bill Clinton was over six feet tall, I am only moderately certain that George Washington was, yet I claim to know both are true. I could, if asked, easily produce good evidence for both. Of course, in some sense it is *possible* that everything I have ever read about these men has been mistaken. But that hardly puts these in the same category as belief in Bigfoot, the Loch Ness Monster, and unicorns.

But Descartes intentionally distanced himself from common sense. While probable knowledge may be good enough for the common man, he thought that for the scientifically minded theorist much more is demanded. Mathematicians, for example, are not satisfied by someone who says that in most cases it is highly probable that 125 divided by 25 is going to be pretty close to 5. No, in *all* cases and with complete *certainty* 125 divided by 25 is going to equal *exactly* five.

The first reason that Descartes insisted on absolute certainty, then, for philosophical and/or scientific investigations is that he believed these disciplines should be held to the same standards as mathematics,[2] which also happened to be his first area of expertise. (It was Descartes who invent analytic geometry and the system of Cartesian Coordinates).

This raises the second question. How does Descartes propose that disciplines other than mathematics could achieve such certainty? His answer was to ground *all* reasoning in what he called "clear and distinct ideas." This comes down to the claim that reason, as opposed to experi-

---

1. Descartes, *Meditations*, First Meditation, 59.

2. To which Aristotle replies, "a well-schooled man is one who searches for that degree of precision in each kind of study which the nature of the subject at hand admits: it is obviously just as foolish to accept arguments of probability from a mathematician as to demand strict demonstrations from an orator." *Nicomachean Ethics* 1.3, 1094b22.

ence, is the only reliable source of knowledge. The problem with experience—i.e., what we see, hear, feel, taste, and smell—is that it is always subject to deception. The lake we think we see turns out to be a mirage; the bird we think we hear turns out to be a squeaky door; and the itch an amputee "feels" on his foot turns out to be a phantom limb experience. And to this list can be added all sorts of dreams and hallucinations, many of which are so vivid and lifelike that sometimes we loose confidence in our own ability to distinguish one from the other.

These sorts of deceptive experiences have been known for centuries. And given the recent advances in medicine and neurophysiology, we are approaching the point where sophisticated brain implants can produce deceptions on demand. Though *The Matrix* was a science fiction movie, that sort of "virtual reality" is now a theoretical possibility.

Descartes, of course, knew nothing about computers and brain implants. But he did speculate about deception on a grand scale. Suppose, he wrote, there was "an evil genius, supremely powerful and clever, who has directed his entire effort at deceiving me. I will regard the heavens, the air, the earth, colors, shapes, sounds, and all external things as nothing but the bedeviling hoaxes of my dreams, with which he lays snares for my credulity."[3] Given such a supposition, how could we know anything? Would nothing remain about which we might not be deceived?

Descartes thought there was. An evil genius could easily deceive us about the lake we think we see or the bird we think we hear. He could even deceive us about the existence of our own hands and feet by producing phantom limb experiences. But not even an evil genius with supernatural powers, said Descartes, could deceive us about our own existence as a *thinking being*. How, after all, could he deceive someone who did not exist? Thus, his famous line—"I think, therefore I exist"— becomes for Descartes an absolutely firm foundation upon which to build his philosophy.

From this foundation of pure reason, devoid of any reliance on experience, Descartes built his rationalist theory of knowledge. As long as we reason well from "clear and distinct ideas," he argues, we can be completely certain that our conclusions are true. But what exactly is a "clear and distinct idea"? According to Descartes, these are ideas that people know to be true as soon as they understand what is being proposed. Here are some examples of "clear and distinct ideas":

3. Descartes, *Meditations*, First Meditation, 62.

- $2 + 2 = 4$

- The shortest distance between two points on a flat surface is a straight line.

- If Tom is taller than Dick and Dick is taller than Sally, then Tom must be taller than Sally.

- Tomorrow it will either rain or it will not rain.

Though these propositions are obviously true, that is not what makes them clear and distinct. Rather, they are "clear and distinct," he says, because at *no* point does our knowledge depend on any experience. To know that it will either rain or snow tomorrow would require meteorological observations and measurements. But no observations are required to know with complete certainty that tomorrow it will either rain or not rain.

"Clear and distinct ideas," in other words, are *not* the same as what everyone believes. For example, everyone believes that:

- Anyone who falls off the Empire State building without a parachute will be seriously injured.

- It is impossible for anyone to high jump fifty-three feet two inches.

- No baseball player can launch a ball into orbit using only his right arm.

- All biological mothers have had sexual intercourse or have been artificially inseminated.

All of these propositions are true and all of them are the sorts of truths upon which we would "bet our mortgage." But they are not "clear and distinct" in Descartes' sense because our knowledge of their truthfulness depends on either our own direct experience or reports of other people's experience. In either case, these experiences could be subjected to the evil genius's deceptions, and hence, such propositions cannot be used ground our scientific and philosophical investigations. Remember, for Descartes, unless we know something *with complete certainty* we do not know it *at all.*

Descartes' rationalism[4] had many supporters, but it also had many critics. These critics were called *empiricists*. (Today we call them positivists.) The most important was David Hume (1711–1776). He said that Descartes got it exactly backwards. Descartes argued that the only reliable source of knowledge was pure reason. Hume argued that the only reliable source of knowledge was pure *experience*—that which we *literally* saw, heard, felt, tasted, or smelt. Or, to use our previous metaphor, pure experience is that which can be captured on a super-camcorder.

Hume's fundamental objection was that all of Descartes' "clear and distinct ideas" are utterly trivial and of no philosophical or scientific use. Rather than being an absolutely certain insight into the nature of reality, such propositions only tell us how we have arbitrarily decided to define words. They are no more informative than the proposition "all truck drivers drive trucks." When a proposition's predicate merely repeats the subject the whole thing is trivial.

Of course, the fact that the predicate merely spells out the meaning of the subject is not always so blatant. Consider a weight lifter who boasts that if he worked hard enough he could bench press 1,000 pounds. Suppose we give him a year of training to make good on his boast. When the year is up, we put his boast to the test. After failing the test he says, "Well, I guess I just did not work hard *enough*." So we give him another year of training. At the end of the second year he again tries and fails. Still, he holds fast to his boast only this time he explains his failure by saying that he did not have *enough* time. So we give him yet another try. But again he fails. This time his excuse is that he did not have a smart *enough* personal trainer! At some point the significance will die what has been called the "death of a thousand qualifications."[5] Rather than being a claim to exceptional strength, the weight lifter's boast seems to be no more than a disguised triviality. By explaining away repeated failures with the word "enough" he has emptied his boast of all meaning. "Trained enough" has simply been defined to meaning "able to bench press 1,000 pounds." But if that is what "enough" means, then anyone who worked

4. In chapter 1 we referred to Descartes as an idealist. Now we are calling him a rationalist. There is no inconsistency here. Philosophers distinguish between ontology (what really exists) and epistemology (how do we know). Ontologically Descartes was an idealist because he argued that ideas were the ultimate reality; epistemologically he was a rationalist because he argued that pure reason is the only legitimate source of knowledge.

5. Flew, "Theology and Falsification," 97.

hard enough, long enough and with a smart enough personal trainer could bench press 1,000 pounds.

Empiricists argue that upon careful analysis all the rationalists' alleged "truths of reason" suffer a similar fate. Consider again the claim that the shortest distance between two points on a flat surface is a straight line. As rationalists themselves admit, if the proposition fails the test, we would question the validity of the test and not the truth of the proposition. But if no conceivable test can count *against* a proposition, then it is equally true that nothing can count *for* the proposition. And if there can be no real world evidence in favor of a proposition, then the proposition must not be about the *world*, but only about how we have *decided* to define the crucial terms. A proposition which can never be falsified must not be empirically meaningful.

The only place to find a firm foundation, according to most empiricists, is in the positive results of modern science. Philosophers, theologians, and moralists have not made any recognizable progress in the last two thousand years. But science has made tremendous progress in only the last two hundred years. Since the scientific method is grounded in observation and experimental testing, we must only rely on what we see, hear, touch, taste, and smell for our firm foundation. The problem with armchair philosophers, theologians, and moralists is that they try to figure out *a priori* (i.e., prior to experience) what is true and what is not. However, unless one is willing to do the painstaking work of the scientist, statements about God, immortality, and the moral law are nothing more than one's own biases dressed up in flowery language.

Hume summed up the empiricists' position in his famous concluding paragraph of *An Enquiry Concerning Human Understanding*: "When we run over libraries, persuaded of these principles, what havoc must we make? If we take in our hand any volume; of divinity or school metaphysics, for instance; let us ask, Does it contain any abstract reasoning concerning quantity or number? No. Does it contain any experimental reasoning concerning matter of fact and experience? No. Commit it then to the flames: for it can contain nothing but sophistry and illusion."[6]

6.2 FLAWS IN FOUNDATIONALISM

Foundationalism is the general term many philosophers use for those who claim that there is no real knowledge unless it is grounded on an

6. Hume, *Enquiry*, sec. 12, part 3, 509.

absolutely certain foundation. Descartes and Hume are both classical foundationalists. If it is even *possible* that a person's sources of knowledge are deceptive or mistaken, then one's claim to knowledge is not really justified. As we saw, Descartes was quite explicit about this.

And though empiricists like Hume are not as explicit about their commitment to firm foundations, when they explain exactly what they mean by "observation" their foundationalists assumptions are clear. When I look at my dog, do I "observe" a mammal, an animal, something that is alive, or merely a physical object? Or do I "observe" all of these things? But how can an "observation" that is so ambiguous be the source of scientific knowledge? To avoid these problems, empiricists argue that we never really see plants and animals, rocks and rocking chairs. What we really see are *mental images* (representations) of plants and animals, rocks and rocking chairs.[7] Statements about "seeing a dog," according to empiricists, are not strictly speaking observations; instead, they are interpretations or inferences based on our own mental images.

While we are sometimes mistaken when we think we have seen a dog, we cannot be mistaken about what we *seem* to see, i.e. our own mental images. If a patient tells his doctor that he broke his big toe, X-rays could show that he was mistaken and that really he had only sprained it. But if a patient merely says that he had a terrible pain in his big toe, X-rays could never show that he was mistaken. Perhaps the patient was being insincere or exaggerating, but it is impossible for anyone to be *mistaken* about their own pain. The same is true of mental images; it makes no sense to say that we could be wrong about our own mental images. Therefore, the firm foundation upon which to ground knowledge, according to empiricists, is our certainty about our mental images (not what we ordinarily mean by "observations").

Realists like Aristotle and Aquinas reject foundationalism. They say that the search for absolutely firm foundations is misguided. They do not deny that knowledge requires *some* justification. Even true beliefs, until they are justified, may be nothing more than lucky guesses. However, both rationalists and empiricists have failed to understand that while

7. We will soon see the problems this creates. "Experience, taken purely as passive and sensory, is impotent to interpret itself. Sense data are disconnected fragments, no one of which ever entails any other. But knowledge consists in the awareness of connections between the items of experience. Therefore, between experience and knowledge, there is and must always be a leap. The central problem of epistemology arises from the necessity to explain this gap." Grene, *Portrait*, 44–45.

belief requires justification if it is to be real knowledge, so too, *doubt* requires justification if it is to be real doubt.[8]

Once this is understood, foundationalism collapses under its own weight. Consider again Descartes' evil genius. Descartes did not introduce this idea because he thought such a being might really exist. Rather, he introduced this idea as a way to combat skepticism. As we have already seen, since the time of ancient Greece, relativists have argued that real knowledge is impossible because there is no way of knowing that our firmest convictions today will not turn out to be mistaken tomorrow. Foundationalists try to counter such skepticism by discovering a philosophical starting point that is beyond doubt. For rationalists the starting point is pure reason; for empiricists the starting point is the images in our mind.

But suppose the doubts of philosophical skeptics turn out to be incoherent? Descartes correctly noted that doubting one's own existence is incoherent. If a thinking mind does not exist, then there is nothing to deceive. Aristotelian realists extend this argument: Unless there are some observations we know are *not* deceptive, we can never know that other observations have been deceptive. It is incoherent to argue that our observations of plants and animals in our immediate vicinity with good light and no drugs or alcohol affecting our minds might be deceptive because there is nothing more obvious that might "correct" our original observation.

Obviously we have been deceived about the existence of some *particular* plant or animal in less than ideal situations. We think we see a deer down the road, but when we get closer we see that it was only a fallen tree that looked like a deer. But notice: we are now assuming that we really do see a fallen tree. However, if we are working with Descartes' assumption, an evil genius might be deceiving us about the tree too. Perhaps the tree really is a deer, in which case I would have been mistaken about my original mistake! The supposition that we might be mistaken about *all* our observations of plants and animals is as incoherent as the supposition that *all* twenty dollar bills might be counterfeit. If there are no real twenty dollar bills, there is nothing to counterfeit.

So too, the skeptic rhetorically asks: How can we be sure that our firm convictions today will not be proven false tomorrow? Again, in

---

8. "Doubt requires justification just as much as belief, and there are many perceptions that we have no real reason to doubt." Putnam, *Fact/Value Dichotomy*, 110.

some cases, of course, such questions are legitimate. If a person has a history of breaking solemn vows, then it is quite legitimate to ask for evidence that she will not break today's solemn vow tomorrow. If a judge has a history of being too quick to convict, then it makes sense for an investigative reporter to look for exonerating evidence. What the skeptical philosopher forgets is that in these cases the starting point is not *doubt*, but rather *knowledge*. The skeptic's *doubt* is always parasitic on his *knowledge*. We legitimately doubt a person's vow when we *know* her history of past vow-breaking. We legitimately doubt a judge's sentence when we *know* his past convictions have been unjust.

The skeptic's doubts are like shadows. Physical objects can exist without shadows; but shadows cannot exist without physical objects. Without opaque objects shadows are impossible. And if there is no real knowledge, then the skeptic cannot coherently say, "The reason your claim is doubtful today is because you have made similar claims in the past and those have been *proven* wrong." Nothing can be *proven* wrong if all knowledge is doubtful. There is no need to refute someone who claims to *know* that all knowledge is impossible—the statement refutes itself.

Foundationalist philosophers assume that the skeptic's questions can only be answered by producing a theory whose assumptions are *proven* to be true. Aristotelians argue that it is both unnecessary and impossible to prove one's starting points. All philosophers begin with assumptions. What is important is that we begin with the right assumptions. For realists those assumptions are: (1) plants and animals exist; (2) square circles do not exist, and (3) nothing comes from nothing.

These assumptions are immediately evident so proof is unnecessary. Only when evidence to the contrary can be presented is proof necessary. Again, it is not possible to present evidence against our most basic beliefs (e.g., the existence of plants and animals) because that would presuppose that we know this evidence to be true. In which case, *that* evidence would become our most basic belief. And again, unless we know that *some* twenty dollar bills are real, it would be impossible for anyone to a counterfeit twenty dollar bill for the same reason it is impossible to counterfeit a three dollar bill. So too, unless we really know that deer exist, we can never *mistake* a fallen tree for a deer.

Second, Aristotelians argue that with our most basic beliefs proof is *impossible*. To prove a proposition means to deduce it from premises.

But by definition premises must be more obviously true than the conclusion. It is absurd to argue for the obvious propositions by producing propositions that are less obvious. But there is nothing more obvious than our above assumptions. All chains of arguments must ultimately end someplace. The very concept of argumentation or proof means that "starting points" cannot be proved.[9]

Thus, the proper goal of a theory of knowledge is to explain *how* we know; it is not to prove *that we know*. The latter is both unnecessary and impossible.

6.3 ARISTOTELIAN REALISM

Aristotelian realists make three points about claims to knowledge. First, they are fallible.[10] Yes, we really do know some things; but we can never know in advance what we do not know. Since knowledge is always dependent upon evidence, and since our evidence is always increasing in ways that we cannot anticipate, we can never know when we *truly* know something and when we only mistakenly *believe* we know something. We know things; but we will not be able to distinguish what we really know from what we thought we knew until the end of history.

In this regard, our knowledge is like the actuarial tables. We know that on average women live longer than men. However, we cannot know in advance whether Sally will live longer than Fred. But that does not

---

9. Aristotle said, "We reply that not all knowledge is demonstrative, and in fact knowledge of the immediate premises is indemonstrable. Indeed, it is evident that this must be so." He goes on to explain, "Thus it is clear that we must get to know the primary premises by induction; for the method by which even sense-perception implants the universal is inductive. Now of the thinking states by which we grasp truth, some are unfailingly true, others admit of error—opinion, for instance, and calculation, whereas scientific knowing and intuition are always true: further, no other kind of thought except intuition is more accurate than scientific knowledge . . . It will be intuition that apprehends the primary premises—a result which also follows from the fact that demonstration cannot be the originative source of demonstration, nor, consequently, scientific knowledge." *Posterior Analytics* 72b19 & II.19.100b3.

Aquinas comments as follows: First principles "become known through the natural light of the agent intellect, and they are not acquired by any process of reasoning but by having their terms become known." Aquinas, *Commentary*, sec. 599; vol. 1, 242.

10. As Aristotle said, "It is hard to be sure whether one knows or not; for it is hard to be sure whether one's knowledge is based on basic truths appropriate to each attribute—the *differentia* [i.e., the distinguishing mark] of true knowledge." Aristotle *Posterior Analytics* 1.9, 76a26. See also John I. Jenkins, *Knowledge and Faith*, 41, and note 31 in chapter 9.

mean that the actuarial tables do not tell us anything. Just because the tables do not tell us everything, does not mean that they tell us nothing. So too, just because we cannot know everything—for example, when new evidence and invention will force us to revise and refine our previous beliefs—that does not mean that we know nothing.

Second, Aristotelian realists argue that rationalists misunderstand reason. Since human experience begins at birth (or perhaps sooner), for Descartes to say that reason is only pure when it is utterly devoid of experience is equivalent to saying that truths of reason are innate. While Aristotelian realists believe that reason is a legitimate source of knowledge (not just trivial truths), they do not believe that such truths are innate. Rather, they argue that the human intellect *abstracts* essential natures (forms) from experience.[11] (We will explain *how* this is done in a moment.)

Third, Aristotelian realists argue that empiricists misunderstand the nature of experience. According to Hume the only pure (and hence trustworthy) experience is of our own mental images. While realists believe that experience is a legitimate source of real knowledge, they believe that the empiricists seriously misunderstand how experience works—people *see* trees and rabbits; they do not, as the empiricists claim, see mental *images* of trees and rabbits (unless they are delusional). Hume failed to distinguish between *what* we see and that *by which* we see. Many people cannot see distant trees without their glasses. But when they see trees *by* looking through their glasses it is not their glasses that they see.[12]

We will now develop these last two points. Descartes argued that our sense experience is always dubious because it is subject to error. Therefore, in his search for indubitable foundations, he looked to reason *stripped of the least trace of experience*. This sort of reason must be innate. But if there is such innate knowledge, why do babies and very young children not know, for example, that the shortest distance between two

11. "Clearly, therefore, it is by induction that we have to get to know the first things. For that is how perception too implants the universal in us." Aristotle *Posterior Analytics* II.19.99b34. A contemporary philosopher explains it like this: "Aristotle now explains how knowledge develops from sense-perception. It is not that men have innate *ideas*, but that they have innate *capacities*: they can perceive, remember, notice similarities, form general ideas, and grasp universals [i.e., concepts]." Ackrill, *Aristotle,* 109.

12. "But the sensible image is not what is perceived, but rather that by which sense perceives. Therefore the intelligible species is not what is actually understood, but that by which the intellect understands." Aquinas, *ST,* I 85.2.

points is a straight line? Rationalists sometimes argue that children really do know such truths of reason; it is just that they are incapable of verbally expressing their knowledge. However, this seems to be an instance of allowing our theory to interpret the evidence rather than allowing evidence to guide the theory. What Descartes said about children can just as easily be said of my water bottle—*maybe* it understands rocket science but is simply incapable of verbalizing its understanding!

The Aristotelian realist's explanation of how reason works is more straightforward. According to Aristotle, truths of reason are understood when the human intellect is able to *abstract* from experience (i.e., to draw out) the most general truths about existence, e.g., nothing can both exist and not exist at the same time and in the same respect. When it does this, experience will be the *occasion* of knowledge, but not its *justification*. For example, a first grade teacher will frequently teach elementary mathematics by showing his students various combinations of two objects plus two more objects. The teacher will then push them together and ask the child how many objects are in the combined group. At first, children may have to count the number of objects in the combined group. But pretty soon they will know the answer *before* having to count.

The experience of children looking and counting the two separate groups came first, but it was not the justification of their knowledge. Suppose, for example, one child said something like this: "I can see that in many cases 2 + 2 = 4, but I remember seeing a magician place two cards in an empty hat, and then placing two more cards in the same hat, and after saying the magic words, he turn over the hat and out came five cards. I saw it with my own eyes; so 2 + 2 does not *always* equal 4!" Clearly, this student has yet to understand addition. He is still looking for justification in what he sees, as opposed to understanding that 2 + 2 = 4 is one of those most general truths of reason that, once understood, no longer require experience for its justification.

Our point here hinges on the distinction between the *temporal* occasion and *logical* justification of knowledge. Sometimes the order in which subjects are taught is of relatively little importance. For example, in some schools world history is taught before state history. In other schools the temporal sequence is reversed. This is possible because there is no logical connection between the two. Temporally speaking, state history and world history can be taught in either order. But in other cases, the temporal priority of instruction is logically fixed. For example, no school teaches analytic geometry before algebra because analytic geometry logically builds on what is learned in algebra.

Realists agree with developmental psychologists who say that children learn best with visual example. As Aristotle never tired repeating: Nothing is in the intellect which is not first in the senses.[13] Therefore, both Aristotelians and developmental psychologists understand that even subjects like simple arithmetic are best taught by using blocks, balls, pens, and other physical objects to help children learn the truths of addition. These provide the experiential background that children need if they are to learn math.

But the mathematical truth that 2+2=4 is not justified by counting physical objects. Again, the child who *sees* a magician turn four cards into five has mistaken an *aid* in learning (the blocks, balls, and pens) for the *principle* to be learned (a truth of reason). Abstracted truths of simple mathematics are just like the meaning which readers "pull out of" the ink on this page—we cannot read and understand without seeing; but we can "see" (e.g., if we are looking at a foreign script) without being about to read or understand. In other words, the *temporal* occasion of coming to understand simple math must never be confused with the *logical* justification of mathematical truths.

On the other hand, the empiricist's (positivist's) mistake is just the reverse. Empiricists misunderstand experience because they have confused *what we see* (e.g., plants and animals) with *what we see by* (e.g., mental images of plants and animals).[14] Here, it seems, we have another instance of using a theory to (mis)interpret common experience as opposed to letting common experience guide our theories. Remember, according to the empiricist's theory we never see plants and animals directly, but we only see mental images of plants and animals. Yet, when we are looking at a tree in good light that is only a few

---

13. Aquinas put it like this: "While the soul is joined to the body it understands by turning to sense images; it cannot even understand itself except . . . through an idea taken from sensed realities." *ST* I 87.1.

14. "[T]he subjective ideas in an individual's mind are always and solely the means whereby he apprehends something other than his own ideas, and never something that he is able to apprehend or be aware of in any manner or degree. He cannot experience his own ideas; they are totally uninspectable by him; he has no awareness of them. This does not preclude his knowing, by inference from effects to their causes, that subjective ideas really exist. We have inferential knowledge of many things of which we have no direct experience." Adler, *Language*, 55–56.

feet away, we never say or think (unless we are delusional) that we see a *mental image* of a tree.

A simple experiment illustrates this Aristotelian point. Consider the following set of letters:

- THE CAT IS ON THE MAT

Now consider an equally complex set of letters:

- BEU MFU GL SB FNI PEO

Now, without looking, try to recall each of the letters in the two sets. Any adult reader of English will have no difficulty remembering all the letters and their order in the first bullet; few adult readers will be able to do this with the second bullet. Why? One bullet is no more complex or longer than the other. The reason we can remember the first bullet, but not the second bullet, is that we do not see the first as a merely set of letters, much less as a set of images; rather, we see words which form a simple statement. In a similar way, Aristotle argues that people do not see *images* of plants and trees; rather, they see plants and trees *by means* of images. In this respect, images are like a clean pair of glasses. When people with glasses see plants and animals, it is not their glasses that they see; instead, they see plants and animals *by means* of their glasses.

The problem, again, is the empiricist's misguided attempt to answer the skeptic's challenge by grounding our knowledge on an indubitable foundation.[15] But Aristotelians will not allow a theory to contradict the obvious unless absolutely necessary. Since the skeptic's challenge has already been shown to be incoherent, there is no reason to deny the obvious—people *see* plants and animals!

But there is a more "philosophical" reason many empiricists want to deny the obvious, namely, they want a world devoid of anything other than matter and motion. Hume could see where Aristotle's epistemology was headed. Neither forms, essential natures, nor the intellect which

15. "With a quite hyper-Cartesian fear of being deluded, he [the positivist] has restricted the realm of philosophy to sense-data [mental images] and psychological states, and anything that cannot be reduced to these is ipso facto excluded from his system. This does not, however, prove that nothing else exists; it only proves that if it does exist the positivist cannot see it. Such an excess of caution is in fact not proper to man; we are far more likely to discover the true nature of the world if we use the faculties with which nature has provided us and learn from our mistakes." Mascall, *Existence and Analogy*, 83–84.

knew them were the sort of things that could be explained merely in terms of matter and motion. So to maintain their philosophical materialism, empiricists (i.e., positivists) are forced to look for an alternative to Aristotle's common sense theory of knowledge.

To understand why a materialist is forced to deny Aristotle's common sense, we need to review points previously made. First, when we say that a person *sees* a plant or a word, "sees" can be understood in two ways. In one sense, we say that a six month old baby smiling at a cat is able to "see the cat." In the same way we say that a toddler can "see the words" in the book from which her mother is reading. But in another sense, neither a baby nor a toddler sees cats and words the way adults see cats and words. To see something in this second (adult) sense is to see *what* something is. From here on out, when we speak of "seeing" a plant or a word, or whatever, we intend the phrase in its "adult sense"—we see that something *is* a plant or that it *is* a word.

In this "adult" sense, seeing a plant or a word means that we understand *what* we are seeing. But plants and words come in a huge variety of sizes, shapes, and colors. Until we are able to *abstract* their form or essential nature from this vast variety of observed features, we do not know *what* it is that we are observing.[16] It is this uniquely human ability to abstract forms that enables us to understand the concept of "plant" or "word" and their definitions. And as we have already stressed, forms, essences, and concepts are all immaterial. Meaning is not in words the way dirt is in a rug. A vacuum cleaner pulling ("abstracting") dirt from a rug is an example of one physical thing (a vacuum cleaner) acting upon another physical thing (some dirt). But when the human intellect abstracts meaning from ink or it abstracts the form of a plant from the physical object it is observing, it is not "pulling out" something physical.

But the physical cannot act upon the non-physical. A physical eraser could theoretically remove all physical representations of the number seven; but no physical tool could (even theoretically) remove the *concept* seven. Like can only act upon like. Since concepts, forms, and essential natures are all immaterial, Aristotelians argue that the hu-

---

16. "Likewise, the things which belong to the species of a material thing, such as a stone, or a man, or a horse, can be thought of apart from the individualizing principles which do not belong to the notion of the species. This is what we mean by abstracting the universal from the particular, or the intelligible species from the phantasm [observed image]; that is, by considering the nature of the species apart from its individual qualities represented by the phantasms." Aquinas, *ST,* I 85.1.

man intellect doing the abstracting must itself be immaterial. (We will develop this further in chapter 7.) Thus, anyone who argues that reality is limited to physical things that are empirically observable is *forced* to deny Aristotle's explanation of *how* humans know.

A single sentence from Thomas Aquinas provides an excellent summary of Aristotle's explanation: "But it should be borne in mind that material substances are not actually intelligible but only potentially; and they become actually intelligible by reason of the likenesses of them which are gotten by way of sensory powers and are made immaterial by the agent intellect."[17]

First point: Plato elevated concepts (often called Forms or Ideas) to the status of timeless truths in an immaterial realm that exists quite independent of the physical world. (These are the "innate ideas" of the rationalists.) Furthermore, he thought this immaterial realm more real than the material realm of "shadows" and "images" in our cave-like existence. Aristotle and Aquinas disagreed.[18] They would have nothing to do with Plato's depreciation of the physical world.

But Aristotle and Aquinas were equally critical of materialists who said that *only* matter and motion was ultimately real. A universe totally devoid of immaterial concepts is ultimately unintelligible. Since Aristotle and Aquinas thought that the universe, at least in part, is intelligible to even humans' finite minds, it follows (by *modus tollens*) that materialism is false.

The "middle way" Aristotle established between Plato's hyper-immaterialism and materialists' total denial of an immaterial realm is summarized by Aquinas: "But it should be borne in mind that material substances are not actually intelligible but only potentially." Again, to say that something is intelligible simply means that humans are able to understand it, i.e. to know *what* it is. Such conceptual knowledge is communicated by means of definitions. On this point Plato and Aristotle are in complete agreement.

17. Aquinas, *Commentary*, sec. 2541; vol. 2, 893.

18. "Lack of experience diminishes our power of taking a comprehensive view of the admitted facts. Hence those who dwell in intimate association with nature and its phenomena grow more and more able to formulate, as the foundations of their theories, principles such as to admit of a wide and coherent development: while those whom devotion to abstract discussions has rendered unobservant of the facts are too ready to dogmatize on the basis of a few observations." Aristotle *On Generation and Corruption*, I.2.5–10.

What separates Plato from Aristotle is the distinction between *actual* and *potential* concepts. According to Plato, concepts come first; they exist eternally. According to Aristotle, material objects come first. The concepts embodied in them are real, but they only exist potentially. In this respect, concepts are like water behind a hydroelectric dam.[19] There is no *real* electricity mysteriously hidden in the water; yet there is *potential* electricity in the water which is quite real. Similarly, the essential nature that makes a pansy a plant does not mysteriously exist hidden between the complex molecules of a pansy. But that does not mean the concept is unreal. Essential natures and the concepts by which they are understood are real potentialities waiting to be abstracted by humans.

Second point: Our concepts come from observations. This is what Aquinas means when he says that "the likenesses of them [intelligible concepts] . . . are gotten by way of the sensory powers." Unlike truths of reason that only require observation as the *occasion* of knowledge, conceptual abstractions require observations as part of their *justification*. Humans are not disembodied spirits with innate knowledge of things' essences. Instead, our knowledge of essential natures requires sensory experience.

Conceptual abstraction also requires experience because the physical characteristics of plants and animals are wholly dependent on accidental occurrences. For example, it is an accidental fact about life on earth that it is based on carbon molecules (see chapter 3.3). There is nothing that says it *had* to be this way or that life *could not have been* based on silicon molecules. And if life based on silicon is one day discovered elsewhere in the universe, its physical appearance would almost certainly be radically different from life on earth. Thus, knowledge of its various essential natures would require a whole new set of observations. Without actual observations, we could not know the essential natures of silicon-based life.

Third point: The essential natures embedded in material objects only become part of our understanding, as Aquinas says, "by the agent intellect."[20] Returning to the dam analogy, we said that in the water be-

19. Aquinas frequently compares the function of the agent intellect to that of light. As the colors of objects are made visible for the eye by light, so material entities are rendered intelligible by the agent intellect. It reveals objects by illuminating the sense images. See Aquinas, *ST*, I 79.3.

20. "The soul has two cognitive powers. One is the act of a corporeal organ, which naturally knows only the singular. But there is another kind of power call the intellect.

hind the hydroelectric dam there is potential electricity just as there are essential natures in plants and animals. Actual electricity to power homes and factories does not exist until the water leaves the dam. Similarly, actual concepts do not exist until they are abstracted from things by humans. Now what is it about dams and humans that enable them to turn potentialities into actualities? In the case of dams, it is the electrical generators. In the case of humans, it is their "agent intellect" (*nous*).[21]

However, the analogy between an electric generator and the agent intellect can be misleading. Generators are physical objects that are *in* dams just as dirt is *in* a rug. But agent intellects are immaterial and hence they are not *in* humans the way generators are in dams. Remember, Aristotelians describe agent intellects as being in humans the way meaning is *in* words. Generators *make* electricity by converting kinetic energy into electrical energy, but agent intellects *abstract* essential natures from things. When the essential natures are stripped of all their material characteristics, then (and only then) do they become the immaterial concepts we use to understand reality.

The distinction between creating and abstracting cannot be overemphasized. The relativists, who we will consider in the next section, maintain that *all* concepts are human creations. Realists disagree. When the human intellect correctly understands reality, its concepts, as Plato said, "Divide nature at the joints." In these cases, the human mind is the abstractor of concepts, not the creator of concepts. Of course, in addition to the concepts that "divide nature at the joint" (and remember, these may be as few as five in number, see chapter 4.3), humans obviously *create* all sort of words to name humanly created objects and distinctions. These are the nominal definitions we discussed in chapter 4. But

---

Though natures [essences] only exist in individual matter, the intellectual power knows them not as individualized, but as they are abstracted from matter by the intellect's attention and reflection. Thus, through the intellect we can understand natures in a universal [conceptual] manner; and this is beyond the power of the sense." Aquinas, *ST*, I 12.4.

21. A contemporary philosopher explains it like this: "What may be called for, then, is a return to the scheme and way of thinking displayed in Aristotle's *De Anima* and in Aquinas' commentary upon it. There the ultimate gap is between intellection and every other activity of animals—human and otherwise . . . The distinctive point about abstract thought is that it calls for a unique form of understanding, the contemplation of natures, which is the preserve of *nous*, the active intellect. Suffice it to say that neither Aquinas *nor* Aristotle supposed that this could be the work of a bodily organ: *immaterial objects; immaterial acts; immaterial power.*" Haldane, "Rational and Other Animals," 28.

Aristotelians insist that these two functions of language be kept distinct. Real definitions *abstract* concepts which truly describe reality; nominal definitions *make* distinctions on continuums where no real (essential) difference exists.

While human's ability to abstract concepts is truly remarkable, like the rest of our knowledge, it is not infallible. For example, part of the definition of pansies is that they are a plant and hence they feel no pain. Now it would be difficult to imagine the sort of observations that would call into question the claim that "pansies feel no pain." Certainly we should require more than the images of "Kirlian" photography or the anecdotal reports of plants growing faster when exposed to music. If it were true that even one pansy really felt pain, then everything in biology books would have to be revised, including the role of the central nervous system in producing feelings. A biological revolution would be in the works.

That is not to suggest that science never undergoes a revolution. Prior to Kepler all philosophers and scientists believed that circular motion was part of the essential nature of planets. Even "revolutionary" figures like Copernicus and Galileo did not challenge the older, essentially Aristotelian, belief that all astronomical objects move in circular orbits. And as we saw in chapter 2, it took over fifty years and Newton's magnificent *Mathematical Principles of Natural Philosophy* before the scientific community could fully digest the implications of Kepler's observations establishing the non-circular orbit of the planets. Copernicus and Galileo were *sure* that they understood the essential natures of planets and that these included circular motion. But the conceptual abstractions of any particular theory are never infallible.

For these reasons we must not consider the proposition that pansies feel no pain an *infallible* deliverance of the agent intellect. Humans' best theoretical understandings have been revised in the past and it is possible, and even likely, that they will have to be revised in the future. But as we have argued, there are two requirements for a successful revolution: First, no single observation should be allowed to overturn our best theoretical understanding; the observational data in favor of a new understanding must be overwhelming. Second, before abandoning the old theory, a new, more comprehensive theory must exist. The problems Buridan observed in the Aristotelian theory of motion were nothing more than anomalies until they were digested in a new, and better, unifying theory (chapter 2.2).

In short, empiricists are right—a "scientific" understanding of reality requires experience. But the experience upon which science builds is never pure; it always has a conceptual and theoretical component.

6.4 POSITIVIST'S AND RELATIVIST'S OBJECTIONS TO ARISTOTELIAN REALISM

Positivists and relativists, of course, would reject pretty much all of Aristotle's theory. The positivism we have considered in the previous chapter clearly has its roots in Hume's empiricism. Defined in contemporary terms, positivism (sometimes called scientism)[22] is the theory that all meaningful propositions are either empirically verifiable or wholly nominal definitions grounded in arbitrary human conventions. If positivists are correct, talk of conceptual abstraction is meaningless. Relativists also deny the possibility of conceptual abstraction, but for slightly different reasons. According to relativists, reality is unknowable, so it is futile to search for essential natures. The best humans can do is to *create* (not abstract) categories for successfully making our way through life.

While we are convinced that both of these challenges can be met, we will be blunt: there *is* something strange and even ominous about the "agent intellect" (*nous* in Greek). Aristotle described it as "akin to the divine."[23] Initial skepticism about such things is understandable and we will flesh out in much greater detail Aristotle's argument for the existence an immaterial agent intellect in the next chapter. But, in this chapter we will only summarize the positivist's and relativist's own theory of knowledge and then outline the realist's response.

---

22. "Scientism is one of the most dangerous contemporary intellectual tendencies. [The critique of it] is a duty for a philosopher who views his enterprise as more than a purely technical discipline." Putnam, "Why There Is Not a Ready-Made World," 147. And again, "For this reason there is an exceedingly subtle and insidious danger in positivism. If you cannot avoid metaphysics, what kind of metaphysics are you likely to cherish when you sturdily suppose yourself to be free from the abomination? Of course it goes without saying that in this case your metaphysics will be held uncritically because it is unconscious; moreover, it will be passed on to others far more readily than your other notions inasmuch as it will be propagated by insinuation rather than by direct argument." Burtt, *Metaphysical Foundations*, 229.

23. Aristotle *On the Generation of Animals* II.3,736b22; see also, Aristotle *Nicomachean Ethics* 10.7; Aristotle *Parts of Animals* 4.10, 686a27–32; Aristotle *On the Soul* 3.4–5.

Positivists argue that statements about entities that can never, even in principle, be directly observed (like essential natures and agent intellect) are simply meaningless. Consider, once again, the example in chapter 2. A self proclaimed "super-scientist" one day announces a momentous discovery: On April 15, 1950 the entire universe doubled in size; everything got twice as big and the speed of light also doubled. No one noticed this because at the same instant they became twice as tall, their clothes also became twice as big, and their table and chairs twice as large.

Here it is plain that the super-scientist is involved in a meaningless "word-game." While his words appear to have meaning, in fact there is no conceivable observation that could count either for or against such a claim. As we have said before, knowing that it will either rain or not rain tomorrow does not make us meteorologists. All truths of reason, positivists say, are reducible to a tautology—a proposition which can never be false because it has no real content. Here positivists are simply updating the argument we considered in the first section of this chapter concerning the weight lifter who boasted that if he were strong "enough" he could bench press a 1,000 pounds.[24] Tautologies are really nothing more than arbitrary definitions about how humans choose to use words. While we must provide meaningful definitions of our terms the only real source of knowledge, according to positivists, is direct empirical observation.

So, if, as the positivists maintain, all meaningful propositions are either (1) observationally verifiable or (2) arbitrary definition, then we must ask: Into which of these two categories do propositions concerning the agent intellect belong? Since they are clearly not empirically observable, statement about them must be either arbitrary definitions by Aristotelians or meaningless word-games. In either case, Aristotle looses.

The positivist attack is rhetorically persuasive, but logically flawed. Consider the following propositions:

---

24. The classic contemporary statement of positivism is from A. J. Ayer. "Like Hume, I divide all genuine propositions into two classes: those which, in his terminology, concern 'relations of ideas,' and those which concern 'matters of fact.' The former class comprises the *a priori* propositions of logic and pure mathematics, and these I allow to be necessary and certain only because they are analytic. That is, I maintain that the reason why these propositions cannot be confuted in experience is that they do not make any assertion about the empirical world, but simply record our determination to use symbols in a certain fashion." Ayer, *Language, Truth and Logic*, 31.

- Lead is heavier than water.

- There is a gold nugget on the backside of Pluto.

- There are fifty states in the Union.

- Hitler was a bad man.

- The agent intelligent exists.

The first is straightforwardly empirically verifiable. All we have to do is watch a piece of lead fall to the bottom of a glass of water. The second proposition is not as easily verifiable; and perhaps, it never will be verified. However, we can specify what it would take to verify: for example, a space probe with very sophisticated instruments capable of flying around Pluto and sending back a highly detailed scientific survey of the planet. In short, the second proposition is *in principle* verifiable.

The third statement is neither straightforwardly nor in principle verifiable. But that is only because it reports the complex legal arrangements governments have agreed to about who is going to rule where. Though the statement is meaningful, according to positivists, it tells us nothing about the universe except the way we have arbitrarily decided to arrange political sovereignty.

The forth and fifth statements are neither verifiable nor do they have an agreed upon definition. They are *not* meaningful, according to positivists, because they are neither true nor false. Rather, they are more like a cheer at a football game expressing the cheerer's emotional reaction to what's at hand.

On the above five propositions, the positivist's position is clear. But suppose we add a sixth proposition to the list:

- The positivist's theory of knowledge is true.

What is a positivist going to say about this statement? What would count as evidence for such a claim? Could the positivist's theory of knowledge be verified by satellites circling the moon or robotic submarines deep in the Mariana Trench? Hardly. It seems the positivist's own thesis is *not* empirically verifiable. By their own criteria, positivism must be nothing more than an arbitrary definition about how some philosophers want to use the word "knowledge." In other words, *the positivist's theory is self-defeating.*

A second major problem with positivism harkens back to chapters 2 and 3. There we argued that when considering cutting-edge scientific problems there is no significant difference between the methods of scientists and the methods of philosophers. Both employ the three Cs of consistency, coherence, and comprehensiveness. And though there is no simple procedure for verifying philosophical claims about the agent intellect, neither is there a simple procedure for verifying the claim that the earth revolves around the sun.

Third, even if scientist were able to straightforwardly verify all their theories, this is no reason to believe that *only* scientific statements are meaningful. The mistake here is simple logic.

"All S is P" (e.g., all scientific theories are meaningful) is *not* logically equivalent to "Only S is P" (e.g., only scientific theories are meaningful). If there are any doubts, think about the statement: "Only citizens are eligible to vote." The point of this statement is to exclude resident aliens and other non-citizens from voting. But "All citizens are eligible to vote" says nothing, one way or the other, about resident aliens being eligible to vote, just as "All Golden Retrievers are friendly" says nothing, one way or the other, about Irish Setters, German Shepherds, etc. So too, "All scientific truths are empirically verifiable" says nothing, one way or the other, about whether philosophical, theological, or ethical truths are verifiable in some other way.

As we said in chapter 1, realists are "double-knowers"; they believe both reason *and* experience are legitimate sources of knowledge. Positivists are "single-knowers"; they believe that *only* experience is a legitimate source of knowledge. Relativists are "know-nothings"; they believe that there are *no* sources of real knowledge. If people want to call some things "plants" and other things "animals" because it helps them navigate the world in which they live, then so be it, says the relativists. But do not pretend, they say, that such distinctions reveal the "truth" about reality. "Truth" is created, not discovered. As Friedrich Nietzsche (1844–1900) said, truth is nothing but a "mobile army of marching metaphors."

Contemporary relativists frequently criticize what philosophers call the "correspondence theory of truth." This is the theory that a proposition is true if and only if what it asserts corresponds to what really exists. Aristotle clearly endorsed such a theory. As he said, "a proposition is true if it says of what is that it is and of what is not, that it is not." The correspondence theory is simply the common sense view that a truth is the conformity of our concepts to reality.

To review the argument of chapter 4, relativists argue that "reality" is never immediately accessible. Reality cannot be observed except through the eyes of a "conceptual scheme" which, roughly speaking, refers a culture's linguistic or logical categories. A culture's conceptual scheme is never a simple reflection of reality. Instead, say relativists, it is a set of distorting lenses through which everything is observed. All theories of reality are thereby reduced to an arbitrary set of assumptions.

It is as if everyone who has ever lived was given different color contact lenses at birth because, without such lenses, everyone was so blind that all they could see was vague and indistinct shadows. Now suppose that in such a hypothetical universe a discussion arose among philosophers as to the *true* color of the things. One group would say that all things are shades of green, while other groups would say all things were shades of red, and still other groups would see different colors. Since no one can distinguish the color of anything without their contact lenses, relativists say that it is simply silly to waste valuable time and energy disputing such "philosophical" questions.

Relativists therefore counsel us to give up our futile attempts to discover "reality." It is impossible to evaluate our own conceptual schemes (and certainly not the conceptual schemes of other cultures) for their correspondence to reality. If we find that a belief in things like human rights, freedom of speech, the separation of church and state, and the other verities of a liberal democracy help us to live together in harmony, then well and good. And if grounding our democratic beliefs in some sort of "philosophical theory" concerning "the Laws of Nature and of Nature's God" helps to strengthen people's resolve, then that's fine too. But we should not pretend that our beliefs somehow reflect reality.

Aristotelian relativists have clearly been effective in getting out their message. It has become a cliché to say that it is *mere arrogance* for us to *impose our understanding* on another individual or culture. Like all clichés this one contains some truth mixed with error. In an attempt to sort out these elements we will examine this piece of conventional wisdom word by word.

First, consider the phrase "mere arrogance." The assumption here is that arrogance is an evil that we ought to avoid. This raises immediate problems for the relativists. It makes good sense for a realist to say that we ought to seek good and avoid evil. But what can such language mean to relativists? If all language creates a set of lenses through which we view everything, then noting that "arrogance is evil" tells us a lot about the speaker's perspective but nothing about reality. If "good" and "evil" are not real categories, then why should one be sought and the other avoided? Why should someone in a culture whose language categorizes "arrogance" as a sign of virility, confidence, and resolution see it as something to be avoided?[25]

Realists agree with Alasdair MacIntyre: "Take away the notion of essential nature, take away the corresponding notion of what is good and best for members of a specific kind who share such a nature, and ...there remains only the individual self with its pleasures and pains. So metaphysical nominalism [i.e., relativism] set constraints upon how the moral life can be conceived. And, conversely, certain types of conceptions of the moral life exclude such nominalism."[26]

Second, consider the notion of "imposing" something on someone else. "Impositions" have two aspects: there is the action (how something is done) and the effect (what is done). The act of imposing suggests some element of force or compulsion. Considered by itself, force and/or compulsion is neither good nor evil. Forcing Nazi soldiers to surrender their tanks is presumably good whereas compelling an innocent man to testify against himself is presumably evil. Here the proper evaluation of an action is based upon the effect: is it good or bad? So, again, we are back to language that can only be accommodated by the relativist's own theory with great awkwardness.

Third, consider what it is that is being imposed, namely, "our understanding." If our goal is merely to persuade someone else to adopt *our* beliefs, then Aristotelians are the first to counsel against such actions. The mere fact that we *believe* something to be true, good, or beautiful is never a good reason by itself. Unless we can produce good reasons and evidence, there is no truth, only rhetoric. And truth (along with the

---

25. "Commonsense realism about the views of my cultural peers coupled with anti-realism [i.e., relativism] about everything else makes no sense. If, as Rorty likes to claim, the notion of an objective world makes no sense, then the notion of 'our culture' cannot be more than Rorty's private fantasy, and if there is no such thing as objective justification—not even of claims about what other people believe—then Rorty's talk of 'solidarity' with the views of 'our culture' is mere rhetoric." Putnam, *Fact/Value Dichotomy and Other Essays*, 143.

26 MacIntyre, *Three Rival Versions of Moral Enquiry*, 138.

good and the beautiful) is not something that any individual or culture "owns."

Besides, "imposed beliefs" do not change beliefs, though they may change actions. It is easy for a misguided teacher to coerce students into writing an essay that agrees with his own ideas. But only a fool believes that he has thereby convinced them. So, if relativists are only calling attention to the ineffectiveness of force and compulsion in changing other people's beliefs, then philosophical realists wholly agree.

In sum, relativism, like its philosophical cousin skepticism, is always in danger of refuting itself. If its goal is only to promote tolerance of things that *ought* to be tolerated, then Aristotelians have no objection. But the arguments whereby relativists seek to achieve their goal undercut the crucial distinction between what we should and should not tolerate.[27]

---

27. We agree with Michael Polanyi: "Modern fanaticism is rooted in an extreme skepticism which can only be strengthened, not shaken, by further doses of universal doubt." Polanyi, *Personal Knowledge*, 298. We also agree with Karl Popper: "I have argued in favor of realism in various places. My arguments are partly rational, partly *ad hominem*, and partly even ethical. It seems to me that the attack on realism, though intellectually interesting and important, is quite unacceptable, especially after two world wars and the real suffering—avoidable suffering—that was wantonly produced by them." Popper, *Quantum Theory*, 2.

Not only does the lack of realism cause harm, but the presence of philosophical realism can be a force for good. The philosophy department faculty at Catholic University of Lublin "began with an ancient conviction—they would be radically realistic about the world and about the human capacity to know it. If our thinking and choosing lacks a tether to reality, the philosophers believed, raw force takes over the world and truth becomes a function of power, not an expression of things-as-they-are. A communist-era joke in Poland expressed this realist imperative in a way that everyone could grasp: 'Party boss: How much is 2 + 2?' 'Polish worker: How much would you like it to be?' The political meaning of the realist assumption . . . was later expressed in the famous Solidarity election poster that read, 'For Poland to be Poland, 2 + 2 must always = 4.' Human beings can only be free in the truth, and the measure of truth is reality." Weigel, *Witness to Hope*, 133.

7

What Does It Mean to Be Human?

What is the mind or soul or self (we use these terms interchangeably in this chapter)? Commonly it is said to be an immaterial substance in a person's body the way a captain is in a ship. The body and soul interact here on earth, but when the body dies, the soul lives on like a captain who escape from a sinking ship. When referring to theories of the mind, this view is called dualism .

Materialism is a second common approach, at least among those who consider themselves scientifically minded. According to this view the "soul" is not a separate substance. Rather, it is a humanly predictable and scientifically understandable function of the brain. Thus, the "soul" is in a person's body the way that "great handling" is in a sports car. And when the body dies, there is nothing left.

Aristotelians take a middle course. On one extreme are the materialists who argue that a functioning body and brain are both a necessary and sufficient condition for being human. On the other extreme, dualists argue that a functioning body and brain are neither necessary nor sufficient for being human. Aristotelian argue that the soul is in the body the way meaning is in words. So the body and brain are necessary, but they are not sufficient. With the materialist, they agree that having a body and brain are necessary, i.e. the soul cannot exist without a body and brain. With the dualist, they agree that a functioning body and brain is not sufficient, i.e. there is something more, namely, the agent intellect discussed in chapter 6. However, unlike the dualist who take the soul to be responsible for all consciousness—feeling, perceiving, remembering, dreaming, etc.—it is only the human's ability to abstract concepts, according to Aristotelians, that requires more than a functioning body and brain.

Aristotle's argument assumes a type/token distinction. If a person has three pennies in his hand, he is holding one type of coin, though he holds three individual tokens. *All things that are humanly predictable and scientifically understandable presuppose a type/type correlation, i.e., whenever type A events occur, type B events will follow. But not all causal relations are like this. Many are token/token relations. For example, the cause of* this *particular coin landing "heads up" was* this *particular person flipping it in* this *particular situation at* this *particular time.*

With the materialist, and against the dualist, Aristotelians argue that the conservation laws of modern physics are never violated in the body and brain. They even agree with the materialist that many brain functions associated with consciousness (feeling, perceiving, remembering, etc.) exhibit type/type relations which can be scientifically explained and are in principle predictable. However, Aristotelians deny that this is the case with conceptual thought. Here there are only token/token relations between brains and concepts.

Their justification for this last claim is simple: no type/type relations exist between the shape *of words, symbols, codes, etc. and the* concepts *(in-form-ation) they communicate. For example, the word TOOL can be written in an infinite variety of ways and mediums. So there can be no type/type relation between the brain states caused by* physical *words, symbols, codes, etc. and the* immaterial *concepts associated with those states in a particular brain.*

Some materialists attempt to circumvent this argument by reducing concepts to "dispositions to behave" in a particular fashion. But their argument is viciously circular. Dualists, on the other hand, object to Aristotelians' timidity in refusing to give the "agent intellect" full standing as an immaterial substance. Aristotelians respond by distinguishing among (1) that which exists, *(2) that which does* not exist *and (3) that which* subsists. *The "individual form" which defines who* we *are subsists after death, but only the supernatural in-forming of a "resurrected" body can bring a dead person back to life and full existence.*

7.1 CARTESIAN DUALISM

W HAT DOES IT MEAN to be human? There are two common answers. The first goes like this: Humans are composed of two distinct substances—a physical body and an immaterial mind. Our immaterial mind or soul or self (these are all roughly interchangeable) is our true essence. Our bodies are merely tools that our souls temporarily control. The relation between the body and mind is like the relation between a captain and his ship. If his ship sinks at sea, the captain can escape and remains who he is. So too, when our body dies, our soul survives to live in a spiritual realm. Descartes and Plato are the two most important philosophers associated with this position. This theory is called philosophical dualism and is supported by several arguments.

First, the mind is the seat of consciousness. It is "where" we experience pain and pleasure, hopes and fears, loves and hates. When we reflect on these sorts of conscious experiences, however, it becomes fairly obvious that "consciousness" has no specific location in space. Hearts are located in chests and neurons are located in brains, but it is exceeding odd to locate consciousness *in* brains. When I stub my toe, it is my toe that hurts, not my brain. Of course, when a doctor asks—"Where does it hurt?"—and I "locate" the pain in my toe, we both understand that it is *me* (my "self") that feels the pain. Neither a toe nor a brain is the sort of thing that is capable of feeling pain.

Second, the freedom and dignity of humans requires an immaterial soul. Without an immaterial soul to intervene in the nexus of physical causes, how could we be free? Besides, if humans were merely biological machines, then we would be no different from other higher animals. But no one seriously believes that humans and animals are of equal worth. If you are driving a car and suddenly a child and two dogs appear, we swerve to miss the child, even if it meant hitting the two dogs. The best way to account for this fact is in terms of human's unique spiritual component.

Finally, the common belief in the immortality of the soul also provides support of dualism. If the soul separates from the body at death, then obviously the soul/mind is a distant substance independent of the body. Some people believe in immortality for explicitly theological reasons. For example, Jesus said you can kill the body but not the soul. Other people believe in immortality on the basis of paranormal experience. Still others do so simply because they are "spiritual."

Since this is a book on philosophy, not theology, we will not say much about this final argument. But it is important that we not dismiss it too high-handedly. The more hard-headed scientifically minded people sometimes reject such reasoning as wishful thinking. They may even employ Freud's argument that religion is the product of deep seated psychological fears. When we hurt ourselves as children, we run to our earthly father for comfort. But when we become adults, and we no longer have an earthly father, our subconscious "invents" a heavenly father to provide spiritual comfort. God did not create humans; humans "created" God because they could not abide the thought of living all alone in a cold, cruel, and careless universe.

However, the opposite is equally true. While we are all prone to wishful thinking, we are equally prone to fearful thinking and turning a blind eye to anything that would cause us to rethink our own actions and attitudes. When there is news that our favorite political candidate acted in a tawdry fashion, we dismiss it as "tabloid journalism." When the same sort of story breaks with regard to our political foes, we welcome it as "good ammunition." Who will deny that we frequently see what we want to see? But if God exists and nothing we do escapes his sight, then we know deep down that our actions and attitudes may need to change. While a "total makeover" of our house or even our body may be desirable, a "total makeover" of our soul would mean a kind of death. And any kind of death is anxiety-producing.

In sum, any topic touching on God and the soul is self-involving. Sometimes we desperately want there to be a God and soul; other times we desperately want there *not* to be a God and soul. For either the religious or non-religious to invoke arguments impugning the *motives* of the other side is an *ad hominem* fallacy that all logic books teach one to avoid. (We will say much more about self-involving knowledge in chapter 12.)

7.2 MATERIALISM

Materialism is the theory that *only* matter in motion exists. Humans are thus incredibly complex and highly evolved machines. Though we clearly surpass all other animals in abilities, all our capacities can be wholly explained in terms of the laws of physics and chemistry. Materialism is the second common answer to our question, though it is much more common in academic circles than with the general public. Without impugning the motives of dualists, they are still able to produce powerful arguments against an immaterial mind.

Materialists assume that it is not rational to believe that something exists without good evidence, especially if the thing in question cannot be seen, heard, touched, smelt, or tasted. The problem with immaterial minds, simply put, is that they are quite odd. Odder still is the idea that an immaterial mind can have an effect on physical bodies. The dualist says that the mind guides the body just as a captain guides a ship. So far, so good. The dualist, however, goes on to insist that the mind is immaterial. Of course, a material brain can guide and control our bodies. But an immaterial mind guiding our bodies is like a captain using mental telepathy to guide the ship! This is the materialists first argument.

Materialistically-minded scientists and philosophers, though, should not put too much stock in the "oddity factor." After all, the "oddity" of much of modern physics is hard to exaggerate. Even to this day, no one has ever *observed* an electron (and by today's standards, electrons are fairly large). It is only the *effects* of electrons that are observable. Scientists' confidence in the reality of electrons is based on an inductive inference to the best explanation (see chapter 2 and 3). Scientists started believing in electrons, for example, because they thought them to be the best explanation of the occasional streaks that are observed in a cloud chamber containing radioactive material. Dualists say that their argument for the existence of immaterial soul is not essentially different. Besides, the "oddness" materialists are so worried about is highly relative. Today we find nothing odd about virtually sending information half way around the world with no visible links. Yet, a materialist of David Hume's era would have howled in protest at such a proposal.

A second, and stronger, argument for materialism is that consciousness can be fully explained *without* positing immaterial minds. The love and pain we feel are real, but they don't exist *in* an immaterial substance. A better explanation is that love and pain are *in* us the same way that "great handling" is *in* a sports cars or "a lot of memory" is *in* a computer. The sports car with "great handling" is not infused with some sort of strange spiritual substance. "Great handling" is simply the predictable properties and dispositions that result from a low center of gravity, a balanced distribution of weight, a wide wheel base, etc. And a "lot of memory" is likewise the predictable result of computers with a huge number of extremely small off/on switches.

In the past, many observable phenomena could only be explained in terms of various kinds of "spirits." Plagues and diseases used to be explained either in terms of divine punishments or demonic agents; today we explain them in terms of germs. Prior to Copernicus, the appearances of comets were thought to be divine signs; today their appearance is as predictable as a clock. Materialists argue that the advances of neurobiology will make immaterial souls as obsolete as these previous "spirits."

And it does not stop there. A mere thirty to forty years ago, school teachers established order in the classroom by praising good behavior and punishing bad behavior. In many cases it worked, but in some cases a child's "misbehavior" was incorrigible. Today, many of these same "problem children" are successfully treated with psycho-active drugs. What was once thought to result from a "lack of discipline," we now know is really the result of chemical imbalances in the brain. Just as poor weight balance will cause a sports car to behave poorly, so too, poor brain chemistry will cause children to behave poorly. With neither cars nor children should we invoke immaterial "souls" to explain what is happening.

Finally, we cannot underestimate the powerful push of evolutionary biology. Until a mere century and a half ago, species were thought to be fixed and immutable and the amazing complexity of the humans appeared to be totally inexplicable in purely materialistic terms.[1] Then it seemed pretty obvious that a divine creator was required to account for the amazing complexities of the human body. Nor was it much of a stretch to think that life itself required a supernatural explanation. Now biologists can explain the amazing complexities of humans as the accumulation of small, but beneficial, chance mutations over billions of years.[2] And if a supernatural designer is not needed to account for the complexities of the human body and brain, then it becomes a *much* greater stretch to assume that our complex mental capacities nonetheless require a supernaturally created soul.

7.3 ARISTOTLE'S MIDDLE WAY

Aristotle argued for a middle way. Humans are neither highly evolved apes nor immaterial spirits temporarily inhabiting bodies. Instead, they

1. Even an outspoken atheists like Richard Dawkins has said that prior to Darwin, the materialistic explain of humans was highly implausible. "An atheist before Darwin could have said, following Hume: 'I have no explanation for complex biological design. All I know is that God isn't a good explanation, so we must wait and hope that somebody comes up with a better one.' I can't help feeling that such a position, though logically sound, would have left one feeling pretty unsatisfied, and that although atheism might have been logically tenable before Darwin, Darwin made it possible to be an intellectually fulfilled atheist." Dawkins, *Blind Watchmaker*, 6.

2. Of course, in the United States there is much controversy about evolutionary explanations. However, Aristotelians and Thomists have no principled objection to evolution and are quite willing to defer to what the majority of scientists say is established beyond a reasonable doubt. See my *In Defense of the Soul*, especially chapter 7, for details.

are an essential unity of both the material and the immaterial. We already considered the Aristotelian claim that *everything* we observe is composed of both immaterial forms and material shapes (see chapter 5). Our argument here will sharpen and synthesize our previous points. This will necessarily involve some redundancy and some hand waving in the direction of previous arguments.

However, let us first define each of the positions in such a way that they can easily be compared and contrasted.

- *Dualism* = Material bodies and brains are neither necessary nor sufficient conditions for humans. All that is necessary is the immaterial mind or soul.

- *Materialism* = Material bodies and brains are both necessary and sufficient conditions for humans. Immaterial substances do not exist.

- *Aristotle* = Material bodies and brains are a necessary condition for humans, but they are not sufficient. Immaterial intellects (i.e., agent intellects, see 6.3) are also required.

Aristotelians argue that Descartes made a crucial mistake when he lumped all sorts of disparate things—pains, memories, mental images, attitudes, and concepts—into a single category we now call "consciousness." Descartes placed all these under one heading because he thought they were all the products or contents of immaterial minds. As a result, he bequeathed to modern philosophy one of its biggest, most discussed questions: Can "consciousness" be reduced to some sort of physical behavior, brain state, or function (as the materialist thinks) or is "consciousness" fundamentally immaterial, something that will forever and necessarily be a mystery to science (as the dualist thinks)? Aristotelians, however, argue that the question is misguided. To illustrate the problem, consider a little question.

During the year or two preceding the turn of the millennium, there was much talk and concern over what came to be called the "Y2K" problem. The issue revolved around ubiquity of computers using programs which only specified the year with two digits. Such computers would be unable to distinguish between the year 2000 and the year 1900. Given our economic reliance on computers and computer chips, there was widespread concern about the problems this would cause. Clearly computer programs used by financial institutions would have to be fixed, as would those used by Admissions offices in colleges and universities. But what about cars with chips to control gas flow? Would they start on the morning of the new millennium?

The little question is this: suppose someone coins a new word, "bork," and uses it to refer to all the things humans have made that somehow keep track of time. The category of "borks" will thus include things like computers, trains, automobiles, programmable coffee pots, and pendulum-powered cuckoo clocks. And let us also suppose that there *are* good reasons to think that computers, trains, automobiles, and programmable coffee pots might succumb to the Y2K bug. Is this any reason to suppose that the fifth "bork" listed—pendulum-powered cuckoo clocks—might also succumb? Of course not. "Bork" is an invented term. It does not, as the ancients said, "divide nature at its joints." Being nothing more than a social construct, it can tell us nothing about the inner workings of things we call borks.

"Consciousness," as Descartes used the term, is also a social construct. He took all sorts of things—pains, dreams, mental images, perceptions, memories, intentions, and concepts—and lumped them into a single invented category. He then asked, "What do all these things have in common and how do they differ from things like rocks, trees, arms, noses, and brains?" His answer involved the invention two kinds of things—1) those that were located in space, and 2) those that lacked a spatial location. The spatially extended objects he called material substances, while the spatially non-extended objects he called immaterial substances and argued that they accounted for consciousness. Thus, his famous mind/body dualism.

Descartes' mistake was to lump radically different sorts of things into a single category of consciousness. Yet, most critics of dualism continue to ask his misleading question: "What is consciousness?" Aristotelians reject, or at least, divide the question. They argue that pains, mental images, perceptions, and memories are all in principle reducible to some sort of physical behavior, brain state, or function. It is only *concepts*—if you will, the fifth "bork"—that point to something transcending physical categories. As Aristotle said, "only the intellect comes from without."[3]

3. "Principle whose activity is bodily clearly cannot be present without a body, just as one cannot walk without feet. So they [such faculties as those of nutrition and perception] cannot enter the body from outside . . . they cannot exist separately . . . It

We introduced the distinction between concepts and precepts in chapter 5. Here we will revisit it here with two thought experiments and one parable.

Thought Experiment One:

Close your eyes and form a mental image of a circle. Now form a mental image of an octagon. Most of us will have no difficulty "seeing" these two images as distinct. But, now, form a mental image of a chiliagon. (A chiliagon is a 1,000-sided regular polygon—an octagon on steroids, if you like.) Can anyone honestly claim that their mental image of a circle is distinct from their mental image of a chiliagon?[4] Nonetheless, we have no difficulty thinking about the difference between circles and chiliagons because our *concept* of a circle is quite distinct from our *concept* of a chiliagon, even though we are unable to form distinct mental images of the two.

Thought Experiment Two:

Imagine you are in a room where there is a piano, a map of North America, and several people who drive cars. Now suppose you are asked to count the number of *keys* in the room. Can you do it? Not until you know whether you are supposed to count both car keys *and* piano keys, or perhaps even the key on the map. And if the request was made verbally, then we would also need clarification about how to count the Florida Keys.

Now imagine you are in the same room and another request is made—this time you are asked to count the number of "things" in the room! Can you do it? Just like counting keys, it is impossible to count "things" until one knows *what* constitutes a "thing." Are we supposed to count each person as one thing? Or do we count their noses, feet and toes as three separate things? Or perhaps we should count the cells in their noses as individual things? Obviously, our questions do not end here!

---

remains that only the intellect enters from outside and only intellect is divine. For *its* activity is not associated with any bodily activity." Aristotle *On the Generation of Animals* II.3.736b22; cf. Aristotle *Nicomachean Ethics* bk. 10 ch. 7; Aristotle *Parts of Animals* bk. 4, ch. 10, 686a27–32; Aristotle *On the Soul* bk. 3, chs. 4 and 5.

4. "Aquinas could not be more forceful in reminding us that entering upon metaphysics means entertaining discriminations quite beyond our capacity to imagine [Burrell's note: 'Aquinas' classic texts are found in his commentary on Aristotle's *Metaphysics*, lectio 1 1162–65']." Burrell, *Knowing the Unknowable God*, 8.

A Parable:

A peripatetic philosopher, a number crunching statistician, and a super-sleuthing forensic scientist are hiking down a trail when they see rocks on the side of a hill shaped like this:

The statistician comments that the odds against rocks arranging themselves by random chance into a shape like this are so great that the rocks *must* be a sign of what is ahead. In a skeptical spirit, the forensic scientist sets about to look for physical evidence that some person or group of people actually arranged the rocks. Yet, using his most sophisticated tools, he discovers no evidence that humans have had any physical contact with these rocks, and concludes that the statistician is wrong. The rocks are nothing more than a highly unusual event, utterly devoid of meaning.

The statistician, not to be out done by the tools of the forensic scientist, gets out his calculator, plugs in some numbers, pushes a button, and out comes a number—10^{87}. He then explains with his favorite illustrations just how big that number is and then repeats his original claim: these rocks *must* be a sign of what's ahead.

Finally, though without much hope, the statistician and scientist turn to their tool-less philosophical friend for assistance. "Well," says the philosopher, "maybe the rocks are a sign and maybe they are not—it all depends on their *form*. If they are only rocks *shaped* like words, then they're not a sign. But if they are in the *form* of a word, then they are a sign." Their initial hunch is confirmed—without the sophisticated tools of math or science, their philosophical friend can only utter meaningless mumbo-jumbo.

So the dispute continues as they walk down the road. Five minutes later they see a taco stand. The statistician is delighted and takes this to be a sure vindication of his tools. The forensic scientist is crest-fallen, wondering why his tools did not uncover evidence of human activity. The philosopher remains agnostic—maybe it was a chance event; maybe not.

A day later, the owner of the taco stand drives up the road and sees the same rocks. He thinks to himself—"What a great advertisement!"—and makes arrangements with his lawyer in New York to purchase the land. When the peripatetic philosopher hears of the purchase, he says to himself: "Whatever they were previously, now the rocks really are words."

The point in all three cases is that *form* is not *shape*. Again, we are using the term "shape" as a shorthand to refer to the totality of a thing's physically quantifiable properties, i.e. its physical shape and size, height, weight, chemical composition, etc., *in its most complete description*.[5]

"Form," once again, is used to refer to a thing's essence or nature. A thing's *form* is that which makes it what it is. For example, we can write the word "tool" in several different ways so that it has several different shapes.

𝒯ool　tool　TOOL　*tool*　Tᴏᴏʟ

Yet any instance of the word "tool," irrespective of its shape, has the exact same form. We know that differently shaped instances of the word "tool" have the same form because they all convey the same in-*form*-ation which is nothing other than the concept tool. It is *what* the word means.

Having stipulated the meaning of "form" and "shape," let me now return to our three examples and unpack them further.

(1) The conclusion that Aristotelians draw from the chiliagon vs. circle example is that humans can conceive of (i.e., think about, reason, and understand) all sorts of things that cannot be perceived. As Hamlet said to Horatio, "There are more things in heaven and earth than are dreamed of in your philosophy." Of course, the precise nature of concepts remains to be determined. But any philosophy that conflates conceiving with perceiving (thinking with visualizing) is subject to a devastating counter-example at the outset.[6]

5. In other words, we are using the term "shape" as Descartes used the term "extension." See also section 4.1.

6. And, as Robert Boyle understood, the confusion of thinking with imagining is equally disastrous for science. "When I say that spirit is incorporeal substance . . . if he should answer, that when he hears the words incorporeal substance, he imagines

(2) The conclusion Aristotelians draw from the ill conceived request simply to "count things" is that our idea of "quantity" is itself a "quality." We should probably fault Galileo and Locke more than Descartes for this mistake; they bear the primary responsibility for dividing our perceptions into primary and second qualities. "Primary qualities," they said, were those perceived features of objects that could be measured, weighed, or otherwise "quantified." "Secondary qualities," according to Galileo and Locke, were somehow caused by an object's primary qualities, yet they were really nothing more than the subjective experiences of perceivers. In other words, what *really* existed in nature were quantifiable properties; qualitative ones were merely subjective experiences and wholly parasitic upon those which are quantifiable.

As we argued in chapter 4, they got it exactly backwards. *Quality* is not parasitic upon *quantity*. Rather, *quantity* is parasitic upon *quality*. There is absolutely nothing that one table, one atom, one person, one baseball game, one pain, one poem, one corporation and one concept have in common except, as Aquinas put it, the transcendental quality of unity. Since all quantities are, by definition, iterations of one, it follows that all quantifiable measurements are conceptually dependent on humans' ability to abstract qualities which distinguish heaps of stuff from integrated wholes. And if our ability to abstract qualities which unify is nothing more than a subjective, airy-fairy, socially constructed and idiosyncratic "feeling," then so is the most scientifically sophisticated set of quantifiable measurements.

And though undoubtedly obvious, we will be explicit—the most fundamental *quality* of things is their form. Until we know *what* something is (i.e. until we have abstracted its form) any kind of counting or measurement is impossible.

(3) The conclusion of the parable is that form is not *in* things the way dirt is *in* a rug. To put dirt into a rug or to pull dirt out of rug

---

some aerial or other very thin, subtle, transparent body, I shall reply, that this comes from a vicious custom he has brought himself to, of imagining something whenever he will conceive anything, though of a nature incapable of being truly represented by any image in the fancy [imagination] . . . Because the use of imagining, whenever we would conceive things, is so stubborn an impediment to the free actings of the mind, in cases that require pure intellection, it will be very useful, if not necessary, to accustom ourselves not to be startled or frighted with every thing that exceeds or confounds the imagination, but by degrees to train up the mind to consider notions that surpass the imagination and yet are demonstrable by reason." Quoted in Burtt, *Metaphysical Foundations of Modern Physical Science*, 183–84.

requires some sort of physical contact with the rug. But the way humans put meaning (in-*form*-ation) into physical shapes is radically different, so too is the way humans pull out meaning (in-*form*-ation) from physical shapes. When we come to understand *what* something is (i.e., when we have abstracted its form) we are not performing a physical process. *At no point did the owner of the taco stand need to make "physical contact" with his rocks to make them words.*

However, Aristotelians never tire of repeating that nothing is in the intellect which is not first in the senses (see chapter 6). To perform the intellectual act of abstraction we must first perform the prior act of perception. Plato famously argued that humans "intuit" the Forms directly. But Aristotelians insist that humans are by nature rational *animals*, not disembodied minds. And as animals, our ability to abstract forms presupposes sensory perception. Sensory perception is a necessary condition for the intellectual act of abstraction. But it cannot be a sufficient condition because *forms* (i.e., *what* something is) are distinct from perceivable *shapes*, even in their most sophisticated description.

But now consider the argument of a contemporary philosopher, John Searle, and notice how his discussion of "consciousness" completely ignores the crucial distinction between perceiving and conceiving. He writes, "At the most fundamental level, points of mass/energy are constituted by the forces that are described by the laws of nature. From those laws the existence of consciousness follows as a logical consequence, just as does the existence of any other biological phenomena, such as growth, digestion, or reproduction."[7]

Searle calls his position "biological naturalism," a term that warms Aristotelian hearts. At the risk of being repetitious, we shall say it again: Aristotelians have no objection to Searle's comparison of pains, perceptions, and memories to other biological phenomena such as growth, digestion, or reproduction. Aristotle was at least as enamored of biology as contemporary evolutionary psychologists. Since Aristotelians insist both (1) that nothing is in the intellect which is not first in the senses, and (2) that the body is a necessary condition for human existence, they have no principled objection to the claim that pains, perceptions, and memories are constituted at the most fundamental level by the same sorts of mass/energy points that constitute digestion and growth.[8] Furthermore,

7. Searle, *Mind*, 130.

8. One objection to Descartes' dualism that we have not mentioned concerns his

there is good reason to believe that all of these are describable by "laws of nature."

Now we must be clear about what is entailed by a "law of nature." Here the "type/token" distinction is helpful. While the term is a little dated, the distinction is not. A "token" is a single instance of a particular thing or event. *This* particular penny as opposed to *that* penny. A "type" is a kind or category of things or events, for example, dimes as opposed to quarters or pennies. So, if I am holding a quarter, a nickel, and a dime in my hand, then I am holding three *types* of coins. However, if I am holding three pennies in my hand, then I am holding one type of coin, but three coin *tokens*.

At a minimum, "laws of nature" must establish "type-correspondences" between things or events (as opposed to a mere token-correspondence). In other words, events of type A are observed to be consistently correlated with events of type B. Given our understanding of neurobiology, it is becoming more and more reasonable to conclude that there are such correspondences between things like pains and perceptions and discoverable events in the brain. Here, Aristotelians are in full agreement with Searle.

However, there are powerful reasons to believe that there are *no* type-correspondences between brain states and concepts. The reason is simple: there is no type-correspondence between the *shape* of words (or any other intentional sign) and the concepts they communicate.

TOOL

and

- --- --- .-..

will reflect photons quite differently, and hence, will have quite different effects on the brain. Yet, "tool" written in the English alphabet and "tool" written in Morse code have the same *form* and communicate the same concept. Since there is no limit to the number of shapes that might physically communicate a particular concept to a particular person, it would be a miracle of supernatural proportion if the infinite number of physically distinct stimuli that communicate the concept tool ended up residing in the same precise place in the brain. Since all scientific

---

denial of "consciousness" in all non-human animals. Since he could not believe—largely for theological reasons—that dogs and cats had immortal souls, he was forced to argue that dogs and cats can feel no pain. All pet owners will find this absurd.

explanations presuppose type-correspondences, a wholly physical explanation of our understanding of concepts must fail.

Having said this, we should add that all Aristotelians assume that there *is* a token/token correspondence between concepts and particular neuronal brain states. Without a brain, we could do nothing. Thus, for every concept "X" there is a brain state "Y" with which it is correlated, though there is no lawful (i.e., predictable) generalization correlating *types* of things.

For example, let us say a C-shaped crack in a particular rock, call it "X," was caused by some physical state/event, call it "Y." In a token/token relation there is no lawful generalization such that whenever rock of type X is in state/event type Y, then a C-shaped crack will emerge. In simple English, a C-shaped crack in a particular rock is the result of random causes which no scientist could, or would care to, predict. But random causes are still physical causes; though they are unpredictable, they in no way violate the conservation laws of mass/energy. (We will say much more about this when we introduce the distinction between *per se* and *per accidens* efficient causes in chapter 9.)

So too, there is nothing in Aristotle's theory of mind, as there is in Descartes', that contradicts the "conservation laws" of modern science. After all, Aristotle knew long ago that "nothing comes from nothing." And again, since Aristotelians insist that humans are rational *animals*, not disembodied spirits, they also insist that the brain is a necessary condition for rational thought (e.g., the abstraction of concepts). Concepts do not "emerge" out of nothing; nor do concepts exist in the "gaps" between mirco-states of the brain. Rather, concepts are correlated in a token/token fashion with brain states/functions in the same way meanings are correlated in a token/token (unpredictable) fashion with ink marks and acoustical disturbances of air.

For example, suppose Fred first learned the concept tool by seeing something shaped like "TOOL" associated with hammers and hand saws. Let us assume for the sake of the argument that one day a neurophysiologist discovers that on the neuronal map of Fred's brain it is neuron 9,346,766 that houses this piece of Fred's perceptual past. Finally, let us suppose that this same scientist is able to hook up Fred's brain to a computer and that every time neuron 9,346,766 is stimulated, Fred reports thinking about tools. Would that demonstrate that concepts really are brain processes? Not unless they could also demonstrate that in *other* people's brain it is neuron 9,346,766 that was correlated with the concept tool.

Might such a demonstration be forthcoming? Well, there is no *logical* contradiction here. But there are huge problems nonetheless. Even though Fred learned about tools by seeing the physical shape "TOOL" associated with things like hammers and hand saws, other people will have learned the concept tool by seeing the physical shape "tool" associated with chain saws and chisels and still others by seeing the physical shape "*instrumento*" associated with ink pens and ice picks. The number of differently shaped physical objects used to communicate a *single* concept like tool is virtually infinite.

Contrast this with *perceptual* states in the brain, for example, feeling a painful burn. The numbers of physically different objects that cause a painful burn are also virtually infinite. Fire, frying pans, hydrochloric acid, and dry ice will all cause the same burning sensation. However, in this case they also have the same physical effect on the body. In other words, with pains we *do* have a type/type relation—same physical effects on the body predictably yield the same burning sensation in one's consciousness.

But is there any reason to believe that all the different physical tokens that mean tool (TOOL, tool, *instrumento*, - --- --- .-.. , etc.) will physically affect the *same* neuron in different brains so as to produce the single concept of tool? If, as Aristotle said, the human intellect is akin to the divine,[9] then how much more akin to the divine would such a massive coincidence be, i.e. the coincidence of millions of different physical tokens all miraculously being coordinated so that they have exactly same effect on the brain? Now, again, we must be clear—nothing Aristotelians claim about the intellect violates the strict conservation laws of physics. There is always, according to Aristotle, a one-to-one correlation between a brain state and a concept; it is just that these correlations are only token/token.

We can summarize this argument[10] for an immaterial intellect like this:

---

9. Aristotle *On the Generation of Animals* 2.3, 736b22; cf. Aristotle *Nicomachean Ethics* 10.7; Aristotle *Parts of Animals* 4.10, 686a27–32; Aristotle *On the Soul* 3.4 and 3.5.

10. I have presented the same Aristotelian argument, but with terms and examples, for an immaterial intellect in chapter 9 of *In Defense of the Soul*.

1. When two events exhibit a type-type correspondence, then it is plausible to claim that the first event explains the second event. However, when two events only exhibit a token-token correspondence, the first event does *not* explain the second.

2. At best, our concepts only exhibit a token-token correspondence to our brain states.

3. From 1 and 2 it follows that our concepts cannot be explained in terms of our brain states (or any other purely physical processes).

4. Therefore, without an immaterial intellect, our conceptual abilities are unintelligible.

7.4 THE CRITICS ON EITHER SIDE

Being in the middle has both advantages and disadvantages. While many people recognize moderation as a virtue, others view it as cowardice. Why are Aristotelians unwilling to take a clear and principled stand on the issue? We shall begin with the charge that they are cowardly materialists.

Materialists welcome Aristotle's willingness to acknowledge that concepts are always correlated with physical brain states. What puzzles materialists is Aristotle's unwillingness to acknowledge the fact that we live in a purely physical world. This strikes the materialists as a sign of mere timidity. Since all concepts have a material cause in the brain, materialists argue, that positing immaterial concepts must be nothing more than airy-fairy fluff for the faint of heart.

Aristotelians respond by invoking the distinction between necessary and sufficient conditions. Clouds are necessary for rain, but they are not sufficient. So too, brains are *necessary* for conceptual thought, but they are not *sufficient*. Remember what words *are* and what they *do*. Words convey concepts, but the same concept can be conveyed by a virtually infinite variety of physical shapes. So conceptual thought cannot be explained merely by the pattern of photons words reflect and are then processed by the brain. What, then, are the alternatives?

One possibility is to argue that there *must*—because the alternative is too spooky—be something physically distinctive and significant about the ink and/or acoustical disturbances which constitute the words; it is just that scientists have yet to figure out what it is. Though now we can find only token/token relations between brain-states and concepts, with further research we will discover type/type correlations. This will demonstrate that brain states and concepts are really identical. In the past, lightning had been interpreted as a sign of divine wrath. But science has now demonstrated that lightening is identical to an ordinary electrical discharge. The same sort of identity-relation will one day be discovered between brains and concepts.

One big problem with this sort of promissory materialism[11] is that it misconstrues the way meaning is *in* words or concepts are *in* the brain. Put simply, the materialist's mistake is their assumption that the only significant way one thing (meaning) can be *in* something else is the way dirt is *in* rugs. Now remember the rocks in the taco "sign." By signing a piece of paper in a lawyer's office the new owner of the taco stand instantaneously in-*form*s the rocks with meaning. But if meaning is conceived in materialistic terms as something that enters into physical relations the way dirt is in rugs, then it is the materialists who have a "spookiness" problem. How can the signing of a piece of paper in one place have an instantaneous physical effect in another place? That sort of "action at a distance" violates Einstein's principle that no physical object can travel faster than the speed of light. So if Einstein is right, the meaning of words and our understanding of them (concepts) cannot be identical to some, as yet undiscovered, physical property of words and/or brains.

The other possibility for materialists is logical behaviorism.[12] This variety of materialism denies that anything of significance vis-à-vis the rocks were accomplished in the lawyer's office. According to behaviorists, there are no immaterial concepts that are conveyed by words. Our understanding of a word's meaning is nothing more than a disposition to behave in a particular way. And dispositions are wholly observable. In this regard, a "concept" is like the brittleness in a piece of glass. "Brittleness" does not refer to something that resides in some immaterial realm. It is nothing more than the disposition of glass to shatter when struck by a hard object. Or think about what we mean when we say that a sports car has great handling. Great handling is not some mysterious "stuff." It is nothing more than the predictable characteristics of a car with a low center of gravity, wide wheel base, and a good weight distribution. So

---

11. See chapter 8 in my *In Defense of the Soul* for another problem with promissory materialism.

12. The classic formulation of logical behaviorism is Gilbert Ryle's, *Concept of Mind*.

too, says the behaviorist, the understanding of concepts is nothing more than the observable dispositions of people to react in predictable ways in the presence of words and other signs.

But is it really true that people who understand a concept act in predictable ways? True, when men and women line up to use the restrooms at the half-time of a football game, they rather predictably separate themselves by gender in front of the doors with the words "MEN" and "WOMEN." But this is only the case if we assume that they share other mental concepts, e.g., of what constitutes proper public decorum. A woman protesting traditional middle class values might very well choose not to stand in line in front of the "Women's Room," and use the "Men's Room" instead.

A logical behaviorist might respond that the protesting woman's concept of "proper public decorum" is itself a disposition to act in a predictable way. So the above example, rather than constituting a counter example to their thesis, is itself another piece of confirming evidence.

The problem with such a rejoinder is that it makes the behaviorist's analysis of concepts and other mental states viciously circular. Consider two Army inductees in the beginning stage of a thirty mile march. They both read and understand English and they both see a sign that reads: "Contaminated Water." Peter, looking for an excuse to be sent back, drinks some of the water. Paul, looking forward to a good hike, refrains. So once again, having the same *understanding* of a concept does not lead to the same action because Peter's and Paul's desires differ.

Okay, so suppose the behaviorist analyzes *desires* in terms of dispositions to act in a predictable way. Well, let's consider two more inductees. David and Dan, like Peter, are both looking for an excuse to return to base. But Dan's understanding of the concept "Contaminated Water" is different from Peter's; he thinks it will kill a person. So Dan refrains from drinking. David, however, understands the concept "Contaminated Water" to mean no more than that it will make you too sick to endure a long march. So he drinks.

So here are the two assertions of logical behaviorism:

- If people have the same understanding, then they will be disposed to the same action, but only if they have the same desires.

- If people have the same desires, then they will be disposed to the same action, but only if they have the same understandings.

But obviously, we can only know the first is true, if we know the second is true. Yet we can only know the second is true, if we know the first is true. The circle is vicious.

This problem with logical behaviorism is serious, though it may not be decisive. Any coherent theory is going to suffer from some degree of circularity. After all, to say that a theory is coherent means that the individual parts of the theory both supports and are supported by all the other parts. So the difference between a good theory and a viciously circular theory becomes the size of the circle. Good theories bring large amounts of data into a coherent circle; bad theories only bring a small amount of data into a circle. In other words, the issue is one of comprehensiveness. Suffice it to say that the behaviorist's "circle" is in danger of being too small.

But even if behaviorists are capable of enlarging their circle of definitions, the behaviorist's attempt to eliminate immaterial concepts in favor of observable behavior flounders on the third "C," namely, consistency. Remember, behaviorism is an attempt to defend the materialist thesis that only "shape" (i.e. measurable quantities that can be observed) exists and that Aristotelian "forms" (i.e. essential natures, concepts, and meanings) do not exist. So let us ask of the ink flowing from the materialist's pen or the acoustical disturbances emanating from his mouth: How did *they* become carriers of information? Where do *they* house their meaning? Why should *they* be any more significance than the rustling of leaves or the pattern of rocks after a landslide? In short, if words are just shapes (not conveyers of concepts) then nothing a materialist says can be a good *reason* for believing that materialism is true.[13]

13. Similar arguments have been made many different times throughout the history of philosophy; the earliest is Epicurus': "He who says that all things happen of [material] necessity cannot criticize another who says that not all things happen of necessity. For he has to admit that the assertion also happens of necessity." Aphorism 40, cited in Popper, *The Self and Its Brain*, 75. Aristotle's much commented on formulation of this argument for the immateriality of the intellect in found in bk. 3, chs. 4 and 5 of Aristotle *On the Soul*.

Darwin himself also seems to see the difficulty, though it is not clear that he understands it to be self-referential. In a letter to William Graham he writes "with me the horrid doubt always arises whether the convictions of man's mind, which has been developed from the mind of the lower animals, are of any value or at all trustworthy." Darwin, July 3, 1881. Though fifty years latter, the biologist, J. B. S. Haldane, clearly understood the self-referential problem: "If materialism is true, it seems to me that we cannot know that it is true. If my opinions are the result of the chemical processes going on in my brain, they are determined by the laws of chemistry, not of logic." Haldane,

We will now consider the critique from the other side.[14] Some would argue that Aristotelians are really cowardly dualists. How can there be any significant difference between a Cartesian mind and an Aristotelian intellect since both are immaterial? An analogy may help.

When Beethoven composed the "Ode to Joy" many years ago, a new song came into existence. Its *form* was specified by a unique set of notes and the mathematical relations that existed among those notes. However, until the song is played or sung by musicians, it had no *shape*. Only when the form and shape exist together is the music heard. Once the music

Inequality of Man, 157. See also Stanley Jaki, *The Purpose of it All*, ch. 6, "Heuristics of Purpose," especially 151–55.

Haldane's argument against a wholly materialist interpretation of evolution was well known in the nineteenth century. The Princeton theologian Charles Hodge wrote, "Unless we are we cannot know. This knowledge of self is . . . , moreover, a knowledge not only that we are a substance, but also that we are an individual substance, which thinks, feels, and wills. Here, then, is a mind, i.e. an individual, intelligent, voluntary agent, necessarily included in the first, and most essential of all truths. If this be denied, then Hume is right, and we can know nothing . . . The Materialist cannot think, or speak, or write, without assuming the existence of mind as distinct from matter." Charles Hodge, *Systematic Theology*, vol. 1, 275, 277, 292.

One of the more popular and clearly-written contemporary formulations of the argument is found in the third chapter of *Miracles* by C. S. Lewis. (I believe the original version of his argument is cleaner and more elegant than his rewritten version after his famous "debate" with Anscombe.) For another literary treatment, see the first chapter of Percy, *Message in the Bottle*.

Karl Popper has formulated the argument in several places. Two of the best are section 21 of *The Self and Its Brain* and chapter 12 of *Conjectures and Refutations*. Mortimer Adler has done likewise, see "Intentionality and Immateriality" in *The New Scholasticism*, and ch. 12 of *The Difference of Man*.

Daniel Robinson, a neurophysiologist, has an especially readable version of the argument in *The Wonder of Being Human*, ch. 4.

Finally, ch. 12 in Alvin Plantinga's, *Warrant and Proper Function*, develops this argument in a style familiar to analytic philosophers.

14. Some would argue that there is a third interpretation of materialism we have yet to consider, namely, functionalism. The identity theorists argued that concepts were really identical to certain brain states. The behaviorist argued that concepts do not really exist. Functionalists argue concepts are identical to certain brain *functions*. A common analogy is the difference between a computer's hardware and its software. The identity thesis likens concepts to computer hardware. The functionalist thesis likens concepts to computer software. Sophisticated versions of functionalism have garnered much support among contemporary philosophers, and rightfully so. The question Aristotelians ask is: How exactly is functionalism different from Aristotle's own theory of mind? After all, software is nothing but a very long code. And what is a code if it is devoid of meaning? Or, consider the very idea of a "function." "Functions" are actions aimed at a goal. How is this different from Aristotle's idea of a final cause?

stops, the song ceases to exist. However, when that same unique set of notes is played again, the song, in its full sense, begins to exist once more. No new song comes into existence. Each succeeding performance of the "Ode to Joy" is the performance of the same song.[15]

So a single song can fully exist at many different times, yet not fully exist in between. But this is the crucial point: those intervals *after* Beethoven composed the "Ode to Joy" when the song is not being performed are quite different from the interval of time *before* Beethoven's composed of the "Ode to Joy." With songs, at least, we need at least three grades of "existence." Prior to Beethoven, "Ode to Joy" did *not* exist; while it is being performed it *does* exist; and in between performances it *subsists*. "Subsistence," like the name implies, is a sub-standard kind existence, though it is nonetheless real existence to which the rule—nothing comes from nothing—fully applies. Without Beethoven, the "Ode to Joy" would neither exist nor subsist.

Intellects (intellectual souls as Aristotle would have said) *only* exist when they in-form a human body. This is what Aristotle meant when he frequently repeated that the soul is the form of the body. So for Aristotle himself, an intellect is radically different from a Cartesian mind, since the death of the body is *ipso facto* the death of the intellect.

For Aquinas, however, things are more complicated. New forms can be created (e.g., Beethoven's composition of the "Ode to Joy"); but once created, they can never be destroyed. How can something essentially immaterial be destroyed? When our sun dies, everything on earth will cease to exist—all musical instruments, all sheet music, all CDs, etc. Yet the set of mathematical relations which constitute the "Ode to Joy" will not cease to exist. So too, Aquinas argued, although our brain undoubtedly evolved, each human intellect is directly created by God. (We will say a lot more about God and creation in chapter 10.) But once given an intellect, we begin to "co-compose" a unique set of attitudes, priorities, loves, hates, beliefs, and habits that makes us *who* we are.[16] God makes us *what*

15. Or to invoke the type/token distinction once more: though only one *type* of song has been performed, each succeeding performance of the song is another *token* of the song.

16. Concerning the analogy that minds exists as songs or computer programs, Aquinas writes "But even though forms are not prior to composite substances, it is still necessary to investigate whether any form remains after the composite substance has been destroyed. For nothing prevents some forms from continuing to exist after the composite ceases to exist; for example, we might say that the soul is of this sort—not

we are, namely humans; both we and God make us *who* we are. Who we are is our "individual form" and, like all forms, it is indestructible.

But even our indestructible "individual form" is quite different from a Cartesian mind. A Cartesian mind is naturally immortal. At the death of the body it is actually improved since it is no longer confined by a body. A Thomistic "individual form" is not naturally immortal. At the death of the body it is severely degraded; it will only *subsist*. However, all hope is not lost. Because Aquinas was a Christian, he believed that at the end of history God would resurrect the body and each individual form would be reunited with a body, though this new body would no longer be a body subject to death and decay. As physicist and theologian John Polkinghorne puts it, God will download our software on his hardware until the end of history when God will resurrect new bodies (hardware) to run our software.[17]

However, now we are moving from philosophy to theology, and that would be a topic for another book.[18] The distinction between consciousness in general and the intellectual understanding of concepts, along with the distinction between existence and subsistence, however, should be sufficient to rebut the charge that Thomists are merely cowardly Cartesians.[19]

---

every soul but only the intellective." Aquinas, *Commentary,* sec. 2451, vol.2, 865. He then explains, "Now we should observe that it is Aristotle's view regarding the intellective soul that it did not exist before the body as Plato claimed, and also that it is not destroyed when the body is, as the ancient philosophers held inasmuch as they failed to distinguish between intellect and sense. For he did not exclude the intellective soul from the generality of other forms as regards their not existing prior to composite substances, but only as regards their not continuing to exist after the composite substance have been destroyed." Aquinas, *Commentary,* sec. 2452; vol.2, 865.

D. M. MacKay makes a similar point in a theological context: "[O]ur personal identity is closely linked with our priorities. In a sense, what identifies me more fundamentally than anything else is my total 'goal-complex' or priority-scheme: what defines and orders all my aims and satisfactions in life, great and small? . . . If we cherish, as an essential part of what identifies us, priorities which are incompatible with God's eternal kingdom, then . . . such priorities can have no existence in the new kingdom, nobody to who these priorities are essential can exist in it either." MacKay, *Human Science and Human Dignity,* 115–16.

17. For the whole discussion, see Polkinghorne, *The God of Hope,* especially 107–12.

18. Almost all of N. T. Wright's books stress the fact that Christianity teaches the resurrection of the body, not the immortality of the soul. See especially, Wright, *Simply Christian;* Wright, *Surprised by Hope;* and Wright, *Resurrection of the Son of God.*

19. In chapter 9 we will add a third distinction: Cartesian minds act by intervening in the physical realm; Thomistic intellects act by the power analogous to the power of

Yet, without engaging in revealed theology, we can distinguish Cartesian minds from Aristotelian intellects in three ways:

- Cartesian minds are said to explain all consciousness; Aristotelian intellects are said to explain only our understanding of concepts.

- Cartesian minds are naturally immortal; Aristotelian intellects are only potential immortal.

- Though this anticipates the argument of chapter 9, Cartesian minds violate the conservation laws of physics; Aristotelian intellects do not.

---

words. In other words, Descartes and Aquinas had radical distinct theories of human freewill.

8

Why Should We Care about Morality?

Many people today consider morality to be an equivalent of unself-
ishness. This assumption naturally raises the question: Why should
we ever put other people's happiness above our own?

Kant's answer was that duty *is the only truly moral motivator*
of action. If we are being "good" because of the benefit it brings us
in the future, then, says Kant, we are not acting with a "good will,"
and hence, we are not acting in a praiseworthy fashion. Today's
Darwinists say that altruism is literally in our genes. A father who
sacrifices his life to save three of his children appears *to be unself-*
ish, but in truth, such actions are evolutionarily "hard wired" into
humans because they increase the number of genes which he will
pass on to the next generation.

Aristotelians reject the assumption. Rather than being primar-
ily about unselfishness, morality is like a recipe for happiness. But
"happiness" is not a feeling, rather, it names life's ultimate goal and
is always achieved indirectly by successfully and properly pursuing
other worthy goals over the course of a whole life.

This means that Aristotelians also reject the modern distinction
between objective "facts" and subjective "values." Rather than being
about a person's "values," morality is about virtues. And virtues are
as much a "fact" about our teleologically ordered universe as the
fact that poisons kill living creatures.

There are four ingredients to Aristotle's recipe for human flour-
ishing which must be correctly mixed to obtain a good and happy
life: (1) the primary need for knowledge where more is always bet-
ter, (2) the secondary need for things like food, drink, shelter, and
sex which are universal, though more is not always better, (3) in-
nocent desires for things like skiing, surfing, singing, and sex which
are neither universal nor is more always better, and (4) harmful
desires for power and fame which never promote human happiness,
and hence, more is never better.

Aristotle's ethic follows a middle way between absolutism and relativism. For example, a fool fights for everything; a coward fights for nothing; but a courageous person fights for the right causes, at the right times, and in the right ways. But it takes much practical wisdom to be able to correctly discern whether one is acting foolishly, cowardly, or courageously. There are no algorithms or "moral phone books" where one finds answers to such questions. Instead, the sources of wisdom are good teachers, much experience, disciplined habits, and good friends. Finally, practical wisdom requires humility and willingness to learn from others, even when one's self-image is at stake.

Finding good teachers and (to a lesser degree) good friends is greatly enhanced by a good society. But a good society requires virtuous citizens which only exist where there are good teachers and friendships. So how do Aristotelians break out of this circle? They do not. Instead, they rely on an "argument to the best explanation" by enlarging the circle so that all the other aspects of Aristotle's teleologically ordered universe support, and in turn, are supported by Aristotle's conception of a good and just society.

8.1 UNSELFISHNESS VERSUS HAPPINESS AS MORALITY'S GOAL

We live in a culture where the question of this chapter—"Why should we care about morality?"—is something of a riddle. On the one hand, no one wants to suggest that morality is unimportant or optional. But on the other hand, as the term is now used, "morality" is virtually equivalent to unselfishness. It seems that a person is "being moral" only when they are acting in a way that benefits someone else. Or even more, a person is "being moral" only when they are acting in a way that benefits someone else *without benefiting oneself.*

Consider, for example, two fathers with young children. Both care deeply about morality and both understand the value of reading to their children. But Aaron looks forward to reading to his children after dinner whereas Phil, who would rather retreat to his study to read philosophy, *chooses* nevertheless to read to his children. In short, both do the right thing, but Aaron acts out of delight; Phil acts out of duty. If asked to rank the "morality" of Aaron and Phil solely with respect to reading to their children, the vast majority of people today would rank Phil higher than Aaron. Why? Because Phil is being "unselfish." Aaron, on the other hand, is simply doing what he *likes* to do.

Hence, the riddle of the chapter: Why should anyone care about morality since there is virtual unanimity that "morality" is costly to one's own happiness? Since everyone wants to be happy, what possible reason could there be for seeking someone else's happiness instead of one's own? The two most common solutions to the riddle come from Kant and Darwin.

Kant's answer can be reduced to a single word: Duty. Though Kant's books are dense and prosaic, his *Critique of Practical Reason* includes a famous hymn to Duty: "Duty! Thou sublime and mighty name!"[1] The only thing that is good without qualification, says Kant, is a good will. Intelligence, strength, beauty, and even the classical virtues of wisdom, justice, temperance, and courage, can all be used wrongly if the will is not good.[2] An intelligent thief is more to be feared than a bungling one. A beautiful woman is more likely to violate her marriage vows than a plain woman. And a businessman treating his customers fairly because he knows that a reputation for fairness is good for business hardly wins our praise. There is only virtue when the will is pure.

This is why many people equate morality with unselfishness.[3] The successful businessman who adopts a policy of honesty to improve sales gets faint praise because he is not being altruistic. So does the person who gives generously to charities for the reputation it brings. Like Kant we assume that morality should be its own reward. Unless a person is

1. Kant, *Critique of Practical Reason*, I.3, 327–28. Though as the quote proceeds, Kant's dense prose kicks in: "Duty! Thou sublime and mighty name that dost embrace nothing charming or insinuating but requirest submission and yet seekest not to move the will by threatening ought that would arouse natural aversion or terror, but only holdest forth a law which of itself finds entrance into the mind and yet gains reluctant reverence (though not always obedience) . . . what origin is there worthy of thee . . . ? It cannot be less than something which elevates man above himself as a part of the world of sense, something which connects him with an order of things which has under it the entire world of sense . . . This power is nothing else than *personality*, i.e. the freedom and independence from the mechanism of nature regarded as a capacity of a being which is subject to special laws, namely, pure practical laws given by its own reason; so that the person as belonging to the sensible world is subject to his own personality so far as he belongs to the intelligible world."

2. "Intelligence, wit, judgment, and whatever talents of the mind one might want to name are doubtless in many respects good and desirable, as are such qualities of temperament as courage, resolution, perseverance. But they can also become extremely bad and harmful if the will, which is to make use of these gifts of nature and which in its special constitution is called character, is not good." Kant, *Grounding*, 7.

3. C. S. Lewis explores this same point in his sermon, "The Weight of Glory."

acting solely for the sake of duty we see no virtue. Only when we are *disinclined* to be good can we be sure we are acting morally.

The only true *moral* motivator, says Kant, is absolute spontaneity of the will.[4] If the will is not acting with complete autonomy, it is not acting freely. We are only acting in morally praiseworthy fashion when we decide to be good, *solely* because it is the right thing to do. We will say more about Kant's conception of freedom in the next chapter. Here we are only concerned with his claim that a truly moral person *chooses* to put other peoples' happiness first. To ask for or to provide a reason or motivation for so choosing is self-contradictory, says Kant. If there was a reason or motive for one's choice other than duty, then the choice for morality and against selfishness would not, by definition, be fully free and autonomous.

The other answer[5] to our riddle can be traced back to Darwin. Though it has yet to inform popular culture, in the academic world "evolutionary psychology," as it is called, has many advocates. Its answer is directly opposed to Kant's. According to evolutionary psychology, we cannot help but be altruistic. Altruism is literally in our genes.

Kant's lofty appeal to duty, human dignity and freedom, say evolutionary psychologists, is nothing more than a rationalization. The truth, they say, is that genes determine behavior and our genes are "hard wired" so that *their* benefit is maximized, not our own. Evolution, for example, favors a father who sacrifices his own life to save three of his children

---

4. Kant, *Religion*, 19. The only thing "which elevates man above himself as a part of the world of sense" is his "freedom and independence from the mechanism of nature." Kant, *Critique of Practice Reason*, 89. Furthermore, the independence of our free chooses is complete and unblemished. "A physical propensity (grounded in sensuous impulses) toward any use of freedom whatsoever—whether good or bad—is a contradiction." According to Kant, the only "incentive," "ground," "inclination," or natural impulse" for any truly free choice is a maxim. Now since a maxim is "a rule made by the will," and since choices of the will are absolutely spontaneous, it follows that a person's maxims—the ultimate ground of one's morality—are themselves adopted with absolute spontaneity. Kant, *Religion*, 17–26.

5. We are not suggesting that there is no disagreement about the proper list of duties which ought to govern our actions. Kant opted for multiple rules—do not lie, do not murder, do not steal, do not commit adultery, etc. Whereas utilitarian philosophers (sometimes called consequentalists) opted for a single rule or duty—always act in such a way that it produce the best consequences (i.e. the best balance of pleasure over pain) for all people affected by one's actions. The point of this chapter is only that Kantians and utilitarians understand morality in terms of the duties that it demands.

because such an action maximizes the number of genes that survive. Genes are always selfish; they never act altruistically.

Of course, it *appears* that the father is acting unselfishly. But in point of fact, it is the genes, not the person, which is deciding what to do. To Martian aliens who knew nothing about missiles and fighter planes, a missile which "chooses" to destroy itself to save the airplane from which it was launched appears to be acting altruistically. But those who know about missiles and fighter planes understand that it is the pilot in the plane that is "calling the shots" and there is nothing altruistic about his choices. So too, it is the genes that calculate and decide when it is in their self-interest to "sacrifice" their host for the benefit of their genetic cousins elsewhere.

A good riddle can challenge our assumptions. Both Kant and evolutionary psychology assume that explaining altruism is the primary point of ethical philosophy. Aristotle rejected the assumption. Instead, he assumed that the primary point of ethical philosophy was discovering how to obtain happiness. And though it may surprise some, ancient Christians made the same assumption. It was Saint Augustine who famously said that "There is no reason why man should philosophize except that thereby he may be happy."[6]

Aristotle, Augustine, and Aquinas all assume that happiness is (and should be) a person's ultimate goal. Here is why: An "ultimate goal" is one where it is silly and senseless to ask, "Why did you want *that*?" Consider the multitude of different things people want. Some people, for example, want cars. But it makes perfectly good sense to ask why someone wants a car. One sensible answer would be—"I need dependable transportation to and from work." Yet once again, it still makes good sense to ask why this person wants to work. Answers may vary, though, "I need the money," would certainly be a sensible answer. Still, money itself is not an ultimate goal. It is not money itself that people want. They want the houses, food, drink, sex, fame, and/or power that money buys.

We are now approaching ultimate goals, though we are not quite there. Along with the food, drink, and shelter necessary to maintain physical life, the penultimate goals of people are pleasure, fame, and power. But none of these are ultimate goals. It is not senseless to ask why

---

6. Augustine, *City of God*, IX, 1. Aquinas is even more explicit: "Well-ordered self-love is right and natural; a self-love by which one wishes for oneself what is suitable." Aquinas, *ST*, I–II 77.4.

a person wants any or all of these things. Some people will call it "success," others "fulfillment," still others "enjoyment or contentment." But for simplicity sake, we will stick with "happiness" as the name for humans' ultimate aim since it is silly and senseless to ask: "Why do you want to be happy?"[7]

The substantive disagreements begin when we seek to determine which penultimate goal makes a person truly happy. Some would say it is pleasure; others would say it is power; still others would say it is fame. But before we consider Aristotle's answer, we must say more about the somewhat paradoxical relation between happiness and these various penultimate goals.

Consider what many philosophers call the "hedonistic paradox." Though all people desire happiness, happiness cannot be sought directly the way pleasure, fame, and power can. For example, if a person desires pleasure, that person might purchase a massage from a skilled masseuse. Or if a person desires fame, that person might purchase the services of a public relations firm. If a person desires power, he can purchase an army. But where does a person purchase happiness?

The reason we cannot purchase happiness, says Aristotle, is that happiness is always the *indirect* result of the successful pursuit of some other worthy goal.[8] Aristotle believed that there was a proper time and way to pursue all of the penultimate goals, even pleasure. Therefore, the occasionally purchasing of a massage might well be a vital element in a happy life. But this is crucial—even though a massage may *result* in happiness, that does not mean that pleasure *is* happiness. The pleasure was

---

7. And here we might note that "life" is used in its broadest sense. Many religious people have "salvation" as their ultimate goal in *this* life. However, "salvation" is not their ultimate goal because they believe that life does not end with the death of the body. It is not at all silly to ask such a person why they want to be saved. Their response is simple—Salvation in this life leads to eternal happiness (or rest, contentment, joy, etc.) in the next life.

O'Meara puts it like this. "Surprisingly the life of knowing, faith, and love has for its specifying goal not religious obedience but happiness. If happiness is the first attraction for the human journey through life to God, this should not surprise us for God's life is joyful and people exist not for servitude or frustration but for happiness. 'The reality which is desired as a goal is that in which this particular being's happiness consists and which make it happy' (Aquinas, *ST*, I–II 3.4)." O'Meara, *Thomas Aquinas*, 109.

8. "The good of man is an activity of the soul in conformity with excellence or virtue." Aristotle *Nicomachean Ethics* 1, 7, 1098a15. See also, bk. 1, ch. 8 1098b31–1099a7 and bk. 9, ch. 9 1169b27. Aquinas is even more succinct: "We arrive at happiness through actions." Aquinas, *ST*, I–II 6.

not the happiness; it was the successful pursuit of a worthy goal at the proper time and through the proper means that produced the happiness. This distinction is subtle, but important.

The hedonistic paradox explains why drugs like cocaine and heroin are ultimately unsatisfying. The problem with these drugs is not the pleasure they produce. Instead, it is that the "pleasure" is not the product of a worthy activity. The drug user is looking for a direct path to happiness. Though it seems paradoxical, there is *no* direct path to happiness. If we are to achieve happiness, we must always pursue some *other* worthy goal. As Aristotle says, "happiness is some kind of activity, and an activity clearly is something that comes into being and not something we can take for granted like a piece of property" (or we might add, a purchased "high").[9]

Closely connected is the distinction between happiness as the ultimate goal of life and "feeling happy." Feelings are by nature transient; they come and go. But the Greeks had a saying that Aristotle happily endorsed: call no person happy until they are dead.[10] Now obviously a dead person feels nothing, so happiness must be something other than a feeling.

Another reason the Greeks would call no person happy until they died is that an apparently "good life"—like an apparently "good play" at intermission—can be utterly ruined by a bad ending. But more significantly, they understood well that feelings in and of themselves are neither good nor bad. Feelings only become good or bad in a context. Aching muscles that signify the onset of a fatal disease are bad; but the same ache that signifies an athlete has worked her muscles well is good. The painful death of a solider in the successful defense of a just cause means one thing. But the painful death of a child caught the cross fire of a gang war means something quite different. Feelings are like fire. Fire which heats a home is good; fire which consumes a home is bad.

Summing up the argument thus far we can say:

- "Happiness" names life's ultimate goal.

- Happiness is always achieved indirectly by successfully and properly pursuing some penultimate goal.

- Happiness is not a feeling, but instead a positive evaluation of activities throughout a whole life.

9. Aristotle *Nicomachean Ethics* bk. 9, ch. 9, 1169b27.

10. See Aristotle *Nicomachean Ethics* bk. 1, ch. 10.

8.2 VIRTUES VERSUS VALUES

Today, moral discussions are typically couched in terms of values, but it was not always so. Previous millennia couched them in terms of virtues. This is not an insignificant difference. As we will explain, it signals the change from a teleological to a dualistic understanding of the universe.

In the previous chapters we defended the older, teleological understanding. There we argued for the distinctions between form and shape, efficient causes and final causes, and the fact that "philosophy" and "science" *complement* each other to form a single coherent and comprehensive understanding of the universe. These are all part and parcel of a teleological universe. If we begin our ethical reflections with such an understanding, then morality will be about virtues, not values. Values are personal (or perhaps societal). They are something that we individually choose. Virtues, on the other hand, have little to do with personal choices. Instead, they are essentially connected with, and flow from, the nature of the universe as a whole.

The modern understanding of the universe, however, has shattered this ancient unity between form and shape, philosophy and science, virtue and human flourishing in a teleological universe. Now we inevitably divide the universe into distinct realms of "facts" and "values." Science, we say, deals with "facts" which are understood wholly in terms of efficient causes. Philosophy, in general and ethics in particular, we say, deals with individually chosen values. When science is speaking, there are no values. This is why Kant argued that morality requires a realm of autonomous choice where science (efficient causes) is absent. (We will say more about this in the next chapter.)

But as we also saw, the hegemony of modern science is hard to stop. In Kant's time, there was only Newtonian physics and biology had little "scientific" standing. Darwin changed that, and within a few decades Darwin became Newton's equal in the modern pantheon of great scientists. So if it was hard for Kant to resist science, today it is even harder. A mere generation ago, the "hard sciences" and the "life sciences" were still distinguished and hierarchically ordered. But with the advent of molecular and cellular biology (and its promise of improved and prolonged health), the financial resources, and cultural prestige have drastically shifted toward biology. And this ever increasing prestige of biology carries in its wake an ever decreasing place for "autonomous choice." Evolutionary psychology's explanation of altruism as a clever ploy by genes to perpetuate themselves is only a single case in point. Whatever one thinks of such explanations, it is clear that the modern dualism of facts and values constitutes a zero-sum game where science's gains are philosophy's loss. Or at least, this is the common perception.

The argument of the first six chapters constitutes an alternative to this modern dualism of facts and values. The rest of this chapter outlines the ethical theory that flows naturally from the Aristotelian realism of the first half of this book.[11] But first, let us say a concluding word about the contrast of virtues and values.

Values, we have said, are essentially personal because they are the product of individual choices. Therefore, they are often thought of as being "subjective." Virtues, on the other hand, are essentially universal because they are the direct result of the nature of things. Originally, "virtue" simply referred to the "power of things." For example, people spoke of the virtue of air to stoke a fire or the contrary virtue of water to extinguish a fire. In the past, one could even speak without any confusion of a poison's virtue to kill. The point here is that "virtue" was not, as it is today, connected with moral goodness. The "virtue" of a poison, or anything else, simply referred to "what it is supposed to do." So in this sense, there is nothing "subjective" about a thing's virtues.

If the language of virtues and vice is to be correctly understood, it must be considered with this historical context in mind. When the ancients spoke of a "virtuous person" they were *not* thinking primarily of a person's "morals/values." "Morals" originally referred to the customs of a group (e.g., Do the men where robes or pants?).[12] Furthermore, the

---

11. As Alasdair MacIntyre writes, "There is then no form of philosophical enquiry— at least as envisaged from an Aristotelian, Augustinian, or Thomistic point of view— which is not practical in its implications, just as there is no practical enquiry which is not philosophical in its presuppositions . . . Take away the notion of essential nature, take away the corresponding notion of what is good and best for members of a specific kind who share such a nature, and the Aristotelian scheme . . . necessarily collapses. There remains only the individual self with its pleasures and pains." MacIntyre, *Three Rival Version*, 128, 138. In short, a person's metaphysics constrains, and is constrained by, their ethics

12. "Morals (adj): c.1340, 'of or pertaining to character or temperament' (good or bad), from O.Fr. moral, from L. moralis 'proper behavior of a person in society,' lit. 'pertaining to manners,' coined by Cicero ("*De Fato*," II.i) to translate Gk. *ethikos* from L. *mos* (gen. *moris*) 'one's disposition,' in pl., 'mores, customs, manners, morals,' of uncertain origin. Meaning 'morally good, conforming to moral rules,' is first recorded c.1386 of stories, 1638 of persons. Original value-neutral sense preserved in moral support, moral victory, with sense of 'pertaining to character as opposed to physical action.'

ancients fully understood that there was great variability in a society's mores (i.e., morals), so in our sense, they were "subjective." But "virtues" were not thought to be part of a person's mores. Virtues were considered a part of the natural universe just as poison's ability to kill was part of its nature.

So when the ancients spoke of a "virtuous person" they were referring to the *abilities* of the person. Now some abilities—like the ability to bench press 200 pounds—are easily observable. Other abilities—like the ability to make wise decisions under pressure—are more difficult to observe. But unless we assume a narrow, positivistic understanding of "observation," the latter abilities are just as "objective" as the former. When the ancients used the term "virtuous person," it referred to someone able to do what people were meant to do. And being able to do this is equivalent to flourishing *as a human being*.

8.3 ARISTOTLE'S RECIPE FOR HUMAN FLOURISHING

"Every art and every inquiry," said Aristotle, "is thought to aim at some good, and for this reason the good has rightly been declared to be that at which all things aim."[13] The point here is simply that all human action is directed toward an end or a goal which the person acting believes is good. Unfortunately, not everything a person *believes* is good in fact leads to their ultimate goal of happiness. Such errors are typically caused by a failure to appreciate the distinction between wants and needs.

At one level, everyone understands this distinction. Many children do not want to eat their vegetables or to sleep when they are tired. But adults know that they need both. Alcoholics may want another drink, but the wise person knows this is the last thing they need. Addicts want drugs, but we know they need something quite different. And the list of "addictions" has now grown to include gambling, pornography, and sex. Some psychologists would even add "unhealthy relations," "co-dependencies," and "eating disorders" to the list of confused wants and needs.

Aristotelians rejoice. The widespread use of such language signals a turning away from the rigid fact/value distinction of fifty years ago. Back then it was generally assumed that if an action only affected one's self,

---

The noun meaning 'moral exposition of a story' is attested from c.1500. Moralistic formed 1865" http://www.etymonline.com/index.php?term=moral.

13. This is the opening sentence of Aristotle *Nicomachean Ethics* (1094a).

then its "morality" was wholly a matter of personal preference. Unless a person's behavior immediately harmed someone else, it could not be wrong. But now we are coming to understand (again) that "addictions" are bad in-and-of themselves. Even if one's behaviors do not harm others, they can harm one's self.

Aristotle's ethical philosophy is fundamentally a more inclusive understanding of such psychological truths. While popular psychology focuses on avoiding self-destructive behavior, Aristotelian ethics takes a wider perspective and includes the cultivation of positive behaviors, i.e., good habits. The classical virtues of temperance, courage, justice, and practical wisdom (which we will discuss later in the chapter) name the habits that promote human flourishing. They are what everyone *needs* to be all they were meant to be and thereby achieve the good and happy life.

Human *needs* are real goods determined by nature. Since the natural is universal, needs are the same for all people, cultures, eras, and places. The list of universal human needs obviously begins with things like food, water, clothing, and shelter. *Wants*, on the other hand, are apparent goods which are individually and socially determined. What people want will vary with time, place, and culture. But it should be noted that defining wants as "apparent goods" does not imply they are not also really good for that particular person. "There appears to be a person coming down the path" does not mean that there *is not* a person coming; it only means that there *may* not be a person coming (see chapter 4.2). So too, what one person wants may also be a "real good" for that particular person, but not for some other particular person. Having a glass of wine after dinner with friends may be a real good for Fred, but not for Sally who is an alcoholic.

Needs include two sub-categories—the highest good and secondary goods. For reasons that we will consider latter, Aristotle argued that humans' "highest good" is knowledge. Here, more is always better. However, with some needs, more is not always better. These are the "secondary goods" which include things like food and drink. While food and drink are real needs for all people, and hence, universally good, it is also true that too much food and drink can be harmful.

Wants are also divided into two sub-categories: innocent desires and harmful wants. Some desires are really good and should be pursued as part of a good life. For example, skiing, surfing, singing, and sex are all real goods, though different people will choose to pursue these goods is varying degrees, or perhaps not at all. We shall call these "innocent desires." And once again, more is not always better.

But some desires are not innocent. In fact, some wants—like the pursuit of power and fame—are always harmful, according to Aristotle. We will explain why he thought them harmful in the last section. For now, we will simply define harmful desires as those where more is never better.

This fourfold distinction between the highest good, secondary goods, innocent desires, and harmful desires grows directly out of Aristotle's understanding of humans' essential nature.[14] We are rational animals. This defines what humans *are*. And what we *are* determines what we were *meant* to be and do.

Consider what it means to be a screwdriver. A screwdriver is a tool (genus) designed to drive screws (difference).[15] Now all tools are durable to some degree. They are not like clouds which come and go with a breath of wind. So, in a pinch, you might successfully use a screwdriver to pound a nail or mark a piece of wood. But clearly, there are other tools—hammers and pencils—that do such jobs better. On the other hand, no tool is better for driving a screw than a screwdriver. Driving screws constitutes a screwdriver's "highest good," while pounding nails and marking wood are only "secondary goods" for screwdrivers.

This example illustrates something important about human flourishing. The distinguishing characteristic of humans is their rationality. No other animals can reason conceptually (see chapter 7). *And what something can do better than anything else is its highest good.* This is why Aristotle argued that conceptual knowledge is the highest good for humans, just as driving screws is the highest good for screwdrivers. But it is crucial that we not take too narrow a view of reason. Clearly it includes the philosophical search for the true, good, and beautiful. Yet it also includes a poet's search for the right word, the composer's search for a harmonious note, and the amateur motorcyclist's search for the most efficient carburetor setting. True, Aristotle showed some narrow-mindedness in his preference for the fine arts compared to the mechanical arts. But there is nothing intrinsic to the art of motorcycle maintenance

14. This fourfold division I owe to Mortimer Adler.

15. Of course, screwdrivers are human creations, and hence, do not constitute a natural kind, so our example is only suggestive.

which makes it inferior to the "fine" arts of poetry and music.[16] In fact, if we are being true to Aristotle, the boy tuning his motorcycle because he loves racing is more fully engaged in a uniquely human activity than the rich advertising executive looking for words and notes that will sell his client's widgets.

Activities are always defined by their goals. The goal of the amateur motorcyclists is to understand well his motorcycle, a small, but not insignificant part of the universe. The goal of the advertising executive is to make money far beyond what is necessary. The advertiser's goal is utilitarian. If he could make more money doing something else, his activity would change. But the motorcyclist, we are assuming, is motivated simply by love of the sport. He would not do other things with his free time to make more money. That is what makes his activity uniquely human. Humans and wolves both need food. Humans get food by making money; wolves get food more directly. So the advertiser and wolf have this in common—their goal is *not* the activity itself. The goal of the motorcyclist, however, is direct—knowing all he can about motorcycles.

Aristotle begins his *Metaphysics* with another example of humans' intrinsic desire for knowledge. His first sentence says: "All people desire knowledge." His next sentence illustrates this by noting the delight people take in vision. Who, for example, would prefer a windowless office to one with a window? Why is this? We frequently use vision for purely utilitarian ends—like escaping danger or obtaining food, drink, and shelter. But even when our purely physical needs are met, we still take delight in seeing the world around us. Why? Because humans gain more knowledge through sight than any of the other four senses. We want to "see what's happening," even when such knowledge serves no utilitarian end, because we can never have too much knowledge.

Of course, all inductive generalizations carry with them an implicit *ceteris paribus* or "other things being equal" clause. If we were disembodied minds with no physical needs, then we could say without qualification that more knowledge is *always* good. But since humans are rational *animals*, and since animals have physical needs, to be looking out the window when there is "work to be done" may not be good.

Our animal nature also explains why Aristotelians include the pleasures of a good glass of wine, massage, or sex as real secondary goods. In

16. As Robert Pirsig classically demonstrated in *Zen and the Art of Motorcycle Maintenance.*

the proper circumstances and portions, pleasure is a necessary ingredient in the good life. Though once again, a *ceteris paribus* clause is assumed. Sex with someone else's spouse (adultery) may be quite pleasurable but it unjustly takes from someone else what is theirs, and injustice can have no place in a good life. In the last section we will explain why.

Finally, animals have not only general characteristics (e.g., all mammals have kidneys), but they also have individual characteristics (e.g., my dog has a birthmark on the back of her tongue). So too, some of us take pleasure in a good glass of wine; others in a good beer; and still others in neither. Therefore, while a certain amount of pleasure is a real good for all animals (including humans), there will be a wide diversity of innocent desires which fulfill this need.

8.4 FINDING THE MEAN THOUGH PRACTICAL WISDOM

Some people value moral clarity above all else. These people are typically attracted to a Kantian ethic. With Kant there are moral absolutes or what he called "categorical imperatives." For example, according to Kant, lying is always wrong. But the clarity of the Kantian imperatives comes with a cost. If you are hiding Jews and a Nazi solider asks if you have seen any Jews, according to Kant, the categorical imperative forbids one from lying about their whereabouts.[17] Aristotelians are unwilling to obtain clarity at such a cost and have learned to live with some ambiguity.

In must be noted, however, that in denying that there are "moral absolutes" in the Kantian sense, Aristotelians are not committing themselves moral relativism. Relativists claim that sincerely *believing* something is right or good *makes* it right or good. Aristotle's ethic is universal, without being either absolutist or relativistic. An absolute is something that is true without exceptions. "2 + 2 = 4" has no exceptions and is therefore an absolute. "A little sun is good for one's health" is universal since all humans need vitamin D. But it is not absolute, since even a little sun can be very harmful for someone who just underwent eye surgery. But

17. "Now it happens sometimes that something has to be done which is not covered by the common rules of actions, for instance in the case of the enemy of one's country, when it would be wrong to give him back his deposit, or in other similar cases. Hence it is necessary to judge of such matters according to higher principles than the common laws." Aquinas, *ST*, II–II 51.4. Aquinas' example alludes to Plato's famous example at the beginning of the *Republic*. There the question is whether it is right to keep a promise to return deadly weapons to a person who has recently gone insane. Plato thinks it would not.

note: it is not merely a matter of opinion whether or not some sun will be good for a person. The amount of sun a particular person needs will vary with the *circumstances* of the person; but it does not vary with the *beliefs* of the person. For Fred to sincerely believing that eight hours of sun a day is required for good health does not make it true *even for him*.

Aristotle's stock example of the middle way between absolutism and relativism concerned courage. While courage is a universal good, it takes much wisdom to know what one should do in a dangerous situation. "Doing the right thing" is typically a mean between two extremes. Personal safety is a good thing, but so is fighting in defense of a just cause. A fool fights for everything; a coward fights for nothing; a courageous person fights for the right causes, at the right times, and in the right ways. This raises the obvious questions: Who determines the *right* causes, times, and ways in which to fight and how is the mean between extremes to be found?

The problem is exacerbated by the fact that the Aristotelian mean is definitely *not* mathematically quantifiable. If 3,000 calories a day is too much for humans and 1,000 calories a day is too little for a human, that does not mean that everyone should strive to consume 2,000 calories a day. For an athlete in training, 2,000 calories is probably too few whereas for a sedentary philosopher it is probably too many. So too, the ethical mean is not quantifiable. There are no algorithms here. Nor is there a "moral phone book" with alphabetically listed answers to our tough moral questions.

Instead, we must rely on practical wisdom to find the proper mix of all real goods, as well as innocent desires. This mix will be determined in part by one's human nature (species nature) and in part by one's individual nature and the society in which he or she lives. Finding this mean and the proper mix of needs and wants requires good teachers, much experience, disciplined habits, and good friends. We'll start with the last.

Aristotle's most significant ethical book is the *Nicomachean Ethics*. It is literally a "self help book" (that is what Aristotelians mean by "practical reason"), though it is much too dense and scholarly for today's bookstores' "self help" sections. Nonetheless, fully a fifth of it concerns friendship since "a man needs morally good friends," according to Aristotle, "in order to be happy."[18]

18. *Nicomachean Ethics* bk. 9, ch. 9, 1170b19.

His first reason is obvious, though it's no less true for being so. Remember, happiness can never be approached directly. It is always the result of worthy activities successfully pursued. Exercise is such an activity. Yet we all know that it is easier to maintain a course of regular exercise with friends than by oneself. And each of us could multiply examples where the pursuit of innocent desires becomes even more enjoyable with a good friend at one's side. Cats and snakes are loners; dogs and humans are by nature social.[19] This is one reason good friends can be an important aid in acquiring disciplined habits.

Second, virtuous friends can improve one's self-understanding.[20] I can scratch other people's backs but I cannot scratch my own. So too, it is sometimes easier to observe attributes and habits in others than it is in ourselves. By observing the actions of virtuous friends, we not only receive pleasure, but we learn by imitation. Remember, virtue is more like a skill than a calculation. Math teachers teach rules, and once the rule is learned, the teacher is unnecessary. Tennis coaches develop skills, which sometimes involve "rules of thumb" (e.g., only come to the net when you hit the ball deep in the opponent's courts). But the skillful player knows when to ignore the rule. What better way to acquire such skills than by watching players better than oneself and then attempting to imitate their actions in one's own play?

Of course, those who seek the clarity of engineers and scientists will attempt to turn "rules of thumb" into either hard-and-fast rules or mere options. But those who actually play tennis know that this is misguided. For beginners, a coach will lay down rules—"always set your back foot

---

19. Ibid., 1169b18

20. Practical wisdom, says Aquinas, "is concerned with particular matters of action, and since such matters are of infinite variety, no one man can consider them all sufficiently; nor can this be done quickly, for it requires length of time. Hence in matters of prudence man stands in very great need of being taught by others, especially by old folk who have acquired a sane understanding of the ends in practical matters. Wherefore the Philosopher [Aristotle] says (*Nicomachean Ethic.* vi, 11): 'It is right to pay no less attention to the undemonstrated assertions and opinions of such persons as are experienced, older than we are, and prudent, than to their demonstrations, for their experience gives them an insight into principles.' Thus it is written (Prov 3:5): 'Lean not on thy own prudence,' and (Sirach 6:35): 'Stand in the multitude of the ancients' (i.e. the old men), 'that are wise, and join thyself from thy heart to their wisdom'" (Aquinas, *ST*, II–II 49.3).

before hitting"—knowing full well that this is not always possible in tournament tennis.[21] The same is true with the practice of virtue.[22]

Yet, little will be learned from the most virtuous friend, coach or teacher if a person lacks a teachable spirit. Freedom to "do it my way" is, in many cases, a good thing. We all have our individual preferences, styles, talents and abilities. Humans cannot be happy if they are forced to do everything in conformity to someone else's rules. But neither are we all-knowing. We require the experience of others if we are to achieve wisdom. Our dependence on the knowledge and aid of others both lasts longer and is more extensive than in any other animal species.[23] Even as

21. Sartre argues that there is no such thing as practical knowledge. To illustrate his point he asks us to consider the situation of a student of his who was faced with the choosing between the care of his elderly mother and leaving her to in order to fight for the French Resistance. Sartre asks, "Which does the greater good, the vague act of fighting in a group, or the concrete one of helping a particular human being to go on living? Who can decide *a priori*? Nobody." Sartre, *Existentialism*, 28–30.

Henry Veatch argues that Sartre is partly correct. Such complex issues are impossible to decide a priori, but this is also true of any "decision involving skill or technical know-how" in a complex situation. As an example, Veatch asks us to consider a skilled fisherman, who has just landed a big fish, which requires both hand for his rod and reel. However, the wind is pushing his boat toward a bed of lily pads where his line will be hopelessly entangled. There are no mathematical rules for this sort of situation. But at the same time it is equally clear that there is a big difference between a skilled fisherman and an unskilled novice. Veatch, *Aristotle*, 115.

Even Plato, much more mathematically-inclined than Aristotle, understood the futility of attempting to reduce skills to rules. The genuine craftsman "must not only know general rules of procedure but also how to supply them to the varying individual matter *on* which he works. Such skill can be gained only from actual practice [*Phaedrus*, 271 D–E], since the accidental variations of material things are too manifold to be encompassed in any 'theory' of essential structure." Wild, *Plato's Theory of Man*, 49.

22. As John Bowlin says, Aquinas "indicates that the complexity of action that accords with *recta ratio* [right reason] cannot be codified in a simple set of principles. For this reason he repeatedly insists that the judgments of the wise and the virtuous are our best measure of good and praiseworthy action and the only standard of excellence in practical reasonableness that we can, with good reason, hope for in this life (*ST* I-II 2.1.1; 100.1; II-II 49.3; 52.1.1)."

Of course, Aquinas understands that there are moral principles which summarize the practical deliberations of the wise. "For this reason Aquinas maintains that this side of Eden laws are framed to discipline the young and inexperienced, not the wise. Pedagogical intentions govern their use and dissemination. Laws withdraw the young from the 'undue pleasures' to which they are inclined and restrain them from evil, 'by force and fear' (*ST* I-II 95.1) in order that they might become good (*ST* I-II 92.1) . . . As such, they provide starting points of actions and the proximate source and origin of moral virtues." Bowlin, *Contingency*, 115–16.

23. For example, most dogs are able to live without their parents by the time they are six months old. And on average, dogs will live to be twelve or so years old or 144

we mature and are capable of living on our own, it is still be true that 95 percent of what we know we learned from others.

Yet only some things are easily learned from others. Information that has little or no affect on our self-image can easily be learned from others. For example, I have been told, and I believe, that the winters in Maine are on average colder than the winters in Northern California where I live. Believing this affects my life very little, and demands virtually no change in my actions. However, other things are much more self-involving. Where this is the case, it is much more difficult to learn from others. Here is a somewhat trivial illustration. I have been told, and I believe, that it is good to floss your teeth. This piece of knowledge makes some demands on my actions (that I take the time to floss), but it has minimal affect on my self-image.

However, other things do affect one's self-image and hence are much harder to learn. Here's a personal example. Many years ago, I was a somewhat talented high school tennis player who went on to play college tennis. My new coach was far superior to my previous coaches and he spotted a significant flaw in my game. Now "my game" was much more closely tied to my self-image than my teeth. So it was much harder for me to admit that I would need to change "my game." Learning this sort of humility is much harder than learning to floss nightly.

And it takes even greater humility to acknowledge our moral "vices" (which are usually obvious to our friends!) simply because they are even more deeply connected to our sense of self. To acknowledge a vice is hard; to be willing to remove it is harder. Good friends and teachers can help with both. (We will discuss the notion of self-involving knowledge from a slightly different perspective in 12.3.)

---

months. Most human children are unable to live on their own until they are eight or nine years old. (For humans, independence requires much more than being weaned.) And the average age for humans is around seventy-eight years. In other words, dogs are only dependent for about 4 percent of their life whereas humans are dependent for at least 10 percent of their life. Aristotelians (and evolutionary biologists) think that these sorts of differences between species have significant implications for the sorts of things that are good for different species. In this case, it explains why education is much more important for humans than dogs.

8.5 A GOOD SOCIETY

Good friends can be found even in bad societies. But teaching is essentially a social institution.[24] So in a bad society it is much more difficult to find good teachers than good friends. Yet all Aristotelians would argue that a good society requires virtuous citizens. So where do virtuous citizens come from, if virtue itself requires good teachers? It seems we have gone in a circle. Individual virtue requires good teachers and good teachers are only wide spread in a good society, but a good society is only possible if it is composed of individually virtue citizens.

The problem must be faced. It is fallacious to argue in a viciously circular fashion. But, as we argued in chapter 2, a circular argument is not vicious if its size and scope is sufficiently large. If Copernicus was right, then we ought to obverse a stellar parallax. But neither he nor any of his contemporary could do so. Nonetheless, because Copernicus's theory explained so many other things, most astronomers concluded that the earth really did revolve around the sun even though observations failed to detect a stellar parallax. Deductively speaking, the argument is circular: the earth really moves because Copernicus was right and even though we do not observe a stellar parallax we know it must be there because Copernicus was right. But inductively speaking, a sufficiently large "circle" of interconnected propositions is the very essence of "an argument to the best explanation." So the Aristotelian's strategy is to enlarge the set of ethically and philosophically interconnected propositions as far as possible.

We can enlarge the circle by considering the place of justice in the Aristotelian ethical map. In doing so we will see how happiness, virtue, disciplined habits, good teachers, a good society, and justice are all symbiotically connected and interrelated. And we must not forget the other more philosophical aspects of the teleologically ordered cosmos we have been considering in the six previous chapters which support and are supported by Aristotle's ethics. Doing so makes the circle quite large.

24. "At the beginning of his *Metaphysics* [bk. II, 1, 993b12–15] Aristotle explains the social character of the acquisition of truth and says: 'It is just that we should be grateful not only to those with whose view we may agree, but also to those who have expressed more superficial views; for those also contribute something, by developing, before us, the powers of thought.' And Saint Thomas adds [in his commentary on the *Metaphysics*] 'These men who disagreed with each other compel us to discuss things more strictly and to seek for a more limpid vision of truth.'" Regis, *St. Thomas and Epistemology*, 57–58.

A just society is one in which the material means necessary for a good life—money, health care, time to develop and enjoy one's talents and abilities—are available to all its citizens. Fleshing this out for a "first world" twenty-first century nation would take us far beyond the scope of this book. But two points are directly relevant to this chapter.

First, we agree with Plato: "The citizen must indeed be happy and good and the legislator will seek to make him so; but very rich and very good at the same time he cannot be."[25] More specifically, Plato argued in his last book, *Laws*, that no just society permits a person to own more than five times as much land as the least favored citizen.[26] In *Politics* Aristotle agrees with the thrust of Plato's principle, though he warns against its mindless application.[27] And it would be mindless to enforce Plato's law in the United States today. In ancient Greece, land was the primary means of production. So if we wished to follow Plato's rule today, we would have to consider *capital*, not land. But even if we move from land to capital, questions remain. Why should the ratio be five to one as opposed to four to one or six to one?

We must remember a fundamental Aristotelian dictum: a wise person only seeks as much precision as the subject matter permits.[28] A wise Aristotelian will therefore refuse to give a precise ratio of permissible inequality. But this hardly means that the ratio of rich to poor is of no ethical significance. Current estimates of income inequality in the United States range anywhere from a hundred to one all the way up to four hundred to one. Again, the precise number is unimportant. What is important from an Aristotelian perspective is that the gap between rich and poor has grown so wide as to make any sense of common justice impossible.

Whether a ratio of ten to one or twenty to one or even forty to one will preserve a sense of common justice is not a question that currently needs an answer. Should a person walk three miles a day or five miles a day? For some people, that is a question worth asking, but to the person who walks no more than thirty steps a day, the important question is already answered—you need to walk much more. Likewise, the important

25. Plato *Laws* bk. 5, 742.
26. Ibid., 744.
27. Aristotle *Politics* bk. II, ch. 7.
28. Aristotle *Nicomachean Ethics* bk. 2, ch. 2, 1104a8.

question for Americans is also answered: we need to drastically reduce our inequality.

The second point is that without a common sense of justice, no society can be more than a disparate collection of individuals. In one of his earlier more theoretical works—*The Republic*—Plato forbid a nation's rulers to own *any* silver, gold, or property because he was fearful that they would seek political power as a way to increase their wealth. Aristotelians have similar fears, though they add another consideration. A couple section back, we distinguished between needs and wants. And while we argued that the pursuit of some wants has a legitimate place in a virtuous and a truly happy life, we said that the pursuit of fame and power should never be pursued because they are always harmful.

The problem with the *pursuit*[29] of either power or fame is that it turns social relations into a zero-sum game—when one person has more, other people by definition have less. Contrast this with the pursuit of knowledge. One person's pursuit of knowledge does not negatively affect other people's pursuit of knowledge. If anything, it makes it easier. The cliché is true—"knowledge wants to be free."[30] The problem with the pursuit of power or fame is that it is de facto the pursuit of inequality. So what is wrong with inequality? Nothing, as long as it is within limits. But the unbridled pursuit of inequality destroys society.

As we already hinted when discussing our dependence on other people's experience, in addition to being rational animals, humans are also social animals.[31] Social relations can only exist among individuals that are in some sense equal. Strong and significant bonds can be formed

29. We must distinguish between the pursuits of power and power itself. Only the former is pernicious. Political power which is *given* to some by others for the good of the whole is not only good; it is necessary. It is the same with fame; only its pursuit is pernicious. The honor that is free bestowed by others for excellent achievements is a spur to virtue. What is more, fame that is manufactured by "PR campaigns" goes as quickly as it comes.

30. Of course, the proprietary search for technical knowledge that is becoming more common in our culture is anything but free. But the pursuit of this sort of knowledge is really the pursuit of money.

31. Actually, humans' rational and social natures are themselves symbiotically related. In the twentieth century, followers of Wittgenstein emphasized the impossibility of a "private language." All languages are essentially social products. As we saw in chapter 7, rationality is the ability to reason conceptually and concepts are given in definitions. Thus, rationality and language are essentially connected. So here we have another "circle."

between people and their pets, but they are not *social* bonds since social relations are necessarily reciprocal relations. The person/pet relation is too one-sided for that. The master/slave relation is also too one-sided to be social in our sense. (Ironically, Aristotle's own blindness to the fact that "barbarians" were as human as Greeks makes this point. It was the "barbarians" who constituted the majority of slaves in the Greek city/states, and of course, "barbarians" were never citizens because it was understood that the relation between masters and slaves was too one-side to be fully social.) The fact that we are social animals explains why the pursuit of power and fame beyond the limits of justice is always destructive of society, and ultimately, self-destructive—it severs the symbiotic circle of relations that result in the good and happy life. These are summed up in the chart at the end of this chapter.

In the next chapter, we will consider freedom—both its nature and place in a good life.

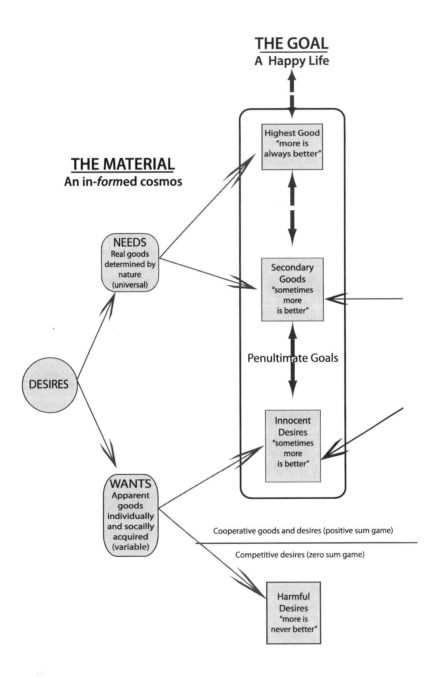

THE MEANS
Ethical/Political
Virtue

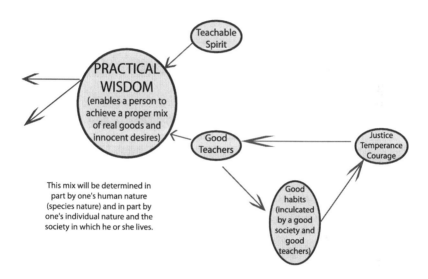

Teachable Spirit

PRACTICAL WISDOM
(enables a person to achieve a proper mix of real goods and innocent desires)

Good Teachers

Justice Temperance Courage

Good habits (inculcated by a good society and good teachers)

This mix will be determined in part by one's human nature (species nature) and in part by one's individual nature and the society in which he or she lives.

They are destructive of the good society which is a necessary means to real goods and to the satisfaction of innocuous desires

9

Are Humans Really Free?

Whether or not humans have a free will depends upon what a person means by the term. Many people assume that having a "free will" means that a person's actions must be physically uncaused.

Most people who are enamored of the sciences are of the opinion that by this definition no "free wills" exist. Everything we know about the physical universe, including human beings, points to the fact that nothing happens without a physical cause. Of course, we do not know *the physical cause of many things, including the physical antecedents which determine human choices. Yet to insist that these have no physical cause stifles the scientific study of the human brain and nervous system. Thus, belief in "free will" must be rejected by all who study humans scientifically.*

Many philosophers accept the reasoning of this last paragraph. But they believe that there is another definition of "free will" which is compatible with a modern scientific understanding of humans. These philosophers are called compatibilists. Compatibilists believe that humans are free whenever (1) their actions are not compelled and (2) they are carrying out their own wants and desires. Compatibilists do not deny that a person's wants and desires also have physical causes which are open to scientific investigation. They only deny that these physical causes in-and-of themselves are coercive. Furthermore, they argue that this understanding of free will makes good sense of our common belief that the whole point of rewards and punishments is to encourage good behavior and discourage bad behavior.

Still other philosophers find the compatibilist definition of "free will" unacceptable because it ipso facto *denies that a person could have done otherwise. These philosophers, called libertarians, argue that the ability "to have done otherwise" is absolutely essential to our understanding of moral responsibility. If our wants and desires are really determined by antecedent physical causes in the brain (as compatibilists maintain), then even when we are doing what we "want to do" we are not truly free (and hence, responsible) because by hypothesis our "wants and desires" could not have been otherwise. Therefore, libertarians reject the assumption of modern science that absolutely everything has a physical cause. When faced with an important moral decision, libertarians argue that the will is absolutely free and independent of all physical causation. Instead, these choices are solely determined by an immaterial volition, i.e., by our autonomous will.*

Finally, Aristotelian realists provide a third definition of "free will". Their position presupposes a distinction between causation and determinism. Events which are humanly predictable are determined, but not all events with physical causes are even in principle predictable. For example, we can predict that a flipped coin will fall down, but we cannot predict whether it will land head or tails. To make such a prediction would require accurate information about "the microscopic structure of the whole world" and this is humanly impossible. In Aristotle's own terminology, events which are determined have a per se *efficient cause whereas all other events only have a* per accidens *efficient cause. A free choice, then, is defined by Aristotelians as one that is (1) caused but not determined and (2) directed by reason to a good (or at least apparently good) end.*

Comparing and contrasting the libertarian and Aristotelian definition of "free will" we can say: 1) The libertarian position presupposes a mind/body dualism; the Aristotelian position does not. 2) The libertarian position assumes that free will is an all-or-nothing affair since every event is either caused or uncaused; the Aristotelian position assumes that freedom is a more-or-less affair since rationality is itself a more-or-less affair. 3) The libertarian position assumes that morality is episodic and that free choices are relatively rare (otherwise any scientific study of human behavior would be impossible); the Aristotelian position assumes that morality is an on-going and ever present condition so that our "big" moral decisions flow naturally from the imperceptible set of values and priorities we are continuously constructing every moment of our waking life.

IN THE PREVIOUS TWO chapters we considered the modern dualisms of body versus mind and fact versus value. And in both chapters we described the Aristotelian alternative integrating these dualisms into a single unified whole. In chapter 6 we argued that our intellect *in*-forms our body as meaning informs words, not as dirt is *in* rugs. In chapter 7 we argued that virtues are universal recipes for human flourishing. As such, they are *both* "facts" about the universe and "values" about how we ought to act. In this chapter we argue that humans are truly free when their actions are guided by reason. This requires that their actions are not physically determined, but it does not require physical *gaps* in the way our bodies and brains operate.

9.1 THE BLOCK UNIVERSE OF DETERMINISM

The most fundamental law of modern science is that mass/energy is always conserved. In other words, there is never more mass and/or energy in an effect than there is in a cause. For example, when one billiard ball hits another billiard ball, the direction and motion of the second ball is wholly determined by the direction and motion of the first ball. In street language, if we imagine:

1. If a perfectly hard and round billiard ball hits another perfectly hard and round billiard ball

2. of precisely the same weight

3. on a table perfectly flat and hard so that there is no rolling friction (or air resistance) and their centers are in perfect alignment, then

4. the second ball must (according to the conservation law) move in a straight line at precisely the same speed as the first.

5. Furthermore, since the cause and effect relation between these two balls is completely specified, we can "chain together" cause and effect relations indefinitely without gain or loss of speed or deviation from a straight line.

$$A \rightarrow B \rightarrow C \rightarrow D \rightarrow E$$

Figure 9.1

Finally, though this may come as a surprise to some, there is nothing that is distinctly modern or scientific about the law of conservation. The third principle of Aristotelian realism—nothing comes from nothing—is its exact equivalent.

The conservation laws of modern science and the third principle of Aristotelian natural philosophy *seem* to imply that we live in what William James (1842–1910) described as a "block universe." In such a universe, he writes, "those parts of the universe already laid down absolutely appoint and decree what the other parts shall be. The future has no ambiguous possibilities hidden in its womb: the part we call the present is compatible with only one totality. Any other future complement than the one fixed from eternity is impossible. The whole is in each and every part, and welds it with the rest into an absolute unity, an iron block, in which there can be no equivocation or shadow of turning."[1]

James unequivocally rejects such a universe because, if the universe really is one big block, then how can humans be free? If our bodies and brains are merely parts in one big block, then is not everything a person does, as James said, "fixed from eternity"? There are three modern responses to this question: Hard Determinism, Soft Determinism (compatibilism), and the libertarian theory of free will.

Hard determinism says in essence, "Get used to it! The idea that everything we do is determined by the laws of chemistry and physics may be hard to accept emotionally, but to deny the universal validity of modern science is a futile attempt to roll back the clock. We must courageously face the fact that we are electro-chemical machines. We are the biological product of evolution here on earth and the chemical product of exploding stars throughout the rest of the universe. That makes us literal 'stardust' and nothing more. Believing anything else returns us to the superstitions of the dark ages." In short, hard determinists argue that "free will" is an illusion.

This is not a uniquely modern theory. The Atomists of ancient Greece and the Stoics and Epicureans of ancient Rome both articulated and advocated this sort of mechanistic universe. They were also the first to argue that, by eliminating the gods and religion, we were free to live without guilt here on earth and fear of punishment after we die.[2]

We have, however, already discussed (chapter 7) the philosophical problems with the materialist's attempts to reduce human's conceptual abilities to brain states or functions. And prior to that we argued that it is

1. James, *Essays in Pragmatism*, 40–41. The reference to a "block-universe" is found on p. 63.

2. The currently popularizers of atheism—Richard Dawkins, Daniel Dennett, Sam Harris, and Christopher Hitchens—are, at their best, contemporary Stoics.

impossible to understand how Socrates sitting and Socrates standing are the same person without some sort of philosophical distinction between form and matter. And even if materialists could solve these difficulties, the materialist's promise of annihilation at death may be a cold, cruel fact about reality, but it is hard for most people to hope that they are correct. In any case, we have nothing more to add to our previous objections to a purely materialistic philosophy.

9.2 THE COMPATIBILIST THEORY OF FREEDOM

"Soft Determinism" is James's sarcastic term for those who celebrate human freedom and dignity while giving free reign to the scientific search for natural laws at the same time. Freedom and determinism, James insists, cannot be reconciled. We can hold fast to human freedom and dignity *or* we can cast our lot with the scientists in their never ending search for laws of nature, including those which govern humans. But we cannot have both; the choice is forced. In the century prior to James, Immanuel Kant made the same point by contemptuously referring to such "freedom" as the "freedom of the turnspit."[3]

Nonetheless, many contemporary philosophers defend "soft determinism." They argue that there is no need to choose between modern science and an ethical understanding in which humans are responsible and free moral agents. Determinism and free will, they say, are compatible. These compatibilists (to use the less contentious term) define freedom as the ability to act on one's *own* wants and desires, even if those wants and desires are ultimately caused by electro-chemical reactions in the brain.

For example, if a thief points a gun at a bank teller and demands money, we hold the thief, not the teller, responsible for the bank's loss, even though it was the teller who physically removed the money from the vault. But if a person has an epileptic seizure and breaks an expensive antique vase, we do not (at least morally speaking) hold him responsible for the antique store's loss. The difference is that the thief got what he wanted (someone else's money), whereas the epileptic neither wanted nor desired to break an expensive vase.

---

3. Kant, *Critique of Practical Reason*, 101. Just before that he says, "it is a wretched subterfuge to seek an escape in the supposition" that there is a kind of causality which is internal to the agent and is therefore compatible with freedom. Ibid., 99.

Furthermore, though all of us have wanted to kick, throw, or somehow "hurt" inanimate objects that cause us harm, we understand how silly and counter productive such acts of vengeance really are. For the same reason, to "punish" the epileptic for breaking the vase would be nothing but an act of childish vengeance. But punishing a thief, when he is caught, is neither silly nor counter productive because it is likely to deter both the thief and other would be thieves from robbing banks. The fact that the thief's desire to rob banks was itself a product of theoretically predictable electro-chemical reactions in his brain is irrelevant according to the compatibilist.

Here is why: A scientific view of humans assumes that a person's wants and desires are ultimately the product of their genetic makeup and the environment in which they were born and raised. So let us assume that some particular person is genetically predisposed to thievery and was never taught that stealing is wrong. And let us also assume that this person's predispositions are so strong that whenever a gun is available and he is short of cash, his brain produces an overwhelming desire to rob a bank. Our immediate reaction is that if this really were the case, then it would be wrong for society to "punish" such a person for robbing banks since he would not have had a choice. After all, people do not choose their own genes or the setting into which they were born.

But our immediate reaction, says the compatibilist, is misguided. First, while this person did not choose his genes or environment, his actions were nonetheless voluntary because they freely flowed from his own wants and desires. It is not as if someone made him act *against* his own will. Furthermore, the fact that the wants and desires of a thief are the causally predictable product of his biological and social setting means that punishing him will *also* have a predictable outcome. Punishment changes both beliefs and brains. And even the credible threat of punishment changes a person's social setting. So by holding thieves responsible for their actions we are, in effect, "reprogramming their brains" and changing their future wants and desires. Next time they find themselves with a gun in their hand and short of cash, their wants and desires will be different. They will, so to speak, "think twice" before robbing another person. And is not this precisely what "holding someone responsible" is all about?

Second, compatibilists argue that their position becomes even stronger when we consider the alternative theory. Suppose a person's wants and desires were *not* the predictable product of biology and so-cial settings. Suppose, in other words, that a person's will was uncaused. Punishment would become senseless. If a free act is uncaused, then appropriate punishment of past actions would have no predictable af-fect on future choices and thus it would have no effect as a deterrent. It is the *denial* of determinism, not determinism itself, which destroys moral responsibility. Uncaused actions, rather than being the paradigm of freedom and responsibility, are in fact nothing but the capricious and meaningless "movements" of one's body.

There is, however, an objection to the compatibilists argument. If a person's wants and desires are the inevitable product of his genes and social setting, then even if a person's actions flow freely from their own wants and desires, his actions are not voluntary because at no point did this person make a real choice. Moreover, if this person's "wants and desires" were fully determined by his genes and social setting, then they *compel* his actions just as much as if he were being physically forced to act.

Compatibilists respond by distinguishing between causation and compulsion. Their justification for this distinction is found in David Hume's theory of causation. Prior to Hume, when people said that "A causes B" they naively believed there was a necessary connection be-tween A and B. But Hume argues that no matter how carefully we *ob-serve* one billiard ball hitting another billiard ball, even with the most sophisticated scientific instruments, we will never detect any "necessity" connecting the two balls. In Hume's own words, "All events seem entirely loose and separate. One event follows another; but we never can observe any tie between them. They seem conjoined, but never connected."[4] Causation is nothing more than "constant conjunction." No one has ever *observed* anything like A *making* B happen. If Hume is right, "force," "compulsion" and "coercion" are never present in any physical relations. Only people can make, force, compel, and coerce other people to do something. Therefore, on Hume's theory of causation it is misleading to say that a person's actions were *compelled* by the electro-chemical ac-tions in his brain.

The reason, in other words, we punish thieves, but not epileptics, is *not* because the thief's actions are uncaused, whereas the epileptic's were caused. Rather, we punish thieves because it will deter future acts

4. Hume, *Enquiry*, Section VII "Of the Idea of Necessary Connection," part II.

of thievery whereas "punishing" epileptics will do nothing to prevent future seizures.

9.3 THE LIBERTARIAN THEORY
OF AUTONOMOUS FREEDOM

Compatibilists want to give science universal reign while retaining human responsibility and freedom. According to libertarians, they end up doing neither. By reducing causation to mere "constant conjunction" they destroy the fundamental distinction between real causation and mere correlation. Remember Emerson Hall (chapter 3.2). There might well be a perfect correlation between entering Emerson Hall and being unable to speak Inuit. But this is not a causal law. Real science requires much more than constant conjunction.

Nor do compatibilists save moral responsibility by reducing it to mere deterrence. When someone is properly punished for their free and wrongful actions, it would be nice if the punishment also had a deterrent affect. But deterrence does not define responsibility. The point of punishment is *not* merely to deter crime. If it were, we might as well "punish" the innocent. Imagine a murder in a small town. Over a period of several months, the police collect much evidence, but no suspect. Finally, they find a person to whom all the evidence points. However, when the chief of police interrogates the person, the alleged murderer hands him a dated picture proving that he was no where near the crime scene.

If the only point of punishment is to deter crime, then the chief of police should take the picture, destroy it and send the man to trial. Everyone else would think that this was a case of a murderer being caught and punished, so the deterrent effect would be the same as if the guilty person was punished. But clearly this would be wrong. And if framing an innocent man for its deterrent affect is wrong, then so is "punishing" people whose genes and social setting left them no real *choice*.

According to libertarians, by misguidedly attempting to reconcile determinism and freedom, compatibilists end up losing both. The only rational course is to place limits on science to make room for morality and freedom.[5]

---

5. Kant famously writes in the preface to the second edition of his most famous work, *The Critique of Pure Reason*, that "I have therefore found it necessary to deny *knowledge*, in order to make room for *faith*." Kant's trinity of faith includes freedom, immortality, and God.

However, limiting science, libertarians insist, is not the same as eliminating science. They are quite willing to give science an unchecked reign over the vast majority of physical events. The growth of the body, digestion, the random blinking of the eyes, the uncontrolled ticks and spasms resulting from electro-chemical defeats in the brain are all fit topics for scientific investigation. It is only moral choices, according to libertarians, that transcend the limits of science.

When the issue is moral choice there is, as Kant said, "absolute spontaneity of the will."[6] The only thing "which elevates man above himself as a part of the world of sense" is his "freedom and independence from the mechanism of nature."[7] Furthermore, the independence of humans' will is complete and unblemished. "A physical propensity (grounded in sensuous impulses) toward any use of freedom whatsoever—whether good or bad—is a contradiction."[8] In short, at the moment of moral choice, the conservation laws of physics are suspended. Frequently, this is referred to as "contra-causal freedom."

We can picture an autonomous will like this.

Figure 9.2

On the left, the letters A through F represent a person's actions as they would be if there was no free will. The arrows represent the causal connections open to scientific study. On the right, a person's free choice (C1) changes the course of a person's actions. The gap between "C" and "D" represents a moral choice were there is no physical cause. Yet, the

6. Kant, *Religion,* 19.

7. Kant, *Critique of Practical Reason,* 89.

8. According to Kant, the only "incentive," "ground," "inclination or natural impulse" for any truly free choice is a maxim. Now since a maxim is "a rule made by the will," and since choices of the will are absolutely spontaneous, it follows that a person's maxims— the ultimate ground of one's morality—are themselves adopted with absolute spontaneity. Kant, *Religion,* 17–26. This is one of the last books Kant wrote and is perhaps the most readable. It was also written to directly address the place of divine grace in Christianity which is the topic of the last chapter. For all these reasons, our discussion of Kant will focus on this work rather than his more famous *Critiques* or his *Introduction to the Metaphysics of Morals.*

effect "D" is not random since it is caused "immaterially" by C^1 which is the autonomous will.

Libertarians acknowledge that "immaterial" causation is utterly mysterious. Kant writes, humans' "ability to master all opposing motivating forces through the bare idea of a [moral] law is utterly inexplicable." He says the "subjective principle of morality . . . lies hidden in the incomprehensible attribute of freedom." He also says that, "the ultimate subjective ground of the adoption of moral maxims is inscrutable."[9] Nonetheless, libertarians say we have the strongest possible evidence for such autonomous freedom. All we have to do is to look inward and consider what happens during the moment of moral choice. Here we have undeniable first hand evidence that our choices are caused by nothing other than our own will.

Furthermore, limiting the scope of science in this way will not result in chaos or "anything goes" since genuine moral choices are relatively rare. Most of what we do, we do out of habit. Here there is no reason to doubt the scientific descriptions of our brains. Nor is the fact that science has yet to observe the will acting contra-causally a conclusive argument. After all, none of Copernicus's contemporaries observed a stellar parallax. But this did not prove that he was wrong. And remember, it was almost three hundred years after Copernicus died that a parallax was first observed. Neural-biology has only been investigating the inter workings of the brain for fifty years. The fact that it has yet to observe the precise location of the will's interventions in brain processes is hardly surprising.

Finally, even though there is no specific evidence of causal gaps in brain process, quantum mechanics has demonstrated the existence of causal gaps at the sub-atomic level. So it is more than idle speculation to suppose that such gaps also exist in our brains.

9.4 CAUSATION VERSUS DETERMINISM

Aristotelians agree with libertarians that hard determinism is inconsistent with our most fundamental moral convictions. Aristotelians also agree with libertarians that properly understood punishment is more than deterrence and that Hume's theory of causation destroys real science (4.3). However, Aristotelians reject the libertarian's notion of an autono-

9. Kant, *Religion*, 52n, 158n, 17n, cf. 133, 179.

mous will and the mind/body dualism it assumes. Instead, Aristotelians argue for a fully integrated universe where human freedom and human rationality are an essential unity, just as the meaning of a word and the ink out of which it is made are an essential unity. But before considering their proposal, we must first discuss the difference between causation and determinism.

Little mistakes at the beginning of an argument, said Aristotle, can have big consequences at the end of the argument. Determinists (of both the "hard" and "soft" variety) and libertarians make such a mistake. Their mistake is to equate causation and determinism. When these are equated there are only two possibilities: 1) every event is caused and therefore determined or 2) some events are not determined because they are uncaused. In this section we will argue that this is a false dichotomy.[10] There is a third alternative. An act can be caused, but not determined.

Furthermore, this third alternative is not the result of esoteric and hair-splitting philosophy. It is simple common sense. Consider, for example, the flipping of a coin or the rolling of dice. We can predict that a flipped coin will soon fall down (rather than orbit the earth) and that a rolled pair of dice will come to a stop (rather than circling the globe). However, we cannot predict whether a flipped coin will land "heads" (as opposed to "tails") or that rolled dice will show an "eleven" (as opposed to a "seven" or "eight," etc.) *even though both of these are wholly the result of antecedent causal factors.*

Whenever the number of causal factors involved makes human prediction impossible, the event is caused, but not determined. According to Aristotelians, events which are determined/predictable are a *subset* of caused events; that is, all determined events are caused, but not all caused events are determined. In short, "caused" and "determined" are *not* equivalent terms. Once this simple distinction is made, there are many examples of events falling inside the set of "caused" events but outside the set of "determined/predictable." It is neither determined nor predictable that:

---

10. Put bluntly, William James is *wrong* when he says of determinism that "Fortunately, no ambiguities hang about this word or about its opposite, indeterminism . . . The truth must lie with one side or the other, and its lying with one side makes the other false." James, *Essays in Pragmatism*, 40–41.

- a single falling oak leaf would land precisely where it did

- Ronald Reagan would die on June 5, 2004, at the aged of ninety-three in Bel Air, California

- a particular rock would have a C-shaped crack on its flat side

- a giant meteorite would hit the Yucatan Peninsula on a particular day 65 million years ago

- a particular person, on a particular day would be struck by lightning

Yet, all of these are caused. Their unpredictability is not due to a gap in the causal sequences.[11] Rather, the unpredictability results from the extreme complexity of the causal factors involved.[12]

Determinists and Libertarians both object to this Aristotelian picture, but for different reasons. Determinists argue that the distinction between "caused" and "determined" is at best verbal. They argue that it is *only* our current lack of knowledge, either of the causal laws involved or of the initial conditions, which make the above list of events unpredict-

11. Contrary to William James, who says in his famous essay, "The Dilemma of Determinism," that "future human volitions are as a matter of fact the only ambiguous [uncaused] things we are tempted to believe in." James, *Essays in Pragmatism,* 44.

12. Here is an example, using purely Newtonian physics, of what we mean by "extreme complexity." Consider the impact of balls on an ordinary pool table. It is fairly easy to calculate what will happen on the first impact. The second is harder, but not impossible. However, by the ninth impact, the calculations become virtually impossible because "you need to take into account the gravitational pull of someone standing next to the table . . . And to compute the fifty-sixth impact, every single elementary particle of the universe needs to be present in your assumptions! An electron at the edge of the universe, separated from us by 10 billion light-years, must figure in the calculations, since it exerts a meaningful effect on the outcome." Taleb, *Black Swan,* 178. The calculations from Michael Berry are found in Berry, "Regular and Irregular Motion, in Topics in Nonlinear Mechanics."

When we consider the human brain, the degree of complexity becomes even greater. "Given 100 billion neurons each with an average of around 3,000 connections, each human being has something like 1,000 trillion (10^{14}) synaptic switches. If each of these synapses can assume 1 of 10 conductive levels we have 10100,000,000,000,000 potentially distinct brain states. If one assumes the 99.9 percent of these make no functional difference, we are still left with 1099,999,999,999,997 functionally unique states. If you further assume that 99.9 percent of these are unconscious, 1099,999,999,999,994 distinct conscious states are possible. By comparison, there is estimated to be something on the order of 10^{87} elementary particles in the universe." From Owen Flanagan, *Consciousness Reconsidered,* 35–37, cited in Brown, *Whatever happened to the Soul?,* 227.

able. *In principle*, determinists argue, all events belong within the smaller circle. Here, libertarians are in basic agreement with the determinist. All the events listed above, they would say, are in principle predictable for the same reason. Their only disagreement with determinists is that they believe there are a few events—those resulting from our free moral choices—that are uncaused. (See figure 9.3 for a picture of these three positions.)

Aristotelian's have several objections to determinism. The first two are conceptual.

First, Aristotelians argue that the phrase "in principle" makes determinism conceptually vacuous. Determinists say: "If a person knew enough, then that person could predict anything."[13] Aristotelians repeat the argument concerning the weight lifter who boasted that if he worked hard enough, he could bench press a 1,000 pounds (chapter 6.1). So too, in this context "enough" means "everything needed to make a prediction." Thus to claim that everything is *in principle* predictable is equivalent to: "If someone knew everything he needed to make all predictions, then that person could make all predictions." True, but not very informative.

Second, determinists ignore the conceptual distinction between predicting and performing. Many things by definition can never be *predicted*; they can only be *performed*. For example, people can make choices, but nobody can predict their own future choices. To do so is to *de facto* make the choice. If a person "predicts" that tomorrow they will *choose* to go swimming, and if the "prediction" is valid, they have in fact made the choice *today* to go swimming tomorrow.[14] Again: People

---

13. This point is frequently referred to as Laplace's Demon. Laplace famously said, "We ought then to regard the present state of the universe as the effect of its anterior state and as the cause of the one which is to follow. Given for one instant an intelligence which could comprehend all the forces by which nature is animated and the respective situation of the beings who compose it—an intelligence sufficiently vast to submit these data to analysis—it would embrace in the same formula the movements of the greatest bodies of the universe and those of the lightest atom; for it, nothing would be uncertain and the future, as the past, would be present to its eyes." Laplace, *Philosophical Essay*, 4.

14. Some have argued that while predicting one's *own* choices is impossible, *other* people can predict one's choice. But even this is impossible. For Sam to be able to predict what Sally will do, Sam will have to obtain the relevant data concerning the initial conditions effecting Sally's choice. But this means that Sam must be in "causal contact" with Sally. So, since Sam cannot predict his own actions, Sam can not predict whether or not he will act in such a way vis-à-vis Sally that would falsify his original prediction. I flesh this argument out in more detail in Chapter 10 of *In Defense of the Soul*. Included there are numerous references to other works which have made the same point.

invent things, but nobody can predict when some new gadget will be invented. Suppose a caveman "predicts" that in the future people use a device made of a flat piece of wood in the shape of a disc that rotates on a shaft or axle to move heavy objects. This caveman will not have *predicted* the invention of the wheel; they will have done it. When we consider how radically people's choices and inventions have changed the course of history, the scope and significance of conceptually unpredictable events like these becomes enormous.

There are also three empirical (i.e., "scientific") objections to determinism. First, there is the threshold argument. Determinism gains much of its plausibility by assuming that small differences in initial conditions will only produce small differences in outcomes. For example, no artillery officer can predict precisely where an artillery shell will land given the viability in temperature, wind directions and velocities, powder density, etc. But as he gains more precise measurements of the initial conditions, he will be able to predict more precisely where the shell will land. In cases like these, it is reasonable to assume that increased knowledge of initial conditions will produce more precise predictions.

But most "predictions" are not like this. Scientists studying "chaos" now realize what common sense has known for ages: nature is riddled with thresholds (or in their jargon, "non-linear systems").[15] In terms of jumping ability, there is not much difference between Aaron who can jump thirty feet and Phil who can jump twenty-nine feet and eleven inches. But if forced to jump a thirty foot chasm, Aaron will live and Phil will die. The old saying, "Close only counts in horse shoes and hand grenades" is a bit of an exaggeration, but nonetheless, there are many instances where a seemingly insignificant difference in a cause will make a huge difference in the effect. A butterfly flapping her wings in Moscow, we now acknowledge, can affect the weather in Montréal three days hence.

Second, there is the measurement problem. There will always be some discrepancy between our measurements and the reality we are measuring (or as philosophers say, between epistemology and ontology). For example, temperature varies along a continuum, but our measurement of temperature will only be accurate to a given number of decimals.

---

15. "Chaotic systems" need not be "complex." The motion of a simple double pendulum is theoretically unpredictable. There are many simulations of double pendulums on the internet. Here's one, http://www.myphysicslab.com/dbl_pendulum.html.

Suppose we have a thermometer accurate to two decimal places. And suppose that a crucial "tipping point" occurs at exactly 32 degrees (e.g., the ice on a lake will not support invading troops). That means that for all readings below 31.99 and above 32.01 a General planning an invasion will be able to predict whether the ice will support his troops. But if the reading is 32.00, no prediction is possible. Such a reading is consistent with *actual* temperatures of anywhere between 31.996 and 32.004.

Third, there is the hopelessly entangled argument. When gathering data concerning extremely small things (e.g., electrons), all measurements will have a causal affect on the object being measured. No one can see a baseball in a dark room. But by turning on a light we cause photons to bounce off of the baseball, many of which then enter our eyes, and thus the location of the baseball becomes visible. But if we are trying to locate an electron, such a strategy will not work. Since photons and electrons are basically the same size, bouncing photons off of an electron will have a significant effect on the location of the electrons. Thus, by the time the photons bouncing off of the electron reach our eyes, the electron will be someplace else.

And we must again remember that very small causes can have very large effects. For example, place a Geiger counter in a box with an explosive device. Set the trigger on the bomb to explode on the 1,000th "click" of the Geiger counter. It will be humanly impossible to predict when the bomb will explode because it is humanly impossible to predict when the 1,000th random alpha-particle will be detected.

While libertarians frequently cite such cases as examples of uncaused events, Aristotelian realists agree with founder of the "Uncertainty Principle," Werner Heisenberg: "We know the forces in the atomic nucleus that are responsible for the emission of the alpha-particle [electron]. But this knowledge contains the uncertainty which is brought about *by the interaction* between the nucleus and the rest of the world. If we wanted to know why the alpha-particle was emitted at that particular time we would have to know *the microscopic structure of the whole world*, including ourselves, and that is impossible [emphasis added]." [16] The uncertainty is not, says Heisenberg, the result of an uncaused event. Rather, it is the result of the number and complexity of the relevant causes, in this case, "the microscopic structure of the whole world." Predicting when the bomb we previously described would explode would literally

16. Heisenberg, *Physics and Philosophy*, 89–90.

require knowledge of the location and momentum of every particle in the universe.[17]

Finally, as we have noted before, the authority and prestige of physicists is now being matched by the authority and prestige of biologists. When physics dominated the sciences, it was easier to assume that "scientific prediction" and "scientific explanation" meant the same thing. After all, the process used to *predict* where a planet will be and to *explain* where a planet has been were one-in-the same. The term "retro-diction" was even used to suggest that prediction and explanations were nothing more than the flip sides of the same coin.

The raising status of biology has changed all that. No biologist has ever suggested that the course of evolution could have been predicted. As they like to say, there are too many "stochastic processes" involved. (A "stochastic process" is one that is governed by random chance. Or in our terminology, it is an event which is caused but not predictable.) While we can explain *after the fact* the evolutionary results of these random processes, it would have been impossible to predict the course of evolution *prior to the fact*.[18] Evolutionary biologists are a little like sports announcers—neither can predict what is going to happen, but afterwards both will explain how random errors produced winners and losers.

While Aristotle wrote on a wide range of topics, they were all informed by his biological investigations. So we should not be surprised to see Aristotle anticipating contemporary biologists' investigations of stochastic processes. He did this with his distinction between "*per se* efficient causes" and "*per accidens* efficient causes." We will explain.

As we said in chapter 4, efficient causes *make* things happen; final causes explain why something happened. "*Per se*" is simply the Latin word for "in or by itself" and "*per accidens*" means "by accident" or "*not* in or

---

17. And even if we had this information, any attempt to actually perform the calculations would be stymied by the "Three Body Problem," i.e., the impossibility of algorithmically calculating the interaction of three or more gravitational bodies.

18. "The theory of natural selection can describe and explain phenomena with considerable precision, but it cannot make reliable predictions, except through such trivial and meaningless circular statements as, for instance: 'The fitter individuals will on the average leave more offspring.' Scriven has emphasized quite correctly that one of the most important contributions to philosophy made by the evolutionary theory is that it has demonstrated the independence of explanation and prediction." Mayr, *Toward a New Philosophy of Biology*, 32.

by itself."[19] For example, all mammals, in or by themselves, have lungs, kidneys, and hair. But not all mammals, in or by themselves, have black hair—some have brown hair; others have white hair. In other words, it is *per se* that mammals have hair; it is *per accidens* that a particular mammal has black hair.

A *per se* efficient cause is grounded in a thing's essential nature and thereby makes predictions possible. Heaviness (or, more precisely, mass) is part of the essence of stones. Thus we can predict that unsupported stones (other things being equal) will fall to the ground. Heaviness (or, more accurately, mass) is also part of the essence of dice. However, it is not part of the essence of the wood or plastic out of which dice are made that any particular side will have three dots (as opposed to one, two, four, five, or six). Thus, while we can predict that dice will fall, we cannot predict that it will land with three dots facing up. There is a *per se* efficient cause of dice falling; but there are only *per accidens* efficient causes for dice landing with three dots up.

We can map this distinction onto the circles in figure 9.3. The innermost circle contains the class of events with *per se* efficient causes. The area inside the middle (but outside the inner circle) contains the class of event with only *per accidens* efficient causes. The area outside the middle circle contains the class of events with no efficient cause. Both Aristotelians and determinist believe this area to be empty; only libertarians believe that some events reside here.

- *Determinism*: all events belong within the inner circle and the outer two circles are empty

- *Aristotle*: the outer circle is empty; the middle circle includes most events; the inner circle contains some events.

- *Libertarian*: the outer circle contains a few events; the middle circle is empty; the inner circle contains the most events.

---

19. Accidents are not uncaused events. "Nor does an accident have any determinate cause, but only a contingent or chance cause, i.e., an indeterminate one. For it was by accident that someone came to Aegina; and if he did not come there in order to get these, but because he was driven there by a storm or was captured by pirates, the event has occurred and is an accident; yet not of itself but by reason of something else." Aristotle *Metaphysics* bk. 4, ch. 30. Aquinas glosses this last phrase, "by another external cause." Aquinas, *Commentary*, sec. 1141; vol. 1, 422.

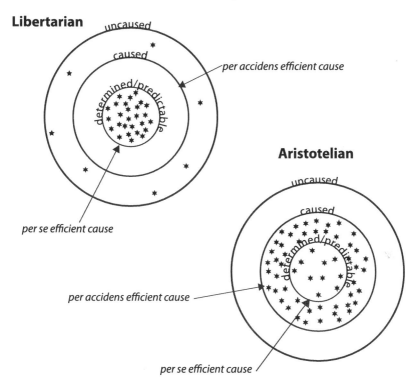

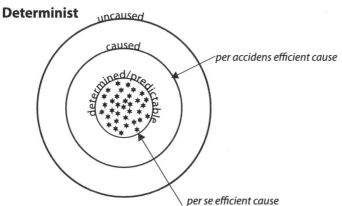

Figure 9.3

9.5 PROBLEMS WITH LIBERTARIANISM

There are three fundamental problems with the Libertarian theory of freedom. First, it presupposes an unnecessary dualism between body and mind. The sort of autonomous will described by Kant (8.1) exists in a realm distinct from everything else we know. We already argued in chapters 2 and 5 that coherence is a crucial test of truth. Any theory that assumes two distinct realms (only connected in the most elusive way) is by definition not as coherent as a theory which integrates the two into a single realm. (That is one important reason Newton's theory—which integrated the celestial and terrestrial spheres—was judged superior to the older Two-Sphere theory of the universe.) In chapter 6, we described how Aristotelians integrate "body" and "mind," so there is no need to say more about that here.

Second, an uncaused choice is not significantly different from a capricious choice. Libertarians correctly assume that whenever a person is morally obligated to act in a particular way, then that person must be *free* (i.e., "able") to act as required.[20] It makes no sense to command a person to do that which is physically impossible to do. While we might reasonably request children to make their bed, but we never request children to fly like birds. Frequently philosophers make this point by saying that "ought implies can." If a person ought to do something, then they must be *able* to do it. And, conversely, if a person is not able to do something, then it cannot be the case that they ought to do it.

Where libertarians go wrong is to assume that moral responsibility requires that a person be able to act otherwise, *even if absolutely everything else about the situation remains the same.* This is simply another way of expressing their idea of contra-causal freedom. If two genetically identical people, with two identical histories, placed in two identical situations are faced with a moral decision, then libertarians believe they are able to make *different* decisions.

Furthermore, since moral decisions are made by an "absolutely spontaneous will," a person's past decisions and habits can have no effect on his future decisions. As Kant said, even a *propensity* toward good or bad is a contradiction.[21] A free will for a libertarian is like a ball on a

---

20. Kant writes that "when the moral law commands that we ought now to be better men, it follows inevitably that we must be able to be better men." Kant, *Religion*, 46.

21. "A physical propensity (grounded in sensuous impulses) toward any use of freedom whatsoever—whether good or bad—is a contradiction." Kant, *Religion*, 26.

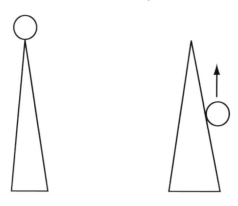

Figure 9.4

tipping point, with no propensity to move one way or the other. Though at the same time, it takes virtually no physical force to move it one way or the other.

And because it takes so little force to move a ball off a tipping point, as opposed to moving a ball that has already slid downwards, libertarians have a plausible explanation of why scientists have been unable to observe the effects of our free will. Just as the telescopes of the seventeenth and eighteenth centuries were unable to observe a stellar parallax, so too, today's functional MRIs are unable to observe the physically uncaused origins of our moral decisions.

On the other hand, we know that a ball perfectly balanced on a tipping point will not move one way or the other unless it is pushed. So too, when a difficult moral decision is made, we know that *something* happened to make the decision. According to libertarians, this infinitesimally small, yet nonetheless decisive force, comes from the immaterial realm. They sometimes call it a volition.

Yet, Aristotelians argue that the notion of "immaterial volitions" only sweeps the problem under the rug. According to libertarians, moral responsibility requires that people be able to act otherwise everything else being *physically* equal. So should not the same be true in the immaterial realm where the volitions reside? If free choices must be uncaused in the physical realm, then should not the volitions in the immaterial realm also be uncaused by all previous volitions? Kant thinks it does. "However

evil a man has been up to the very moment of an impending free act . . .
[it is as if] he had stepped out of a state of innocence into evil."[22]

Though we might criticize Kant's prose, we applaud his consistency.
"Absolute spontaneity of the will" requires complete absence of both
a physical history *and* a moral history. If either our previous physical
circumstances or our previous moral habits have any *influence* on our
present choices, then we lack autonomous freedom. Freedom, as the
libertarian conceives it, is an all-or-nothing affair. But now we are right
back where we began: How are we to distinguish between an absolutely
spontaneous will and a will that acts capriciously?

Third, while it increases libertarianism's scientific plausibility to
picture the will as a ball on a tipping, it significantly decreases its moral
plausibility. The whole point of moral instruction and training is to move
people off the tipping point, so that their good actions become *more*
automatic and *less* a matter of conscious choice. In fact, one significant
measurement of successful instruction—either in tennis or morality—is
how well the student does without conscious effort. If students and children ever got to the point where they *always* did the right thing without
thought or effort, coaches and parents would be elated. Of course, complete success is humanly unattainable. Nonetheless, it is the goal. And we
can certainly move people away from the tipping point where the least
temptation moves them the wrong way. Parents and teachers want their
children and students to move easily and frequently in a good direction
and only with great temptation and rarely in the wrong direction.

Iris Murdoch is correct when she described the structure of morality like this:

> If we consider what the work of attention is like, how continu-
> ously it goes on, and how imperceptibly it builds up structures
> of value round about us, we shall not be surprised that at crucial
> moments of choice most of the business of choosing is already
> over . . . The moral life, on this [Aristotelian] view, is something
> that goes on continually, not something that is switched off in

---

22. Kant, *Religion*, 36; see also 62. Benjamin Warfield's analysis of Pelagius's understanding of freedom is directly applicable here. It applies without modification to Kant's
libertarianism, and we suspect to other forms of libertarianism as well. "After each act of
the will, man stood exactly where he did before: indeed, this conception scarcely allows
for the existence of a 'man'—only a willing machine is left, at each click on the action of
which the spring regains its original position, and is equally ready as before to perform
its function." Schaff, *Select Library*, xvi.

between the occurrence of explicit moral choices. What happens in between such choices is indeed what is crucial.[23]

In the next section we will develop this Aristotelian understanding of freedom. Unlike the libertarian understanding, it is not an "all-or-nothing" affair nor does it undermine the importance of moral education and developing good habits.

9.6 THE FREEDOM OF RATIONAL INTEGRITY

According to Aristotelians, a human action is free when (1) there is no *per se* cause of the action (though there are *per accidens* causes) and, (2) the action is directed by reason toward a good goal, or at least an apparently good goal. This means that freedom looks both backwards and forwards. A released prisoner is *free from* past bondage. A doctor who has graduated is *free to* practice medicine. Libertarians are solely concerned with the past—being released *from* bondage. Aristotelians add a second element—being *free to* pursue a worthy and significant goal.

Aristotelians are concerned with both the past and the future. If a person's past allows us to predicate future behavior (as it does in the case of epileptics), then with respect to these predictable actions, a person is neither free nor responsible. But instead of requiring freedom from all prior physical causation, Aristotelians only require that a person be free from *per se* efficient causes. *Per accidens* efficient causes, they argue, are not inconsistent with freedom.[24]

The Aristotelian understanding of freedom, however, is also oriented toward the future. Only actions which move a person toward their primary goal are truly free. And that goal, as we argued in chapter 8, is none other than the happiness which results from being all you were meant to be. We will call this the freedom of rational integrity. Such freedom is a function of both will and reason.[25]

---

23. Murdoch, *Sovereignty of the Good*, 37.

24. As we argued in chapter 7, there is good reason to believe that token/token (but not type/type) correspondences exist between brain states and our concepts. Here, we are simply refining that same point with the distinction between *per se* and *per accidens* causation.

25. "Moreover, judgment is within the power of one judging insofar as he can judge of his own judgment. For we can judge of whatever is in our power. Indeed to judge of one's own judgment belong only to reason, which reflects upon its own act and knows the relations of things of which it judges and through which it judges. The root of all

"Integrity" involves both "facts" and "values." Consider, for example, the integrity (or lack thereof) of an airplane's wing. A wing without structural integrity will collapse when it should not. This is bad. However, the structural integrity of an airplane wing is not an ethereal "value" that exists only in some airy-fairy subjective world. It is as much a part of the physical structure of the wing as its length and width.

The same is true of a person's integrity. It is pointless to distinguish between "factual" and "evaluative" aspects of personal integrity. To describe a person as "having integrity" is clearly to praise the person (a "value"). But our evaluation here is as much a description of his or her psychological nature as it would be for a doctor to describe a patient as "clinically depressed" (a "fact"). A person of integrity is one whose will exhibits a consistency appropriate to the situation. Such a person is not easily distracted by passing passions.[26]

Plato defined the "democratic man" as one who "will set all his pleasures on a footing of equality, denying to none its equal rights and maintenance, and allowing each in turn, as it presents itself, to succeed, as if by the chance of the lot, to the government of his soul until it is satisfied . . . His life is subject to no order or restraint, and he has no wish to change an existence which he calls pleasant, free, and happy." To this, Plato rather sarcastically quips, "A wonderfully pleasant life, surely, for the moment." Rather than being truly free, the democratic man is en-

---

liberty, therefore, is found in reason. Hence according as something is related to reason, so is it related to free choice." Aquinas, *On Truth*, question 24, article 2. Found in Goodwin, *Selected Writings,* 124.

A contemporary philosopher put it like this: "Whenever anyone allows his appetitive power to be spontaneously (and hence conditionally) moved by anything short of the ultimate end, to that extent will the actions be less free. Freedom, then, admits of degrees without ceasing to be originative and a source of responsibility. By insisting on the transcendence of the ultimate end, furthermore, Aquinas can press his analysis to offer complete freedom to a person, without generating the paradoxes that accompany the notion of freedom as autonomy or absolute indeterminacy." Burrell, *Aquinas,* 124. By the paradoxes of absolute indeterminacy, Burrell is referring to the "caused or capricious" arguments against libertarianism that we considered above in 9.5.

26. "To apprehend the true relation of freedom to causality, it is helpful to ask this simple question: 'where do we find the most unmistakable examples of whatever we call freedom, free choice, free will, liberty?' Do we find these distinguished examples in the perplexed, irresolute, weak-willed and highly suggestible people? Or should we consider as the most certain exemplifications of the free man persons in firm control of their images and emotions, persons who know what they want and who will not be deterred from their goals by accidents of imagination or affectivity, pressure or lure, disease or poverty?" Simon, *Freedom of Choice,* 158. The question is rhetorical.

slaved by his own unregulated passions. He has succumbed to the many-headed beast.[27] People of integrity, on the other hand, direct their actions toward achieving the proper mix of the needs and innocent desires we discussed in the previous chapter.

To achieve this "proper mix" a disciplined will is necessary. Nonetheless, the will is greatly aided by reason. When faced with trials and temptations, reason speaks: "Remember what you set out to do and be. You must neither ignore nor be surprised by these temptations. You know that the 'lust of the eyes and the pride of life' is part and parcel of this mortal life. Why are you surprised that the path you've chosen is not steady and smooth? Suffering and frustrations are unavoidable. Be strong; be steady; be courageous!"

When faced with a difficult decision, reason counsels: "Consider your goals carefully. Do your individual talents really match your goal or are you pursuing this course for the sake of pride or power? Have you honestly considered the advice of close friends and others who know you well? Or are you arrogantly assuming that you alone have wisdom in these matters? Are your goals realistically achievable or are you foolishly ignoring the cultural and historical setting in which you find yourself?"

Finally, when things are going well, when there are no looming trials, temptations, or difficult decisions, reason declares: "Life is good, enjoy it, but remember to use your present freedom to grow in wisdom. Read good books; seek out good teachers. You know that fortune is fickle. Take this opportunity to search out the truth in all matters, to embrace what is good and to delight in what is beautiful. This way, when trials and temptations return—as they surely will—you will be better equipped to fight the good fight."

A theme that runs throughout this book is that big philosophical (or even "scientific") ideas should never be analyzed in isolation. The ecology of ideas will not allow it; how a person answers one big question effects and is affected by how other big questions are answered. Nowhere is this interconnection more apparent than with the relation between the question of this chapter and the question of the previous chapter. "Why be moral?" and "What is freedom?" are ultimately inseparable. If a person thinks of morality primarily as a list of onerous rules which nonetheless *ought* to be followed, then it is likely that this person will think of

27. Plato *Republic* VII 558–61.

freedom primarily as an autonomous *choice* for which no reason can or should be given other than—that's just what *I* choose to do.

On the other hand, if a person thinks of morality primarily as recipes for human flourishing, then it is likely that this person will think of freedom primarily as an ability and/or skill which continually needs to be developed and improved. In this case no reason can or should be given to the question—"Why be moral?"—other than I want to flourish as one who is fully human and enjoy the resultant happiness.[28]

We will close with a thought experiment to clarify what is at stake with these competing conceptions of freedom. Imagine a teacher and classroom so perfect that students end up always "doing the right thing" when faced with a difficult moral decision. This is a highly "idealized" hypothesis, perhaps even more idealized than Galileo's imaginary balls rolling down frictionless ramps with no air resistance. Nonetheless, let us ask: Is a 100 percent success in matters of morality a worthy goal?

Libertarians and Aristotelians both have their doubts, but for different reasons. Libertarians worry that a teacher who was 100 percent successful would *ipso facto* be coercing her students and denying them their freedom. When dice are rolled several times and they always comes up "seven," we have strong evidence that the dice are "fixed." Without variation, we suspect some kind of foul play. So too, if students never disagree with their teacher, libertarians suspect some kind of coercion on the part of the teacher.

Aristotelians, on the other hand, worry that teachers who made 100 percent success their goal would *ipso facto* be denying the fallibility of their own instruction. In principle, they have no greater objection to 100 percent success in moral matters than they do in math tests. Nor do they assume that "critical thinkers" must always challenge what others have said and only believe what they have verified for themselves. Aristotle was explicit: "He who wishes to learn must believe."[29] Life is short. No

---

28. "When there are rules, they are not removing the liberty of the believing people but are rather impeding the slavery of sin which is repugnant to spiritual freedom." Aquinas, *ST*, I–II 108.1.

29. Aristotle *Sophistical Refutations* ch. 2.2; 165b; see also Aristotle *Nicomachean Ethics* bk. 1. ch. 2, 1095b; and Aquinas, *ST*, II–II 2.1; *ST*, II–II 5.2. As Gilson puts it, "'It is said with justice,' St. Thomas asserts, 'that if a person wishes to learn, he must begin by believing his teacher; for he would never attain to perfect knowledge unless he accepted the truth of such doctrines as may be offered to him at first, the justification of which he cannot, at that time, discover for himself' [*De Verit.*, qu. XIV., art. 10, ad Resp.]." Quoted

one has the time or energy to independently and autonomously verify everything they know.[30]

The real reason teachers should not make a 100 percent success their goal is that it presupposes the epistemic certainty of foundationalism (section 6.2). Our knowledge about the world (as opposed to the purely formal realm of logic and mathematics) can never be complete until history comes to an end.[31] Thus, everyone—both students *and* teachers—must always be open to new observations and new arguments. The difficulty with our imaginary super-teacher is *not* that his power would overwhelm the students' freedom, but that we are being asked to imagine something that is impossible. No human teacher teaches the whole truth and nothing but the truth. As we said before, the best teachers realize that a significant portion of all they teach will turn out to be false. Yet, they continue to teach because until history ends they will never be able to infallibly distinguish truth from error.

But, again, we must not confuse fallibilism with relativism. There is a right answer to even the most difficult moral questions, but there are no moral algorithms which infallibly guide humans to these right answers. So while we ought to follow a sincere and humble conscience, acting with sincerity and humility is not the *definition* of acting virtuously. A doctor who sincerely and humbly believes that a particular drug will improve his patient's health is not guaranteed success just because his decision was made with sincerity and humility. So too, difficult moral

---

in Gilson, *Philosophy of St. Thomas Aquinas*, 56. Augustine made a similar point only stronger and more theologically: "The fact is that a rational creature is so constituted that submission is good for it, while yielding to its own rather than its Creator's will is, on the contrary, disastrous." Augustine, *City of God*, bk. XIV, ch. 12.

30. Josef Pieper tells a story about a naturalist who around 1700 was trying to describe pollen grains. While he could see some of the detail with a simple magnifying glass, "suppose he is visited by a colleague who has seen such pollen at Delft under one the first microscopes made by Antonie van Leeuwenhoek ... Let us assume further that our naturalist has had no opportunity to look through a microscope himself and has never observed these things that his visitor reports. Granted these assumption, would not our naturalist be grasping more truth, which means more reality, if he did *not* insist on regarding as true and real only what he has seen with his own eyes, if, on the contrary, he could bring himself to 'believe' his visitor?" Pieper, *Faith, Hope, and Love*, 44.

31. In one of his books intended for a popular audience, Aquinas writes: "Our knowledge is so imperfect that no philosopher has ever been able to discover perfectly the nature of a single fly." Aquinas, *Three Greatest Prayers*, 6. Catherine Pickstock adds, "Thus in Aquinas, there is much more sense than with Aristotle, of knowledge as a never completed project." Milbank, *Truth in Aquinas*, 15.

decision always raise two questions. First, did the person make the best judgment possible given the available information? Second, did he in fact flourish as a human being as a result of his judgment?

We must not *blame* a sincere and humble person whose decision in a difficult case turns out wrong. To do so would be to hold him to a standard no fallible human can meet. But on the other hand, we must never minimize the fact that *we* are neither the arbiters of truth nor the creators of reality. Aristotelians will always encourage aeronautical engineers to do their very best to design wings with the integrity required to withstand the forces of nature. But even more, they encourage all of us to do our very best to design a *life* with the integrity required to withstand the "slings and arrows of outrageous fortune."

10

Does God Exist?

Aristotelian realism is inherently theistic. If rocks, plants and animals all have distinct forms (essential natures), and if form is not shape, then the question naturally arises: Who or what in-formed nature? Wanting to rid the world of God, Nietzsche attempted to rid words of meaning so that such questions would no longer be asked.

But scientists cannot do science without assuming that words refer to real differences in nature. Otherwise it would be impossible to explain why dropped rocks fall but dropped birds fly. Rather than following Nietzsche, many who are scientifically minded turn to Darwin to account for the real differences between rocks, plants, and animals.

Though it is frequently assumed that Darwin destroyed traditional arguments for the existence of a divine In-former, contemporary Aristotelians argue the exact opposite. Prior to Darwin it could be argued that since rocks, plants, and animals have always existed just as they do now, there is no need to explain how they came to exist. However, while Aristotle himself assumed the fixity of species, he nonetheless argued that a divine In-former is required. But to do so, he first had to make a philosophically sophisticated distinction between temporal and conceptual causation.

Today, sophisticated philosophical distinctions concerning causal priority are unnecessary. Since we now know that rocks and dirt existed long before plants and animals, the question—How did rocks and dirt produce plants and animals?—becomes scientifically inescapable. And once it is established that form is not shape (i.e. a physical property), it follows that no purely physical cause can account for the difference between rocks, plants, and animals. Thus, the existence of a divine In-former is itself inescapable.

We must emphasize, however, that this argument has nothing in common with the currently popular "Design Argument" which argues eyes and brains are mathematically too complex to have evolved by chance. Aristotelians reject this argument for a couple of reasons. First, it is form, not complexity that requires explanation. Second, arguments based on mathematical complexity make two unwarranted assumptions: 1) nature had only a finite amount of time to shape complex organs and 2) simple observation tells us "what to count" when we are comparing mathematical complexities.

This chapter also considers Aquinas' "cosmological conjecture" that only a transcendent Creator adequately answers the philosophically puzzling question: "Why is there something rather than nothing?" Though many would like to ignore or reject this question, Thomists argue that this cannot be done without ceasing to be a philosopher. On the other hand, this is a question that does not stand by itself. How philosophers respond to the biggest of questions is pretty much determined by their answers to the relatively smaller philosophical questions we addressed in prior chapters. So once more, the ecology of ideas is evident.

"I AM AFRAID WE shall not get rid of God until we get rid of grammar," said Nietzsche.[1] He realized that philosophical realism is inherently theistic. The ability of words to convey in-*form*-ation about the world presupposes an in-former and this in-former has traditionally been referred to as God.[2] Nietzsche wanted to rid the world of the Christian God. So he set out to destroy "grammar" (i.e., realism).

Aristotelians' response to Nietzsche is always indirect. Positively speaking, they never attempt to "prove" that realism is true or that our words have meaning. Our knowledge that plants and animals exist is immediately evident. It is rock-bottom. There are no more obvious prem-

---

1. Nietzsche, *Twilight of the Idols*, 3.5, 483. Not quite a century later, Sartre made s similar point: "There is no such thing as human nature because there exists no God to think it creatively." Sartre, *Existentialism is a Humanism*, quoted in Pieper, *Silence of St. Thomas*, 52.

2. *God* is a tricky word. At first blush *God* appears to be a proper noun. This raises the contentious question of whether Jews, Christians, and Muslims all use the word to refer to the same "God." And then there is Pascal's famous distinction between the "God of Abraham, Isaac, and Jacob" and the "God of philosophers." But even in a book with as grand a scope of this, some questions must be put aside. So though questions about the precise reference of the term *God* are important, I will stick with the old conventions of capitalizing *God* whenever the term is used leaving its precise reference deliberately vague. For those looking for greater precision, and a more historical and theological perspective, see Wright, *New Testament and the People of God*, xiv–xv.

ises from which the existence of plants and animals could be deduced or inferred. However, negatively speaking, Aristotelians do point out that all attempts to "prove" that words have no meaning are self-refuting, or in Aristotle's colorful metaphor, they reduce humans to a "vegetable."[3] Proofs use words. If all words are meaningless, then all demonstrations that words have no meaning are themselves meaningless.

And we have already explained *how* words like "plant" and "animal" get their meaning. The human intellect, after observing plants and animals in various situations, is able to abstract their respective forms. These abstracted forms are the essential natures of what is being observed. Humans then take their conceptual knowledge and by agreed upon conventions assign meanings to certain shapes and sounds (words) to be used to communicate these concepts. Of course, in one sense, nothing could be simpler. But, in another sense, nothing is more mysterious than words and the intellects which create them. Both exist on the cusp between the material and immaterial. Words are material shapes and sounds, but they are not *just* shapes and sounds. Intellects require material brains to function, but they are not *just* brains. But now we are merely repeating previously covered ground.

10.1 THE DIVINE IN-FORMER

We are on new territory, though, when we ask about the origin of the forms (essential natures) themselves. Who or what in-*formed* the plants and animals? As we just said, it was our human ancestors who in-formed the *word* "plant" and the *word* "animal." But the plants and animals themselves were not human creations. So they could not have been in-formed by our ancestors.

---

3. "It is impossible for anything at the same time to be and not to be, and by this means we have shown that this is the most indisputable of all principles. Some indeed demand that even this shall be demonstrated, but this they do through want of education, for not to know of what things one should demand demonstration, and of what one should not, argues want of education. For it is impossible that there should be demonstrations of absolutely everything (there would be an infinite regress, so that there would still be no demonstration) . . . we can, however, demonstrate negatively even that this view is impossible, if our opponent will only say something. And if he says nothing, it is absurd to seek to give an account of our views to one who cannot give an account of anything, in so far as he cannot do so. For such a man, as such, is from the start no better than a vegetable." Aristotle *Metaphysics* bk. 4, ch. 4. In his commentary, Aquinas puts it like this: "For he who 'destroys reason,' must uphold its significance, because he can only express what he denies by speaking, and by signifying something." Aquinas, *Commentary*, sec. 611, vol. 1, 248.

In ordinary language, the divine in-former argument can be reduced to a simple deductive argument that goes like this:

1. Information exists.

2. Nothing comes from nothing.

3. Matter cannot create information.

4. Therefore, there must be an immaterial in-former.

There is no question about the validity of the argument, though obviously many philosophers have questioned one or more of its premises. Again, Nietzsche's attempt to rid the world of "grammar" was an attack on the first premise. And, again, we've already said all we have to say in opposition to Nietzsche's attack.

Though it is contrary to conventional wisdom, it is easier to defend the second premise *after* Darwin than before. Aristotle, and his Greek contemporaries,[4] assumed that the universe had always existed just as it does now. This meant that pre-Darwinian materialists could argue that the existence of plants and animals was simply a "brute fact." They did not *come from* anywhere, so they neither could nor needed to be explained. However, today, we know that plants and animals have not always existed. They have a history, a "coming to be" story. It is the causal history of the coming to be of plants and animals that concerns us in this chapter.

Of course, many contemporary Darwinians (like Richard Dawkins) argue that evolution proves that God *does not* exist. They implicitly either reject or ignore the third premise, just as the ancient materialists. But as Aristotle argued, materialism is too simple and is incapable of accounting for the fact that our universe is a cosmos, not a chaos. Materialists forget that questions about origins are ambiguous. Are we asking about the origin of the shape or the form (see 4.1)? "Where did plants and animals come from?" can be inquiring about either: (1) the immediate events which created their shape or (2) the responsible agent who in-*formed* their shape. Let us return to our stock example. Biologists are now able to give a fairly complete explanation of the electro-chemical causes of how people move their hands. They might one day even be able to explain the efficient causes operating in people's hands and brains

4. By Aristotle's time, many of the ancient Hebrews undoubtedly believed in a Creator God, but there is no evidence that the belief in creation *ex nihilo* (out of nothing) had made its way to Greece.

when they move a pen over a piece of paper to produce ink marks that look like—TOOL. But this does not explain how the ink in the pen became in-formed with meaning (see chapter 7).

Frequently people object to the divine in-former argument like this: "Okay, perhaps it is impossible for mere matter to be the cause of information. But why not suppose that both matter and information have always existed? Why do we need a divine in-former?"

The answer returns us to the distinction between a *per se* and *per accidens* efficient cause (see chapter 9). We frequently speak of *the* cause of some event. But in the vast majority of cases, things or events will have many causes. For example, biologists have long wondered about the extinction of the dinosaurs. Most scientists now believe the cause was a massive asteroid which struck the earth about sixty-five million years ago. Of course, they do not mean that a single asteroid broke into millions of pieces and that each of these "miraculously" hit each individual dinosaur. Instead, they are saying that the asteroid was the originating cause in a whole series of causal events (clouds of dust shooting high into the atmosphere, trade winds distributing the dust around the entire globe blocking the sun, plants dying for lack of sunlight, dinosaurs dying for lack of plants to eat, etc.).

So in what sense was the asteroid an originating cause? It was certainly not original in the sense that nothing came before it. Rather, we say of the almost infinite number of events that preceded the death of the dinosaurs that this is the one that *explains* their death. It is the one which elicits the response, "Ah, now we understand why the dinosaurs became extinct." This is the *per se* efficient cause of the dinosaurs' extinction.

Contrast this with the sort of causes captured by the old rhyme,

> For want of a nail the shoe was lost.
> For want of a shoe the horse was lost.
> For want of a horse the rider was lost.
> For want of a rider the battle was lost.
> For want of a battle the kingdom was lost.
> And all for the want of a horseshoe nail.

The rhyme captures an important fact about our world—much that happens, happens by random chance or, in Aristotelian terms, *per accidens* efficient causes. The last line of the rhyme is ironic. It is *not* suggesting that the nail was the originating cause of the kingdom being lost since clearly there was a long series of accidental causes preceding the loss of a nail. No one, after learning about the lost nail, says, "Ah, now we understand why the kingdom was lost."

In the older language of Aristotle and his scholastic followers, this point is made by saying that an infinite series of causes is impossible. Moderns frequently respond: Why not? The series of numbers is infinite. So why cannot a series of causes also be infinite? The dispute rests on an ambiguity. When Aristotelians say "an infinite series of causes is impossible" they are speaking in a kind of short hand. What they mean is that an infinite series of *per se* causes is impossible.

Aristotelians have no objection to an infinite series of *per accidens* causes. (Again, Aristotle himself thought the universe was itself infinite in this sense.) Their only claim is that if the universe is composed exclusively of *per accidens* causes, then scientific understanding is impossible. Aristotle's argument goes like this: if a series of causes is infinite, then by definition no cause is first or primary. But if no cause is first or primary, then every cause is *per accidens* and *per accidens* causes do not explain *why* something happens. To say that something occurred as the result of a random (*per accidens*) cause is tantamount to saying that we cannot understand it. That is, we would never say, "Ah, now I know why the dinosaurs became extinct."[5]

So, in the more technical language of Aristotle, the divine in-former argument[6] looks like this:

5. Aristotle's argument against an infinite series of *per se* efficient causes is explained by Aquinas in his *Commentary on Aristotle's Metaphysics* like this: "In any finite series where there is a first, intermediate, and last it is clear that the first must be the cause of the other two (and hence of the series), since the last is cause of none and the intermediate the cause of only one. The same argument holds whether the intermediates are one or many. Now if the intermediates become infinite, then by hypothesis there is no first or last, only intermediates. Yet the same argument against the intermediates being the efficient cause remains." Aquinas, *Commentary*, sec. 302–3, vol. 1, 125.

Per se causes are transitive, e.g., *a* moves *b* which causes *b* to move *c*. In this series of causes, we can say that *a* moves *c* through the intermediary *b*. An infinite regress in *per se* causes is impossible. *Per accidens* causes are intransitive, e.g., *a* being the father of *b* and *b* being the father of *c* does *not* allow us to say that *a* is the father of *c*. Since each cause by itself is a complete explanation, there is no reason why such a series cannot proceed to infinity, i.e. even if the series is infinite, each individual answer to "What caused x?" will be intelligible, though there will be no end to the possible questions. As Aquinas says, "Hence it is not impossible for a man to be generated by man to infinity." Aquinas, *ST* I 46.2. See also Brown, "Infinite Causal Regression."

6. Philosophers frequently refer to this as the teleological argument for the existence of "God." The name comes from the Greek, "*teleos*" which means "end, goal or purpose." When we say something so simple as "The first pair of claws on a lobster are pinchers" we are speaking "teleologically" since we are explain *what* something is in terms of its

1. Only *per se* causes explain why things happen (chapter 5)

2. *Per se* causes assume the existence of forms/essences (chapter 9.3)

3. Matter by itself can never create a form/essence (chapter 7, et. al.)

4. Therefore, if we are to understand anything in this universe, there must be an originating agent that in-*forms* matter.

Again, the argument is clearly valid; the only philosophical question concerns the truth of its premises (see chapter 1). A more thorough justification of the premises is found in the parentheses, though here is a one sentence summary for the argument in each of the listed chapters.

- Why-questions require a final cause and by definition *per accidens* causes are not *lawful*.

- Until we know *what* something is it is impossible to predict its behavior.

- Shape is not form, so purely physical characteristics can never define *what* something is.

Again, the conclusion is conditional so it says nothing to the skeptic who asserts that "science" itself is a social construct. It only concludes: if science is possible, then the universe cannot be composed exclusively of an infinite series of *per accidens* efficient causes. There must be a *per se* in-former.[7]

---

end, goal, or purpose. Aristotelians disagree with all those who say that such language is obsolete. See chapter 7 of my *In Defense of the Soul* for a more detailed response to Aristotle's contemporary critics on this point.

7. "To put it succinctly, things are knowable because they have been created . . . Do not think that it is possible to do both, to argue away the idea that things have been creatively thought by God and then go on to understand how things can be known by the human mind!" Pieper, *Silence of St. Thomas*, 56.

With regard to the possibility of an infinite series of causes, a contemporary Thomist says that Aquinas' "point is not to show that there cannot be such a series, perhaps even infinite, of moved movers; it is rather that, without an unmoved mover or principal cause that does not depend on something else for its motion, the motion of nothing will be explained. To drive home this point here, however, he simply turns to the analogy with the carpenter's tools without a carpenter." Wippel, *Metaphysical Thought of Thomas*, 441. The carpenter's tool analogy is from Aquinas' *Compendium of Theology*, part 1, ch. 3.

We suggested earlier that pre-Darwinian Aristotelians had a more difficult time establishing the existence of God. We can now say more. Darwinians assume that life has not always existed on earth; instead, they argue that the earth existed for billions of years before life evolved. Though the originating process is something that we do not yet understand, we do know that DNA plays an important part. Aristotle, on the other hand, assumed that life had always existed; it did not *come from* anywhere. Therefore, Aristotle's own argument for a supernatural Informer needed to explain how it could be that A was responsible for (i.e. caused) B even though A did not temporally precede B.

Beginning with David Hume, many philosophers have assumed that *all* causes must temporarily *precede* their effect. We have already criticized Hume's reduction of causation to mere constant conjunction (chapter 4.3). And there are other problems as well. There are several stock illustrations of causes which do not *precede* their effect. Rather, they are *simultaneous* with their effect. If we imagine a table with an apple on it and suppose that both the apple and the table have always existed, by hypothesis there will be no time when the table existed but the apple did not. Nonetheless, it is obvious that the table is supporting the apple, not vice versa. So, even though Aristotle thought the universe and all its species of animals were eternal, he understood that that does not make the search for an originating cause superfluous. Yet, such illustrations by themselves appear slightly *ad hoc*, so a full defense of the Aristotle's argument requires a fuller fleshing out of the first two premises. We did this in chapters 4 through 7.

But if we assume a Darwinian perspective on life, the conclusion follows from the third premise alone. As we have frequently repeated, form is not shape. There is no shape which is the form of *any* word, symbol, sign, or code. But as Darwinians rightfully insist, DNA is a *code*. They sometimes even use explicitly Aristotelian terminology. For example, Cairns-Smith, an important researcher on biogenesis, writes: "In biology both goods and messages are passed on from one generation to the next. But it is the messages that are the most important inheritance: only they can persist over millions and millions of years. This distinction between goods and information is a case of the ancient distinction between *substances* and *form*. While a message may have to be written in some material substance, the message is not to be identified with the substance. The message as such is form."[8] Even the italics are in the original!

---

8. Cairns-Smith, *Steven Keys to the Origin of Life*, 12.

In short, Darwinian explanations presuppose a form/shape distinction. Since matter by itself can never create a form, an immaterial and self-subsisting In-former (God) must exist.

10.2 WILLIAM PALEY'S DESIGN ARGUMENT

We are deliberately being a little provocative since so many people simply assume that Darwinian ideas have refuted traditional arguments for God. And those that do not make this assumption typically make the opposite assumption, namely, that a rational belief in God can only be saved by refuting Darwinism. Given these opposing, but equally mistaken assumptions, a little provocation seems appropriate.

It is hard to know whether the Darwinian refuters of theism or the Christian refuters of Darwin are more to blame for this philosophical misunderstanding. We will leave that question to the historians. But it is clear that the dispute centers on William Paley's "Design Argument."

Paley (1743–1805) argued that if a person who had never seen a watch before came across one in some out of the way place, then that person would nonetheless know that the watch had a designer. Something so complex could not have been created by the random actions of wind and waves, fire and ice, even over indescribably long periods of time. But when we look at eyes and hearts, we see the same degree of complexity and order, so how could we rationally conclude that they are the product of random chance?[9]

9. Actually, the Design Argument goes back to at least Newton: "If the planets had not received a push to give them an inertial (or tangential) component of motion, he [Newton] said, the solar attractive force would not draw them into an orbit but instead would move each planet in a straight line toward the sun itself. Hence the universe could not be explained in terms of matter alone." Cohen, *The Birth of the New Physics*, 165.

And again, "Because the inverse-square law of gravitation was compatible with parabolic and hyperbolic paths, the planet's assumption of a closed, elliptical orbit depended on its receiving exactly the right 'flick' at exactly the right time. It was an exquisite calculation on the part of the deity who had to consider the 'several distances of the primary planets from the sun and secondary ones from Saturn, Jupiter and the Earth, and the velocities with which these planets could revolve at those distances about those quantities of matter in central bodies.'" Brooke, *Science and Religion*,146. This quote is from the Dec 10, 1692, letter from Newton to Bentley. It can also be found online at "The Newton Project": http://www.newtonproject.sussex.ac.uk/texts/viewtext.php?id=THEM00254 &mode=normalized.

Newton also invoked God as a "fine tuner" who corrected for the gravitational interaction among the planets to ensure a stable universe. The French mathematician Pierre Laplace (1749–1827), however, demonstrated that the universe did not require such a "fine tuner." Using Newton's laws and a step-by-step iterative technique, Laplace calcu-

Paley's conclusion is correct, but his argument is confused. Occasionally, Paley distinguishes between "order" and "complexity." But more often than not Paley assumes that complexity implies order and vice versa, thus confusing form and shape. It is not the "complexity" of a word that is responsible for its "orderliness." "KDOVENAPPFGN" is more "complex" than "TOOL," but "TOOL" is more orderly than "KDOVENAPPFGN."

Nor is this confusion between complexity and orderliness merely a verbal slip. By making "complexity" the issue, Paley and his contemporary followers, [10] have turned a strong philosophical argument into a weak

---

lated, that the shrinking and expanding of the orbits of Jupiter and Saturn followed a 929 year cycle. Hence, there was no need for God to "intervene" to keep the solar system from collapsing. This was the point of Laplace's famous quip to Napoleon that he "had no need of the God hypothesis." Gribbin, *Deep Simplicity*, 13–16.

Many readers will (and should) understand that Newton's and Paley's arguments are the forerunners to the "Intelligent Design Movement."

10. William Dembski, a leader in the "Intelligent Design Movement" frequently refers not just to complexity, but what he calls "specified complexity." This poses a dilemma for the intelligent design movement. I have two sets of channel lock pliers in my garage—one is a 6-inch pair of pliers, the other is a 12-inch pair of pliers. Which is more complex? The question is ambiguous. Until we know what constitutes the parts of these two pliers, we will not know what we are to count. Are the parts the two arms plus the pin that hold them together? Or are the parts each of the quarks in the two pliers? (I'm using quarks as the stand in for whatever physics finally decides is the fundamental unit of mass/energy.)

Obviously, we get two very different answers. If the parts are the "middle-size" arms and pin, then these two pliers have the same complexity. If the parts are the "mirco-size" units of the atomic physicists, then the 12-inch pliers are more complex than the 6-inch pliers. Presumably it is the "middle-size" parts that specified complexity would have us consider, while complexity by itself (i.e., apart from "specification") would have us consider the "micro-size" parts. But the challenge for the Intelligent Design movement is to sketch an empirically detectable test which concludes that the 6-inch and 12-inch pliers have the same complexity without smuggling into the test that it is *pliers* whose parts we are counting.

Why the prohibition against mentioning "pliers"? Simply this: "pliers" names a form (albeit an artificial form) and "form" is another word for "species" and "species" is the root of "specified." It is a tautology to say that two things of the same form/species have the same specified complexity. Unspecified complexity is what can be quantifiable; specified complexity is not. Until the human intellect abstracts the form/species, we will not know what it is that we are to count. The chief virtue of Intelligent Design according to its defenders is that it proceeds in a wholly mechanical/algorithmic fashion. "*Specified* complexity" lacks this virtue because "specificity" cannot be reduced to an algorithm. Any appeal to specificity is implicitly an appeal to the sort of teleological argument that Aristotle developed and we are here defending. But no teleological argument can proceed in a wholly mechanical/algorithmic fashion. See the appendix of my *In Defense of the Soul* for further details.

"scientific" argument concerning mathematical probabilities. Paley's contemporaries argue like this: assume that an eye has ten parts and that there are ten different ways the parts can be attached to one another and there are ten different temporal orders in which they can be assembled. In that case there are 1,000,000,000,000,000,000,000 different ways these parts can be randomly arranged. If we make the reasonable assumption that only a very small number of these ways produces a functional eye, then it seems highly probable that the parts in an eye were not randomly assembled, but instead, were assembled by a designer.

There are a couple problems with this seemingly "scientific" improvement of Aristotle's argument.

First, it assumes a uniquely western understanding of time. If the odds against something happening by chance are extremely high, then, if after only a few tries the highly improbable happens, it may be reasonable to assume that it was not chance alone that accounts for the thing in question. However, if we have an extremely high number of attempts to produce by chance an extremely improbable event, this is no longer true. For example, if on the *first* ten flips, a coin lands head each time, then it may be reasonable to suppose that someone may have "fixed" the coin. But if a person finds a series of ten straight heads in a series of a hundred billion flips of a coin, then that is *not* good reason to suppose that the coin has been "fixed." All calculations of probabilities require both a numerator (how "complex" something is) *and* a denominator (how many "attempts" are available).

We in the West believe that the universe is some where between six thousand years old and thirteen billion years old. We also assume that there is a big difference between a six thousand year old universe and a thriteen billion year old universe. Both of these assumptions reflect our "western" understanding of history. In the East,[11] it is generally assumed that history is a series of endless cycles. "The time frame of Indian cosmology boggles the imagination," says Huston Smith. He continues, "The Himalayas, it is said, are made of solid granite. Once every thousand years a bird flies over them with a silk scarf in its beak, brushing their peaks with its scarf. When by this process the Himalayas have been worn away, one day of a cosmic cycle will have elapsed."[12] Not only does such a time frame boggle the Western mind, it makes the denominator in any

11. An everlasting and/or endlessly cyclical understanding of the universe was also common in Aristotle's Greece.

12. Smith, *World's Religions*, 68.

calculation of probabilities inestimably big for even a single cycle. If we assume that the cycles themselves are endless, then our calculations are meaningless since the denominator is infinite.

But even if we knew the denominator was a small finite number (whatever that means), real statisticians know how tricky calculations of probability can be. Factor in thresholds and seemingly minor differences in the initial assumptions (see chapter 9) and calculations about what is or is not "mathematically probable" in something as big as the universe begins looking a little like a "star wars" missile defense system that can never be tested—not something that inspires great confidence!

Finally, those who would calculate the probabilities of our universe developing by chance have failed to understand that "quantity" is itself a "quality." Again, there is nothing that one table, one animal, one baseball game, one essay, one play, one corporation, one ocean have in common except the quality of "unity" (chapter 5.2). So we cannot know *what* we are counting until we understand its form—an essentially qualitative judgment of the intellect. For example, suppose someone is asked to calculate the complexity of two pairs of pliers. Both are composed of precisely the same number of functional parts, but one is twice as large as the other. Which is more complex? The question is impossible to answer *until* we know what we are supposed to count. If we count the functional parts, their "complexity" is the same. If, on the other hand, we count their atomic parts, then the bigger pliers are more complex. Once again, we are face-to-face with the confusion of form and shape. It is impossible to know what something *is* merely by observing its shape with a super-camcorder.

The second problem with turning Aristotle's argument into an argument concerning complexity is that it *invites* competing calculations. Richard Dawkins, for example, blithely makes the same assumptions as Paley about the usefulness of probability calculations in thinking about God.[13] But he comes to the opposite conclusion as Paley. After making estimations (guesses[14]) about the "complexity" of the simplest forms of

13. Dawkins, *Blind Watchmaker,* ch. 6.

14. Michael Behe in, *The Edge of Evolution,* in our opinion, appropriately chides Dawkins for his *a priori* estimates of the "complexity" of the simplest life forms. Behe argues that such questions should be addressed in the laboratory studying relatively simple microbes like malaria. Unfortunately, in the end Behe also assume that it is meaningful to talk about issues of "complexity" without first addressing philosophical issues about *what* it is we are supposed to count.

life that are able to reproduce, he then borrows the astronomers' estimations about the size and age of the universe. It turns out, he says, that the chance coming to be of "replicators" is not all that improbable. Once replicators exist, a process of cumulative selection begins.[15] "Cumulative selection" is like a game of Yahtzee. Instead of having to roll all three dice after each throw, the player gets to leave selected die on the table to build on in the next roll. Using such a strategy, Dawkins demonstrates something *in itself* highly improbable, like monkeys typing the phrase "Me thinks it is like a Weasel," is not at all improbable using a process of cumulative selection.

So who is right, Paley or Dawkins? Is the eye really extremely complex and thus highly improbable? Is even the simplest of life forms so complex that it is statistically impossible for them to have evolved by chance? Aristotelians never attempt to answer such questions. To do so would be like trying to answer the question: How many atoms does it take to make a meaningful word? Or to extend the analogy: Paley and Dawkins are like someone who assumes that before we can determine if a book had an author we should first consult literary critics to see if the plot and character development is sufficiently complex. Aristotelians know better. First, it is silly to think that "plot" and "character development" are quantifiable. Second, it is not merely probable that even a simple children's book has an author. Any book, no matter how simple, *must* have an author.[16]

In sum, Aristotle's argument for the existence of God has nothing to do with "complexity" and therefore it can be neither supported nor refuted by the sort of empirical observation made by scientists.

10.3 THE COSMOLOGICAL CONJECTURE

Quantum mechanics provides an excellent understanding of how very small things behave. General relativity provides an excellent understanding of how very big things behave. Unfortunately, these theories are mutually incompatible. Scientists have been looking for over fifty years for

15. We will grant Dawkins' point concerning the power of cumulative selection to produce remarkably "complex" organisms. However, the origin of the first "replicator" raises the hard philosophical questions which Dawkins simply begs. See my review "No Chance" in *Books and Culture*.

16. Ch. 7 of my *In Defense of the Soul* is a much more detailed consideration of these issues.

some more general theory that would unify these into a single coherent theory. For a while, it looked like "string theory" might be the answer, but it seems now that more and more scientists are looking elsewhere.

Now imagine a skeptical scientist who argued like this: "There is no answer to this puzzle. It is simply a brute fact about the universe that it is incoherent. Quantum Mechanics and General Relativity are the best answers there are. We should stop wasting time and money looking for a better answer to a senseless question."

Is the skeptical scientist's argument rational? Is there an argument that would prove such a scientist wrong? Well, clearly, if ten years hence scientists do discover a more general theory that unifies quantum mechanics and general relativity, then the skeptical scientist will have been refuted. But suppositions about what will happen in the future cannot be used *today* to refute such skepticism.

On the other hand, one could argue historically that in the past scientific puzzles have been resolved, so it is irrational to believe that this present puzzle will not also be solved. It is unlikely, however, that this will turn the skeptic into a believer. There is an obvious objection to such extrapolations: "There's a first time for everything. A turkey may give thanks every morning to the farmer who feeds him. But on Thanksgiving, it is the farmer who will be thanking the turkey."

The best a scientist can say to their skeptical colleagues is: "You must believe. While we do not now know *what* the answer is, we must believe *that* there is an answer. The only alternative is to give up on science. Of course, you are free to do so and we will respect your choice. However, you will lose our respect if you continue to call yourself a scientist *and* to argue that there is no solution to the puzzle."

Aristotelians like Thomas Aquinas make a similar argument with respect to God and the universe. Here is the puzzle: Why is there something rather than nothing? Everything *in* the universe has a cause. No thing simply "poofs" into existence. And when we do not know a thing's cause, we nonetheless insist that there is a cause. Therefore, even though we have absolutely no idea *what* the cause of the universe is—all we can do is call it God—we know *that* there is such a cosmological Cause.[17]

Before we consider criticisms of this argument, we must rule out another "scientific" attempt to improve on the ancient argument. One of the corollaries of General Relativity theory is that the universe is ex-

17. See note 7 in ch. 4.

panding. In fact, one of the successes of Einstein's theory is that it predicted an expanding universe prior to detecting experimental evidence for expansion.[18] But if the universe is now bigger than it was a billion years ago, that means that at some point in the past it must have been infinitesimally small, i.e., virtually non-existent, what scientists call a "singularity." So what caused the universe to become what it is today? There must have been something temporally prior to the Big Bang that caused the expansion. Here, some would say, we have a scientific demonstration for the existence of a First Cause.

There are a number of reasons to reject this new interpretation. First, the fact that there was a "Big Bang" about thirteen billion years ago does not mean that this was the first "Big Bang." An eternally oscillating cycle of "Big Bangs" followed by "Big Crunches" is also consistent with General Relativity. It all depends on whether the force of the Big Bang is stronger than the gravitational force of the mass of the universe. Though right now, most scientists seem to think that there is insufficient mass in the universe to cause a Big Crunch, this says nothing about conditions prior to the singularity exploding.

Furthermore, to assume on philosophical grounds that the universe has a beginning in time begs all sorts of crucial questions. Much better, Aristotelians argue, to remember that "efficient causes" means "responsible agent," not temporally prior agent. Sometimes, causes are simultaneous with their effects. Other times, they operate at a different "level," as in the case of the intellect which in-forms a word with meaning. And as we will soon see, there is a radical difference between picturing God as a "First Cause" which initiated the series and picturing God as the "Creator" responsible for the existence of the series itself (see figure 10.1).[19]

In an important sense, the point of the cosmological conjecture is to rule out certain ways of understanding the Divine In-former argument we considered in the previous section. As Aquinas said, "Because

18. While Einstein's theory predicted an expanding universe, Einstein himself was wedded to a static model of the universe so he introduced the "cosmological constant" to neutralize the expansion implied by the theory. Latter he confessed that this *ad hoc* "solution" was the biggest mistake of his scientific life.

19. "Properly speaking, neither a motion nor change, the act of creation will be located not in the category of action or passion, but in that of relation (*de Pot* 3.3). A relation of dependence would be compatible with either temporal arrangement: creator and creature coextensive, or creature being with time." Burrell, *Aquinas: God and Action*, 136–37.

Figure 10.1

it is not possible for us to know *what* God is, but rather what God is *not*, we cannot consider how God exists, but rather how God does *not* exist."[20] Here is part of what God is not. First, if God merely stands for the first in time or biggest member in a series of causes, then God becomes a part of the universe, not the responsible agent for its existence. Second, we must not think of God as a Supreme Craftsman. In the last section we argued that if there is in-*form*-ation, then there must be an In-former. But that raises a question: What is it that the In-former (i.e., God) in-forms? One answer is that God in-forms pre-existing matter. At first blush, that appears to be Aristotle's answer. After all, it was Aristotle who first insisted that we distinguish between matter and form.

Yet, a more careful reading of Aristotle makes this interpretation impossible. "Matter" is a relative term. Bricks may be the "matter" out of which a house is built. But in relation to clay, bricks are not "matter." They are an in-formed substance. And again, clay is the "matter" of bricks, but in relation to molecules, clay is also an in-formed substance. Obviously, at some point, this reduction must stop. When it does, we will have reached pure matter. But what is this? Ancient materialists coined the term "atom" for that which is "not divisible." For them, atoms were thought of as little bits of "pure" matter.

Aristotle argued that the Atomist's analysis was incomplete. Atoms, no matter how simple, are substances in-formed at least with geometrical shape and mass.[21] So what is it that is so in-formed? There must be

20. Aquinas, *ST*, I.3.

21. "For even though first matter is in potentiality to all forms, it nevertheless receives them in a certain order. For first of all it is in potency to the forms of the elements, and through the intermediary of these, insofar as they are mixed in different proportions, it is in potency to different forms. Hence not everything can come to be directly from everything else unless perhaps by being resolved into first matter." Aquinas, *Commentary*, sec. 2438, vol. 2, 860.

something more basic than even atoms. Aristotle called it pure potentiality. The potentiality behind a house is a bunch of bricks. The potentiality behind a brick is a lump of clay. The potentiality behind a lump of clay is a bunch of atoms. Since an atom is itself an in-formed substance, we must not stop our analysis there. We must continue until we reach pure potentiality, something that is not itself an in-formed substance.[22]

So what is pure potentiality? One thing is clear: it is not a material substance. Nothing can be made out of pure potentiality, even by a Supreme Craftsman. Though Aristotle said that everything is "composed" of both form and matter, the scare quotes around "composed" are absolutely necessary. They indicate that we are reaching limits of definition (chapter 3.3). "Composed" in all other contexts suggest that two or more things come together to make something else. But in this context, "composed" cannot mean that. Everything is "composed" of form and matter only in the sense that we can distinguish two "principles"—that which acts (the form) and that which receives the action (the matter).

Yet how helpful is this? "Principles" do not exist, they only describe how *existing* things act. "Principles" by themselves cannot *do* anything. So in one sense, we have gotten no closer to answering our question: where do the things that God in-forms come from?

A different answer to our puzzle is that while everything in the universe must come from some efficient cause, the universe itself does not *come from* anything, it just is. To think otherwise is to commit a fallacy of composition, that is, assuming that what is true of the parts is also true of the whole.[23] The universe has no efficient cause and it needs no efficient

22. Speaking of the probability wave of modern quantum mechanics, Heisenberg writes, "It was a quantitative version of the old concept of '*potentia*' in Aristotelian philosophy. It introduced something standing in the middle between the idea of an event and the actual event, a strange kind of physical reality just in the middle between possibility and reality." Heisenberg, *Physics and Philosophy*, 40–41.

23. This is the substance of Bertrand Russell's famous response to Father Copleston in their 1948 debate on the BBC. It has been transcribed and published in several places, including, Edwards, *A Modern Introduction to Philosophy*, 1973.

Part of Russell's argument is that the universe has no beginning in time so therefore it exists non-contingently. This assumption *appears* reasonable because it is true that anything that has a beginning in time exists contingently. However, logically speaking, it is an illicit contraposition to move from "If something has a beginning in time, then it exists contingently" to "If something has no beginning in time, then it exists non-contingently." (On the right side of figure 10.1 we "picture" what it would mean to speak of an eternal universe that nonetheless exists contingently.)

If Russell had been more logical, he would have understood that from the true premise, "If something has a beginning in time, then it exists contingently" what logically

cause. The individual molecules which make up a plant are not alive, but that does not mean that the plant itself is not alive. The same is true of the universe—while everything *in* it has an efficient cause, the universe as a *whole* has no efficient cause.

There are three problems with this answer. First, the fallacy of composition is an *informal* fallacy. Whether any particular inference from the parts to the whole is or is not fallacious depends on the *content* of the argument. True, we *cannot* infer from the fact that carbon based molecules are not alive, that the plants composed solely of carbon based molecules are not alive too. But we *can* infer from the fact that all the exterior wood on my all wood house is brown that therefore my house is brown. Sometimes the inference from parts to whole is fallacious; sometimes it is not.

Second, scientists estimate that there are approximately 10^{87} fundamental particles in our universe. And this number (10^{87}) is not something scientists discover by pure reason, the way mathematicians calculate the ratio of a circle's circumference to its radius (3.14). In other words, the universe did not have to be composed of 10^{87} number of particles—it could have been 10^{77} or 10^{66} or 10^{55} or even 10! This means that the number of particles in the universe is a contingent truth; not a mathematically necessary truth like the ratio of the circumference of a circle to its radius. (As we said in 4.2, to "exist contingently" simply refers to a thing that would not exist were it not for some other efficient cause.) Finally, by definition, fundamental particles are essentially alike. They must all have the same properties. One cannot be blue and another green. Or one cannot have a measurable mass while another has no measurable mass. So if one of them exists contingently, then *all* of them must exist contingently. Therefore, if *individual* fundamental particles exist contingently, then collectively the *whole* universe must also exist contingently.

The third problem with this answer returns us to the "cosmological conjecture." It is *possible* that the universe "just is" and philosophers should stop worrying about why anything at all actually exists. But that does not solve the puzzle; it ignores the puzzle. And just as a scientist is always free to change vocations, a philosopher can stop asking philo-

---

follows is "If something exists non-contingently, then it has no beginning in time." And of course, that is exactly how Christians have traditionally understood the Creator, i.e., as a non-contingent being that exists outside of time.

sophical questions. But a person who does this cannot reasonably demand that other philosophers stop asking such big questions. Nor can they justifiably accuse philosophers who continue to push their discipline to its limits of acting irrationally.

The difference between a scientist and a philosopher is nicely summed up by a joke circulating on the internet.

> One day a group of atheists got together and decided that humans had come a long way and no longer needed God. So they picked a spokesman to go and tell God that he was no longer needed.
>
> The spokesman walked up to God and said, "God, we've decided that you're no longer needed. We're to the point that we can synthesis new elements, we can create the building blocks of life in a test tube, we can clone sheep and soon we will be able to clone people. There's no end to the miraculous things we can do. You've become irrelevant."
>
> God listened patiently. After the spokesman finished talking, God said, "Very well! How about this? Let's have a person-making contest." To which the spokesman replied, "OK, great!"
>
> But God added, "Now we're going to do this the old fashion way, just as I did it originally."
>
> The spokesman said, "Sure, no problem" and bent down and grabbed a handful of dirt.
>
> God smiled and said, "No, no, no . . . You get your own dirt!"

A scientist is one who smiles at the joke and then continues his work. A philosopher is one who smiles at the joke, and then realizes that the joke *is* his work.

10.4 THE ECOLOGY OF IDEAS

This chapter is relatively short. That may seem surprising since it asks what many take to be a very big question—Does God exist? The surprise, however, comes from our culture's refusal to take the ecology of ideas seriously. We now understand that seemingly small and insignificant changes in one part of a *biological* ecosystem can have significant effects on all the other parts of the ecosystem. In any biological system—be it a single cell or the entire "web of life"—each part supports, and is in turn supported by, all the others.

The same is true of philosophical ideas. Once the seemingly small and insignificant ideas are in place—plants and animals exist; square circles do not; nothing comes from nothing—all the resources necessary to answer the "big" and "exciting" questions about immortality, morality, free will, and God are readily available. And since we have already addressed the small and unexciting questions at some length, the big and exciting questions about God *should*, in one way, seem almost boring. After all, the heavy lifting has already been done.[24]

On the other hand, it is anything but boring to learn that there must be an In-former of all that exists and that this In-former must *not* be thought of as a First Cause or Supreme Craftsman. In fact, the In-former must not be thought of as any *thing*. Instead, the In-former of all that exists can only be known as the agent responsible for the *existence* of everything else. As such, the In-former cannot simply exist as the biggest, the oldest, the most powerful, and most intelligent *thing* that exists. The traditional term which makes this point is "Creator." *That* there is a Creator we know philosophically; *what* the Creator is will forever remain a philosophical puzzle.[25]

In the last book of the *Nicomachean Ethics*, Aristotle warns against heeding those who say we should ask only little questions, questions humans are fully capable of answering. "On the contrary," he said, "we should try to become immortal as far as that is possible and do our utmost to live in accordance with what is highest in us."[26] We agree.

24. I thank my colleague Dan Barnett for the ecology analogy.

25. John Haldane writes, "My earlier reasoning demonstrated the existence of this stone fragment not *qua* (as a) piece of masonry but simply as existing blockage. So we might say that I proved that there is a blockage but did not show anything about its nature ... Thus it is with the causal proofs of the existence of God. They aim to establish the existence of a Transcendent Cause of being, change, and order and so on, from its effects in the world ... Oversimplifying, one might observe that they attempt to prove the *thatness* and not the *whatness* of God." Smart, *Atheism and Theism*, 128–29.

26. Aristotle *Nicomachean Ethics* bk. 10, ch. 7, 1177b32.

11

How Can God Allow Evil?

This chapter discusses the oldest and most powerful objection to the Christian conception of God: If God is good and is also the Creator whose power knows no limit, then why is there so much pain and suffering?

The most common response today is grounded in a libertarian conception of freedom. Since freedom is a great good, and since free people will sometimes chose to misuse their freedom, God was faced with a dilemma: (1) He could create a world populated by truly free people who sometimes cause pain and suffering, or (2) He could create a world in which there is no pain and suffering, but only because there are no truly free people. The libertarian Christian then argues that the first sort of world is better than the second and that therefore the existence of pain and suffering does not disprove the existence of an all loving and all powerful God.

Such a defense is not available to the Thomistic Christian who conceives of human freedom in terms of rational integrity, not autonomous (libertarian) freedom. Instead, they begin their defense by emphasizing the radical distinction between the Creator and the creature. Our existence and God's existence are not the same kind of existence. God and humans, so to speak, inhabit radically different "ontological realms" in the same way Shakespeare and the characters in Hamlet *exist in ontologically distinct realms. And though Hamlet (the character), in one sense, is free to act as he chooses, in another sense, he can do nothing apart from Shakespeare's intentions. So too, Thomists argued that while humans are free to act with rational integrity, they can never act apart from God's intentions, and hence, they never have the kind of autonomy presupposed by libertarians.*

The fact that God and humans inhabit distinct ontological realms leads to several "paradoxes of omnipotence." For example, humans can commit suicide; God cannot. Human parents some-

time succeed in raising children who can flourish independently;
God's children can never flourish apart from him. Humans can
sometimes do their very best; God can never "do his very best" since
he can always do something better. God can no more create "the
best of all possible worlds" than we can name the "biggest number."

Therefore, Thomists' ultimate response to pain and suffering
will always be a "studied silence." Evil is the ultimate mystery, the
mathematical surd, the impossible possibility. Why? Because evil is
ultimately a privation—a lack, a "nothingness"—that nonetheless
reeks havoc in a good creation.

However, penultimately humans can catch a glimpse of the
Creator's intentions by reflecting on the nature of beauty. A single
pane of red glass is costly (because of its gold content) and, in one
sense, might even be beautiful. But it cannot have the beauty of a
skillfully crafted stain glass window because it lacks richness and
diversity. Likewise, we live in a world where all *have been given*
different gifts and asked *to carry different burdens. Right now this*
great diversity of gifts and burdens appears pointless and random.
But Christians believe that a Divine Choreographer is at work and
that one day, in a new heavens and new earth, we will all praise
the beauty of the grand dance in which we danced a small but sig-
nificant part.

S o far this book has focused on Aristotle's solution to classic philosophical problems. But Aristotle was a pagan. Not in the sense that he
was irreligious or hedonistic, but only in the sense that he lived prior to
the Christian era and was at least a nominal adherent of Greek polythe-
ism. So the question of this chapter—How can God allow evil?—never
arose for him the way it did for his Christian and Islamic followers. But
once medieval Islamic and Christian philosophers began to read and
adopt Aristotle's philosophy, the problem of evil was inescapable. In this
chapter we will focus primarily on Aristotle's great Christian interpreter,
Thomas Aquinas.

The problem is this: If we *know* philosophically that there is an In-
former and Creator of all that exists, and we *believe* by faith that this
God is the same one spoken of in the Bible as one who is "merciful and
gracious, slow to anger, and abounding in steadfast love,"[1] then why is
there so much pain and suffering in the world? In the pagan world, the
question does not arise. Even if Zeus was the most powerful god, he was

---

1. Exodus 34:6.

not without rivals. So even if we assumed that Zeus *wanted* to practice "steadfast love," there would be no expectation that his intentions would be unimpeded by other gods.

But if God abounds in steadfast love *and* is also the Creator whose power knows no limit, then the existence of pain and suffering is puzzling, to say the least. Aquinas summed up the problem like this: "Any wise guardian wards off harm and evil from his charges as much as he can. Yet we see many evils in things. Either God cannot prevent them, and so is not almighty, or he does not really care for all." Either way, the traditional Christian conception of God seems to be open to a devastating philosophical objection.[2]

11.1 THE LIBERTARIAN DEFENSE

A common response to this "problem of evil" begins by assuming a libertarian conception of freedom. It then distinguishes between statements which are false and those which are literally meaningless. "Mount Everest is 18,000 feet above sea level" is false (in fact, Everest is more like 27,000 feet above sea level). "Fred made procrastination lay lazily under the seven" is meaningless; it does not even "rise" to the level of falsehood. (Of course, we are assuming that "other things are equal" and that these words are not part of a secret code with a pre-established coherent sense.)

If God is really all-powerful, he must be able to make false statements true, say by sending a massive lightening bolt to knock off the top of Mount Everest so that now it *is* only 18,000 feet above sea level. A God who was unable to do this would not be all-powerful. However, not even an all-powerful God can make procrastination lay lazily under the seven because no possible action is described by such a meaningless phrase. An incoherent string of words does not magically become intelligible when it is applied to God.

The same is true of anyone who asks God for something self-contradictory. An all-powerful God can certainly create a cube of gold that weighs 10,000 pounds. But no God could make a cube of gold with seven sides, since cubes by definition have only six sides. God's "inability" to create seven-sided cubes is not a weakness, since it too is a meaning-

---

2. Aquinas, *ST*, I 22. 2. The problem is much the same for traditional Jewish and Islamic understandings of God. See Burrell, *Freedom and Creation.*

less string of words. Not even an all-powerful God can make or do that which is self-contradictory. "All-powerful" only means that God can do or create anything that is logically self-consistent. This is the first premise of the libertarian defense.

Second, freedom is a great good. An all-powerful God could certainly have created a universe with creatures pre-programmed never to hurt either themselves or others. But such creatures would lack a free will and not be fully human. At best, they would be "human-like" creatures. God could also have miraculously insured that forces of nature would never cause pain or suffering. But if he had chosen to create such a hedonistic paradise, then humans' could never learn to make responsible choices. In such a universe, knives would cut an apple, but would never cut another human being when wielded in anger; and heavy objects would *usually* fall toward earth with a uniform acceleration, but when careless contractors dropped tools from a third floor their acceleration would be "retarded" until all by-passers below had cleared the area. Such a universe is logically possible. However, it would eliminate all opportunities for making responsible choices, and therefore human freedom would also be eliminated.

The third premise follows directly from the second. God could have created a world with only *human-like* creatures pre-programmed to never cause pain or suffering. And as we just illustrated, there is nothing logically impossible about such a world. However, it would not be as good as a world like ours with truly free humans capable of doing good *or* evil. Nor would a hedonistic paradise with no opportunities for responsible choices be as good as one like ours where irresponsible choices result in pain and suffering.

This means that a world with truly free human beings must (in the logical sense) include pain and suffering caused directly by human choice or indirectly by human negligence. It is self-contradictory to think that God could create a world with truly free human beings *and* that he could *ensure* that all his creatures would never cause harm to themselves or others (either directly by wielding a knife on another person or indirectly by carelessly dropping heavy objects on their heads). A world in which humans are truly free and responsible agents *logically* requires the existence of at least some pain and suffering. The idea of truly free people who only do what is good and never suffer as a result of bad or irresponsible choices is logically contradictory.

In sum, the Libertarian Defense looks like this:

1. Even an all-powerful God can only create that which is logically consistent.

2. It is logically impossible to create truly free people who *always* do good.

3. A world with truly free people and pain is *better* than a world without pain but also without truly free people.

4. Therefore, there is no logical contradiction in believing that our world was created by a good and all-powerful God.

It must be emphasized that the point here is purely negative or defensive. No attempt is being made to positively demonstrate that there is such a God (that was the point of the previous chapter). The only point of the libertarian *defense* is to show that the existence of pain and suffering does *not disprove* the existence of a good and all-powerful God.[3]

Furthermore, logic alone cannot tell us *how much* pain and suffering God can justifiably allow. Some skeptics argue that while the existence of a little pain and suffering is consistent with the existence of a good and all-powerful God, it is simply obvious that our world has *much more* than is required by pure logic. But this objection "moves the goal post" in the middle of the game. Again, the libertarian defense only seeks to show that the existence of pain and suffering does not *logically* contradict belief in an all-powerful and good God. For the skeptic to now raise concerns about *how much* pain and suffering exists is to implicitly admit that the purely logical question has been decided in favor of the believer.

And even if we move to this new question—Why *so much* pain and suffering?—the skeptic is caught in an awkward dilemma. If logic alone does not tell us how much pain and suffering is acceptable, then where did the skeptic learn that our world has too much? Let us grant the existence of horrendous pain and suffering. Still, it is horrendous evils that make possible equally heroic choices for good. Now one may

---

3. It is frequently said that "two negative make a positive." That is not true here. "Not disprove" does *not* mean "prove." No one can disprove the existence of flying purple people eaters because no one is able to observe what kinds of creatures exist in other galaxies. But the fact that we cannot disprove the existence of flying purple people eaters is *not* a reason to believe (much less a proof) that such creatures exist. Logicians call this an argument from ignorance.

choose to believe that a world with only a little freedom and a little pain is better than a world like ours where there is both unspeakable pain and superhuman virtue. But this is truly a *choice*. It is not something either evidence or logic compels.

The libertarian defense we have just outlined seems to have become the virtual default position for most Christians today, including many Christian philosophers.[4] And there is no denying its appeal and simplicity. But before considering the alternative, more traditional Christian response to the problem of evil, a standard criticism of the libertarian defense must be considered. It centers on its second premise.

Why should we assume that it is *logically* impossible for truly free people to always make the right choice? There is, after all, no contradiction in supposing that the first choice a truly free human makes is a *good* choice. Nor is there a contradiction in supposing that the second, third, fourth and fifth choices are also good. This may be unlikely, just as it is also unlikely that an honest coin will come up heads the first five times it is flipped. Nonetheless, the latter is not logically impossible. Why, then, should it be *logically* impossible that the first five choices of a truly free person are also good choices? Of course, as we add to either series, it becomes more and more improbable that an honest coin will *only* land heads and that free people will *only* make good choices. It may even become miraculous. But a God who is unable to perform miracles is not all-powerful.

Libertarian Christians would reject the analogy. Yes, by chance it is possible for an honest coin to land heads five (or five hundred) times in a row. But if God or someone else *ensures* that it lands heads, then by definition it is not an honest coin. So too, they say, that a truly free person might by chance make five (or five hundred) good choices in a row. But if God *ensured* that they would, then by definition they would not be free. So, unless God freely chooses to limit his own power for the sake of human freedom, human autonomy will be destroyed. And without autonomy, there is no real freedom (see chapter 9.3).

---

4. Alvin Plantinga and Richard Swinburne are two of the most prominent advocates of the libertarian defense. Plantinga himself calls it the "Free Will Defense." We do not because it suggests that the "countra-causal freedom" of the libertarian is the only proper understanding of free will. As we argued in chapter 9, there are powerful philosophical and moral reasons for understanding "free will" in terms of rational integrity, not autonomous choice. And as we will see later in this chapter, there are also theological reasons to think of freedom in terms of rational integrity.

Such a response, however, comes with a fairly high price. First, it *ipso facto* denies the traditional Christian belief that God controls the *whole* of his creation, including both the *per accidens* efficient causes behind the roll of dice *and* humans' choices. Second, at the heart and center of the Christian faith is the claim that Jesus was fully human, yet without sin. He was crucified, not because he was guilty, but because the rest of humanity was guilty. But God is not a God of confusion. "In him [Jesus]," says Karl Barth, "there is no paradox, no antinomy, no division, no inconsistency, not even the possibility of it."[5] So, if Jesus was fully human, and humans all have a free will, it follows that it is *not*, contrary to the thesis of libertarian Christians, impossible for a free creature *always* to chose what is good.

Whether these difficulties are a price worth paying is something we can only decide in comparison with Augustine's and Aquinas's more traditional response to the problem of evil. Their response acknowledges the reality of evil, yet argues that evil is a privation, and hence, not a *part* of God's creation. But before we can understand their point we must first explain the notion of "Ontological Space."

11.2 ONTOLOGICAL SPACE

"Ontology" is that part of philosophy which studies the various ways things exist. In chapter 5, for example, we distinguished between substances and their forms. Both exist, but they do not exist in the same "ontological space." Forms are real, but they are not *in* things the way dirt is *in* a rug. Rather, they are *in* things the way meaning is *in* words.

We argued in the previous chapter that the world has a Creator. But we also argued that it is a mistake to picture God as either a First Cause or the Supreme Craftsman. To do so places the Creator and the created in the same ontological space. The problem here can be illustrated by considering the relationship between Shakespeare and Hamlet. Both *Hamlet* the play and Hamlet the character are quite literally Shakespeare's creation. True, written copies of the play and actors playing the role of Hamlet existed in the same space/time continuum as Shakespeare. However, the character of Hamlet that Shakespeare created does not. How could he? Shakespeare lived in the sixteenth century whereas the historical setting of *Hamlet* is somewhere around the eleventh century.

---

5. Barth, *CD*, IV.1, 186.

If we try to think of Hamlet and Shakespeare on the same "ontological level," then we are left with the absurdity of Shakespeare creating Hamlet *before* Shakespeare was even born!

Generally speaking, Augustine and Aquinas agree that it is no real limitation on God's power to say that he is "unable" to perform self-contradictory actions. Yet, in addition to being "unable" to make both halves of a contradiction true, God is also "unable" to perform actions which are contrary to his own nature. For example, God is "unable" to commit suicide. And note: we are using scare quotes around "unable" to indicate that such inabilities do not constitute a real limitation of God's power. In other words, we are extending (not denying) the first premise in the libertarian defense.

The ontological distinction between God and everything else also creates certain "limitations" on what God is able to create. Consider, again, the relation between Shakespeare and Hamlet. Shakespeare can write a play in which some of Hamlet's actions are free, while others are not. For example, when Hamlet blindly reacts to a noise behind the curtain and ends up killing Polonius, he is acting with diminished responsibility. However, when he berates and belittles Ophelia, it is pretty clear that Hamlet is fully responsible for his actions.

Yet even when Hamlet is acting freely, he is not acting independently of Shakespeare. How could he? His very existence is dependent on his author, Shakespeare. Shakespeare is free to have his characters do many different things. He is even free to write plays in which the gods miraculously intervene to save the day. But Shakespeare is not free to write a play where his characters act *independent of him*. By definition, Shakespeare is the author of everything Shakespeare's characters do.

The libertarian defense pictures God as "limiting his power" so that humans can act freely and independently of their Creator. But this sort of "self-limitation" by God only makes sense if the Creator and the created are both occupying the same ontological space. Augustine and Aquinas argue that God could no more limit his power over his creatures than Shakespeare could limit his power over his characters. It is self-contradictory to suppose that a creature or a character could act independent of its creator or author.

Before proceeding, however, we should make explicit how various ideas about God and freedom are interrelated and symbiotically connected. First, notice that what libertarians say God *cannot* do, Augustine and Aquinas say God *did* do. Libertarians say it is logically impossible for God to create a free moral agent over whom he has complete and ultimate control. But Augustine and Aquinas say that this is precisely what God did do because it is logically impossible for God to create a free moral agent over whom he *lacks* complete and ultimate control. There is no middle ground here. If the libertarian defense is right, then Augustine and Aquinas are wrong; and vice versa. The choice is forced.

Second, we must admit that there is something paradoxical[6] with Augustine's and Aquinas' claim that humans can be truly free even though everything they do is ultimately dependent upon God. We will address these difficulties with the Augustine's and Aquinas' understanding of freedom presently. And though we believe their arguments are strong and that the apparent paradoxes can be resolved, problems remain.

Yet, we must not lose sight of the bigger picture. We argued in chapters 2 and 3 that no good scientific theory is rejected just because it has unresolved problems. Until a more consistent, coherent, and comprehensive theory is developed, we must settle for the best (even if imperfect) explanation of *all* the data. So too, we must not judge the relative worth of the "libertarian defense" vis-à-vis "the privation defense" in isolation from our previous discussions of morality and science.[7] As we saw in chapter 7, there are some significant problems—both philosophical and scientific—with the sort of mind/body dualism assumed by libertarians. And as we argued in chapter 9, there are also some significant moral problems—with respect to character development—in the libertarian notion of "contra-causal freedom." And finally, as we argued in chapter

---

6. We are using "paradoxical" in its strict, etymological sense of "contrary to popular belief." We are not using "paradox" to mean self-contradictory.

7. One aspect of the problem of evil that has recently been receiving attention by libertarians concerns animal pain. In the past, many Christian libertarians have argued that even animal pain is the result of human freedom. Adam's disobedience in the garden, so it is argued, caused not only his own sorrow and eventual death, but also the corrupt of the whole of creation, including that of the animal kingdom. But now, some of these same philosophers (e.g., John Russell, director of the center for the study of science and religion at the Graduate Theological Union in Berkeley, California) are puzzling about how this response is to be reconciled with the almost universally-recognized proposition that animals have been suffering and dying long before there were any humans on earth.

Here, the thesis that evil is a privation has the advantage and is more comprehensive since it does not assume that all pain and suffering is caused by humans' misuse of their freedom.

10, there is a significant difference between a Creator and a First Cause or Divine Craftsman.

11.3 THE DIVINE CHOREOGRAPHER

God, say Thomists, is like a choreographer.[8] While he is the ultimate cause of everything, the dancers are real secondary causes of their individual movements.[9] This distinction between primary and secondary causes permeates our common language. We speak of architects and contractors as the builders of buildings, even though they never pound a single nail or lift a single brick. We speak of generals winning wars, even though they never fired a single shot. And we speak of doctors healing their patients, even though in modern medicine it is often the nurses who do the actual work.

So too, Thomists say that the Creator is the ultimate and primary cause of everything his creatures are and do,[10] but nevertheless, humans

8. "A thing can escape from the control of a particular cause, but not from that of the universal cause ... So far, then, as any effect escapes the control of some particular cause it is said to be causal or fortuitous in relation to that particular cause, but in relation to the universal cause, from whose control it cannot be withdrawn, it is said to be foreseen. Thus, for example, the meeting of two servants, although it may be fortuitous so far as they are concerned, has nevertheless been foreseen by their master, if he has deliberately sent them to the same place without letting either of them know about the other." Aquinas, *ST*, I 22. 2; cf. *ST*, I 19. 6 and *ST*, I 116.1.

9. Herbert Butterfield uses the analogy of a composer: "We might say that this human story is like a piece of orchestral music that we are playing over for the first time. In our presumption we may act as though we were the composer of the piece or try to bring out our own particular part as the leading one. But in reality I personally only see the part of, shall we say, the second clarinet, and of course even within the limits of that I never know what is coming after the page that now lies open before me. None of us can know what the whole score amounts to except as far as we have already played it over together, and even so the meaning of a passage may not be clear all at once—just as the events of 1914 only begin to be seen in perspective in the 1940s. If I am sure that B flat is the next note that I have to play I can never feel certain that it will not come with surprising implications until I have heard what the other people are going to play at the same moment. And no single person in the orchestra can have any idea when or where this piece of music is going to end." Butterfield, *Christianity and History*, 94.

10. "People are in charge of their acts, including those of willing and of not willing because of the deliberative activity of reason, which can be turned to one side or the other. But that someone should deliberate or not deliberate, supposing that one were in charge of this too, would have to come about by a preceding deliberation. And since this may not proceed to infinity, one would finally have to reach the point at which a person's free decision is moved by some external principle superior to the human mind, namely by God, as Aristotle himself demonstrated. Thus the minds even of healthy

are free and rational agents. When they act, they are real secondary causes of what they choose to do.[11]

In chapter 4, we distinguished modes of existence. Now we need to introduce a corresponding distinction between modes of actions. In English, different modes of actions are typically reflected in the order of adverbs. This is analogous to the order of operations in mathematics. Consider, for example:

- $(2 + 3) \times 4$

- $2 + (3 \times 4)$

These two mathematical operations have different results. The first equals 20; but the second equals 14. Now consider the following propositions:

- If the Creator makes Socrates sit, then it is necessarily true that Socrates is sitting.

- If the Creator makes Socrates sit, then Socrates is sitting necessarily.

---

people are not so much in charge of their acts as not to need to be moved by God; and much more the free choice of man weakened by sin, by which it is hindered from good by the corruption of the nature." Aquinas, *ST*, I–II 109. 3.

11. "By the very fact of being a cause, a being has a certain likeness to God." Aquinas, *SCG*, III 75. "On account of the abundance of his goodness (but not as a defect in his power), God has communicated to creatures the dignity of causality." Aquinas, *ST*, I. 22.3. "It is not out of Gods' incompleteness or weakness that he gives to creatures causal power but out of the perfect fullness which is sufficient to share itself with all." Aquinas, quoted in O'Meara, *Thomas Aquinas*, 75.

Not surprisingly, one of Aquinas' illustrations for independent causality was teaching: "For a professor does not just want his students to be knowledgeable but to be the teacher of others." Aquinas, *ST*, I 103.6. God gives independence to creatures "not by a lack of power but by an immensity of goodness; he has wished to communicate to things a resemblance to him in that they would not only exist but be the cause of others." Aquinas, *SCG*, III 70.7. "Therefore, God so communicates His goodness to created beings that one thing which receives it can transfer it to another. Therefore, to take away their proper actions from things is to disparage the divine goodness." Aquinas, *SCG*, III 69.16. "It is also apparent that the same effect is not attributed to a natural cause and to divine power in such a way that it is partly done by God, and partly by the natural agent; rather, it is wholly done by both, according to a different way, just as the same effect is wholly attributed to the instrument and also wholly to the principal cause." Aquinas, *SCG*, III 70.8.

In the first, "necessarily" modifies the proposition "Socrates is sitting;" it tells us nothing about *how* or *why* he is sitting. In the second, "necessarily" modifies "sitting." In other words, it describes *why* he is sitting; in this case, that he is being compelled to sit. Following the math analogy the difference looks like this:

- If God wills X, then necessarily (X comes to be)
- If God wills X, then (X comes to be necessarily)

Therefore, the first statement in each pair of bullets is always true. No creature can resist the direct action of the Creator. But the second statement in each pair of bullets is not always true; sometimes the Creator may choose to choreograph the *per accidens* efficient cause so that Socrates sits as the result of his own free choice. There is a lot packed into this last sentence, so a quick review of the argument in chapter 9 is in order.

According to Aristotelians, a person is free when two conditions are met: 1) the person's action is directed toward a rational goal, and 2) the person's actions is the result of *per accidens* efficient causes, not *per se* (i.e. humanly predictable) efficient causes. The Creator is certainly able to make Socrates sit via *per se* efficient causes. If the Creator orders events so that a bear chases Socrates for a couple of miles and consequently Socrates is utterly exhausted, then there would be a *per se* and humanly predicable cause of his sitting. Hence, we would say that Socrates is sitting necessarily.

Now the only way humans can make things happen necessarily is through the use of *per se* efficient causes. For example, hitting someone else over the head with a baseball bat is a humanly predictable cause of their collapsing. And when one human forces someone else to act via such causes, there is no freedom. However, a God who is also the Creator of all that exists has another alternative for making things happen. A Creator can choreograph the *per accidens* efficient causes. And the Creator of all that exists will never have his intentions thwarted. So when the Creator intends for Socrates to sit, there is never a need to add the qualification, "other things being equal." But when Socrates sits as the result of *per accidens* efficient causes, his actions are caused, but not determined (see chapter 9 and the type/token distinction of chapter 7).

Since humans do not occupy the same ontological space as the Creator, there can be no perfect human analogy for making someone else act via *per accidens* efficient causes in such a way that their freedom is not violated. But we can imagine situations in which there is a clear difference between:

- Sally made Fred's choice (so Fred was not free).
- Sally made Fred choose (though Fred was also free).

Suppose, for example, that Sally, a Thomistic philosopher, just won a million dollar lottery and throws a party to celebrate. One of the guests celebrating with her is her libertarian friend and colleague, Fred. Unbeknownst to Fred, Sally tells the other guests that she is going to arrange things so that Fred *freely* chooses to reach out and touch Sally's right hand.

This is what she does. Walking up to Fred she takes a hundred dollar bill from her purse and places it in her right hand. She then places a penny in her left hand. This is done in such a way that Fred clearly sees what is in both hands. Turning to Fred, she says, "You may have the contents of my hand that first makes contact with yours." Fully appreciating the hilarity of the situation, Fred quickly moves his hand so that it touches Sally's right hand. Here we have a situation plausibly described as one where Sally made Fred choose, even though Fred's choice was free.

Contrast this with a second example. Fred jokingly asks to play this game again. Sally, to Fred's surprise and delight, says "Of course." So she reaches into her purse, pulls out another hundred dollar bill for her right hand and a penny for her left hand. However, this time, before Fred can act, Sally moves her left hand so that it touches Fred's hand. She then gives him the penny! This time we have a situation plausibly described as one where Sally made Fred's "choice." Here we place "choice" in scare quotes since clearly Fred was not acting freely.

There are two crucial differences here. In the first case, Sally was, so to speak, working *through* Fred's own actions. Furthermore, Fred's action was directed toward a good goal. Assuming as we are that "other things are equal" (e.g., the money is not stolen, it was not the product of oppression or fraud, etc.), it is better to have a hundred dollars than a penny. However, in the second case, Fred was not an active participant. Instead, he was the passive recipient of Sally's action. And, unlike the first case, the results for Fred were not good. In short, the first case conforms to both Thomistic criteria for freedom. The second conforms to neither libertarian nor Thomistic criteria.

However, a libertarian would undoubtedly describe the first case differently. Though in one sense, Fred's choice was predicted by Sally. In another sense it was not. After all, Sally was not *totally* in control of the situation. It is perfectly possible that one of the guests who heard her prediction would "leak" it to Fred, and Fred, just to make his libertarian convictions clear, deliberately chose the hand with the penny.

This is a real possibility. But far from refuting Thomists point, it confirms their very thesis. Only the Creator of all that exists can infallibly choreograph the *per accidens* efficient causes. With the Creator, there is never a need to attach an "other things being equal" clause. In the case of humans, knowledge must conform to reality. *Believing* that something will happen, does not ensure that it will happen. But in the case of the Creator, believing that something will happen *does* ensure that it will happen.[12]

An important corollary of the Creator's choreography of *per accidens* efficient causes is that the results are always good. This brings us to the critical asymmetry between good and evil.

One variety of ancient dualism conceived of good and evil as two equal and opposite primordial principles. Frequently "good" was identified with spiritual things and "evil" was identified with material things. Here, good and evil are related as white paint and black paint. They both exist as independent substances. However, Christians have always rejected this dualism.[13] The Bible itself begins by declaring that God created heaven and earth and *they were good*. Christians have, therefore, traditionally likened "good" and "evil" to light and dark. "Darkness" is not an independently existing substance. Rather, it is the absence of light.

---

12. Strictly speaking, we should have put scare quotes around "will happen" since the Creator is not our ontological equivalent and therefore we should not use future tense verbs to describe him.

13. It is the original and perhaps most enduring of Christian heresies. It first appeared with the Gnostics. Among other things, Gnostics taught that the god of the Old Testament and the god of the New Testament were distinct supernatural beings. The Old Testament god was composed of flesh; while the New Testament god was composed of spirit. And while flesh is inherently bad, spirit is inherently good. The Manicheans, against whom Augustine wrote many polemics, taught this same doctrine. In the thirteenth century, this misconception was embraced by the Albigensians, against whom Aquinas engaged in polemics.

Again, we must not think of evil as the opposite of good. God is uncreated and wholly good; Satan is God's creation gone bad. Satan cannot be wholly bad the way God is wholly good. If he were, he would cease to exist. Instead, evil is essentially a lack, a missing of the mark, a privation. When a parasite kills the organism on which it feeds, it too dies. So too, for something to become *wholly* corrupt is for it to pass out of existence.

We said earlier that there are at least three things that the Creator of all things cannot do. He cannot make both sides of a logical contradiction true. Nor can he violate his own nature, for example, by committing suicide. Finally, he cannot act in such a way that the ontological distinction between Creator and creature is violated, for example, by creating a creature which is not totally dependent on him. Now we need to add a fourth—the Creator cannot create nothing. "To create" is necessarily to create something. It is easy to make a flashlight. But not even the Creator of all that is can make a "flashdark." Since Augustine and Aquinas both conceive of evil as a privation,[14] it follows that everything the Creator creates must be good, because not even the Creator can create "darkness" or "nothingness."

This argument is so foreign to modern modes of thought that it is likely to be misunderstood. "How," moderns will say, "can a person seriously argue evil is not real? Have not Thomists heard of the Holocaust? Do they honestly think that this is 'the best of all possible worlds?'"

First, Thomists are certainly not Holocaust deniers. Nor do they minimize the pain and suffering caused by Hitler and his minions. Evil is no less real because it is not a thing or substance. Second, Thomists explicitly argue that the notion of "the best of all possible worlds" is incoherent. So he certainly did not create one, since the "best of all possible worlds" is not something an all-powerful Creator *could* create, even if he wanted to. Here is why:

---

14. In the ecology of ideas, conceiving of evil as a privation fits much better with the theory of evolution than does the libertarian defense. If evolution is true, then animal pain and suffering existed long before the first bad choice by a human. Some try to argue that it was Satan's bad choice to rebel against God that is responsible for animal pain and suffering, but this seems a little *ad hoc*.

11.4 THE PARADOX OF OMNIPOTENCE

"Omnipotence" is philosopher's jargon for "all-powerful." We are deliberately using such jargon to call attention to something quite paradoxical.[15] It is one thing to say, as we already have, that there are some things even an all-powerful Creator cannot do. Now we want to add that there are some things we can do that God cannot do! These all flow from the fundamental logical truth that God cannot create another God.[16] God is omnipotent. But it is logically impossible that *two* omnipotent beings exist for the same reason that there cannot be *two* "best Presidents of the United States."[17] In other words, it is logically impossible for the Creator to create what is best or greatest because he already holds those positions. Anything which God creates must necessarily be less-than-the-best. This simple logical truth has several corollaries.

Suppose an omnipotent and good Creator created a universe in which there were exactly a billion people with real freedom, yet there was *no* pain and suffering. Would this be the "best of all possible worlds"? Hardly. Presumably each of these billion people enjoys their existence. So what could possibly be wrong with such a universe? Perhaps nothing. But it still does not warrant the description, "best of all possible worlds" because it is quite easy to conceive of a *better* universe, namely, one just like this one, only it is populated with a billion and one people. A demigod shaping pre-existent material might run out of stuff to make the billionth and first person, but this cannot be a problem for an omnipotent Creator who creates out of nothing. There is nothing that could prevent such a God from choosing to create this second, "better" universe. Yet, it is equally obvious that we have now entered a regress that will never end.

The first paradox of divine omnipotence is that while humans can occasionally do the "best possible job," God can never "do his best." God can create a good universe; he can even create a very good universe.

---

15. Again, we are using the term in its strictly etymological sense of "contrary to popular belief."

16. Augustine writes, "for that which was made of nothing could not be equal to Him [God], and indeed could not be at all had He not made it." Augustine, *City of God*, bk. 12, ch. 5. The rest of this chapter is a clear exposition of evil as a privation.

17. "For it is not possible that there be two highest goods, since that which is said by superabundance is found in only one being." Aquinas, *SCG*, I 42.2.

But he cannot create the "best possible universe."[18] When humans do less than their best, they may be morally culpable. But God could not be morally culpable for doing less than his best because it is logically impossible for a God who creates out of nothing to ever "do his best."[19]

Second, in many contexts, striving for perfection is praiseworthy. Yet, perfectionism can also be self-defeating. If a gymnast is awarded a perfect 10 or a student earns an A+, it is hard for a perfectionist to continue. Nothing a perfectionist does can top the previous performance and most likely anything one does will fall short. Such thoughts can be paralyzing. But *good* gymnasts and students are not perfectionists; they know that even though they cannot top their last performance, they must act, even if their actions will be less than perfect. What is true of gymnasts and students is *always* true of the Creator. If the Creator waited to create until he had a "perfect plan," none of us would exist. The second paradox of omnipotence is that it is *good* for us that the Creator is not a perfectionist. If he were, we would not exist.

That's why Thomists insist that creation is not a product of calculation. It is an act of love.[20] The Creator creates, not for his own benefit, but solely for the benefit of his creatures. As Christians tell the story, God "knew in advance"[21] that the most privileged of his creatures— humans—would rebel out of envy. To be made in the very image of God and to reflect God's glory was not enough. We wanted to shine on our own and be what we were not and could not be—our own creator and God. With Milton's Satan, we said to ourselves: "We know no time when we were not as now; Know none before us, self-begot, self-raised"[22]

18. See Aquinas, *ST*, I 25.6; Aquinas, *SCG*, II 45.

19. Theologians make this same point when they insist that God is perfectly free. If there *were* a "best of all possible worlds" then, because God is good, he would be constrained to create that universe instead of some other universe.

20. "The knowledge of the divine persons was necessary [for us] for two reasons. The first was to give us the right idea of creation. To assert that God made all things through his Word is to reject the error according to which God produced things by natural need; and to place in him the possession of love is to show that if God has produced creatures, this is not because he needed them for himself nor for any other cause extrinsic to him; but rather through love of his goodness." Aquinas, *ST*, I 32.

21. The scare quotes are necessary since the Creator and the created do not inhabit the same ontological space or *time*.

22. Milton, *Paradise Lost*, bk. V, 859–60. Compare with Isaiah 47:10—"You felt secure in your wickedness; you said, 'No one sees me.' Your wisdom and your knowledge led you astray, and you said in your heart, 'I am, and there is no one besides me.'"

Absurd as it is, we demanded equality with our creator. Nonetheless, God freely chose to create what he knew would be good, but not perfect, because only he is perfect.

A final paradox of omnipotence is that God, unlike human parents, cannot raise his children to flourish independently on their own. Good parents do not want their children to remain dependent upon them for the whole of their life; God does. And good earthly fathers frequently succeed in raising children capable of flourishing independently. But this is something that God is incapable of doing. So even though Christians refer to God as a father, God the Father is *not* like a good earthly father.

While the Kantian paradigm of freedom and dignity is a fully autonomous human, it is not God's. Nor could it have been. Creating fully autonomous humans is not something he *could* have created, even if he had so chosen. In this respect, God is more like an engineer than a parent. No engineer can design a screwdriver that is better at sawing wood than at driving screws. Screwdrivers are made to drive screws; that is by definition what they do best. So too, for God to create human beings that could flourish apart from him would be like creating a screwdriver that is better at cutting wood than driving screws. Both are self-contradictory.

E. L. Mascall got it exactly right: "When a man tries to exclude God from the act and make himself the primary agent, all that he manages to do is to introduce an element of sheer destruction and negation, an element which contravenes the man's own nature as fundamentally dependent upon God, an element which is not genuine activity but is rather deficiency in actuality, an element which goes against the creature's own inbuilt finality and is therefore self-frustrating and self-destructive."[23]

The problem of evil as it is classically formulated presupposes that God should be good in the same way humans are good. But this assumption overlooks a fundamental fact of logic—God cannot reproduce himself. It is good for a person to always do the best she can and it is good for a parent to raise children who grow to be independent flourishing adults. God does neither of these and his failure to be good in these ways is what gives the "problem of evil" its apparent force. Yet, when we consider the paradoxes of omnipotence, it is clear that God's failure to be good in these distinctly human ways points neither to his malevolence nor his impotence.

---

23. Mascall, *Openness of Being*, 254.

We can illustrate the point with a series of questions. Suppose we were omnipotent and given an opportunity to create out of nothing anything we desired. Surely, we might think, we would not create a universe with cancers, hurricanes, tsunamis, and earthquakes. But why stop there? Why not create a universe in which everyone lived to one hundred and twenty before dying a peaceful death in bed? Then, again, why not create a universe in which everyone lived forever, with no physical pain or mental anguish? Would not this be a better universe than our own?

Perhaps. But would it include baseball games with winners and losers, tennis matches with victors and vanquished? If so, then it seems a minimal amount of mental anguish would be acceptable. But where would we draw the line? Would there be high stakes poker or would all poker be penny ante?

And how many people would we create to populate our universe with no death, no physical pain, and only a minimal amount of mental anguish? And would "potential people" who were denied an unending life of everlasting bliss have reason to protest their exclusion? Of course, we could always create one more person, but we could not create an infinite universe, since we are pretending that we are now God, and hence, the only infinite being. So should we create some arbitrarily limited number of blissful people or not create at all?

Rather than attempting to *answer* such questions, Augustine and Aquinas are simply silent. Knowing what questions *not* to answer is as important as answering ones that should be answered. The paradoxes of omnipotence make it clear that we only see through a glass dimly.[24]

One implication of such studied silence is that we must steadfastly resist the temptation to identify evil with particular people (like Hitler) or groups of people (like evil empires). Augustine once prayed: "The good I do is done by you in me and by your grace; the evil is my fault."[25] If good and evil were related like black paint and white paint, Augustine's prayer

---

24. In his commentary on Job, Aquinas wrote: "After the debate of Job and his friends about divine providence had been premised, Elihu had assumed for himself the office of determining the debate, criticizing Job on certain points but his friends on others. But *since human wisdom is not sufficient to comprehend the truth of divine providence,* it was necessary that the debate just mentioned be determined by divine authority." (emphasis added, Aquinas, *Job,* 460–70). David Burrell and Brian Davies make similar points in their books *Deconstructing Theodicy: Why Job Has Nothing to Say to the Puzzle of Suffering* and *The Reality of God and the Problem of Evil.*

25. Augustine, *Confessions,* 209–10.

would be unintelligible. When we conceive of good and evil as opposite ends of a continuum, then *either* God would be responsible for both the good that we do and the evil that we do *or* we would have to be ultimately responsible for both the good and evil. To split responsibility—so that God gets credit for the good and we get blamed for the evil—would be like the old joke about the Soviet Union: "What's ours is ours; what's yours is negotiable." Yet, once we understand that good and evil are *not* opposite ends of a continuum, but instead, are related like light and dark, Augustine's prayer is no longer puzzling, but profoundly humbling.[26] But for God's grace, I would be nothing.

Only God can create out of nothing. Satan cannot create a single clod of dirt; he can only ruin what God creates.[27] The same is true of humans. We can make many good things, but when we do so, we are making them out of other good things supplied by God.[28] We have the power, however, to corrupt good things, so to speak, "out of nothing." We say "out of nothing" because when we corrupt good things, we are not making them bad by *adding* bad things to them. Nothing God has created is intrinsically bad. When people make bad things they are only

26. Some theologians reject the asymmetry between good and evil. They argue that just as God predestines some to heaven he also predestines others to hell. (Notes 17 and 18 in the next chapter consider Karl Barth's "single predestination.") The problem with double predestination is twofold. 1) By maintaining that God intentionally creates humans with irredeemable sin whose end is damnation, it treats evil as if it were a created substance. 2) It fails to distinguish between that which is foreseen and that which is intended. For example, a doctor may foresee that a drug will cause a patient to lose his hair, but his only intent is to kill cancer. Similarly, God's intention is to create a "very good" universe, but to do so, he must permit evil since the only perfect Being is God (Luke 18:19). That is not to say that there is no puzzle in the doctrine of predestination. But the mystery is *not* that moral freedom and God's sovereignty are logically contradictory. Instead, it is the mystery of creation itself: why did God create people to glorify him forever? He certainly does not need children the way a mother needs a baby to suckle. Nor does the praise of his creatures somehow increase his glory. As Robert Sokolowski perceptibly put it: God plus nothing is no less great than God plus everything else.

27. "At the end of the poem [*Paradise Lost*] Adam is astonished at the power 'that all this good of evil shall produce' (XII, 470). This is the exact reverse of the programme Satan had envisaged in Book I, when he hoped, if God attempted any good through him, to 'pervert that end' (164); instead he is allowed to do all the evil he wants and finds that he had produced good. Those who will not be God's son become His tools." Lewis, *Preface to Paradise Lost*, 67–68.

28. "Nothing can act beyond its species, since the cause must always be more powerful than its effect." Aquinas, *ST*, I–II 112.1.

ruining the good things created by God. To make something good is an act of addition; to make something bad is an act of subtraction.

Remember, evil is a parasite; it has no independent existence as either a force or a person in opposition to God. Paradoxically, if evil ever succeeded in corrupting everything, like a virus which killed the last living cell, it too would cease to exist.[29] God cannot create bad things. But it would be misleading to think of this as one of God's *moral* virtues. The fact that good and evil are related like light and dark means that God *could not* create something evil. God is good, but not like morally good people. Morally good people are able to resist temptation; God never resists temptation, because nothing *can* tempt God.

Human bakers make two kinds of donut holes. First, there is the literal hole in the center of a donut; second, there is the ball of dough that bakers bake and sell as "donut holes." These two kinds of donut holes are quite distinct. No baker can sell the void in the center of a donut apart from selling the donut. Though bakers make donuts with *real* holes in

---

29. Aquinas puts it like this: "every thing that is must necessarily be good so far as it is being. For every thing loves its own being and desires its preservation, an indication of which is the fact that every thing resists its own dissolution; and *the good is that which all things desires* [here he is quoting Aristotle] . . . Hence, a thing must be evil so far as it is a non-being. But this is a being deprived of being; . . . indeed, evil is itself this very privation." Aquinas, *SCG*, II 41.5-10. See also Blanchette, *The Perfection of the Universe*, 116.

Jesus said "Without me you can do nothing" to which Jacques Maritain says, "That text can be read in two ways, . . . Without Me you can not commit the slightest act in which there is being or good; but if it concerns the line of evil, then the text should be otherwise interpreted: . . .without Me you can do nothingness . . . Thus we must reason in two different ways according to whether we are considering the line of evil or the line of good. Such dissymmetry is absolutely necessary from the very fact that the line of good is the line of being, and the line of evil is the line of non-being and of privation." Maritain, *St. Thomas and the Problem of Evil*, 24–38.

Finally, Karl Barth puts it like this: "There is opposition and resistance to God's world-dominion. There is in world-occurrence an element, indeed an entire sinister system of elements, which is not comprehended by God's providence in the sense thus far described, and which is not therefore preserved, accompanied, nor ruled by the almighty action of God like creaturely occurrence . . . This opposition and resistance, this stubborn element and alien factor, may be provisionally defined as nothingness." Barth, *CD*, III, 3, 289.

The fact that Barth, the leading Reformed theologian of the twentieth century, whose tradition is in many ways opposed to Thomism, also equates evil with nothingness makes it all the more puzzling that most Christian philosophers respond to Hume with the "libertarian defense" and not the older Augustinian/Thomistic response which treats evil as a privation.

the center, these holes cannot be made the way bakers make and sell fried balls of donut dough.

Though we risk repetition, nonetheless we will be explicit: on the Thomistic understanding of creation, evil is like literal donut holes—it is an absence, a lack, a missing of the mark; it is not an independently existing substance. Evil is not something that God could create nor is it something he refrains from creating. That is why it is misleading to frame the problem of evil as a question about God's *moral* goodness as if God made a *choice* about the kind of universe to create while we sit in judgment to determine if he made the *morally* correct choice.[30]

11.5 DIVERSITY AS A PERFECTION OF THE COSMOS

Nonetheless, though we are in no position to judge God's moral goodness, we do know that evil is an absence or lack of a special sort. Both rocks and people born blind lack the ability to see. But the rock's inability to see is not evil; rocks were never intended to see. However, the inability in humans to see is an evil because people were intended to see. Rocks lack sight, but only people (and other animals) can be *deprived* of sight.[31]

Thomists picture creation as a vast chain of being (see chapter 3) where all members make an essential contribution to its beauty and glory, though they do not make an equal contribution. There is a hierarchy. Rocks and people do not make the *same* contribution. Rocks are necessary and people are necessary, but they make different contributions to the beauty of creation. The part played by rocks does not require sight; the part played by humans does. So for people to deprive either themselves or someone else of sight is to corrupt the goodness and beauty of the divinely intended order. But for God to "deprive" rocks of sight is not to corrupt anything. Rocks were never meant to see. Or at least, this is how Thomists understand the great chain of being. But how plausible is this story?

---

30. See Davies, *The Reality of God and the Problem of Evil*, especially ch. 4.

31. "Although generation is from not-existing, one should realize that we maintain, not that negation is a principle, but rather that privation is, for negation does not determine a subject for itself ... Privation is attributed only to a determinate subject in which the missing perfection is meant to be. For example, blindness is attributed only to those things that were born to see." Aquinas, *Principles of Nature*, ch. 2.

Modernity has rebelled against all hierarchies. Any hierarchical arrangement is assumed to be the product of oppressors. Yet, at the same time, it seems that any and all diversity is held to be worthy of praise.[32] But how can this be? Have we forgotten that hierarchies and diversity are flip sides of the same coin? Mere difference is neither good nor bad. In a garbage dump there is much diversity and in a mountain there is a great diversity of rocks. Yet such "diversity" is hardly praiseworthy. Diversity is only worth celebrating when it results in a well ordered whole where the whole is more than the sum of its parts.

For example, in a stain glass window, the red glass is more costly than the other colors of glass. But that does not mean that the more valuable windows are the ones with the most red glass. When a skillful artist *orders* different colors of glass into a beautiful picture, the whole window takes on a value greater than the value of its individual parts.[33] Though there is an ascending order value to various colors of glass, that does not mean that a window composed solely of the most costly glass is best. Such a window would lack the proper diversity.[34]

32. Jürgen Habermas once challenged Hilary Putnam to give him as example of a value that was more than a mere preference. Putnam responded: "I believe that, other things being equal, a world in which there are a variety of (morally permissible) conceptions of human flourishing is better than one in which everyone agrees on just one conception ... [O]ther things being equal, a world in which there is this kind of diversity is *better*." Putnam, *Collapse of the Fact/Value Dichotomy*, 112–13.

33. "In the organization of the world, the inequality of the parts ... has as its goal the perfection of the totality—as we see in works of art." Aquinas, *ST*, I 47.2. "The perfection of the universe requires a certain inequality in beings so that all levels of good can be present ... God makes what is better in the totality but not in each part ... and if there are in the universe some beings which can defect from good, at some time some of them will defect. Still it belongs to providence not to destroy nature but to preserve it ... God is so powerful that he can even do well from evil realities." Aquinas, *ST*, I 48.2. Also see Aquinas, *ST*, I 96.3 on hierarchy in the state of innocence before the fall.

34. "It is written (Romans 13:1): 'The things which are of God, are well ordered.' But order chiefly consists in inequality; for Augustine says (*The City of God*, xix, 13): 'Order disposes things equal and unequal in their proper place.' Therefore in the primitive state, which was most proper and orderly, inequality would have existed." Aquinas, *ST*, I, 96, 3.
Again, "In a whole the good is the integrity which results from the order and composition of the parts. Hence it is better for a whole that there be a disparity among its parts, without which there cannot be the order and perfection of a whole, than that all its parts be equal, with each one of them attaining the degree of the most noble part. Yet any part of an inferior degree, considered in itself, would be better if it were in the degree of a superior part. This is evident in the human body: the foot would be a more worthy part if it were to have the beauty and the power of the eye; but the body as a whole would be imperfect, if it lacked the function of the foot." Aquinas, *SCG*, III 94.11.

Aquinas explicitly makes this same point concerning God's cosmos. "Those reason falsely," Aquinas declares, who say that "since an angel is better than a stone, therefore two angels are better than one angel and a stone ... Although an angel, considered absolutely [i.e., by itself] is better than a stone, nevertheless two natures are better than one only; and therefore a universe containing angels and other things is better than one containing angels only; since the perfection of the universe is attained essentially in proportion to the diversity of natures in it, whereby the diverse grades of goodness are filled, and not in proportion to the multiplication of individuals of a single nature."[35]

It is crucial that we not forget the distinction between the value of a whole and value of its parts. When a doctor prescribes chemotherapy, he can foresee that the patient's hair will fall out. Yet, that is not the intended goal. Considered *by itself* the loss of hair is not good and is not intended by a good doctor. However, considered *as a whole*, the loss of hair is good since it is necessary for the patient's recovery.[36]

Yet, a God who can move mountains, turn water into wine and resurrect the dead does not face similar constraints on his power to act. If God were the cancer patient's doctor, he could kill the cancer without also causing a loss of hair. So in God's case, it is frequently objected, it is incoherent to speak of an unintended effect which is nonetheless foreseen. Anything foreseen by God would also be intended by God.

But this objection fails to consider the paradoxes of omnipotence. Again, we all ought to thank God that he is not a perfectionist. Were God unable to tolerate privations of good, none of us would exist. Only God would exist. Anything God chooses to create is necessarily going to exist in a less perfect way.[37] Remember, not even God can create a *second* "best President of the United States." Only God is wholly good. Privations which are evil are a logically necessary element of anything God chooses to create. But the evil in creation will not be something that

---

35. Aquinas, *I Sent. Dist.* XLIV, q.1, a.2. quoted in Lovejoy, *Great Chain of Being*, 77. Also quoted in Blanchette, *The Perfection of the Universe*, 298–99. See also Aquinas, *ST*, I 47.1 and 2; I 65.2.

36. In Thomistic terms, this is the distinction between the antecedent and consequent will of God. "Antecedently considered" (i.e. considered by itself) God never wills evil. However, "consequently considered" (i.e. considered as a whole), God sometimes wills that the individual parts be of lesser value thereby increasing the value of the whole.

37. Aquinas, *ST*, I 7.2. See also I 19.4

he chooses *in itself* to create. Rather, it is the necessary consequent of any good he creates. Evil will be foreseen, but not intended.

On the other hand, there is a sense in which Aquinas' believes that the created order is "perfect." But we must remember that the word "perfection" means something radically different than it did eight hundred years ago when Aquinas wrote. Back then, "perfection" only meant "complete" or "fully formed."[38] Aquinas never suggested that God's cosmos was the highest possible grade in a series of value—"good, better, and best." And he was definitely *not* saying that on a scale of 1 to 10 our universe deserves a "perfect 10." (Again, the notion of God creating the "best of all possible universes" is incoherent.) A "perfect" cosmos for Aquinas was one that contained everything necessary to accomplish its fundamental goal—to give glory to God and to enable humans to enjoy him forever. There is simply no end to the beauty of God and his creation. The redeemed of the Lord will praise his beauty for ever and ever without end.[39]

Yet, such a high and lofty goal for creation transcends anything that philosophy is capable of knowing. If this is God's goal in creation, it is something humans will only know through faith in God's own self-revelation. (We will say much more about this in the next chapter.) Philosophy can never demonstrate that God loves us; that is an essentially theological task. All philosophy can do is to counter the assertion that the existence of so much pain and suffering refutes the belief that our cosmos was created by a good God.

Furthermore, philosophy must never presume to explain how *individual* instances of pain or suffering can give glory to God or allow

---

38. "Thus, in its original meaning as seen by Aristotle and Aquinas, perfection does not refer to any special kind of excellence, but simply to a kind of expected completion at the end of a process. 'What we call the nature of each and every thing is what is fitting for it when its generation has been perfected: as the nature of man is what he has after the perfection of his generation; and similarly for the horse and for the house, as long as by the nature of the house is understood its form' (*In I Pol.*, lec. 1, n. 32)." Blanchette, *Perfection of the Universe*, 45.

39. Karl Barth writes, "If we can and must say that God is beautiful, to say this is to say how He enlightens and convinces and persuades us. It is to describe not merely the naked fact of His revelation or its power, but the shape and form in which it is a fact and is power. It is to say that God has this superior force, this power of attraction, which speaks for itself, which wins and conquers, in the fact that He is beautiful, divinely beautiful." Barth and Aquinas may be in opposition on some matters, but his words here will certainly warm the hearts of Thomists everywhere. Barth, *CD*, II.1, 650.

humans to enjoy God more fully. Evil is like mortality rates. Actuaries can determine with a high degree of precision the mortality of various *classes* of people. But they are no better than fortune tellers at determining when any *particular* person will die. Thomistic philosophers take God's condemnation of Job's friends seriously and never pretend to know why any particular person is suffering. [40] Aquinas' statements about evil are all propositions about *classes* (like statements by actuaries); they are not *generalizations* applicable to any particular case.[41]

We must never forget: according to Aquinas all we can know while here on earth is *that* God exists; we will never know *what* God is in his essence, and hence, we will never know his specific purposes. Thomists do not even presume to explain how specific classes or kinds of pain and/or suffering *in fact* give glory to God. But here is one way the diversity of human experience *may* contribute to God's glory and human's ability to enjoy God forever.

If it is true that no two human beings have the same fingerprints, it is certainly true that no two humans on earth have had the same life experiences. Some have been blessed with a long life largely devoid of suffering. Others have had to endure countless agonies, only to die before seeing even a glimmer of good growing out of their pain. Some have been required to courageously face the amputation of a leg without anesthetics. Others have felt the pain of hearing the doctor say, "I'm sorry, you have cancer." If there is one thing we know for sure, it is that life is not fair.

St. John wrote in the *Apocalypse* that in the new heavens and earth each person will be given "a white stone with a new name written on it, known only to him who receives it."[42] To which C. S. Lewis asks, "What

---

40. See Boethius, *The Consolation of Philosophy*, bk. IV, ch. 6 for possible ways privations may increase the value of the whole. For God's condemnation of Job's friends, see Job 42:7.

41. "Model T Fords are rare" is a *class* statement. "Model T Fords have four cylinders" is a *generalization*. Generalizations make a statement about every member of the class. To say that "Model T Fords have four cylinders" is to say that if one looks at any particular Model T Ford, they will see that it has four cylinders. But to say that "Model T Fords are rare" is a statement about the class as a whole, i.e., there are not many Model Ts left. This means, among other things, that they are seen infrequently while driving. However, if one spots a Model T on the road, it is no harder to "see" than any other car one sees on the road. In other words, we "see them infrequently" because the class of Model T Fords is small; not because any particular Model T Ford is too small to see.

42. Revelation 2:17.

can be more a man's own than this new name which even in eternity remains a secret between God and him? And what shall we take this secrecy to mean?" His own answer is perfect.

> Surely, that each of the redeemed shall forever know and praise some one aspect of the divine beauty better than any other creature can. Why else were individuals created, but that God, loving all infinitely, should love each differently? . . . Aristotle has told us that a city is a unity of unlikes, and St. Paul that a body is a unity of different members. Heaven is a city, and a Body, because the blessed remain eternally different: a society, because each has something to tell all the others—fresh and ever fresh news of the "My God" whom each finds in him and whom all praise as "Our God."[43]

Yes, God is not fair.[44] We have not been dealt equally good hands. No Thomist will quibble with this obvious truth.[45] Nor will any Thomist deny that much unfairness in this life is the result of human injustice. Therefore, it is morally incumbent for all of us, but especially those who are blessed here on earth, to work for the correction of injustices wherever they are found.[46] To whom much is given, much is required—both

43. Lewis, *Problem of Pain*, 154–55.

44. John Rawls famously argued that justice *is* fairness. If this is true, then acknowledging that God is unfair is tantamount to saying that he is unjust. But no Thomists draw such a conclusion. Instead, they argue that Rawls was mistaken about the definition of justice. One of Aquinas's most quoted passages in the Bible was the story of parable of the workman (Matt 20:1–16). In that parable, a farmer promises to pay a standard days wage to laborers in his field. Many start their work in the morning; some start at noon; a few do not begin work until an hour before quitting time. When the farmer paid all the laborers the standard day's wage, those who began work in the morning protested that the farmer was being unfair. And, of course, he was. But where was the injustice? As the farmer himself said to one of the protesting laborers, "Friend, I am doing you no wrong; did you not agree with me for a denarius [the standard day's wage]? Take what belongs to you, and go; I choose to give to this last as I give to you. Am I not allowed to do what I choose with what belong to me? Or do you begrudge my generosity?"

45. In fact, the Christian doctrine of grace which we will discuss in the next chapter insists that God is not fair, but again, he is just.

46. The "ecology of ideas" is nicely illustrated in the following. Aquinas wrote, "To man these means were provided in general, inasmuch as he was given hands by nature by which he is able to devise for himself a variety of shelters and defenses. This is so because man's reason is so multiple and extends itself to diverse things in such a way that determinate instruments could not devise thing things that would suffice its." Aquinas, *On Truth* 22.7. In his Commentary on the *Epistle to the Ephesians* he then adds, "God wants man to have the hand, so that it may serve reason, and man to have reason,

in acts of justice, but also, in acts of mercy and love. And though *in itself* injustice is always evil, in the cosmos *as a whole* it also makes possible the highest human virtues of mercy and love which otherwise would be logically impossible.[47]

But beyond all this Thomists never tire of repeating that the Christian hope is for the resurrection of the body and the life of ever-lasting glory that it will bring. And it will be a glorious existence because each of the saints will take turns praising an aspect of the infinite God which their unique experiences on earth have enabled them to under-stand in a way previously unknown to all the other saints. And when their turn is over, while waiting for another turn to praise their Creator, they will not be bored. Because each person's experiences on earth was *different,* their unending adventure of discovery will be enhanced each time they hear other saints praising some aspect of God's inexhaustible glory that they had previously missed.[48]

But if the saints in the new heavens and new earth count their earthly suffering as nil when compared to their present glory,[49] the same

---

because He wanted man to be, and He wanted that there be man for the perfection [full formation] of the universe." Quoted in Blanchett, *The Prefection of the Universe.* 285. Blanchette explains the last phrase: "The proper activity of the rational creature, however, is not just to understand truth and love the good, but also to do justice— *operari justa.* This is the work of its hands, so to speak." Blanchette, *The Perfection of the Universe.* 285.

47. "Then, too, a thing approaches to God's likeness the more perfectly as it re-sembles Him in more things. Now, goodness is in God, and the outpouring of goodness into other things. Hence, the creature approaches more perfectly to God's likeness if it is not only good, but can also act for the good of other things, than if it were good only in itself; that which both shines and casts light is more like the sun than that which only shines. *But no creature could act for the benefit of another creature unless plurality and inequality existed in created things.* For the agent is distinct from the patient and superior to it. In order that there might be in created things a perfect representation of God, the existence of diverse grades among them was therefore necessary." Aquinas, *SCG,* II 45.4; emphasis added.

48. "There are in fact two things that we must remember about God's gifts to us. The first is that whatever God has given to us is more than we had any right to demand. The second is that, whatever God has given us, it is always in his power to give us more. The attitude of the Christian before God should thus combine gratitude and contentment with expectancy and wonder; and it is difficult to conceive of anything more exhilarat-ing than this." Mascall, *The Importance of Being Human,* 60–61.

49. Commenting on Psalm 8:4–5—"What is man, that thou art mindful of him?"— Aquinas remarks, "It is as if an artist were to make great things, and then among them make the very slightest of things, such as a needle. By making the needle, he showed that

is not true of the damned. What, then, could possibly justify hell? Only this: hell is a real possibility, but it is not a part of the created order. Rather, hell is made by and for those whose chief end in life is finding happiness apart from God. Heaven and hell must never be thought of as analogous to white and black paint. Heaven is *created*; it is God's addition to the other good things he created. Hell is *made*; it is humans' subtraction from the good things created by God. We must remember, as C. S. Lewis says, that "the doors of hell are locked on the inside."[50]

As we have already argued, it is logically impossible for God to create creatures who can flourish as autonomous individuals. No part of God's creation can exist apart from God. God can no more create a place where autonomous individuals flourish than he can create "nothingness." However, what God cannot create, humans *can* realize by preferring a life of miserable autonomy to a life of glorious integrity. But to say that humans *can* make their existence hellish, is not to say that they *will*. A real possibility need never become actuality. Aquinas argues that God cannot "undo" the past. Fornication can be forgiven, but God cannot return a fornicator to a state of virginity.[51] So it is senseless to pray that he would. However, we can (and are also commanded to) hope and pray that, *by God's grace*, hell will be empty.[52] Since evil is a privation, there is nothing irrational in such a hope and prayer.

In the final chapter, we will consider this all important phrase, "by God's grace."

---

he knows about it. But if in planning for his works he *cared* about that needle, this would be utterly astonishing." Quoted in Pasnau, *Thomas Aquinas on Human Nature*, 404.

Robert Pasnau goes on to explain Aquinas' perspective like this: "When taken seriously, the presence of an infinite being in the universe changes everything. The moral center of the universe tilts away from us, and modern humanism looks as provincial as Ptolemaic astronomy. The effect is to leave us feeling grateful for whatever attention God bestows, rather than resentful or doubting because he has not done more." Pasnau, *Thomas Aquinas on Human Nature*, 404.

50. Lewis, *Problem of Pain*, 130.

51. Aquinas, *ST*, I, 25, 4, reply 3.

52. See Hans Urs von Balthasar, *Dare We Hope "That All Men Be Saved"?* (1988). See also Neuhaus, "Will All Be Saved?" 77–80.

12

Why Should We Believe in God?

"Why should we believe in God?" is a doubly ambiguous question. Sometimes it asks: "Are there good reasons to believe that God exists?" Other times it asks: "Should I put my trust in God or something else?" "Believing in" versus "believing that" marks the first ambiguity.

The second ambiguity concerns the distinction between reasons and causes. Here we take a third person point of view and ask— "Why do people believe in God?" One response points to the kinds of reasons we considered in chapter 10. A second response points to the faith one has been given, that is, the cause of one's belief.

These are two distinct kinds of answers which must not be confused or conflated. They are not, however, competing answers where we must chose one or the other. Rather, Thomists argue that reasons and causes complement each other just as do efficient and final causes (see 5.3).

Skeptics sometimes claim that the real explanation for belief is a kind of wishful thinking or even a lack of courage. Thomists do not deny that Christian faith is self-involving, i.e. that faith carries with it certain emotional and psychological benefits. But such an admission is not much of a concession to the skeptic. First, all answers to big questions are self-involving, the skeptic's—no less, though no more—than the believer's. Second, explanations in terms of causes never by themselves destroy reasons. (For example, a person may see a doctor because he is fearful that the growth on his face is cancerous, but that does not mean that he lacks good reason for consulting a doctor.)

Finally, just as there is nothing properly called the "scientific method" (see chapters 2 and 3), so too, there is no single explanation of "religious belief"—the various religions of the world are simply too diverse to be adequately explained by a single theory. We therefore limit ourselves to explaining Christian faith.

We begin by distinguishing between the "preambles of faith" and "doctrines of faith." Thomists argue that positing an all powerful Creator God is the best philosophical explanation of the common sense propositions that plants and animals exist, square circles do not, and nothing comes from nothing. (This is a preamble.) On the other hand, the uniquely Christian belief that this Creator is one substance with three distinct natures can only be known "by faith"; the Trinity is not philosophical demonstrable.

However, "faith" must not be understood as a uniquely "spiritual" source of knowledge. It is not an essentially "inner" and private kind of knowledge as is a person's awareness of a pain in his or her big toe. In one sense, the Christian belief that Jesus was the first person to be raised from the dead is just as public and rationally discussable as is a doctor's belief that his patient's big toe is not broken, only strained.

Yet, in another sense, there is an aspect of Christian faith which is ultimately private and inexplicable. When one person "falls in love" with another person (1) the lover "sees" something in their beloved that they "can't help but love," (2) the lover thinks of their beloved as the supreme source of their own happiness, and (3) the lover frequently has good reasons for their belief that their beloved is the supreme source of their own happiness. All three are also true of Christians who have "fallen in love with Jesus."

THE QUESTION OF THIS chapter is deliberately ambiguous. It invites answers which range anywhere from "I choose to believe so that I won't burn in hell" to "I've fallen in love with Jesus and can't help but believe." But before considering such uniquely theological answers, we need to consider belief in general.

12.1 DEFINITIONS AND DISTINCTIONS

Many people believe that in a right triangle the square of the two sides will always equal the square of the hypotenuse, that is, $A^2 + B^2 = C^2$. And, of course, this belief is true. But people believe this for different reasons. Some people believe this algebraic formula because teachers they trusted told them it was true. They were probably also told that an ancient Greek mathematician name Pythagoras proved it was true. Other people, however, believe the Pythagorean Theorem to be true because they have done the mathematical proof themselves.

So we have to make a decision about our use of the word "believe." Some people, including Aquinas, would say that those who have proven the Pythagorean Theorem no longer *believe* that it is true; they *know* that it is true.[1] Others would say that they both believe *and* know the Pythagorean Theorem to be true. After all, if someone who understands Pythagoras' proof was asked—"Do you or do you not believe that $A^2 + B^2 = C^2$?"—they might sensibly respond: "I not only believe it to be true; I know that it is true."

There is no need to choose between these two uses of "believe." There is ample usage to justify either. However, it is important that we distinguish between the inclusive and exclusive sense of "believe." Otherwise, our thinking will be confused. So, when we use "believe" to be the contrary of "know," we will call this the exclusive sense. And when we use "believe" in a way which is consistent with claims to know, we will call this the inclusive sense. Thus, the mathematician who can prove the Pythagorean Theorem believes it to be true in the inclusive sense, but she does not believe it to be true in the exclusive sense since she also *knows* it is true.

Yet for an Aristotelian, the relation between *believing* and *knowing* is even more complicated. Classical foundationalists argue that knowledge requires an absolutely firm foundation or proof. Aristotelians disagree for all the reasons given in chapter 6. While I have never personally been in Maine, I know that on average the winters in Maine are colder than the winters where I live in Northern California. Here my justification

1. "Science and faith [belief] cannot be about the same object and in the same respect because the object of science is something seen whereas the object of faith is the unseen." Aquinas *ST*, II–II 1.5. Josef Pieper explains such statements like this: "What we are at present discussing is not the theological concept of belief but belief in general, taken in its most comprehensive but nevertheless strict and proper meaning. And an essential element of this meaning is the fact that the believer cannot know and verify *out of his own knowledge* the matter to which he assents." Pieper, *Faith, Hope and Love*, 25, emphasis added. Aquinas and Pieper are here referring to what I have stipulated as the exclusive sense of "belief." The inclusive sense of "belief" follows necessarily from the classical definition of "knowledge" as justified, true belief, where "true belief" is the genius and "justified" is the specific difference. The need for an inclusive sense of "belief" is also hinted at by Aquinas' narrow use of the term "science" to mean what is "thought impossible to be otherwise." Aquinas, *ST*, II–II 1.5. This is what Pieper meant by verified out of one's "own knowledge." However, today we use "knowledge" more broadly to include, among other things, historical knowledge. It would be extremely strange for anyone today to say that no one *knows* that George Washington was the first President of the United States because this cannot be logically deduced from first principles.

is the testimony of trustworthy witnesses. Of course, in a purely logical sense it is possible that my witnesses were all joking, lying, or simply mistaken. If this were the case, then I too would be mistaken. I would not have known it; I would only have *believed* wrongly that the winters in Maine are colder than in Northern California. Now classical foundationalists would object to using "know" to describe situations subject to error, but we have already argued that the classical foundationalist's highly restrictive use of "know" is misguided. Thus, Aristotelians are quite willing, even insistent, that we use the word "know" in situations where foundationalists would only use the word "believe."

Some accommodation, however, can be made with foundationalists by distinguishing between the epistemology and psychology of belief. Aristotelians insist on using the word "know" whenever we have *good* reasons and/or evidence for the truth of a belief. Foundationalists insist that "know" should only be used when we have *irrefutable* reasons and/ or evidence for the truth of a belief. Both "good reasons" and "irrefutable reasons" address issues of epistemology.

But we must not ignore the psychology of belief. Someone who is slightly unsure of himself might work a complicated mathematical proof perfectly, and yet, be *psychologically* uncertain about his proof. His reasoning, epistemologically speaking, could be flawless, even irrefutable, yet psychologically speaking, he might be uncertain. And the converse is also possible. Someone else may work the same problem and, psychologically speaking, be absolutely certain that she has proven her conclusion, when in fact her proof is fatally flawed. The epistemological strength of reasons and evidence is not directly correlated with the psychological certainty of the person. This distinction between epistemological strength and psychological certainty will become critical when we discuss the "certainty of faith" in a religious context.

12.2 REASONS AND CAUSES FOR BELIEF

Suppose that Fred believes that $A^2 + B^2 = C^2$ in a right triangle. Fred's belief can be explained in two distinct ways. First, we could explain Fred's beliefs in terms of its causes. For example, one answer might begin by noting that Fred lives in the United States where there are compulsory education laws and geometry was one of the classes he was required to take. This sort of causal explanation of Fred's belief could be fleshed out in many ways. Many more details could be provided concerning the sociological, legal, educational, and psychological setting in which Fred grew up. Neurophysiologists might even be able to specify in general terms the regions in the brain that are activated when Fred is consciously thinking that $A^2 + B^2 = C^2$. And sometime in the future, according to Aristotelians, they might even be able to specify (after the fact) the *per accidens* efficient causes of Fred's belief.[2] All of these are causal explanations of beliefs.

However, we can also explain Fred's belief in terms of reasons. Fred may be one of those fortunate children who had a geometry teacher who insisted that students were able to *prove* Pythagoras' Theorem for themselves, not just memorize a formula. If this was the case, the reasons for Fred's belief would ultimately be the rational insight of an agent intellect. If Fred was one of those less fortunate children whose geometry teacher was content to have her students memorize a formula, then the reasons for Fred's belief would have been different. In this case Fred's reason to believe would be the observed credibility of his teacher. Or perhaps Fred drew several right triangles on paper and checked to see if their measurements agreed with Pythagoras' formula. In either case, Fred's reasons would be a kind of empirical induction from past experience.

We discussed these various kinds of reasoning in chapter 6 and have nothing further to add here except to acknowledge that the sort of empirical induction mentioned above would *not* satisfy real mathematicians. In these cases, there is a sense in which Fred's reasons for believing that in a right triangle $A^2 + B^2 = C^2$ would not have been very good. Nonetheless, they were the *reasons* for Fred's belief, not the *causes* of his belief. Our only point here is that we can answer the question "Why does anyone believe anything?" by either specifying the causes of their belief (we will call this the C-because answer) or by specifying the reasons for their belief (we will call this the R-because answer).

This distinction between a C-because and R-because parallels closely the distinction between efficient and final causes in chapter 5. In both cases, the relationship is complementary, not contradictory. A C-because explanation of a person's belief in no way prohibits, contradicts or diminishes an R-because explanation of the same belief. And the converse is equally true. An R-because explanation does not rule out a C-because explanation. And remember, as we argued in chapter 7, according to Aristotelians, there *must* be a C-because answer when-

2. See chapter 7.3.

ever we ask why someone believes anything. This follows directly from Aristotle's claim (1) that brains and bodies are a necessary (though not sufficient) condition for all mental activities, including beliefs and (2) their rejection of the libertarian idea that some beliefs or action are totally independent of any physical cause. Of course, we will probably never know what causes people's individual beliefs since the causes of a person's beliefs will usually be astronomically complex and whenever they are rational beliefs they will always[3] be the result of *per accidens* (not *per se*) efficient causes.

12.3 SELF-INVOLVING BELIEFS

It is one thing to believe *that* George Bush was President of the United States. It is quite different to believe *in* George Bush. Believing *that* something is the case only involves assent to a proposition. Believing *in* something (usually a person) also involves assent to a proposition (e.g., that the thing you believe in actually exists). But it also involves trust, loyalty and obedience. So when a person believes *in* another person there is an implicit obligation to act in a certain way.

For example, believing *that* George Bush was President implies no particular set of actions. However, if someone says that they believe *in* George Bush, then that person is implicitly saying that they will act in a particular fashion. For example, they might work for his re-election and/or verbally support legislation he has proposed and/or attend his campaign rallies and/or defend him when he is criticized, etc. If people do not do *anything* like this when given the opportunity, then their claim to believe *in* George Bush is insincere, or even hypocritical.

In short, believing *in* someone else is always self-involving. It commits one to act with trust, loyalty and/or obedience toward the person. As we argued in chapter 8, these moral commitments need not be onerous. The goal of Aristotelians is always to work toward becoming a person for whom "doing the right thing" is matter of delight, not duty. Nonetheless, "doing the right thing" frequently *begins* by doing one's duty even when it is contrary to one's immediate desires and interests. Until one's emotions, desires and attitudes are properly trained, "doing the right thing"

---

3. The "almost always" qualifier is necessary because it is possible that certain neurotic beliefs for which a person is not him or herself responsible may have predictable *per se* efficient causes.

typically involves a kind of death to self. This is why we say that "belief *in*" is self-involving.

On the other hand, "believing *that*" something is the case typically involves little or no "death to self." When we learn *that* there are nine planets in our solar system, *that* silver melts at over 500 degrees, or *that* every cell in the human body is replaced over a ten year period there is nothing we are obligated to do other than to assent to such propositions when asked. In these cases, belief costs virtually nothing. However, as we hinted in chapter 8, sometimes a "belief that" can inaugurate a train of reasoning where "cost to self" begins to mount. For example, for Fred to learn *that* his favorite movie star is pregnant costs Fred little. But for Fred to learn *that* Sally, his former girlfriend, is pregnant costs Fred more.

This movement from a "belief that" to a self-involving "belief in" further complicates our prior distinction between epistemology and psychology. If one of Fred's friends tells him that his favorite movie star is pregnant, Fred will typically hear what his friend says with purely epistemological ears. That is, he may want to know if his friend is serious or just kidding. He may even ask questions about his friend's sources. In either case, Fred is simply evaluating the reliability of his friend's testimony much like a lawyer might examine the testimony of a witness.

But now consider the second scenario where Sally is Fred's former girlfriend. And suppose a friend now says to Fred: "You know, Sally hasn't slept with another man since you broke up." Assent to such a statement moves beyond epistemology and into psychology. Here Fred cannot help but ask himself questions like: "Should I help Sally raise our child?" "Should I try to convince her to abort her pregnancy?" "Will I have to pay child support since we were together for more than seven years in a state which practices common law marriage?" This second set of questions is highly self-involving. Whether Fred will believe *that* Sally has slept with no other man is as much a psychological question as it is an epistemological question.

And more than mere psychology, Fred's ability to correctly evaluate the epistemology of his friend's statement has much to do with his moral character, or, as the ancients would have said, his virtue. If Fred is a man of integrity, then he will do his very best to separate his epistemological questions—"How could my friend really know that Sally has slept with no other man?"—from his self-interested questions—"What will I do if a judge makes me pay child support?" Only his moral integrity will enable him to distinguish these two questions. Without virtue, what Fred ends up believing will have less to do with the evidence (epistemology) and more to do with his own self-interest (psychology).

All this means that the question—Why should we believe in God?—is doubly ambiguous. First, the "why" could be a request for a good reason or it could be a request for the psychological, sociological, and/or historical causes of belief. Second, the phrase "believe in God" could mean 1) believe *that* God exists or 2) believe *in* God as one who deserves, even requires, one's trust, loyalty, and obedience.

12.4 BELIEF *THAT* GOD EXISTS

In chapters 2 and 3, we argued that there is no such thing as *the* scientific method. Philosophers and scientists use pretty much the same techniques (i.e., the three Cs of consistency, comprehensiveness, and coherence) to answer their cutting edge questions. And as philosophers and historians of science are now beginning to realize, even the individual disciplines in the sciences are quite different with respect to the kinds of arguments they use. The methods of physicists are not the same as the methods of evolutionary biologists. Physicists' final court of appeal is experimental data which must be repeatable. But, as we saw in chapter 3, for an essentially historical disciple like evolutionary biology there is very little repeatable experimental data. As Darwin put it, *The Origin of Species* is "one long argument." In this respect, Darwin was more like a lawyer who "built a case" for his client than a Galileo repeatedly measuring the acceleration of balls down an inclined plane.

The same sort of specificity is necessary in the study of religion. There is no general answer to the question: "Why do scientists believe what they believe?" So too, there is no general answer to the question: "Why do religious people believe in God?" The answers that a Hindu, Buddhist, Jew, Christian, and Muslim give would all be different. So we have no choice but to narrow down the question. In this chapter, we will only consider a traditional Christian answer.

Our goal in what remains of this book is to first clarify the double ambiguity of the phrase "believe by faith" as it is commonly used. Second, we will argue that a complete answer to the question of this chapter—Why believe in God?—includes philosophy, historical testimony, common grace, and saving grace as essential elements (see chart below).

	belief *that* God exists	belief *in* God
R-because	philosophy	historical testimony
C-because	common grace	saving grace

Figure 12.1

According to Thomistic Christians, the reason (R-because) they believe *that* God exist is philosophy. Thomists believe that the teleological and cosmological arguments discussed in chapter 10 provide the best explanation of our ability to abstract concepts and the very existence of a cosmos. Furthermore, they believe that the existence of evil is not a decisive argument against the existence of an almighty and good God (see chapter 11).

That is not to say that all people who consider these arguments will be convinced. Textbooks have frequently included the couple of pages from Aquinas' multi-volume *Summa Theologica* that constitute his summary of these arguments. But no Thomist has been so silly as to expect that these few pages would convince skeptics. The arguments included in his *Summa* were mere outlines intended for students who had already completed a bachelor's degree course of study which would have included the whole of Aristotle's metaphysics. Obviously, this is not true of most who read Aquinas' arguments today. So it should surprise no one that the number of students who have been psychologically convinced by Aquinas' "Five Ways" can be counted on less than one hand.

Furthermore, Thomists teaching Aquinas' arguments today will count themselves lucky if they have more students than can be counted on one hand who have the time, energy, and prior education necessary to seriously consider Aquinas' arguments. And even those teachers who are fortunate enough to have such students must remember that most students do not find self-fulfillment in philosophy—many will look to the sciences or the arts. The number of psychological, sociological, and historical pre-conditions (what we have called "C-becauses") for understanding Aquinas are beyond counting. Nonetheless, sometimes all these pre-conditions are fulfilled and a person is either confirmed in his childhood belief that there is a God or perhaps even begins to believe that there is a God as the result of philosophical study. All this, Thomists say, is a matter of common grace, namely, the time, talent, and disposition to reason philosophically.

But for a person to actually be psychologically convinced by the teleological and cosmological arguments there is an additional set of preconditions (C-becauses). Grammatically speaking, believing *that* God exists is no different than believing *that* silver melts at over 500 degrees. But considering reasons to believe *that* God exists typically starts a train of thought rolling which is significantly more self-involving than beliefs concerning the melting temperature of silver. Believing *that* God exists is frequently a first step toward believing *in* God.[4]

And as all Jews, Christians, and Muslims agree, no belief is more self-involving than belief *in* the God of Abraham, Isaac, and Jacob since this is a God who makes serious (and sometimes even onerous) claims on one's life. Someone seriously studying reasons to believe *that* such a God exist is likely to encounter the sort of psychological resistance that Fred encountered when he was considering reason to believe that Sally has slept with no other man. To overcome such resistance, more than common grace is required according to Aquinas. Here saving grace is necessary. We will say more about that in the next section. But first we must consider an objection.

The last paragraph will undoubtedly raise the hackles of many readers. It sounds like we have accused atheists of "bad faith" or even worse. And, in a sense, we have. Without a willingness to ruthlessly follow the arguments wherever they lead, no one can ever be forced to believe in God as the result of Aquinas' arguments. Arguments which are self-involving can never "force" belief the way physical coercion or threats can force action. So, if a good argument which is well presented does not convince a student, then there is necessarily a kind of "bad faith" on the part of the student.

But atheists ought not to take too much offense. Thomists have only reversed the arguments of Marxists, Freudian, and some contemporary atheists who argue that theists are guilty of bad faith because they are looking for "metaphysical comfort" and not dispassionately considering the arguments.

---

4. C. S. Lewis' autobiography, *Surprised by Joy*, describes his own movement from a philosophical belief *that* there was a God to his Christian belief *in* the God revealed in Jesus Christ.

Can this dispute be resolved? Perhaps, but only in a limited case, and even then, we must begin by rigorously distinguishing epistemological and psychological questions. Questions concerning what *in fact* convince people are psychological; questions concerning what *ought* to convince people are epistemological. Our suggestion is to acknowledge that the psychological, sociological, and/or historical causes behind any person's beliefs are so numerous and complex as to forever defy human understanding. The number of *per accidens* efficient causes preceding any particular belief is literally astronomical.

True, psychologists, sociologists, and historians can make some truthful observations about why people, cultures, or historical eras have *in general* believed or not believed particular philosophical arguments. But this tells us little about whether we *ought* to believe these arguments. We must, therefore, rest content to examining these arguments on their own merits and resist every temptation to explain the *causes* of belief or disbelief.

The only exception to this principle is when we are inquiring into the causes of our *own* belief or disbelief. Only then are we in a position to make informed judgments about the psychological, sociological, and historical causes of our own belief or disbelief. And even in our own case, knowing that we *ought* to ignore such irrelevant causes does not mean that we *will* ignore such causes.

12.5 BELIEF *IN* GOD

We need to reiterate that "religion" is no more uniform than "science." Scientists seek to discover the efficient causes of things and events in the material world. And since these are so different, there are many different ways scientists go about their work. The same is true of religious people. Some focus on philosophy, others on meditation and mystical insight, still others on divine revelation. Furthermore, different religions have radically different notions of ultimate reality. Large segments of the Hindu and Buddhist tradition, for example, have nothing that corresponds to the Jewish, Christian, or Islamic concept of God.

So, again, our goal in this final section is not to find the lowest common denominator among the various religions in the world. Instead, we will be considering how one substantial segment of the Christian tradition—that of Augustine and Aquinas—answer the question: why do you believe *in* God? Their answer, simply put, is that they have fallen in love with Jesus.

But before unpacking the notion of "falling in love with Jesus," we must make explicit the connection in Christianity between believing *in* God and loving Jesus. As we said at the beginning of this chapter, when "belief" is used in the exclusive sense it typically refers to trusting a person's testimony. A person who has spent many winters in both Maine and Northern California has first hand knowledge about the relative winter temperatures. But a person who has only lived in Northern California can only know this if he is willing to trust credible witnesses.

As Aristotle said long ago, "He who wishes to learn must believe."[5] If we will not believe credible witnesses, there is very little that we can learn. However, for someone to be a credible witness they must themselves be in a position to know that to which they are testifying. Thus, belief in the exclusive sense always presupposes the *knowledge* of someone else. So too, according to Augustine and Aquinas, belief *in* God presupposes a credible witness who has firsthand knowledge of that to which he testifies. For Christians that someone is Jesus.

Here we must stress again the distinction between "belief *that*" and "belief *in*." According to Aquinas, the teleological and cosmological arguments provide a person firsthand evidence for the existence of God. But that hardly makes one a Christian. "You believe that God is one; you do well. Even the demons believe—and shudder," said St. James.[6] Christians have always understood their faith to be far more than an assent to a set of propositions, i.e., belief *that* statements. Believing *that* God exists, *that* he is one, *that* he is a spirit, and *that* he is both intellect and will are what Aquinas called the Preambles to Faith. These are the true propositions about God that philosophical argumentation by itself are able to establish. Here a person can have "first hand" knowledge without relying on someone else's testimony.

But beyond these philosophical truths about God, Aquinas argued that there were a whole set of theological truths about God that could only be known through God's self-revelation. These he called the Doctrines of Faith. Aquinas illustrated the distinction between the Preambles and the Doctrines of Faith like this. Based only on one's vision a person might

5. Aristotle *Sophistical Refutations* chap 2.2: 165b (Josef Pieper's translation in *Faith, Hope and Love*, 13). See also Aquinas, *ST*, II–II 2.1 and II–II 5.2.

6. James 2:19.

know that an approaching object far down the road is a person—not a dog, deer, or car. This is the analogue for the Preambles. Yet, one would have no idea whether it was Peter, or Paul, or someone else unless the person called out, "It's me, Peter." This is the analogue for the Doctrines of Faith.[7]

That is not to say that there is not some overlap between the Preambles and Doctrines of Faith. While the mere existence of God is philosophically knowable, as we have said, it is rare that a person has the time, talent, and inclination to study the necessary arguments.[8] Therefore, Aquinas said, God chose also to reveal his existence in the Bible. In other words, the existence of God is *both* part of the Preambles *and* Doctrines of Faith.

It is also worth noting that, according to Aquinas, the possibility of demonstrating the existence of God through wholly philosophical means was itself one of the revealed Doctrines of Faith. Here Aquinas cites Rom 1:20, "Ever since the creation of the world his [God's] invisible nature, namely, his eternal power and deity, has been clearly perceived in the things that have been made." In other words, Aquinas claims to know by faith that the existence of God is not *only* knowable by faith; it is also knowable by reason.[9]

What Aquinas never disputes, doubts, or qualifies is that *who* God is (i.e., his essence) can only be known by faith.[10] Were it not for God's self-revelation in Jesus, for example, no philosopher would ever know that God is one substance with three essential natures—Father, Son, and Holy Spirit. Now this is not a book of theology, so we mention the Christian doctrine of the Trinity only as an illustration of what Aquinas means by a Doctrine of Faith.

We have used the phrase "know by faith" several times in the last couple paragraphs. It is obviously crucial for Christians in general and for Aquinas in particular. It is also a phrase open to multiple interpreta-

7. Aquinas, *ST*, I 2.1.

8. Some may wonder why God would reveal that which can be philosophically demonstrated. Ralph McInerny answers, "It is in the *Metaphysics*, bk. XII, that we find the most remarkable natural theology ever achieved. *But its cogency can be appreciated only if we have taken the long path to it.* And that is the first reason for the fittingness of the revelation of the preambles." McInerny, *Praeambula Fidei*, 30-31, emphasis added.

9. See Ralph McInerny's Gifford Lectures, *Characters in Search of Their Author*, for an excellent discussion of these matters.

10. "We do not know the essence of God." Aquinas, *ST*, I 2.1.

tions. One common interpretation today is that "faith" refers to an additional way of knowing beyond reason and the five senses. When "faith" is used in this sense it frequently functions as a discussion stopper.

Here is what we mean. Suppose Ron tells a doctor that he broke his big toe. Such a claim is neither indisputable nor does it rule out further investigation. The doctor, for example, can take an x-ray to determine if his toe really is broken. However, suppose Ron merely says that he has a sharp pain in his big toe. Again, the doctor can take an x-ray. But if the x-ray comes back perfectly normal, that would *not* be a good reason to think that Ron was mistaken about having a pain in his big toe. Here, Ron's claim that he has a pain in his big toe (if it is sincere) *is* a discussion stopper. There is no further way to investigate or dispute his claim. So too, some people use the phrase "know by faith" as a kind of knowledge that can neither be disputed nor subjected to further investigation. That is *not* how Aquinas uses the term.

Instead, Aquinas uses the phrase "know by faith" to mean nothing more than "know as the result of someone else's testimony."[11] Epistemologically speaking, there is nothing essentially mysterious about such knowledge.[12] It is not indisputable. Some witnesses may exaggerate. Others may have lied. Still others may simply have been mistaken. But like the doctor investigating a break in a patient's big toe or a lawyer cross-examining a witness, we know how to evaluate testimony to determine whether or not it ought to be believed. A person's testimony is not, by itself, a discussion stopper.

But there is a significant difference between believing testimony about the winters in Maine and believing testimony about *who* God is. Unless a witness is in a position to know that to which he is testifying

11. "Belief cannot establish its own legitimacy; it can only derive legitimacy from someone who knows the subject matter of his own accord." Pieper, *Faith, Hope and Love*, 42. In Aquinas' own words, "Faith presupposes natural knowledge" and "Faith is a kind of knowledge, in so far as the intellect is determined by faith to some knowable object. But this determination to one thing does not proceed from the vision of the believer, but from the vision of Him who is believed." Aquinas, *ST*, I 12.13. And again, "Since man can only know the things that he does not see himself by taking them from another who does see them, and since faith is among the things we do not see, the knowledge of the objects of faith must be handed on by one who sees them himself." Aquinas, *SCG*, III 154.1.

12. "Faith is not meritorious because it is enigmatic, i.e. obscure cognition, but because the will uses such knowledge rightly, namely, by assenting on account of God revealing them to those things that it does not see." Aquinas, *On Evil*, I 3.11.

and unless his cognitive abilities are "up to the task," his testimony will be dubious. Living in Maine and observing its weather takes no special expertise. But it does, to say the least, take special expertise and a unique position to know first hand the God of all creation. Such knowledge is miraculous. It transcends the standard canons of epistemology. So it is reasonable to require extraordinary, even miraculous, confirmation that such a witness *knows* what he is talking about.[13] According to Christians, Jesus was "designated Son of God in power . . . by his resurrection from the dead" (Rom 1:4). The bodily resurrection of a person three days after his death clearly transcends our standard understanding of how the world works. Only something like this would give a person good reason to believe that Jesus has something to teach them about God.

Whether or not there are good reasons to believe that Jesus really was dead on Friday and alive on Sunday is a matter for historians to investigate. And it is obviously an extremely large and contentious issue to which we cannot do justice here.[14] So we will say nothing more about the R-because for belief *in* God, i.e. about why Christians place their trust and give their obedience to God above all else. Yet, there is more to be said about the C-because behind belief in God. In fact, it returns us to the question: why have Christians fallen in love with Jesus?

First, people do not *choose* to fall in love. The lover is captivated, enthralled, awe struck, mesmerized, enchanted, gripped, smitten, and carried away by his beloved. All these words indicate that the lover is the *recipient* of something, not the initiator of an action. Sometimes the beloved is quite unconscious of her effect on her lover. Her beauty may enchant the lover without any conscious action on her part. Other times, however, a lover may be consciously wooing her beloved. In such cases, much time and effort may be required before her beloved "falls in love." But in either case, the person who has fallen in love is being *acted upon*, not acting. Upon this last point Augustine and Aquinas are absolutely

---

13. "To believe in Christ is good in itself, and necessary for salvation. But the will is not born toward this unless it is proposed by the intellect as such." Aquinas, *ST*, I–II 19.5.

14. Of course, in one sense, Paul's testimony itself needs to be evaluated—was he and the other witnesses to Jesus' resurrection in a position to know that Jesus was dead on Friday and alive the next Sunday? If so, were their cognitive powers up to the task? These are clearly questions for historians, not philosophers. For the serious student, it is hard to surpass N. T. Wright's, *Resurrection of the Son of God* and the two volumes that precede it.

insistent. God is the active suitor; Christians are the passive recipients of God's love for them.[15]

The theologically savvy will notice that we have just backed into the doctrine of election or predestination. Libertarians obviously have strong objections to predestination. If Christians were predestined to "love Jesus," then where, they ask, is their free will? And what would it mean to talk about our love of Jesus if it turned out that we were "predestined" to love him before we were even born? Puppets can *say* they "love" their puppeteer, but libertarians insist that this is not genuine love.

We have discussed this issue before in "The Divine Choreographer" (10.3). We will not repeat all that we said there about God instructing us for our own good through the use of *per accidens* efficient causes. But we will make one concession to the libertarian. As libertarians themselves willingly acknowledge, there is a sense in which a "choice," as they understand it, defies comprehension. According to libertarians, a free choice literally "comes out of nowhere" with absolutely no cause, either *per se* or *per accidens*. Augustinians and Thomists are half in agreement. As Augustine prayed, "The good that I do is done by you in me and by your grace: the evil is my fault."[16] A "choice" to reject the Creator's love defies comprehension. There can be no good reason for it. Nor is it something that is caused by God or some part of his good creation. [17] A "choice" to

15. "God does not justify us without us, since while we are being justified, we consent to God's justice by a movement of free choice. But that movement is not the cause but the effect of grace. Thus the whole operation belongs to grace." Aquinas, *ST*, I–II 111. 2.

16. Augustine, *Confessions*, bk. 10, sec. 4, 209–10. And again, "The movement of a will away from you, the supreme Being, towards some inferior being does not derive from you." Augustine, *Confessions*, bk. 12, sec 11, 287.

17. "Evil is *per accidens* in that it occurs when agents fail to attain their appropriate end or the good which is intended *per se*. Even if we try to think of causes of evil, there is no order between them as causes of evil, but only dis-order, and hence no possibility of a first cause among them." Blanchette, *The Perfection of the Universe*, 116.

David Burrell puts it like this: "Creatures are indeed capable of an utterly initiatory role, but it will not be one of acting but of failing to act, of 'refusing' to enter into the process initiated by actively willing 'the good.' In that sense, we can be 'like unto God,' but only in a self-destructive manner." Burrell, *Freedom and Creation*, 91. See also 157.

In other words, we are here rejecting the Calvinist doctrine of "double predestination," i.e. that God predestines some to eternal bliss and other to eternal damnation. With Augustine we are assuming that all good things are "predestined" by God and that is evil is our fault. (See chapter 11 for a philosophical defense of the asymmetry between good and evil). Evil is a privation; it is literally nothingness. Thus, it cannot be caused by God since not even God can create "nothingness." Yet the result of human perversity

reject eternal happiness in favor of a life of misery and frustration can never be understood. It is a "choice" with neither a reason nor a cause. It is the ultimate surd.[18]

Secondly, we need to consider Aquinas' dictum: "A man loves a thing because he apprehends it as his good."[19] Libertarians and moderns in general think of our will as that which makes choices. The ancients thought of the will as that which loves, affirms, and wants. When people are looking at a tree in good light they do not *chose* to believe they are "seeing a tree." They simply see a tree. So too, when someone "falls in love" with another person, they do not *chose* to believe that the other

---

is that we can love that which will ultimately destroy us. Here Augustine, Aquinas, and Barth would all agree with the libertarians: humans have autonomy. But, again, the only autonomous choice a person can make is to reject God's love in favor of nothingness. That is why Barth counsels Christians to never forget that evil constitutes the "impossible possibility" that is "a real threat." Barth, *CD*, III.3. See his *CD*, II.2.32.1, especially pp. 13–18 for his discussion, and ultimate rejection of, double predestination. This is all the more noteworthy given Barth's typically high praise for Calvin.

18. Christians have always defined hell as the place and/or state of those who have rejected God's love as revealed by Jesus' death and resurrection. Nothing that we have said here is inconsistent with such a definition. Nor is describing hell as the "ultimate surd" in any way an attempt to deny or minimize the reality of hell. However, we agree with Karl Barth: "we know [via biblical revelation] of only one certain triumph of hell—the handing-over of Jesus—and that this triumph of hell took place in order that it would never again be able to triumph over anyone . . . We know of none whom God has wholly and exclusively abandoned to himself. We know only of One who was abandoned in this way, only of One who was lost. This One is Jesus Christ. And He was lost (and found again) in order that none should be lost apart from Him." Barth, *CD*, II.2 496.

More explicitly, Barth is saying that we must never minimize either the threat or reality of hell. Nonetheless, he argues that there is no biblical evidence that hell currently is (or will be) populated. Jesus was handed-over to hell; but he also triumphed over hell so that we can now rationally hope and pray that hell will forever remain empty. Whether our hope turns out to be true and our prayers are answered in the affirmative is something, says Barth, which only God knows. Once again (cf. "The Paradox of Omnipotence" 11.4), our questions must end in a "studied silence."

Though the Reformed tradition in which Barth works grew directly out of the Augustinian tradition, there is no question that he is going beyond anything that is explicitly found in either Augustine or Aquinas. Nonetheless, the argument of chapter 11—that evil is *privation*—and hence, that hell is the ultimate surd is nicely complemented by Barth's argument for a real, but hopefully unpopulated hell.

And finally, it we should note the convergence between a realist metaphysics where epistemology and ontology are kept distinct and Barth's notion of a real, but possibly empty hell. In an idealist metaphysics where "to be" and "to be known" are one-in-the-same it is probably nonsense to speak hell as real, but not *known* to be populated.

19. Aquinas, *ST*, I–II 62.4. See also Pieper, *Faith, Hope and Love*, 39.

person is good for them. They cannot help but believe that that person is good for them and will make them happy. Imagine someone saying to their beloved, "You may or may not be good; nonetheless, I *chose* to love you." This would be more of an insult than a profession of love. A lover is not merely of the *opinion* that their beloved is good for them; they are psychologically certain.

To believe *in* God because one has fallen in love with Jesus is to believe that God is the *only* source of goodness and ultimate happiness. And this too is a belief which is held with psychological certainty. Nonetheless, there is an element of what Josef Pieper calls "mental unrest."[20] Even though the believer is convinced that Jesus is a credible witness of God's goodness and love, there will still be an ongoing search, argumentation, and debate within the believer's own mind. As Aquinas says, "The cognition of belief does not quiet the craving [for certainty] but rather kindles it."[21] But, on the other hand, the believer has totally and completely placed their life in God's hand in the way that a patient may fully place his life in the hands of a doctor or a solider in his Commander-in-Chief.

"Mental unrest" names that state where certainty and doubt co-exist. With respect to "belief *that*," Aquinas says that faith "does not attain the perfection of clear vision, in which respect it agrees with doubt, suspicion, and opinion." But with respect to "belief *in*," he says that faith "cleaves firmly to one side, in which respect belief has something in common with science and understanding."[22]

The third point to be made about falling in love with Jesus is that like all "C-because" explanations it does not exclude the giving of reasons. Love can be blind, but it need not be. The goal of love is not misery;

20. Pieper, *Faith, Hope and Love*, 51.

21. Aquinas, *SCG*, III 40.5. Pieper translation, *Faith, Hope and Love* 53.

22. Aquinas, *ST*, II–II 2.1. Of course, the kind of "mental unrest" that Christians experience will be highly variable. For one like Aquinas for whom the existence of God is a *preamble* to faith, the epistemological element of the faith is typically in the foreground. But for Christians without the time, talent or inclination toward philosophical reflection the existence of God will be one of the *doctrines* of faith. Consequently, in such cases it is quite possible that the psychological issues will typically be in the foreground. When this is the case, then the epistemological questions concerning "belief *that* God exists" will probably move to the background, and more psychological questions concerning the faithfulness of God to provide in times of trouble will come to the foreground. Hence, it is "belief *in* God" that will be the subject of "doubt, suspicion and opinion."

it is happiness. The saying is true—"we must watch who we give our heart to." We do not put our life in the hands of a doctor without creditable credentials. Likewise, Aquinas says of the believer: "For he would not believe unless, on the evidence of signs, or of something similar, he saw that they ought to be believed."[23]

John Newton's song, *Amazing Grace*, makes these three points beautifully.

> Amazing grace! How sweet the sound
> That saved a wretch like me!
> I once was lost, but now am found;
> Was blind, but now I see.
>
> 'Twas grace that taught my heart to fear,
> And grace my fears relieved;
> How precious did that grace appear
> The hour I first believed.

"I once . . . was blind, but now I see." What changed Newton's life? Why was he suddenly able to see? He says that his blinders were removed C-because grace taught his heart to fear. (Here he is echoing the proverb that the fear of the Lord is the beginning of wisdom.) But an R-because is also implicit in this answer. Yes, his ability to see clearly is attributed to God's grace. Yet, at the same time, it was clarity of *vision* to which Newton sings praise.

Skeptics will say that Newton was only given a kind of "metaphysical comfort." Others will say that he took a "leap of faith." Augustine and Aquinas would disagree. They would take Newton at face value: God removed his blinders so that now he could see. Alcohol may provide drunkards with a kind of comfort and relief from their trials and troubles. But this is not a kind of *seeing*. And very rarely someone takes a leap of faith by purchasing a lottery ticket and solves their financial problems. But winning a lottery is not *seeing* the solution to one's difficulties.[24] If John Newton was asked, "Why do you believe?," his answer would be two-fold: "C-because grace taught my heart to *fear*, and R-because I now can *see*."[25]

23. Aquinas, *ST*, II–II 1.4. See also II–II 2.1; II–II 5.2.

24. "It [the act of belief] does not stop at something that is said but at something that is." Aquinas, *ST*, II–II 1.2.

25. Referring to Augustine and Aquinas, Josef Pieper writes that "the great teachers have had no scruples, on occasion, about breaking down the linguistic barriers they

12.6 EPILOGUE

In the first chapter, we said that our primary focus would be the dispute between realists and relativists. Until the final section in the final chapter it looked as though the tide of the argument was clearly behind the realist. But now it looks like the tide has turned. We just argued that the explanation for our beliefs about ultimate reality utterly transcends our earthy understanding. True, Christians speak of God's grace which removed their metaphysical and theological blinders. But how different is this from relativists who say that *all* beliefs are ultimately the product of genes, social environment, and education?

Remember the relativist's "argument." No one, they say, can *see* the world directly. All vision, both with our literal eyes and our "mind's eye," is a seeing that takes place *through* a set of linguistic lenses. We cannot see "reality" directly; we can only see things via the medium of language. Perhaps we cannot help but *believe* that we see plants and animals. Yet, the data that our brains receive is only *interpreted* as seeing plants and animals because we have been born, raised, and educated in a culture in which plants and animals are basic linguistic categories. It may be evolutionarily impossible for human life to survive without such categories. Nonetheless, these are *human* categories, wholly contingent on the vagaries of evolution. Whether they are also the categories of reality is a question we are utterly powerless to answer. "So why try?" say the relativists.

Realists will remind the relativists of the absurdity of "arguing" that all arguments are impossible. Relativists will reply that logical consis-

---

themselves have set up [distinguishing belief from knowledge] and calling belief 'cognition,' 'insight,' and 'knowledge,' or even speaking of the '*light* of belief,' by which 'one sees what one believes.'" Pieper, *Faith, Hope and Love*, 54.

It is also worth noting how Karl Barth, usually thought of as a great critic of Aquinas, is in complete agreement on this point. "Illumination, however, is a seeing of which man was previously incapable but of which he is now capable. It is thus his advancement to knowledge. That the revelation of God shines on and in him, takes place in such a way that he hears, receives, understands, grasps, and appropriates what is said to him in it, not with new and special organs, but with the same organs of apperception with which he knows other things, yet not in virtue of his own capacity to use them, but in view of the missing capacity which he is now given by God's revelation. 'Jesus, give me sound and serviceable eyes; touch Thou mine eyes.' It is as He does this that they become serviceable and can be used for the function which is here ascribed to them to which they are appointed and in which they are actually used. It is all a process which like others really implies knowledge in man. But it is all an original creation of the One who enables him to know." Barth, *CD*, IV.3.2 509.

tency is itself a humanly constructed category. Is there any end to this sort of tit for tat?

The recurring slogan of this book has been that plants and animals exist; square circles do not; nothing comes from nothing. Oddly enough, the one thing realists and relativists agree about is that these three propositions can be believed or not believed, but they cannot be proved. Nietzsche was right: "we shall not get rid of God until we get rid of grammar."[26] There are only two options: (1) grammar and God or (2) no grammar and no God. Herein lays *the* fundamental choice for those who philosophize.

---

26. Nietzsche, *Twilight of the Idols*, 3.5, 483. See also chapter 9.

Bibliography

Note on Sources: When citing classical sources, so many of which are readily available on the Web with a simple Google search, standard divisions by book, section, chapter, paragraph, etc. are typically used, though sometimes pages numbers which correspond to the edition cited in the Bibliography are also included.

Academy of Natural Sciences Home Page: http://www.ansp.org/museum/jefferson/megalonyx/history-02.php.

Ackrill, J. L. *Aristotle the Philosopher*. Oxford: Oxford University Press, 1981.

Adler, Mortimer J. "Intentionality and Immateriality." *New Scholasticism* 41 (1967) 312–450.

———. *Problems for Thomists: The Problem of Species*. New York: Sheed & Ward, 1940.

———. *Some Questions about Language: A Theory of Human Discourse and Its Objects*. La Salle, IL: Open Court, 1976.

———. *Ten Philosophical Mistakes*. New York: Macmillan, 1985.

———. *The Difference of Man and the Difference It Makes*. New York: Fordham University Press, 1993.

Aquinas, Thomas. *Commentary on Aristotle's Metaphysics*. Translated by John P. Rowan. Library of Loving Catholic Thought. Chicago: Regnery, 1961.

———. *Compendium of Theology*. Translated by Cyril Vollert. St. Louis, MO: Herder, 1958.

———. *On Evil*. Translated by Jean Oesterle. Notre Dame, IN: University of Notre Dame Press, 1995.

———. *On Truth*. Chicago: Regnery, 1952–1954.

———. "Principles of Nature." In *Aquinas: Selected Writings of St. Thomas Aquinas*. Translated by Robert P. Goodwin, 7–28. Indianapolis: Bobbs-Merrill Educational, 1965.

———. *Summa Contra Gentiles*. Translated by Anton C. Pegis. Notre Dame, IN: University of Notre Dame Press, 1975.

———. *Summa Theologica*. Translated by Fathers of the English Dominican Province. Great Books series. Chicago: Encyclopedia Britannica, 1952.

———. *The Literal Exposition on Job: A Scriptural Commentary Concerning Providence*. Translated by Anthony Damico, interpretative essay and notes by Marin D. Yaffe. Atlanta: Scholars, 1989.

———. *The Three Greatest Prayers: Commentaries on the Lord's Prayer, the Hail Mary, and the Apostles' Creed*. Manchester, NH: Sophia Institute, 1990.

Aristotle. *History of Animals*. Great Books of the Western Tradition, vol. 9. Chicago: Encyclopedia Britannica, 1952.

———. *Metaphysics*. Great Books of the Western Tradition, vol. 8. Chicago: Encyclopedia Britannica, 1952.

———. *Nicomachean Ethics*. Translated by Martin Ostwald. The Library of Liberal Arts. Indianapolis: Bobbs-Merrill, 1962.

———. *On Generation and Corruption*. Great Books of the Western Tradition, vol. 8. Chicago: Encyclopedia Britannica, 1952.

———. *On the Heavens*. Great Books of the Western Tradition, vol. 8. Chicago: Encyclopedia Britannica, 1952.

———. *Physics*. Great Books of the Western Tradition, vol. 8. Chicago: Encyclopedia Britannica, 1952.

———. *Politics*. Great Books of the Western Tradition, vol. 9. Chicago: Encyclopedia Britannica, 1952.

———. *Posterior Analytics*. Great Books of the Western Tradition, vol. 8. Chicago: Encyclopedia Britannica, 1952.

Augustine. *City of God*. Great Books of the Western Tradition, vol. 18. Chicago: Encyclopedia Britannica, 1952.

———. *Confessions*. Penguin Classics. Translated by R. S. Pine-Coffin. New York: Penguin, 1961.

Ayer, Alfred J. *Language, Truth and Logic*. New York: Dover, 1952.

Balthasar, Hans Urs von. *Dare We Hope "That All Men Be Saved"?* San Francisco: Ignatius, 1988.

Barth, Karl. *Church Dogmatics*. Edited by G. W. Bromley and T. F. Torrance. London: T. & T. Clark, 2004.

Baum, Richard, and William Sheehan. *In Search of Planet Vulcan: The Ghost in Newton's Clockwork Universe*. New York: Plenum Trade, 1997.

Behe, Michael. *The Edge of Evolution: The Search for the Limits of Darwinism*. New York: Free, 2008.

Blanchette, Oliva. *The Perfection of the Universe According to Aquinas*. University Park: Pennsylvania State University Press, 1992.

Boethius. *The Consolation of Philosophy*. Revised edited by Translated by Victor Watts. London: Penguin, 1999.

Bowlin, John. *Contingency and Fortune in Aquinas's Ethics*. Cambridge: Cambridge University Press, 1999.

Brooke, John Hedley. *Science and Religion: Some Historical Perspectives*. New York: Cambridge University Press, 1991.

Brown, Patterson. "Infinite Causal Regression." In *Aquinas: A Collection of Critical Essays*, edited by Anthony Kenny, 214–36. Garden City, NY: Anchor, 1969.

Brown, Warren et al. (eds.), *Whatever Happened to the Soul? Scientific and Theological Portraits of Human Nature*. Minneapolis: Fortress, 1998.

Burrell, David B. *Aquinas: God and Action*. Notre Dame, IN: University of Notre Dame Press, 1979.

———. *Deconstructing Theodicy: Why Job Has Nothing to Say to the Puzzle of Suffering*. Grand Rapids: Brazos, 2008.

———. *Freedom and Creation in Three Traditions*. Notre Dame, IN: University of Notre Dame Press, 1993.

———. *Knowing the Unknowable God: Ibn-Sina, Maimonides, Aquinas.* Notre Dame, IN: University of Notre Dame Press, 1986.

Burtt, Edwin Arthur. *The Metaphysical Foundations of Modern Physical Science.* Revised edited by Atlantic Highlands, NJ: Humanities, 1952.

Butterfield, Herbert. *Christianity and History.* New York: Scribner, 1950.

———. *The Origins of Modern Science.* Revised edited by New York: Free, 1965.

Cairns-Smith, A. G. *Seven Clues to the Origin of Life: A Scientific Detective Story.* New York: Cambridge University Press, 1985.

Carre, Meyrick H. *Realists and Nominalists,* London: Oxford University Press, 1946.

Cohen, I. Bernard. *The Birth of the New Physics.* Garden City, NY: Anchor, 1960.

Copernicus, *Revolutions of the Heavenly Spheres.* Great Books of the Western Tradition 16. Chicago: Encyclopedia Britannica, 1952.

Darwin, Charles. "Darwin Correspondence Project." Online: http://www.darwinproject .ac.uk/home.

Davies, Brian. *The Reality of God and the Problem of Evil.* New York: Continuum, 2006.

Dawkins, Richard. *The Blind Watchmaker: Why the Evidence of Evolution Reveals a World Without Design: With New Introduction.* New York: Norton, 1996.

Decaen, Christopher A. "Aristotle's Aether and Contemporary Science." *The Thomist* 68 (2004) 375–429.

Descartes, René. *Discourse on Method.* In *Discourse on Method and Meditations on First Philosophy.* 3rd ed. Translated by Donald A. Cress. Indianapolis: Hackett, 1993.

———. *Meditations on First Philosophy.* In *Discourse on Method and Meditations on First Philosophy.* 3rd edited by Translated by Donald A. Cress. Indianapolis: Hackett, 1993.

Dirac, Paul. "The Evolution of the Physicist's Picture of Nature." *Scientific American* 208.5 (1963) 45–53.

Duhem, Pierre. *To Save the Phenomena: An Essay on the Ideas of Physical Theory from Plato to Galileo.* Chicago: University of Chicago, 1969

Edwards, Paul, and Arthur Pap, editors. *A Modern Introduction to Philosophy,* 473–90. London: Collier-Macmillan, 1973.

Einstein, Albert. "On the Ether." In *The Philosophy of Vacuum,* edited by Simon Saunders and Harvey R. Brown, 13–20. Oxford: Clarendon, 1991.

Feyerabend, Paul. *Against Method.* Revised ed. London: Verso, 1988.

Flew, Antony. "Theology and Falsification." In *New Essays in Philosophical Theology,* edited by Antony Flew and Alasdair MacIntyre, 96–99. London: SCM, 1955.

Galileo. *Two Chief World Systems.* Berkeley: University of California Press, 1967.

Gilson, E. *From Aristotle to Darwin and Back Again: A Journey in Final Causality, Species, and Evolution.* Translated by John Lyon. Notre Dame, IN: University of Notre Dame Press, 1984.

———. *God and Philosophy.* New Haven: Yale University Press, 1941.

———. *The Philosophy of St. Thomas Aquinas.* Translated by Edward Bullough. New York: Barnes & Noble, 1993.

Goodwin, Robert P. *Selected Writings of St. Thomas Aquinas.* Indianapolis: Bobbs-Merrill, 1965.

Gould, Stephen Jay. *The Structure of Evolutionary Theory.* Cambridge: Harvard University Press, 2002.

Grene, Marjorie. *A Portrait of Aristotle.* Chicago: University of Chicago Press, 1963.

Gribbin, John. *Deep Simplicity: Bringing Order to Chaos and Complexity*. New York: Random House, 2004.

Haldane, J. B. S. *The Inequality of Man, and Other Essays*. Harmondsworth, UK: Penguin, 1937.

Haldane, John. "Rational and Other Animals." In *Verstehen and Humane Understanding*, edited by Anthony O'Hear, 17–28. Cambridge: Cambridge University Press, 1996.

Hawkings, Stephen. "My Position." In *Black Holes and Baby Universes and Other Essays*. New York: Bantam, 1994.

Heisenberg, Werner. *Physics and Philosophy: The Revolution in Modern Science*. Great Minds Series. Amherst, NY: Prometheus, 1999.

Hetherington, Norriss S. *Planteary Motions: A Historical Perspective*. Westport, CT: Greenwood, 2006.

Hodge, Charles. *Systematic Theology*. Grand Rapids: Eerdmans, 1981.

Holton, Gerald, and Brush, Stephen G. *Physics, the Human Adventure from Copernicus to Einstein and Beyond*. New Brunswick, NJ: Rutgers University Press, 2001.

Hume, David. *An Enquiry Concerning Human Understanding*. Great Books of the Western Tradition 35. Chicago: Encyclopedia Britannica, 1952.

Jaki, Stanely. *Brains, Minds, and Computers*. New York: Herder & Herder, 1969.

———. *Means to Message*. Grand Rapids: Eerdmans, 1999.

———. *The Purpose of It All*. Washington, DC: Regnery-Gateway,1990.

———. *The Relevance of Physics*. Chicago: University of Chicago Press, 1966.

James, William. *Essays in Pragmatism*. New York: Hafner, 1974.

Jenkins, John I. *Knowledge and Faith in Thomas Aquinas*. Cambridge: Cambridge University Press, 1997.

Kant, Immanuel. *Critique of Practical Reason*. Great Books of the Western Tradition 42. Chicago: Encyclopedia Britannica, 1952.

———. *Critique of Pure Reason*. Translated by Norman Kemp Smith. New York: St. Martin's, 1965.

———. *Grounding for the Metaphysics of Morals*. Translated by James W. Ellington. Indianapolis: Hackett, 1981.

———. *Religion Within the Limits of Reason Alone*. Translated by Theodore M. Greene and Hoyt H. Hudson. New York: Harper & Row, 1960.

———. *The Critique of Pure Reason*. Translated by Norman Kemp Smith. New York: St. Martin's, 1965.

Koestler, Arthur. *The Sleepwalker*. New York: Macmillan, 1968.

Kuhn, Thomas. *The Copernican Revolution*. Cambridge: Harvard University Press, 1957.

Lakatos, Imre. "Falsification and the Methodology of Scientific Research Programs." In *Criticism and the Growth of Knowledge*, edited by Lakatos and Musgrace, 91–196. Cambridge: Cambridge University Press, 1970.

Langford, Jerome J. *Galileo, Science and the Church*. Ann Arbor: University of Michigan Press, 1992.

Laplace, Pierre Simon. *A Philosophical Essay on Probabilities*. Translated from the 6th French ed. by Fredrick Wilson Truscott and Frederick Lincoln Emory. London: Chapman & Hall, 1902.

Lewis, C. S. *Miracles: A Preliminary Study*. New York: Macmillan, 1947.

———. *Preface to Paradise Lost*. London: Oxford University Press, 1942.

———. *Surprised by Joy: The Shape of My Early Life*. New York: Harcourt, Brace & World, 1955.

————. *The Problem of Pain*. 1940. Reprint, New York: HarperCollins, 1996.

————. *The Weight of Glory*. 1940. Reprint, New York: HarpersCollins, 2001.

Laudan, Larry. "Underdetermination." In *The Routledge Encyclopedia of Philosophy: CD-ROM*. Version 1.0, edited by Edward Craig, no pages. London: Routledge, n.d.

Lovejoy, Arthur O. *Great Chain of Being: A Study in the History of an Idea*. Cambridge: Harvard University Press, 1964.

Machuga, Ric. *In Defense of the Soul: What It Means to Be Human*. Grand Rapids: Brazos, 2002.

————. "No Chance." *Books and Culture* (July/Aug 2007) 38–39.

MacIntyre, Alasdair C. *Three Rival Versions of Moral Enquiry: Encyclopedia, Genealogy, and Tradition: Being Gifford Lectures Delivered in the University of Edinburgh in 1988*. Notre Dame, IN: University of Notre Dame Press, 1990.

MacKay, D. M. *Human Science and Human Dignity*. Downers Grove, IL: InterVarsity, 1979.

Maritain, Jacques. *Saint Thomas and the Problem of Evil*. Milwaukee: Marquette University Press, 1942.

Mascall, E. L. *Existence and Analogy*. Hamden, CT: Archon, 1967.

————. *He Who Is*. London: Longmans, 1962.

————. *The Importance of Being Human*. New York: Columbia University Press, 1958.

————. *The Openness of Being: Natural Theology Today*. Philadelphia: Westminster, 1971.

Mason, Stephen F. *A History of Science*. New York: Collier, 1962.

Maxwell, James Clerk. "Ether." In *Encyclopedia Britannica*. 9th ed. Vol. VIII, 568–72. Chicago: Encyclopedia Britannica, 1986.

Mayr, Ernst. *One Long Argument: Charles Darwin and the Genesis of Modern Evolutionary Thought*. Cambridge: Harvard University Press, 1991.

————. *The Growth of Biological Thought: Diversity, Evolution, and Inheritance*. Cambridge: Harvard University Press, 1982.

————. *This Is Biology: The Science of the Living World*. Cambridge, MA: Belknap, 1997.

————. *Toward a New Philosophy of Biology: Observations of an Evolutionist*. Cambridge, MA: Belknap, 1988.

————. *What Evolution Is*. New York: Basic, 2001.

————. *What Makes Biology Unique? Considerations on the Autonomy of a Scientific Discipline*. New York: Cambridge University Press, 2004.

McAllister, James W. *Beauty and Revolution in Science*. Ithaca, NY: Cornell University Press, 1996.

McInerny, Ralph. *Characters in Search of Their Author: The Gifford Lectures Glasgow 1999–2000*. Notre Dame, IN: University of Notre Dame Press, 2001.

————. *Praeambula Fidei: Thomism and the God of the Philosophers*. Washington, DC: Catholic University of America Press, 2006.

Meynell, Hugo A. *The Intelligible Universe: A Cosmological Argument*. Totowa, NJ: Barnes & Noble, 1982.

Milbank, John, and Catherine Pickstock. *Truth in Aquinas*. London: Routledge, 2001.

Milton, John. *Paradise Lost*. Norton Critical Edition. 2nd ed. New York: Norton, 1993.

Murdoch, Iris. *The Sovereignty of the Good*. London: Routledge & Kegan Paul, 1970.

Neuhaus, Richard John. "Will All Be Saved?" *First Things* 115 (Aug/Sept 2001) 77–80.

Newton, Issac. *Mathematical Principles of Natural Philosophy*. "Rules of Reasoning in Philosophy." Great Books of the Western Tradition 34. Chicago: Encyclopedia Britannica, 1952.

————. "Third Letter to Bentley." In *Isaac Newton's Papers & Letters on Natural Philosophy*, edited by I. Bernard Cohen, 300–309. Cambridge: Harvard University Press, 1958.

————. "Fourth Letter to Bentley." In *Isaac Newton's Papers & Letters on Natural Philosophy*, edited by I. Bernard Cohen, 310–12. Cambridge: Harvard University Press, 1958.

Nietzsche. *Twilight of the Idols*. In *The Portable Nietzsche*, edited and translated by Walter Kaufmann, 439–563. Viking Portable Library. New York: Viking, 1968.

O'Meara, Thomas F. *Thomas Aquinas Theologian*. Notre Dame: University of Notre Dame Press, 1997.

Pasnau, Robert. *Thomas Aquinas on Human Nature*. Cambridge: Cambridge University Press, 2002.

Percy, Walker. *The Message in the Bottle: How Queer Man Is, How Queer Language Is, and What One Has to Do with the Other*. New York: Farrar, Straus, & Giroux, 1975.

Pieper, Josef. *Faith, Hope and Love*. San Francisco: Ignatius, 1997.

————. *Guide to Thomas Aquinas*. San Francisco: Ignatius, 1991.

————. *The Silence of St. Thomas: Three Essays*. Translated by John Murray and Daniel O'Connor. South Bend, IN: St. Augustine's, 1999.

Pirsig, Robert M. *Zen and the Art of Motorcycle Maintenance: An Inquiry into Values.* New York: Morrow, 1999.

Plantinga, Alvin. *Warrant and Proper Function*. New York: Oxford University Press, 1993.

Plato. *Laws*. Translated by Trevor J. Saunders. New York: Penguin, 1970.

————. *Republic*. Translated by Francis M. Cornford. London: Oxford University Press, 1941.

————. *Timaeus*. Great Books of the Western Tradition 7. Chicago: Encyclopedia Britannica, 1952.

Polanyi, Michael. *Personal Knowledge: Towards a Post-Critical Philosophy*. Chicago: University of Chicago Press, 1974.

Polkinghorne, John. *The God of Hope and the End of the World*. London: SPCK, 2002.

Popper, Karl R. *Conjectures and Refutations; The Growth of Scientific Knowledge*. New York: Basic, 1962.

————. *Logic of Scientific Discovery*. New York: Basic, 1959.

————. *Quantum Theory and the Schism in Physics*. Totowa, NJ: Rowan & Littlefield, 1982.

Popper, Karl, and Eccles, John C. *The Self and Its Brain: An Argument for Interactionism*. New York: Springer, 1977.

Putnam, Hilary. "Why There Isn't a Ready-Made World." *Synthese* 51 (1982) 141–67.

————. *The Collapse of the Fact/Value Dichotomy and Other Essays*. Cambridge: Harvard University Press, 2002.

Regis, Louis-Marie. *St. Thomas and Epistemology*. Milwaukee: Marquette University Press, 1946.

Rescher, Nicholas. *Objectivity: The Obligations of Impersonal Reason*. Notre Dame, Indiana: University of Notre Dame Press, 1997.

Robinson, Daniel N., and John Eccles. *The Wonder of Being Human: Our Brain and Our Mind.* New York: Free, 1984.

Ryle, Gilbert. *The Concept of Mind.* New York: Barnes & Noble, 1949.

Sartre, Jean Paul. *Existentialism.* Translated by Bernard Frenchman. New York: Philosophical Library, 1947.

Schaff, Philip, editor. *A Select Library of Nicene and Post-Nicene Fathers of the Christian Church*, vol. 5. Grand Rapids: Eerdmans, 1971.

Searle, John. *Intentionality.* New York: Cambridge University Press, 1983.

———. *Mind: A Brief Introduction.* Fundamentals of Philosophy Series. Oxford: Oxford University Press, 2004.

———. *Mind, Language, and Society.* New York: Basic, 1998.

Simon, Yves R. *Freedom of Choice.* New York: Fordham University Press, 1969.

Smart, J. J. C., and J. J. Haldane. *Atheism and Theism.* 2nd ed. Great Debates in Philosophy. Oxford: Blackwell, 2003.

Smith, Huston. *The World's Religion.* New York: HarperCollins, 1991.

Taleb, Nassim Nicholas. *The Black Swan: The Impact of the Highly Improbable.* New York: Random, 2007.

Veatch, Henry B. *Aristotle: A Contemporary Appreciation.* Bloomington, IN: Indiana University Press, 1974.

———. *Intentional Logic: A Logic based on Philosophical Realism.* Hamden, CT: Archon, 1970.

———. "Two Logics, or One, or None?" *New Scholasticism* 47 (1973), 350–60.

Wallace, William. "Science and Religion in the Thomistic Tradition." *The Thomist* 65 (2001) 441–63.

———. *The Modeling of Nature: Philosophy of Science and Philosophy of Nature in Synthesis.* Washington, DC: Catholic University of America Press, 1996.

Weigel, George. *Witness to Hope: The Biography of Pope John Paul II.* New York: HarperCollins, 1999.

Weinberg, Steven. *Dreams of a Final Theory: The Search for the Fundamental Laws of Nature.* New York: Vintage, 1993.

Whitehead, Alfred North. *Science and the Modern World*, New York: Pelican Mentor, 1948.

Wild, John. *Plato's Theory of Man: An Introduction to the Realistic Philosophy of Culture.* Cambridge: Harvard University Press, 1946.

Wippel, John. *The Metaphysical Thought of Thomas Aquinas: From Finite Being to Uncreated Being.* Washington, DC: Catholic University Press, 2000.

Wright, N. T. *The New Testament and the People of God.* Christian Origns and the Question of God 1. Minneapolis: Fortress, 1992.

———. *The Resurrection of the Son of God.* Christian Origns and the Question of God 3. Minneapolis: Fortress, 2003.

———. *Simply Christian: Why Christianity Makes Sense.* New York: HarperCollins, 2006.

———. *Surprised by Hope: Rethinking Heaven, the Resurrection, and the Mission of the Church.* New York: Harper Collins, 2008.

Index[*]

---

[*] Definitions are in **bold** fonts.